Once Upon a Kingdom

ONCE UPON A KINGDOM

Myth, Hegemony, and Identity

Isidore Okpewho

INDIANA UNIVERSITY PRESS   BLOOMINGTON & INDIANAPOLIS

This book is a publication of

Indiana University Press
601 North Morton Street
Bloomington, Indiana 47404-3797 USA

www.indiana.edu/~iupress

Telephone orders   800-842-6796
Fax orders   812-855-7931
Orders by e-mail   iuporder@indiana.edu

The paper used in this publication meets the minimum requirements of American National Standard
for Information Sciences—Permanence of Paper for Printed Library Materials, ANSI Z39.48-1984.

Manufactured in the United States of America

Library of Congress Cataloging-in-Publication Data

Okpewho, Isidore.
Once upon a kingdom : myth, hegemony, and identity / by Isidore Okpewho.
p.   cm.
Includes bibliographical references (p.   ) and index.
ISBN 0-253-33396-2 (alk. paper). — ISBN 0-253-21189-1 (pbk. : alk. paper)
1. Igbo (African people)—Folklore. 2. Mythology, Igbo. 3. Folklore—Nigeria—Delta State—
History and criticism. 4. Benin (Kingdom)—Legends—History and criticism.   I. Title.
GR351.32.I34056   1998
398.2'089'96332—dc21   98-19792

1   2   3   4   5   03   02   01   00   99   98

Dedicated to

My uncle, Chief S.N.O. Attoh, who watched me with

delight read as a child, and in more recent years

listened with pleasure to the tales I was recording

CONTENTS

Preface   ix

1. A Kingdom and Its Discontents   1

HISTORICAL AND CULTURAL RELATIONS   4

MYTHOLOGICAL RELATIONS   13

HISTORY AND THE FOLK IMAGINATION   25

2. The Hunter Who Became a King: Heroism and Social History   27

HEROISM AMONG THE WESTERN IGBO   31

OJIUDU'S STORY   37

HUNTER, HERO, AND SOCIETY   48

HISTORICAL CLAIMS   53

3. Male Manqué: Divinity, Authority, and the Individual   61

"EHI" AND THE DIVINE KING   63

OKOOJII'S STORY   75

"CHI" AND THE KING IN EVERY MAN   87

THE OBA IN THE STORY   92

4. The Old Woman on the Outskirts: Myth, Gender, and Power 97

THE TALES AND THEIR TELLING 98

THE IMAGE OF BENIN 116

THE OLD WOMAN ON THE OUTSKIRTS 126

5. The Singer in the Tale: Two Profiles 135

SOME THEORETICAL ISSUES 137

THE PAUPER PRINCESS: A MODERN WOMAN'S STORY? 142

ODOGWU: THE SINGER ALSO WRITES 154

A MYTHOLOGY OF THE SELF 169

6. Myth, Empire, and Self-Determination 173

INFLUENCE OF BENIN ON OTHERS 174

INFLUENCE OF OTHERS ON BENIN 178

NATION, NARRATION, AND SELF-DETERMINATION 183

WILL THE SUBALTERN PLEASE SPEAK UP? 190

Notes 193

Bibliography 225

Index 241

Preface

The old west African kingdom of Benin in Nigeria, which flourished from about the tenth century until it fell to British forces by the end of the nineteenth, continues to hold a powerful sway on the imaginations of many. From the late fifteenth century, when it struck commercial relationships with various European nations, Benin began a career of military campaigns whereby it brought many communities far and wide under political and economic control. It was a hard-won ascendancy. Today, those communities that once lived in the pale of Benin's power still tell stories that show traces of their ingrained resentment of the kingdom.

The career of Benin has been the subject of diverse scholarly interest, due largely to the fascination of artistic relics housed in numerous public and private collections throughout the world. In 1956 the University of Ibadan, Nigeria, established a Scheme for the Study of Benin History and Culture, under which scholars from various disciplines (especially anthropology, history, archaeology, and art history) were to collaborate in investigating the enormous achievement of the old kingdom. The picture as seen from Benin's point of view became something of a master-text for this project. Unfortunately, the Benin Scheme was shortlived, primarily because Nigeria became involved in a hegemonist crisis—inspired largely by this agenda of privileging one group over others—that grew into a civil war and continues to threaten the fragile political unity of the country.

Set within the metonymic frame of the Benin Scheme, *Once Upon a Kingdom* investigates the contending images of dominance and self-assertion in the conflict between privileged elements (the "center") and others (the "margins") who are determined to defend their defining interests and identities. I have used oral narratives I collected from Igbo communities west of the Niger, an area once under Benin influence, to explore ways in which any group of people define or construct themselves in the face of a dominant political presence or hegemonic control. It becomes clear that every community has a strong sense of its identity and its culture, which it expects to be recognized and taken into account. Failure to establish a level playing field for their constituent communities has often led nations like Nigeria (and others elsewhere that are plagued with sectional conflicts) into costly errors of political and social engineering that threaten their very existence. Building on the concept of *myth* that I developed in an earlier work (Okpewho 1983), but mindful also of other contributions on the subject, *Once Upon a Kingdom* reveals not only how myth reflects the structure of relations between peoples but ultimately the implications for contemporary society of prejudices inscribed in those relations.

I have, consequently, tried to adopt as broad-based and interdisciplinary an approach as I could to the interrogation and analysis of my material, made up mostly of tales that I collected within the last two decades. Chapter 1 lays the lines for this approach: in exploring the broad social, cultural, and political geography of Benin's relations with her neighbors, I have had to consult the findings of scholars across various related fields of social research. Chapter 2 has a more directly historical thrust, although even here I deal with a legacy of cultural and political tensions that are rooted in a centuries-old contest for social space. In chapter 3, I probe the influence of metaphysical systems on civic attitudes and ethical standards. In chapter 4, I isolate a motif from my tales that addresses issues of gender relations undergirding the resistance to hegemonic structures, which I consider the real thrust of the traditions I study here. Chapter 5 shifts the focus from these *traditions* to the *persons* who give life to them: a different analytical angle, to be sure, but one no less fruitful for investigating hegemonic stresses. Chapter 6 once again unites a variety of disciplinary foci, as I try first to understand the ideological basis of the resistance enshrined in the tales, and then to trace the links between the stresses they reveal and the political crises facing countries like Nigeria that have improperly managed the contending claims of their plural identities.

So far, I have drawn attention to the discernible *content* of the tales I analyze, which justifies my concentration on issues of history, religion, gender, politics, and culture that underlie the construction of self and society through the tales. It is evident, however, that I have also taken serious interest in the *form* in which my narrators present these issues, by which I mean the circumstances contingent upon their performances and the ways in which I have chosen to order the emergent texts.

For instance, in chapter 2 I have read Ojiudu's battles with the disco music from a nearby room against his performance of a tale that deals, on the surface, with his people's war with Benin but underneath explores stresses in their cultural and political history. In chapter 5 I have also given detailed attention to the relevance of contextual factors to the narrators' efforts at self-projection through their tales. Given the hegemonic basis of the tales these narrators tell, such projections of the ego can hardly be considered out of place.

It should be equally clear that, to appreciate the relevance of such factors as the above to our interrogation of the tales, we need to take more interest in the physical shape of the texts than has been the case so far. Most analytical studies of oral narratives have depended on texts presented in the grey landscape of undifferentiated prose; even with the convincing cases made by scholars like Dell Hymes (1981) and Dennis Tedlock (1983) for a careful ethnopoetic, dialogic scoring of narrative texts, there are still too few investigators who think the oral evidence worth the level of diligence accorded "sophisticated" literature. I am convinced, however, that the full impact of Christy's narration (chapter 5) would have been lost had I left Arinze's interventions out of the text.

Although for considerations of price I have been constrained to leave the original Igbo texts out of this book, the question of translation is just as crucial, and has been subject to some division of opinion. One side in this may be best represented by a point Adam Kuper makes in a slightly different context, that "the natives . . . be given their unedited say" (1994:542), which may be seen as urging an almost literal loyalty to the indigenous text. The other side emerges in the concern variously raised by Gordon Innes (1990), Anthony Appiah (1993), and myself (1983:131) about our duty, as translators, to properly represent cultures whose texts we take into our charge. Each case has its strengths and limitations, of course. I can only say that these tales were told in a language in which I grew up and which I speak fluently, despite a few dialectal differences with which I am very much at ease. In my translations, I have tried to strike a fair balance between the two positions outlined above. I have also, in the endnotes, raised some key issues of idiom and diction that would enable the general reader of the texts to see the nuances of the narrators' representational labors.

It remains for me to state what I consider the relevance of this study. I think it is about time we broke the monotony of our glorification of great "emperors" and "warrior kings" of the romantic past and looked at the other side of the equation. What about the peoples they destroyed in pursuit of their greatness: have they no stories of their own to tell? If they do, isn't time running out on those stories? If we continue to sing the praises of successful warmongers and usurpers of other peoples' lands and wealth, what right do we have to chastise European colonizers who did exactly the same? And do we not see a disturbing resemblance between some of these figures from the "heroic" past and the ignoble villains who continue to lead their nations to ruin in the Africa of our own day?

It is especially urgent for African scholars and leaders to reflect how seriously they weaken the chances of national unity when they continue to treat some sections of their people as if their interests can be compromised, just because they did not build great empires in the past. Everyone counts and should be made to feel as relevant to the national purpose as everyone else. As our narrator Odogwu Okwuashi would say, "The mouse eats, but so does the maggot."

Let me also stress that this study is not aimed at promoting a divisive ideology of *différence/différance* wherein all fruitful engagement is deferred or erased and social reality is headed for irreparable ruin. That these Igbo tales advertise an outlook different from what obtains among the Bini does not suggest that the two peoples are as distinct from each other as east is from west. On the contrary, I think it is clear enough from the study that the various peoples in this region lived so closely with one another that tale motifs and types floated freely between them. I also suggested the possibility that in some cases emigrants from the hostile environment of the kingdom may have carried with them tales they had learnt there. It stands to reason that whatever differences there are between Benin and western Igbo tales may be due partly to divergences in outlook and partly to the latter's resentment of a kingdom that did them wrong; their quarrel is with the leadership, not with the people with whom on the whole they are united by what may be called the "same differences." It is important to grasp this point, because the political course I urge in this study rests as much on common ground as on mutual regard.

Finally, I would like to thank all those who made this study worth the effort it took. Top of the list are the narrators of the tales used in this study: Messers Christopher Ojiudu Okeze and James Okoojii of Igbuzo (Ibusa), Charles Simayi of Ubulu-Uno, Okafor Nwambuonwo Odagwue of Idumuje-Uno, and Odogwu Okwuashi Nwaniani of Onicha-Ugbo, and Madam Christy Mmaduaburochi Arinze of Asaba. Ojiudu, Okoojii, and Odogwu have passed on, but I remain immensely grateful for the wisdom I have gained from these artists (and others not included in this study), for the warmth and patience they have shown me throughout my work with them.

Next is my brother-in-law Patrick Ibe Arinze, who has accompanied me to every performance I have ever recorded and has recorded some for me since my absence from home. Indeed he arranged my meeting with practically every artist I have recorded so far, and has continued to make courtesy calls on those of them still alive, so they can be assured we have not simply made away with their secrets and disappeared. If my work is judged a success, much of the credit is due to him. I should also thank Mr. Ignatius Osadebe, who not only sought out some of our key artists (especially Charles Simayi of Ubulu-Uno, his townsman) but also accompanied Arinze and me to not a few of our recording sessions. My old student Nduka Otiono has very kindly helped me in maintaining cordial relations with Simayi, for which I am grateful.

My uncle, Chief Sylvester Ofili Attoh of Umuaji Quarters, Asaba, to whom I gladly dedicate this book, has not only been a great mentor since my early youth, but listened very intently to my recorded texts and provided the most articulate answers to my queries in the course of my field investigations. I also gained some wisdom and inspiration from my (admittedly brief) sessions with the Asagba of Asaba, Obi Chike Edozien—formerly Professor J.C. Edozien, first of the University of Ibadan and later of the University of North Carolina at Chapel Hill—and Chief (Dr.) J.B. Azinge of Umudaike Quarters, himself a committed student of Asaba oral traditions.

At Igbuzo I was the guest of friends who shared with me useful information about the cultural traditions of their great town: the Obuzo of Igbuzo, Obi Louis Nwoboshi (formerly Professor of Forestry at the University of Ibadan), and Chief Nosike Ikpo, former senator in Nigeria's Second Republic. Here in the United States, I have spent numerous hours in fruitful conversation with Igbuzo sons like Professors Don Ohadike of Cornell and Joe Chimgo Nwabueze of CUNY. Professor Tess Onwueme of the University of Wisconsin at Eau Claire, a noted playwright whose work is deeply informed by the oral tradition, has also very kindly shared with me some insights from the folklore of her native Ogwashi-Uku.

I am immensely grateful also to old Ibadan friends who now live in the U.S. for the same reason I do. Professors Michael Echeruo of Syracuse, Abiola Irele of Ohio State, Peter Ekeh of SUNY Buffalo, and Chikwenye Ogunyemi of Sarah Lawrence have each given of their time and wisdom as readily as in the past. I am especially thankful to Chikwenye for reading virtually every draft chapter of this book and offering frank, incisive comments. My gratitude also goes to Dan Ben-Amos, the doyen of Benin oral narrative study in the U.S., who also read some chapters, sent comments, and responded kindly to my queries over the telephone. I am also grateful to Paula Girschik Ben-Amos for useful clarifications on several points of Benin culture and art history, on which she remains an unquestioned authority. Former Ibadan students, whose fieldwork helped sharpen my insights, are too numerous to acknowledge, but my indebtedness to them is evident enough especially across the pages of chapter 1.

A research grant from Binghamton University has enabled me to visit Nigeria for further investigations and keep my fieldwork alive through Patrick Arinze. I thank the university for this. My wife Obi and our children—Ediru, Ugo, Afigo, and Onome—have, however, given me gifts far more precious than money: love, total sympathy with my quaint pursuits, and patience with quirks of conduct that such pursuits inevitably induce. I can never thank them enough.

Obviously it was hoped that this collaboration might result in the publi-
ion of a "cultural history" of Benin. But the collaboration never truly
terialized. Bradbury busied himself in turning out a series of indepen-
nt studies strictly along anthropological lines: first, a quite informative
onograph on *The Benin Kingdom* (1957)—developed from his doctoral
sis for London University—and subsequently a string of papers, later to
collected and edited by Peter Morton-Williams (Bradbury 1973). In these
relied on some material from the oral tradition. The historian of the
eme, Alan F.C. Ryder, showed scant regard for the oral tradition. In his
in and the Europeans, 1485–1897 (1969), he has relied almost entirely on
dence derived from European documents on the period and in a few
ces treats the claims of the oral evidence somewhat cavalierly. Other
mbers of the Benin Scheme have made independent contributions: the
historian Philip Dark (1960, 1975), the archaeologist Graham Connah
66, 1967, 1975), and others. Bradbury returned ill to England in 1961,
, even by the time he died in 1969, there was little hope that the inter-
ciplinary history of Benin would take anything like a concrete shape
ayi 1990:48).
Although the Scheme has recorded some successes, we can, in retro-
ct, recognize some of its shortcomings, especially in the vision of Brad-
y, its guiding genius. As an anthropologist, he was somewhat solidly
ded to the functionalist prejudice that marked British social research;
s, under him, the work of the Scheme seemed geared toward the speci-
lly pragmatic purposes of historical reconstruction, in which aesthetic
siderations played a rather limited role.
wo aspects of Bradbury's disregard of aesthetic principles may be seen
is brilliant study of *ikegobo*, emblems for the Benin "cult of the hand"
73:251–270). First, he begins his analysis by telling us, in connection with
bronze effigy used in this cult, that he "shall not be concerned with the
nical or aesthetic qualities of the casting." He admits that the events
cted in the figurine are narrative in intent, but goes on to reveal a rather
ow, functionalist appreciation of the nature of the narrative:

> By narrative I mean simply that they were intended to convey some
> information about specific events or particular persons. Provided that
> they can be properly dated and interpreted such bronzes are potential
> sources of certain kinds of historical information, but dating and interpre-
> tation present many difficulties.[2]

second and more glaring weakness emerges when he presents his (on
whole) thorough explication of the *ikegobo*. A casual look at the first
ine, which Bradbury reproduces in a series of plates devoted to the
ct, shows a marked difference in the spaces given to the Oba and his

Once Upon a Kingdom

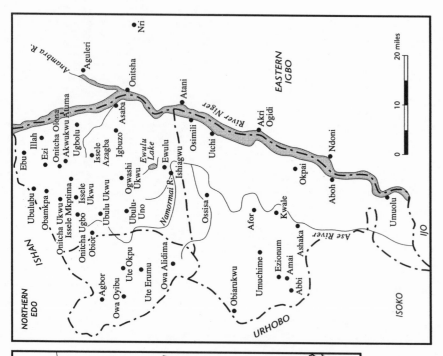

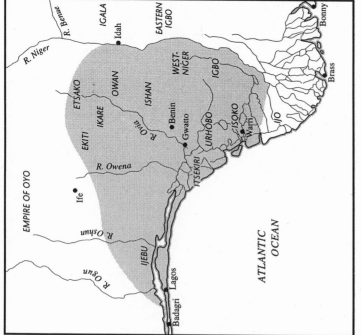

Map 1 (above). Map of south-western Nigeria, showing areas of Benin influence by the mid-sixteenth century

Map 2 (right). Map of the Western Igbo area of Delta State, Nigeria

A Kingdom and Its Disconte

1

The old west African kingdom of Benin (midwestern N: manded the attention of scholars of African history, art, a very long time. The reason for this may be that it continu with new challenges, either because various pieces of evider this field invite further examination, or because the ever-gr ity in the political landscape of Nigeria forces us to rec images and symbols that, in "happier" times, inspired us n than to cavil.

An interesting point of reference is provided by the Sch: of Benin History and Culture (generally known as the inaugurated in 1956 by Dr. Kenneth Onwuka Dike, then University College, Ibadan (from 1961, the University Scheme had a rather chequered life, due largely to a certai approaches between the main disciplines supporting it. ! ologists and art historians were coopted into it at some s was primarily in the hands of scholars trained in history and anthropology on the other. At a period in humanistic historians and anthropologists debated which of the tv better qualified to study traditional or (more fashionably eties,[1] Benin was seen as a test field where it was hoped a tion could be achieved. "The Scheme for the Study of I Culture," says Bradbury, the anthropologist and chief group, "is an experiment in interdisciplinary cooperatic to discover how much can be learnt of the history of Be ever sources and methods are available and practical, and tion for further historical studies in the central area of (1973:17).

war minister, the Ezomo. The *ikegobo* is structured into three tiers: the top tier depicts the Oba surrounded by a group of figures; the middle tier shows the Ezomo surrounded by another group of figures; and the bottom tier consists of a ring of sacrificial animals. The *ikegobo* is said to record the military services of Ezomo Ehenua to the Oba, Akenzua I, at a time when the latter was assailed by trouble from rebellious court officials and relatives (Bradbury 1973:254–255). But it is clear that in this representation the Ezomo is accorded an importance that far outweighs that given to the Oba. Each of the two is attended by the appurtenances of power symbolized by military personnel; but the company attending the Ezomo is much fuller, and it is quite clear that, in commissioning the making of the figurine, the Ezomo has taken care to give notice of his importance in the structure of power within the kingdom, even at the expense of the Oba.

This point should be borne in mind as this study develops to take account of the ways in which persons, no less than peoples, seek to assert their interests and identities against overarching power and authority. In the specific circumstances of the Benin monarchy, Bradbury should indeed be the first to understand why an Ezomo would have such an exaggerated sense of his importance in relation to his Oba, given the ways in which this class of officials—as Bradbury has himself acknowledged—asserted their position and influence within the monarchical power structure.[3]

It is in the oral narratives, however, that this tendency toward self-assertion is most glaring, and for that we shall have to look beyond the limited horizon defined by the Benin Scheme. This book is going to be concerned essentially with exploring the narrative traditions of communities with which Benin came into conflict in the course of its history, and I have chosen to concentrate on the Igbo west of the River Niger. Specifically, I shall be concerned with the ways in which Benin loomed so large in the imaginations of these peoples that they felt the need to define and assert their identities in reaction to this external stimulus, in the process painting a negative image of Benin.

In this chapter, I put the subject of my study in a broad contextual frame that establishes the pattern of Benin relations with communities within its immediate geographic region and zone of influence.[4] Although Benin is reputed to have controlled an empire that stretched far beyond this region, especially to the west,[5] it was in this zone that its presence and might were felt most palpably. In the survey that I give below, I will be using a selection of stories recorded by various investigators: past students of the University of Ibadan who did fieldwork, under my supervision, in their hometowns (especially among the Etsako, Isoko, Ndokwa, and Ijo areas); the renowned poet-dramatist, John Pepper Clark[-Bekederemo], in his classic edition of *The Ozidi Saga* from the Ijo; Joseph Sidahome, in his collection of Ishan tales under the title *Stories from the Benin Empire*; and myself, among various western Igbo towns and villages.

Historical and Cultural Relations

For a long time, the federal government found it convenient to leave the political geography of midwestern Nigeria pretty much intact. This was because, despite the changing political fortunes of the country and the concomitant boundary adjustments (designed both to reduce the areas of inter-ethnic friction and to evolve a manageable administrative framework for the nation), this area has continued to demonstrate a high degree of cultural uniformity between its constituent units. One notable aspect of this uniformity may be seen in language. There are twelve major ethnic units in the area which may be conveniently reclassified into four linguistic group-ings: Edo, Igbo, Ijo, and Yoruba, all part of the Kwa group of the Niger-Congo language family. Alagoa has pointed out that these four groupings are estimated to have parted ways about 5,000 years ago (1966:282); but, in their daily speech, the overlaps between these peoples so outweigh the gaps that "there can be an argument, at least theoretical, that [they] all . . . be-long to one language stock" (Otite 1977:44).

Although the fortunes of history and politics have bred in the various peoples of this area certain sensitivities which must be respected, it may safely be said that for a long time Benin presented itself as the principal member of that social stock. I am, of course, aware of the implications of this acknowledgment. This chapter will be concerned with how various commu-nities in the region so respected the presence and power of Benin that they consecrated their mythic traditions to its overarching image. But the influ-ence of Benin is just as noticeable in contemporary cultural scholarship. Although the Ishan, Etsako, Urhobo, Isoko, and other peoples have scarcely been in the habit of calling themselves Edo, scholars have continually imposed that identity on them, presumably in acknowledgment of the high degree of similarity in social institutions between these peoples and the Bini (i.e., natives of Benin).

The name "Edo" is reported by Egharevba to have originally belonged to the slave who helped to save the life of Oba Ewuare in the course of his struggle for the kingship of Benin; on the death of the slave, the Oba "caused the country to be known as Edo after his deified friend" (1968:16). This may be no more than an eponymous claim, and there is even less justification for the same claim being extended by scholars to peoples who have hardly any illusions about what names to call themselves. In an other-wise stimulating paper, Otite tells us:

Once Upon a Kingdom

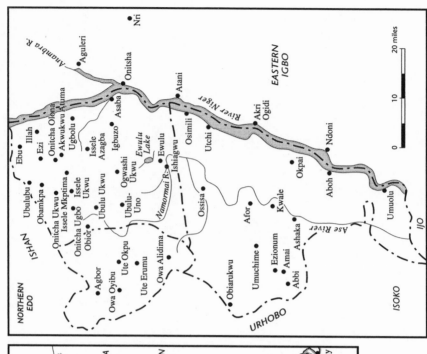

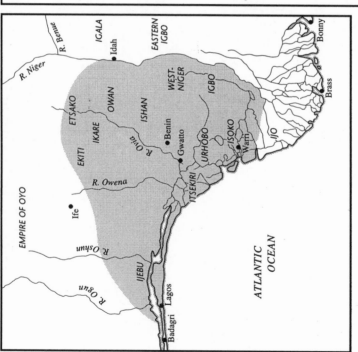

Map 1 (above). Map of south-western Nigeria, showing areas of
Benin influence by the mid-sixteenth century

Map 2 (right). Map of the Western Igbo area of Delta State, Nigeria

A Kingdom and Its Discontents

1

The old west African kingdom of Benin (midwestern Nigeria) has commanded the attention of scholars of African history, art, and culture for a very long time. The reason for this may be that it continues to present us with new challenges, either because various pieces of evidence discovered in this field invite further examination, or because the ever-growing complexity in the political landscape of Nigeria forces us to reconfigure certain images and symbols that, in "happier" times, inspired us more to celebrate than to cavil.

An interesting point of reference is provided by the Scheme for the Study of Benin History and Culture (generally known as the Benin Scheme), inaugurated in 1956 by Dr. Kenneth Onwuka Dike, then Principal of the University College, Ibadan (from 1961, the University of Ibadan). The Scheme had a rather chequered life, due largely to a certain disalignment of approaches between the main disciplines supporting it. Although archaeologists and art historians were coopted into it at some stage, the business was primarily in the hands of scholars trained in history on the one hand and anthropology on the other. At a period in humanistic scholarship when historians and anthropologists debated which of the two disciplines was better qualified to study traditional or (more fashionably) "primitive" societies,[1] Benin was seen as a test field where it was hoped a fruitful collaboration could be achieved. "The Scheme for the Study of Benin History and Culture," says Bradbury, the anthropologist and chief researcher of the group, "is an experiment in interdisciplinary cooperation. Its main aim is to discover how much can be learnt of the history of Benin through whatever sources and methods are available and practical, and so to lay a foundation for further historical studies in the central area of southern Nigeria" (1973:17).

.   Obviously it was hoped that this collaboration might result in the publication of a "cultural history" of Benin. But the collaboration never truly materialized. Bradbury busied himself in turning out a series of independent studies strictly along anthropological lines: first, a quite informative monograph on *The Benin Kingdom* (1957)—developed from his doctoral thesis for London University—and subsequently a string of papers, later to be collected and edited by Peter Morton-Williams (Bradbury 1973). In these he relied on some material from the oral tradition. The historian of the scheme, Alan F.C. Ryder, showed scant regard for the oral tradition. In his *Benin and the Europeans, 1485–1897* (1969), he has relied almost entirely on evidence derived from European documents on the period and in a few places treats the claims of the oral evidence somewhat cavalierly. Other members of the Benin Scheme have made independent contributions: the art historian Philip Dark (1960, 1975), the archaeologist Graham Connah (1966, 1967, 1975), and others. Bradbury returned ill to England in 1961, and, even by the time he died in 1969, there was little hope that the interdisciplinary history of Benin would take anything like a concrete shape (Ajayi 1990:48).

Although the Scheme has recorded some successes, we can, in retrospect, recognize some of its shortcomings, especially in the vision of Bradbury, its guiding genius. As an anthropologist, he was somewhat solidly wedded to the functionalist prejudice that marked British social research; thus, under him, the work of the Scheme seemed geared toward the specifically pragmatic purposes of historical reconstruction, in which aesthetic considerations played a rather limited role.

Two aspects of Bradbury's disregard of aesthetic principles may be seen in his brilliant study of *ikegobo*, emblems for the Benin "cult of the hand" (1973:251–270). First, he begins his analysis by telling us, in connection with the bronze effigy used in this cult, that he "shall not be concerned with the technical or aesthetic qualities of the casting." He admits that the events depicted in the figurine are narrative in intent, but goes on to reveal a rather narrow, functionalist appreciation of the nature of the narrative:

> By narrative I mean simply that they were intended to convey some information about specific events or particular persons. Provided that they can be properly dated and interpreted such bronzes are potential sources of certain kinds of historical information, but dating and interpretation present many difficulties.[2]

A second and more glaring weakness emerges when he presents his (on the whole) thorough explication of the *ikegobo*. A casual look at the first figurine, which Bradbury reproduces in a series of plates devoted to the subject, shows a marked difference in the spaces given to the Oba and his war minister, the Ezomo. The *ikegobo* is structured into three tiers: the top tier depicts the Oba surrounded by a group of figures; the middle tier shows the Ezomo surrounded by another group of figures; and the bottom tier consists of a ring of sacrificial animals. The *ikegobo* is said to record the military services of Ezomo Ehenua to the Oba, Akenzua I, at a time when the latter was assailed by trouble from rebellious court officials and relatives (Bradbury 1973:254–255). But it is clear that in this representation the Ezomo is accorded an importance that far outweighs that given to the Oba. Each of the two is attended by the appurtenances of power symbolized by military personnel; but the company attending the Ezomo is much fuller, and it is quite clear that, in commissioning the making of the figurine, the Ezomo has taken care to give notice of his importance in the structure of power within the kingdom, even at the expense of the Oba.

This point should be borne in mind as this study develops to take account of the ways in which persons, no less than peoples, seek to assert their interests and identities against overarching power and authority. In the specific circumstances of the Benin monarchy, Bradbury should indeed be the first to understand why an Ezomo would have such an exaggerated sense of his importance in relation to his Oba, given the ways in which this class of officials—as Bradbury has himself acknowledged—asserted their position and influence within the monarchical power structure.[3]

It is in the oral narratives, however, that this tendency toward self-assertion is most glaring, and for that we shall have to look beyond the limited horizon defined by the Benin Scheme. This book is going to be concerned essentially with exploring the narrative traditions of communities with which Benin came into conflict in the course of its history, and I have chosen to concentrate on the Igbo west of the River Niger. Specifically, I shall be concerned with the ways in which Benin loomed so large in the imaginations of these peoples that they felt the need to define and assert their identities in reaction to this external stimulus, in the process painting a negative image of Benin.

In this chapter, I put the subject of my study in a broad contextual frame that establishes the pattern of Benin relations with communities within its immediate geographic region and zone of influence.[4] Although Benin is reputed to have controlled an empire that stretched far beyond this region, especially to the west,[5] it was in this zone that its presence and might were felt most palpably. In the survey that I give below, I will be using a selection of stories recorded by various investigators: past students of the University of Ibadan who did fieldwork, under my supervision, in their hometowns (especially among the Etsako, Isoko, Ndokwa, and Ijo areas); the renowned poet-dramatist, John Pepper Clark[-Bekederemo], in his classic edition of *The Ozidi Saga* from the Ijo; Joseph Sidahome, in his collection of Ishan tales under the title *Stories from the Benin Empire*; and myself, among various western Igbo towns and villages.

Historical and Cultural Relations

For a long time, the federal government found it convenient to leave the political geography of midwestern Nigeria pretty much intact. This was because, despite the changing political fortunes of the country and the concomitant boundary adjustments (designed both to reduce the areas of inter-ethnic friction and to evolve a manageable administrative framework for the nation), this area has continued to demonstrate a high degree of cultural uniformity between its constituent units. One notable aspect of this uniformity may be seen in language. There are twelve major ethnic units in the area which may be conveniently reclassified into four linguistic groupings: Edo, Igbo, Ijo, and Yoruba, all part of the Kwa group of the Niger-Congo language family. Alagoa has pointed out that these four groupings are estimated to have parted ways about 5,000 years ago (1966:282); but, in their daily speech, the overlaps between these peoples so outweigh the gaps that "there can be an argument, at least theoretical, that [they] all . . . belong to one language stock" (Otite 1977:44).

Although the fortunes of history and politics have bred in the various peoples of this area certain sensitivities which must be respected, it may safely be said that for a long time Benin presented itself as the principal member of that social stock. I am, of course, aware of the implications of this acknowledgment. This chapter will be concerned with how various communities in the region so respected the presence and power of Benin that they consecrated their mythic traditions to its overarching image. But the influence of Benin is just as noticeable in contemporary cultural scholarship. Although the Ishan, Etsako, Urhobo, Isoko, and other peoples have scarcely been in the habit of calling themselves Edo, scholars have continually imposed that identity on them, presumably in acknowledgment of the high degree of similarity in social institutions between these peoples and the Bini (i.e., natives of Benin).

The name "Edo" is reported by Egharevba to have originally belonged to the slave who helped to save the life of Oba Ewuare in the course of his struggle for the kingship of Benin; on the death of the slave, the Oba "caused the country to be known as Edo after his deified friend" (1968:16). This may be no more than an eponymous claim, and there is even less justification for the same claim being extended by scholars to peoples who have hardly any illusions about what names to call themselves. In an otherwise stimulating paper, Otite tells us:

Just as the Bini are "the Edo of the Benin Kingdom" . . . so also the Urhobo are the Edo of their various kingdoms/states and the Ishans the Edo of their various chiefdoms etc. Academically it is currently a non-question to say who is the original or genuine Edo and who is not (1974:19).

Although I recognize the hegemonic stress to which Otite may be reacting here, I do not consider it particularly urgent that the name Edo should be enthusiastically embraced by people who have perfectly respectable names by which they have been called for as long as anyone can remember.[6]

Still, the power and position of old Benin within this large social stock can hardly be denied. Whether or not we accept that the visible kinship derives from the impact and imprint of Benin's "imperial" might, we should at least recognize various shades of cultural similarity between Benin and other groups in this area, both Edo and non-Edo. We cannot, of course, expect perfect uniformity across the entire region. However extensive the contacts may have been between Benin and the other groups, the latter have for a long time had historical and other links with communities beyond the region—especially across the River Niger to the east and northeast and the creeks of the delta to the southeast—that have inevitably left some imprints on their cultures. But the cultural kinship with Benin is substantial. Perhaps the most noticeable aspect of this is in the pattern of social and political organization. In most areas of midwestern Nigeria, it has been found that the basic unit of government is the village or town (Thomas 1969, Bradbury 1957); even though Ikime has argued for the clan as the broader context of village institutions and traditions among the Urhobo and Isoko, he nonetheless acknowledges the fundamental autonomy of the village in the day-to-day government of the two related groups (1969:14–16, 1972:28–42).

The control of affairs within this basic unit also reveals a considerable kinship between Benin and the other communities. Casting a broad, comparative glance on evidence assembled by various scholars working in the area, Otite has noticed a general pattern of dual or plural organization in the sociopolitical life of the various communities, arising partly from the convergence of several streams of migration and partly from the imposition of an alien-derived rulership system on the indigenous village structure (1977:43–53). At the bottom of this structure, on the level of indigenous organization, we find the male population of each village is divided into three age-grades—or four, as in the case of the Urhobo and Isoko (Ikime 1969:15–16). On the average, the youngest age-set, covering the ages from ten to about twenty-five, are responsible for some of the lesser duties needed to keep the environmental, social, and cultural life of the village functioning properly: these include the cleaning of its streets, building and maintenance of the ruler's premises, digging of graves, and other basic but demanding tasks. The age-set(s) immediately following this represent the main executive class of the society; not only is the first age-set directly answerable to them, but they are generally charged with conducting some of the duties relevant for the survival of the community, such as (in the past) waging war on other communities with which they might have scores to settle, e.g. boundary disputes, gross affronts to the community, refusal to pay mandatory tributes or levies, and so on. The final age-set is made up of the elders—aged roughly from fifty onward—who not only superintend the duties of the median age-sets but constitute the ultimate authority on the key issues of the cultural and religious life of the community.

Such a portrait might leave the impression that the village political organization in this area is essentially gerontocratic in character. But the structure is complicated, or perhaps enhanced, by a system of titled organizations into which male citizens are qualified to enrol on attainment of certain kinds of achievement (e.g., killing dangerous animals or, in the past, claiming human heads in war) or, as frequently nowadays, on the payment of enormous fees. So much more highly are these titles rated than age in the conferment of status, in both the social and political life of the village, that a man may suffer some humiliation if he does not take any title. Among the Urhobo, for instance, the members of the final age-set are called the *ekpako* (sing. *okpako*), and the corresponding titled organization into which they could enrol is that of the *edion* or *ehonmwonren* (sing. *odion* and *ohonmwonren*); any *okpako* who does not take the title is excluded from the major deliberations relating to the life of the village and is commonly derided as an *okpako igheghe*, meaning "ordinary" or "worthless elder." In Asaba, a man of forty who has taken the *alo* title could interrupt a nontitled man of fifty in the course of his speech simply by dropping his goatskin fan on the ground and standing up; the ensuing scene may be awkward and a few objections raised, but the untitled older man would normally have no choice but to let the titled younger man take precedence over him.[7]

At the top of the village political structure is the ruler of the community. There is no strict uniformity across this region in the method of choice of such a ruler. In many villages the office is traditionally awarded to the oldest man within the titled group in which old men are entitled to enrol—in effect, a unification of the principal merits of age and title in the village status-system. In Benin, however, the rulership has always been hereditary. Despite the periodic internal strife the monarchy is known to have experienced throughout its history—due largely to contests over primogeniture (see Igbafe 1979:2)—all available evidence suggests that the kingship has stayed in the Oranmiyan-descended line of rulers, beginning with Eweka I.[8] Some communities, especially among the Ishan where the earlier rulers (*enigie*, sing. *onogie*) were appointed by the Oba of Benin from among his sons or top state officials, have also observed the hereditary system of rulership.

Both in Benin and in the other communities in this area, the relationship of the titled organization to the rulership is essentially conciliar. The inherent potential for confrontation between the ruler and his advisers is perhaps obvious. Benin history abundantly shows how far a monarch could go in satisfying his whims or his emotions. A good case in point is Oba Ewuakpe who, grieving the death of his mother, "ordered a wholesale massacre of his people" (Egharevba 1968:38); there is also the example of the earlier Oba Ewuare who, lamenting the death of two of his sons by mutual poisoning, "made a strict law forbidding anyone in the land of either sex to wash and dress up, or to have carnal intercourse for three years" (15). Given this likelihood of abuse of power, the titled organizations have traditionally acted as a counterweight to the king's prerogatives, an insurance against having all power concentrated in the hands of one man (Thomas 1914:7, 40; Ikime 1969:25); in the case of Benin, several conflicts are known to have ensued between the Oba and his titled advisers over the latter's desire to maintain a balance of power and privilege (Ryder 1969:6–9, 15; Bradbury 1973:57). In more recent times, however, the benefits of the conciliar relationship of the titled class to the rulership have become equally obvious, especially in the more rural communities. Many traditional titles are nowadays taken by middle-aged sons of the village who have acquired Western education and know the wider world, and can thus counsel their less-exposed ruler in his efforts to bring to his people the benefits of modern technological progress.[9]

From our survey so far, it is evident that Benin shares with most of the communities in this region certain institutional features: first, there is the village (or town) as the basis of the sociopolitical structure, marked by a division of the male population into three or four age-sets for effective distribution of labor; superimposed on this is a rulership system working in studied counterpoise with a network of titled organizations into which men of achievement and of means could enrol. A final point of similarity must be mentioned, and that is a marked agnatic or patrilineal basis in the kinship system of most communities (Bradbury 1957:15), as against a tendency toward matrilineage in some Ijo communities (Hollos and Leis 1989; cf. Alagoa 1964).

Considering the well-advertised power of Benin in most if not all of the period of history of the other groups available for investigation, there is a real temptation to conclude that Benin had something to do with the cultural uniformity hitherto observed. It is entirely possible, of course, that Benin was preceded by some other power that it succeeded in crushing. Egharevba mentions the village of Udo as a power that gave the Benin kingdom a good deal of trouble in the latter's infancy (1968:11). Otite also cites Amaury Talbot as well as Urhobo oral tradition in suggesting that Udo preceded Benin as a power and source of migration (1974:21). And of the Ishan kings, Bradbury tells us: "Some *enigie* claim descent from chiefs who ruled before the founding of the present Benin dynasty or before the village or chiefdom in question was incorporated in the Benin state" (1957:33).

Despite all this, a large majority of the oral traditions of communities across this region invariably make a place for Benin somewhere in the origins of their peoples and various aspects of their culture. Although many scholars would agree, with Ryder, that such claims are "certainly the product of a hankering after prestige, or simply the adoption of the most likely story, given the canons of traditional historiography" (1969:3), there is no doubt that Benin had such an impact on these peoples' lives as to dominate their historical imagination.

Let us quickly survey some of these historical traditions. Of the Ishan, Okojie tells us that their name derived from the Benin phrase *esan fua,* meaning "those who fled," a reference to their ancestors who migrated from Benin following the terrible regimen imposed—as we saw above—by "Oba Ewuare the selfish" (Okojie 1960:21; cf. Ayewoh 1979:1); Egharevba, however, takes Ishan origins further back to the *ogiso* dynasty (1968:5). Of the "Edo" group of peoples, the Ishan are perhaps the most influenced by Benin. For not only were some of the earliest *enigie* actually appointed by Obas of Benin, primarily as guardians of military or ritual outposts, but even later *enigie* independently installed by their own communities had to seek validation of their offices from Benin. Besides, there existed a curious vassal relationship whereby each Ishan chiefdom had as its intermediary in Benin one of the major Benin ministers (Ezomo, Uwangue, etc.) through whom they sent tributes (e.g., livestock, food crops, slaves) to the Oba so as to maintain good relations with him (Bradbury 1973:75–76). Further north of the Ishan, the relationship with Benin was somewhat looser, evidently because Benin had to reckon with other dynastic and military powers like Nupe and Igalla bearing down southward across the Niger. Yet Benin continues to be cited as the original homeland of some of these peoples. "All the Etsako tribes," Bradbury tells us, "refer to a period of oppression and civil war in Benin which led to an exodus of refugees to the North" (1957:101; cf. Edemode 1972:187).

Of the Niger delta communities, most of the Urhobo and Isoko clans claim Benin origin (Ikime 1969:6, 1972:21), although there was input from Igbo and Ijo sources to the east and southeast. Here again, control from Benin was not so strong, due largely to the distance involved and the hostile terrain (mangrove forests and swamps) which obviously proved an encumbrance to invasion. For instance, when an Oba of Benin sent a punitive force against one of the Urhobo communities, Ewu, and had their town burnt down because the people did not seek sanction from Benin upon the installation of their king, the Ewu quietly rebuilt the town and would still not seek the required sanction; the Oba's forces did not return to the place (Ikime 1969:14). Otherwise, most of these communities felt compelled, out of regard for the political and ritual power of Benin, to repair to Benin and seek the Oba's blessing on the appointment of a king (*ovie*, linguistically akin to the Bini *ogie*), receiving royal tokens in return.

Of the non-Edo groups in the Niger delta, most Ijo clans consider themselves indigenous or autochthonous, tracing their distribution to only a few "dispersal centers" within their own area (Alagoa 1972:187). Still, a few of the clans point to roots in Benin. The Mein clan, judged by Alagoa "obviously influential over all of the Western Delta" (67), is reported by tradition to have been founded by an ancestor of the same name who left Benin "because of internal wars" and settled first at Aboh and later at Ogbobiri on the Sagbama-Igbedi Creek. From here, some of his descendants dispersed to found other settlements, like Kiagbodo under the leader Mgbile, and Akugbene under Kalanama. Once established, each leader sought legitimacy (encouraged no doubt by antecedent Urhobo and Isoko practice) by making contact with the Oba of Benin and receiving political sanction of his title (*pere*) as well as material tokens (bronze insignia, etc.) in return for allegiance to Benin, especially in matters of trade (52–53, 63–66).[10] The Tarakiri clan—ancestral home of *The Ozidi Saga* (Clark-Bekederemo 1991) —also looks to Benin sources. Although the eponymous (?) Tara or Tara-kiriowei is said to be related to the Kolokuma east of the Sagbama-Igbedi Creek, it is held by tradition that their father Ondo "lived at Benin, but left with his three sons because the Oba seized private lands and levied heavy taxes." Wars with the Mein and other clans caused much dispersal among the Tarakiri, but Orua remains the principal settlement of this clan (Alagoa 1972:71). As with the Urhobo-Isoko neighbors, the physical presence of Benin here was rather negligible.[11]

By far the largest non-Edo group in midwestern Nigeria are the Igbo communities west of the Niger, embracing the present-day Oshimili, Aniocha, Ndokwa, and Ika local government areas. Here the sources of derivation are varied, but it is clear that Benin exercised an early influence in the history of the area. In Asaba, for instance, traditions speak mainly of the founding of the town by one Nnebisi from Nteje near Awka, east of the Niger. But there were confrontations with Benin, one of which followed an invitation by an autochthonous unit (Obodo-Achala) contending with Nnebisi's descendants (Ohadike 1988:194–195).

A variety of sources have been claimed for other west-Niger Igbo communities. Some, like Isele-Uku, claim autochthony. The village of Obior is reported by Egharevba (1968:4) to have been founded by a rich Bini noble-man named Ovio who fell out of grace with the reigning *ogiso* and was forced to migrate with his followers. Of the others, Igbuzo (Ibusa) is said to have been founded by two strands of migration from the east-Niger Igbo, one led by Umejei from Isu (the exact location of which has not been established) and the other by Edini from the old Nri civilization close to Awka. Edini's brother, Odaigbo (or Adaigbo), who had set out on the journey with him, went further on to found another community, naming the place Ogwa-Nri Ukwu—meaning "the large meeting-place of the Nri settlers"—the original name of the town we know today as Ogwashi-Uku. Other communities, however, like Ezi, Onicha-Ugbo, Onicha-Olona, and Onicha-Ukwuu claim to have been founded by a certain Eze Chima who, following a quarrel with an Oba, was pursued from the Benin kingdom and settled with his followers in this area. In time, Benin continued its harassment of the area, causing many of the settled immigrants to continue their flight until they crossed the River Niger at Asaba and settled at what is today called Onitsha. In fact, the name Asaba is said by some to have derived from a Benin statement *A'i sa ba*, meaning "We cannot cross," made by the pursuing imperial troops; a different account, however, traces the name from a statement made by the founding ancestor to the effect that he has made his choice (*A habaa m*, i.e., "I have chosen") of a place to settle.[12]

Benin is known to have enforced its presence and influence quite visibly in this area which, unlike the delta country, was readily accessible to Benin forces. Several oral accounts claim that the paramount rulers of some com-munities were imposed on the people by Obas of Benin, who demanded tributes from them and made war on them when these tributes were not forthcoming. In most of the accounts, however, Benin is said to have lost the war either in a direct military confrontation with the people or as a result of the people's clever strategy of evasion. Whatever the case may be, Benin found the territory here so easy to penetrate that it made frequent incur-sions upon the communities: raiding for slaves or for overdue tributes, visiting punishment upon those thought to have offended against the mon-archy, and other such activities, by which the kingdom sought to impose its power upon the communities. Consequently, Benin's presence in the area was so palpable that, as we shall see in chapter 2, the kingdom was thought to be within earshot.

Granted that the presence of Benin was so pervasive, why did it loom so large in the narrative imagination of these peoples as to appear to be just around the corner? In discussing Isoko traditions, Ikime suggests "it is reasonable to expect that those clans which left Benin as refugees would not be anxious to maintain close links" (1972:22). It could equally be urged that the memory of Benin origins and contacts among these communities would hardly have been so dramatic and pervasive had that history been a happy one. It is true that some narratives portray the Oba as just and wise, even Solomonic, in his decisions: we shall see one of those portraits in chapter 3. But a large majority of these narratives recall experiences so harsh that the Oba, like Benin generally, frequently emerges as a menace that must be confronted and overcome or exorcised.

These stories were no doubt inspired by the physical cruelties and generally harsh demands of life in old Benin. It might be easy to dismiss the evidence cited by European scholars and agents as having been cobbled together to support the larger imperial designs of the European presence there. For instance, one of Vice-Consul Gallwey's official reports on a visit to Benin in 1892 speaks of such a proliferation of human sacrifices and of corpses "strewn about in the most public places" that the city "might well be called 'The City of Skulls.'" However, the real aims of the imperial officer emerge clearly enough: "The rule appears to be one of Terror, and one can only hope that this Treaty may be the foundation of a new order of things throughout the vast territory ruled by the King of Benin" (Ryder 1969:347).

Still, the oral traditions of various peoples paint such a vivid picture of terror that one could hardly blame those who fled to save life and limb. According to an Abraka tradition, their founding ancestor "Avbeka was a son of an Oba of Benin whose birth it had been necessary to keep secret in order to save his life because the then Oba, his father, had given instructions that all male children born to him should be killed so that there would be no obvious heir to the throne who would become the center of palace plots" (Ikime 1969:7).

Other stories point to an equally capricious urge for blood and vengeance on the Oba's part. In the Agboghidi epic from Uzairue, the Oba is shown to have annihilated the town of Iyololu and enslaved whatever was left of its population, and on another occasion to have demanded the head of the newborn child of his adversary Agboghidi (Edemode 1977:10, 12). In the Ukwuani story of Onodi Onye-mma, the Oba, incensed that he is losing the favor of a young girl to the hero Gbodumeh, orders that the girl's womb be "tied" to prevent her from ever getting pregnant (Anene-Boyle 1979:96). Despite Sidahome's dedication of his anthology of Ishan tales "to the Oba of Benin" and the frequently favorable image of the Oba in these stories, standard references to cruelty emerge now and then.[13] For instance, on learning that the hero Elonmo had intruded into the apartment of one of his wives, the Oba "ordered Elonmo to be executed without delay that very evening, and ordered the execution to be one of shame. That meant that Elonmo was to be hacked to pieces, and the pieces dumped in a special enclosure near the sacred tree which stood opposite the city market. There the pieces would be eaten by dogs, vultures, and night-prowling wild beasts"

(Sidahome 1964:133). In the story of Okodan, we are told that "the daily prayer of the Oba's subjects was: 'From the anger of the Oba, O God, deliver us'" (26).

Such terrors are echoed by no less an authority than the Benin nationalist historian Egharevba. Lamenting "the atrocious hearts of the people" (1968:5) as responsible for the numerous migrations from Benin, he documents throughout his *Short History* the most horrific incidents that had become characteristic of the sociopolitical life of the city and kingdom, from reckless fratricide (13, 26, etc.) to the most whimsical disregard, by the monarchy, for the life of the average citizen (21, 38, etc.). And if anyone still questions Gallwey's report, perhaps the following epitaph by Egharevba on the rule of Oba Ovonramwen, who died in Calabar whither the British had exiled him, will prove convincing:

> That the character of the Benin people had sunk very low was shown by the numberless human sacrifices which they offered, and oaths such as *Oba o gha gb-ue* (May the Oba kill you) showed that they feared the Oba more than God or the gods. The old Benin, with its barbarities and horrors, had to fall before the new Benin could rise and take its place (60).[14]

But perhaps the most dramatic element in the memory of the emigrants—the most solid context within which they have sought to take their revenge on old Benin in their stories—is war. Numerous traditions of origin in this region speak of internal or civil wars in the kingdom as the primary cause of migration. Not the least of these were the grim fratricidal contests within the rulership, like the one between the sons of Oba Ozolua or the war over primogeniture between the two eldest sons of Obanosa (Egharevba 1968:26, 43); there were also struggles between the Oba and his dignitaries, like the fight between Oba Ehengbuda and his Iyase (Ryder 1969:15). Having left Benin, however, the emigrants and their hosts did not know much peace from the kingdom. For war became firmly established as an instrument of Benin policy, ordered by a hierarchy of generals (or, perhaps more accurately, war ministers) beginning with the Iyase, and followed by the Ezomo and then the Ologbosere. Egharevba says that "it usually happened that a king would declare war about three years after his accession to the throne" (1949:35); the period of utmost warmongering in the kingdom was the reign of Oba Ozolua, evidently the most bellicose on record (Egharevba 1968:23, Ryder 1969:12).

These wars would appear to have been inspired by the anxiety to secure the widest area of economic control, especially in the face of European commercial activities along the Atlantic coast (with respect to slaves and other commodities); the Obas must have felt an urgent need to keep alive the transit routes and sources of supply within their zone of influence (Bradbury 1973:47–51, Ryder 1969:15). Thus, if any "vassal" community within Benin's area of influence did not secure validation from the Oba of the installation of its paramount ruler (Onogie, Obi, Ovie, etc.) or present yearly tributes to Benin, this was usually taken as an act of insubordination or rebellion and visited with a punitive expedition.

But the military machine soon degenerated into a reckless display of adventurism, to such an extent that the Oba would send soldiers to a community simply "as a matter of routine. They did not interfere with the local government, but it was customary to entertain them lavishly or face condign punishment like the burning down of an entire village" (Ikime 1969:14). The wanton arrogance was epitomized by the careers of the Ezomos, who became so much the centerpiece of the war organization that they rivaled the Oba in riches if not in power. "They delighted in warfare," Egharevba says of them, "as a hungry man delights in food and if their history could be written it would make a big volume" (1968:81).[15] Is it any wonder, then, that the communities in this region, living constantly in fear of attack from Benin, developed such a psychology about war that in their narrative imagination they have repeatedly sought to exorcise the bogey of Benin? Let us now turn to a sample survey of their narratives.

Mythological Relations

In a sense, these stories from outside Benin may have been inspired by stories told within Benin; the emigrants may thus be seen to be striving to recall the archetypes (in some instances at least, notably in Ishan) but to have succeeded only in bending the original imagery and symbolism in the warp of time. Dan Ben-Amos gives us an insight into the main concerns of the tales:

> The Benin kingdom was one of the main West African empires and its traditional history is abundant with tales of intra and intertribal warfare, conquests, and victories. . . . The Oba is certainly the political, religious, and social center of Benin culture. Yet, throughout its folklore, art, beliefs, and even its political system, there are undertones of tensions between the rural areas and the court (1972:106–107).

Ben-Amos goes on later to cite instances of performances by semiprofessional Bini storytellers he has himself recorded, regarding contests between the Oba and his nobility (110–111). The outcome of these contests is obvious, as Ben-Amos elaborates elsewhere in a discussion of Benin folklore and ethnomusicology:

> Finally, in the expressive dimension, the heroes of the professional story-teller are rural magicians and other powerful rural people, or suffering characters on the margins of Benin society. The Oba himself looms in the background as a threatening figure whom the hero cannot combat (1975:54).

This may well be true of performances by narrators within Benin, who would not be expected to put the dreaded Oba in an inferior position. Besides, these narrators are probably the descendants of those who had faith enough in the nation to stay while others left it. But Ben-Amos's observation is far less true of stories told outside Benin, where the image of the Oba (or the Ogiso of the antecedent dynasty) is frequently negative. Even the Ishan, who may be considered the closest to the Bini culturally and territorially, tell stories in which the will if not the personality of the Oba is successfully combated by local heroes.

Let us refer again to some of Sidahome's representations of confrontation between local heroes and the Oba in Ishan stories. In the first story of his collection, titled "Eneka," the hero's action in interrupting the Ezomo of Uzebu's obeisance to the Oba and later flooring the Oba's champion wrestler Igbadaken clearly has an undertone of revolt to it. In the story titled "Elonmo," the hero infiltrates the Oba's palace and abducts one of his wives (an abomination in Benin), overcomes all the obstacles put in his way by the imperial system, and is triumphantly installed Onogie (local king) in place of the incumbent, who had aided the Oba against him. "When the news . . . was reported to the Oba of Benin as required by custom," we are told in the closing lines, "the Oba accepted the fact and confirmed the appointment. He realized that the feud between himself and Elonmo was directed by fate, and decided to end it with good grace." The Ishan, we must recall, were also victims of the obsessive militancy of ancient Benin, so that, even if they were to tell "Benin stories" among themselves, they could not help giving vent to some of their repressed feelings about the sad old days. Heroes like Eneka and Elonmo are a reification of that resentment.

Further away from Benin, however, the revolt is stronger. The stories may conceivably hark back to Benin backgrounds, as in one Ukwuani (Kwale) tale, which starts by recalling "those times, long before we settled here" and "the great men—men like the Oba of Idu (Benin), men like Izomo the warrior, Igwara of Idu, Ologbo-selem and Akpe" (Anene-Boyle 1979:10).[16] But there is a progressive reduction of the image of Benin the further we move from the kingdom, so that we can recognize the following general pattern. First, the major figures of the imperial organization (the Oba, his generals, and his principal warriors) are set up for humiliation and sometimes destruction, or at least portrayed as representing the dangers and evils that must be eliminated for the peace and well-being of the community.

Secondly, the kingdom of Benin is conjured as a terror that lurks menacingly around the peripheries of the community, attracting other symbols of evil that may not easily be identified with any known figures in Benin history and society.

Let us examine a few of these images and figures inspired by the memory of Benin in the traditions of its old adversaries.

Agboghidi: The story of Agboghidi, Ben-Amos tells us, "is one of the corner-stones" of professional storytelling in Benin and is frequently used as an opening piece:

> The plot concerns rural chiefs, their conflicts with each other, collisions between father and son, and struggles to gain the favors of women. . . . Agboghidi, the rural chief, fights not only against the other country rulers, but also against the chiefs of Benin City, though not against the Oba himself (1975:52).

Agboghidi is certainly one of the principal figures in Benin oral tradition, and it is arguably from this random source that Egharevba has composed his "historical" portrait of that figure. But in Egharevba, Agboghidi is not so much the name of a specific individual as a title, a sort of commander or military governor, first appointed by Oba Ehengbuda in the late sixteenth century and stationed at Ugo "to keep the warlike people of Iyekorhionmwo from attacking Benin City" (1968:33). The better known Agboghidi of Ugo comes up, however, in the reign of Oba Akengbuda in the eighteenth century, where his real name is given as Emokpaogbe. I quote the account in full so as to put the personality of this particular Agboghidi in proper perspective:

> Soon after the accession of Akengbuda, a prince of the house of Oboro-Uku came to Benin City to be invested as Ogie or Obi (king) of Oboro-Uku. While dancing round the city after his investiture, according to custom, he called on the Ezomo at Uzebu, who presented kolanuts to him through his beautiful daughter Adesua who had been betrothed to the Oba. When the Obi caught sight of her he wanted to marry her, but she insulted him, calling him "Bush Ruler" in derision. The Obi was indignant, and when he got home he used charms to bring Adesua to Oboro-Uku. Against the advice of her servant, she asked leave of her parents to go to Oboro-Uku to demand a debt owed to her for the sale of goats. When the Obi heard she was there he sent for her, and when she again refused his attentions and insulted him he had her murdered.
>
> When the tidings reached Benin City the Ezomo went to the palace to break the news to the Oba, and to tell him of his intention to make war against Oboro-Uku. The Oba, however, said that he would avenge his lover's death himself.

Akengbuda sent troops under the command of Imaran Adiagbon, and another contingent under Emokpaogbe the Agboghidi (Onogie) of Ugo. After severe fighting the town of Oboro-Uku was captured and the head of the Obi was sent by Imaran to the Oba. A dispute then arose between the two generals, each endeavouring to convince the Oba that the victory was due to his personal valour, though in fact the credit belonged to Emokpaogbe.

Emokpaogbe was very dissatisfied with the rewards given to him by the Oba, and when he returned home to Ugo, acting on the advice of his head slave Arasomwan and a war drummer, he behaved in such an unbecoming manner that a serious report was made to the Oba against him. The Oba sent for him to come to Benin City, but he refused and had the messengers killed. He then declared war against the Oba, who at first refused to engage in conflict with this general who had distinguished himself in the Oboro-Uku campaign, and offered to pardon him. But Emokpaogbe would not desist and began to harass the city. The Oba was compelled to despatch three companies of warriors, Obakina, Igbizamete, and Agbobo, dressed in red uniforms, under the command of Ologbose and Imaran. They camped at Ugboko-niro, and fought several battles, and Ugboko-nosote, one of the villages allied to Ugo, and a fierce battle was fought about a mile distant from the town. Emokpaogbe was defeated, but he escaped, and before he could be overtaken he drowned himself in the Janieson (Igbaghon) river. It is said that Emokpaogbe's wife Emokpolo, who was a sorceress, helped her husband greatly (41–42).

Sidahome's Ishan version of this story (1964:45–72) follows essentially the same lines: as earlier discussed, it is entirely possible that it was from the same general pool of performances, spanning the Benin-Ishan area, that Egharevba drew for his historical reconstruction. In Sidahome, however, we get more of the details that the empiricist Egharevba must have felt inclined to eliminate, apparently because they were of little interest to the monarchically centered history of Benin.

In Sidahome, then, the following details about Agboghidi, reflecting the general pattern of the folk hero's life, emerge. He is born to the Onogie (king) of Ugo and his wife who, having had a succession of daughters, are told they will bear a son (Emokpaogbe) who will cause great trouble but will be a mighty warrior. He emerges from his mother's womb with a complete set of teeth and in six months is a fully grown, formidable, but repulsively ugly adult. In an effort to get rid of him, his father the king charms him with an illness which defies every remedy. In the end his mother takes him to Obolo, whose famed sorcerer-king Ogiobolo not only cures Emokpaogbe but makes him impervious to all dangers and powers (including those of Ogiobolo himself) as well as weapons; they also enjoin on each other an eternal bond of loyalty. Upon Emokpaogbe's return the king, his father, makes further plans to kill him, but is killed instead, and Emokpaogbe succeeds him as Onogie of Ugo, assuming the name Agboghidi.

Fate brings Agboghidi into marriage with the extraordinarily beautiful lady Emokpolo, born on the same day as he and likewise with a complete set of teeth. He also acquires a slave from Obolo who plays enchanting music that drives Agboghidi into wild acts of heroism. He forms all kinds of amorous liaisons, acquiring a new wife Udin and falling into a near-fatal love affair with a river goddess, Igbaghon. The rest of Agboghidi's career follows essentially Egharevba's account of the confrontation between Benin and Oboro-Uku (Obolo) and Agboghidi's role in it, down to the treachery of Ima of Ogbelaka (Egharevba's Imaran) and the war between Agboghidi and the forces of the Oba. There are, however, a few interesting twists to Sidahome's version. While Egharevba tells us that the Oba sent "three companies of warriors . . . dressed in red uniforms" against Agboghidi, Sidahome makes the army "a band of children" dressed in red "as a dancing company," a combination found to be taboo to Agboghidi. He continues to flee from this army until, in the end, he turns into a rope "although it is also believed by many that Agboghidi drowned himself." His wife Emokpolo, appropriated by the Oba, later rejoins Agboghidi in the spirit world, where he continues to threaten that he will destroy the world. The story ends on an etiological note:

> This explains the great thunderstorms. The lightning flashes are the brandishing of Agboghidi's great sword, Ghoma-Gbesin. The thunder is Agboghidi's showing his rage to the world. The dull echoing which follows the thunder is, of course, his dear wife Emokpolo, soothing and calming him down in order to protect the world she loved.

On October 12, 1980 I recorded the story of the war between Benin and Ubulu-Uku from Charles Simayi of Ubulu-Uno, a sister town to Ubulu-Uku (Okpewho 1992:192–201). Although the figure Agboghidi does not feature at all in Simayi's story, the details of the latter are clearly a variation on those in Egharevba's and Sidahome's accounts. Whereas in these versions the Ubulu king goes to Benin to secure validation of his title by the Oba, in Simayi's the leader Ezemu, an expert medicineman, goes to Benin in response to an open invitation to traditional doctors anywhere to save an incumbent Oba from dying soon after his coronation, as successive Obas before him have done. Having cured the Oba, Ezemu is rewarded with the Oba's first princess as wife and her younger brother as page. On his way from Benin, Ezemu is accosted by the Ezomo, who will not let a mere provincial chieftain take a Benin princess away to wife. Ezemu demurs, but on reaching Ubulu-Uku spirits the princess away to himself with a spell. In the ensuing war between the Bini and the Ubulu, the former's forces are seriously trounced, losing one contingent after another to a mere band of seven hunters led by Ezemu. In the end, Benin is forced to sue for peace; as a cardinal part of the settlement, the village of Ugonoba[17] is earmarked as the boundary between the two peoples, with a firm injunction that the Bini should never again kill the Ubulu.

Besides the disappearance of the Agboghidi figure in this version, there is a significant reduction in the image of Benin: an imperial power is brought to its knees by a small provincial community.[18] Especially remarkable is the treatment of the Oba of Benin's image. In Egharevba he is portrayed as master of his decisions and actions. In Sidahome the peace-loving Oba continues to advise patience against his people's urgent pleas for war with the Obolo. But in the Ubulu version the Oba is cast alternately as bloodthirsty (he orders the execution of one candidate after another as each fails the test that will qualify him to be the Oba's doctor) and pliable (he allows himself to be driven to war by the Ezomo, earning the reproof of his soothsayer in the end); in fact it is the Oba himself who timorously leads the Benin peace party to meet Ezemu and his men at Ugonoba!

The Agboghidi figure reemerges in an epic from the "Edo-speaking" Etsako (Edemode 1977). Here again, in an area fairly distant from the kingdom of Benin, the image of the latter and particularly of the Oba suffers a considerable reduction. In this story, Agboghidi is presented essentially as a symbol of the revolt of a provincial people aginst the imperious, high-handed government of the Oba of Benin. Briefly, the Bini annihilate the town of Iyololu and enslave whatever remains of its population; the young hero Agboghidi is received into the Oba's household. But he suffers one humiliation after another (e.g., being cheated of game he has killed) simply because he is an outsider, not one of the Oba's children. He continually protests against these acts of degradation, until one day someone confronts him in a public gathering with the truth of his background, i.e., the fate of his community. This is the final blow. Agboghidi makes away with one of the Oba's princesses, against the latter's warnings, and war is summarily declared on him. Agboghidi returns to the annihilated village of Iyololu, where he is eagerly received by a sorceress, Oledo, who offers him magical aid as well as regular warnings of attack from Benin. The Oba sends one imperial army contingent after another, but Agboghidi exterminates them all until, as we are told, Benin "is empty of men. . . . There are only women in Edo now" (24). The Oba tries other schemes, working in consultation with sorcerers who devise antidotes to Agboghidi's mystical power. But the war drags on for several more years. In the end, the sorcerers discover Agboghidi's secret power: On one day, all the women left in Benin suddenly become pregnant without sexual intercourse; on the last day of the ninth month they all give birth to male children, who begin to walk and talk that same day; they are then equipped with red uniforms and sent to destroy Agboghidi. Unable to fight off this last challenge, Agboghidi and Oledo decide to commit suicide, drowning themselves and the children in a sea.

This Etsako story of Agboghidi reveals its kinship with the Benin tradition in a few places. Besides the details of red-uniformed warriors and the hero's death by drowning (along with a sorceress), the injustices visited on Agboghidi in the Oba of Benin's palace may be seen as a variant on the Benin detail of Agboghidi's being cheated of his achievement in the Benin-Oboro war. Besides, Benin and Iyololu are shown to be so close that the Oba and Agboghidi can see one another from their respective houses (12)—an echo, perhaps, of the nearness of Benin and Ugo in the "original" story. However, the revolt against Benin in this provincial story is just as striking. The Oba is portrayed as powerless and helpless before the humiliating career of the hero; a song which begins "I threaten, I threaten the king" (28) underscores the antimonarchical spirit of the tale; another song urges the hero "Agboghidi kill Edo!" (24) for, after all, "It's not brutal, it's no waste / That men killed one another in Edo" (31); and all through the story the Oba's blood-lust is emphasized by his constantly calling for the head of adult and child alike.

The character Agboghidi also appears in the Ijo epic, *The Ozidi Saga*, edited and translated by the renowned poet-playwright John Pepper Clark-Bekederemo (1991). The Ijo occupy perhaps the furthest reaches of Benin's imperial influence in this region. Although, as I pointed out above, a few Ijo clans invoke Benin roots, this is one of those areas where the kingdom's political and cultural control could be said to be weakest. It is therefore not surprising that the principal figures of Edo folklore do not enjoy quite the same prominence in the traditions of this non-Edo people.[19]

To be sure, Benin continues to be evoked as a large mythical setting for Ijo stories. In his introductory essay to *The Ozidi Saga*, Clark-Bekederemo makes the following observation on the attitude of the various narrators he has recorded to the setting of the story:

> In the Okabou text the stress is on Orua, or Oruabou, that is, the city seen as a state set in some remote time and place, although within the present boundaries of Tarakiri Clan. Both Afoluwa and Erivini make no such insistence on the Ijo setting of the story, being content to use Ado, the other name for Benin City, the conventional setting of Ijo tales and fables. This, of course, is no evidence that these stories derive from Benin or that the city is the original home of those who own them. Rather, Ado, to the Ijo imagination, is the embodiment of all that is distant and mysterious, the empire of improbable happenings that together with the world of spirits help to explain the events of their own lives. Okabou in fact was always self-conscious when, prodded on by Madam Yabuku of Inekorogha, leader of the recorded session at Ibadan, he toed the clearly patriotic line of preferring the local name to the foreign one of Ado. Beyond this, he retains all other names that are clearly non-Ijo, principal ones like Ozidi, Oreame, Orea, Temugedege, and Ogueren which in all likelihood are Benin, while Odogu is obviously Ibo (xxxvii).

I think we should take seriously the quandary revealed in Clark-Beke-deremo's doubting, on the one hand, that either the story or its bearers traced from Benin and conceding, on the other, that the names of its principal characters are of Benin derivation. It should be clear, however, that the extensive physical separation of the Ijo homeland from the heart-land of the Benin kingdom would tend to attenuate the impact of Benin on the content of the story, which may be responsible both for the loss of the standard elements in the Agboghidi canon—dying in a body of water, red-uniformed soldiers, etc.—and indeed for the fairly subordinate position this character occupies in the Ozidi story. For despite its Benin echoes, this story emphatically proclaims its Ijo ecology and cultural setting, so that the respective characters, whatever their derivations, are subordinated to the superior image which the Ijo oral tradition has created for its culture hero. Thus, although Agboghidi is one of the principal opponents of Ozidi and indeed the first of his father's assassins assigned to confront him, it takes Ozidi the least time of all to dispose of him. In this story, then, we have one of the clearest examples of what might happen to images or symbols from Benin (a) in an area where Benin political and cultural hegemony was not so strong, and (b) when the local tradition tended to assert itself.

Aruanran: A similar pattern may be seen in the fortunes of the character Aruanran. There is a much larger fabulary shroud covering this figure, it seems, and perhaps for this reason he gets rather short shrift in the empiri-cist program of Egharevba. There are basically four references to him in the *Short History* (pp. 24–26). First, in the warmongering reign of Oba Ozolua, "Okhumwu was conquered by Prince Aruanran one of the Oba's sons, who brought a large number of captives to Benin City" (24). Next, we are told that he was one of the first three sons of Ozolua, the others being Osawe and Ogidogbo; to find out who was the strongest among them, the three were made to pole-vault over a pond in the palace quarters, and while Aruanran and Osawe succeeded, Ogidogbo fell down and was crippled, thus losing the contest for the succession to the Obaship. The third reference to Aruanran concerns the contest for primogeniture between Osawe and Aruanran. Though he was born first, Aruanran's birth was announced later than Osawe's, and a struggle later ensued during which Aruanran "went to an old woman at Uroho village who trained him in the art of black magic, which he used after the death of his father in his struggle with Osawe." The final reference deals with Aruanran's fratricidal war with Osawe, now crowned Oba Esigie. According to Egharevba, Esigie

> was greatly worried by his brother Aruanran, chief of Udo, a man of giant stature. At last a punitive expedition was sent against Udo. Many battles were fought, sometimes one side being victorious and sometimes the

other. The fiercest went by the name *Okuo-Ukpoba* (Battle of Blood) in which Oni-oni, the only son of Aruanran, was killed. To avoid being taken prisoner, Aruanran drowned himself in the lake Odighi n'Udo.

As we can see, the only concessions Egharevba makes to the folk imagination are to Aruanran's being "a man of giant stature" and his being equipped with magical skill. In Ben-Amos, however, we get a little more insight into his image in Benin oral tradition. Ben-Amos sees him as one of the "folk anti-heroes, tragic figures who were part of the king's family but failed to live up to their royal status . . . a foolhardy giant" who was cheated out of his inheritance and ended his life by drowning in a lake" (1972:109). More pertinently, Ben-Amos tells us that in these Bini stories, Aruanran is represented as "a giant who had twenty toes and twenty fingers, and one who could never tell whether he was coming or going" (1975:44).

There is a rather detailed treatment of the Aruanran story in Sidahome's anthology of Benin/Ishan stories (1964:164–196). As with the Agboghidi story, there are striking similarities in detail between Sidahome and Egharevba (although the latter, as we have seen, is a much more abbreviated and selective account); but there are also striking departures and elaborations. We first meet Arualan (as he is called in Sidahome) in his protolife as the troublesome and hateful spirit Ekatakpi. Worried about their childlessness, Oba Ozolua of Benin and his favorite queen, Ohomi, send to the land of spirits for a solution; Ekatakpi, after much solicitude, and violating all the injunctions laid on him by the king of the spirit world, is incarnated in Benin as the child of Ohomi and named Idubo. But he is born at the same time as another child—Esigie, son of queen Idia—whose birth is announced first. Robbed of his primogeniture, and hated by the Oba in his early childhood, Ekatakpi withdraws to live with the sorceress queen of Uroho, Iyenuroho, better known as Iyenugholo. Under her, this extraordinary child, with ten digits on each limb and a mighty head, grows by leaps and bounds to be a towering giant. The sorceress names him Arualan (giant), and fortifies him with all kinds of magical power to ensure total invincibility, including the power to cause her own destruction. Arualan loses no time in putting his powers to the test: he turns Iyenugholo into a bee and she disappears forever.

Arualan (as his protoself Ekatakpi) came into the world destined to become a great warrior. His first military feat upon leaving Iyenugholo's palace is his victory over Esohen, king of the remote town Amagba; Arualan destroys the town and brings the head of the intractable Esohen to Oba Ozolua, thus winning the love and attachment of a father who once disowned him. Reinstated with pomp and honor in Benin, Arualan goes on to perform his most endearing feat. The town of Okhumu is ruled by a powerful king (who has continually harassed Benin) and defended by the giant

Egbamarhuan, who happens to have been fortified with magic by the same
Iyenugholo who made Arualan invincible. The war between the Benin and
Okhumu forces proves long and fierce; but Arualan is able to summon his
most infallible tools of sorcery to destroy the enemy and lead a triumphant
army and numerous hostages back to Benin.

As Ozolua advances in age and declines in wit, a conflict between the
princes Arualan and Esigie becomes inevitable. By a slip of the tongue which
is quite contrary to his earnest intent, the Oba irrevocably names Arualan
king of Udo, rather than Edo. All attempts by Ozolua to rectify the situation
fail, and prince Esigie is crowned Oba of Benin on Ozolua's death. In the
end, the two brothers are drawn into war, which Arualan loses by a tragic
error: He orders that his entire possessions be thrown into the lake Odighi
if he does not return triumphantly from his march against Benin. Meanwhile the Benin citizens, fully aware they cannot withstand Arualan, withdraw from the city to a person. Arualan returns to Udo disappointed but
hoping to strike again at Benin someday; however, his subjects at Udo, seeing
their king returning without the customary sounds of triumph, dump all his
possessions into the lake in obedience to his instructions. This is the final
despair; Arualan jumps into the lake, to be lost forever. But he is deified, and
his point of disappearance "is regarded as sacred ground to this day."

The native Benin versions of the Aruanran story, as we find them in
Egharevba and Ben-Amos, are certainly not positive. A palace historian,
Egharevba is as patronizing as ever. Ben-Amos is scarcely more charitable.
Grouping "Arhuanran" with the eighteenth-century Oba Ewuakpe, Ben-
Amos says, "Both were deviant persons within the court, failures within a
hierarchical society, rejected by the system because of their own misdoings"
(1975:44). Both Egharevba and Ben-Amos also talk of Aruanran as suffer-
ing defeat, with Egharevba specifically suggesting military defeat in which
Aruanran took his own life "to avoid being taking prisoner" (1968:26).

The picture is, however, not so negative in Sidahome's Ishan portrait of
the hero. Although in his protolife Arualan proves rather recalcitrant and
destructive, in the human world he shows himself a hero very much in
control of his stupendous urge for action. This is most visibly demonstrated
in his treatment of the emissaries from Okhumu: he repeatedly sends them
back with a warning to their king to desist from testing the wrath of Benin.
On the eve of the Okhumu war, we are told, Oba Ozolua

> prayed that Arualan might strike his enemies hard, but that his enemies
> should be powerless to strike him.
> Arualan objected to this last prayer.
> "This is to be a battle between men, and it should not be one-sided," he
> said. "Pray that my enemies should be able to strike me, but that I shall
> emerge victorious" (1964:186).

Far from suffering any military defeat, he comes to grief only as the victim of a tragic flaw in his massive self-confidence. On the whole, therefore, we could safely consider Sidahome's Ishan portrait of this character quite sympathetic. He is presented as an undeserved loser in the Benin game of political intrigue, and in the Ishan oral tradition stands as a legitimizing symbol of revolt against an overbearing imperial machine.

Much further away from Benin City, in the delta regions to the south, the image of Aruanran undergoes essentially two kinds of transformation. First, he is portrayed as a giant constantly putting his restless energy at the service of the oppressed. In one of the Ukwuani narratives collected by Anene-Boyle, this giant of twenty toes defends his father, the Oba of Idu (Edo, or Benin), against the men of Atu who have come on the last of the quinquennial missions to pluck the tooth of the Oba for their festival; Igwara (as Aruanran is called among the Ukwuani) kills them to a man and puts an end to the hateful ritual (1979:75–78). In another story, Igwara defends his sister-in-law Oyibo against the seducer Okalimadu and kills the latter in a brutal fight, though he goes on to turn Oyibo into an anthill, evidently because he sees her, an exceptional beauty, as a possible source of further troubles in the future (90–93). Although the giant's old grudge against Benin survives in his sometimes turning around, unprovoked, to slaughter fellow-citizens of Idu (75), in these Ukwuani stories the emphasis in Igwara's representation seems to be on his using his stupendous energies for the destruction of those who constitute a menace to society.

A second transformation of the Aruanran image puts him in very much the same position that we saw Agboghidi: in the context of Ijo folklore, as far from the heart of the old kingdom as we could get in this region. Once more, there are strong traces of affiliation with Benin oral tradition in the character Ogueren (or Oguaran), as he is called in *The Ozidi Saga*. He is a giant of disproportionate size, a man "of twenty hands, twenty feet," uprooting silk cotton and iroko trees as he tramples along the way.[20] As with Agboghidi, however, this legendary figure is simply a victim of the urge of the local tradition to assert its own heroes; so that, although he gives Ozidi a great deal more trouble than Agbogidi does, Ogueren crashes to his ruin in the face of Ozidi's irrepressible onslaught.

Other images: The above discussion of some major characters in the narrative traditions of communities within Benin's pale of influence has revealed that to a large extent the tales, insofar as Benin is their point of reference, have served the communities in asserting their sense of themselves against whatever pressures Benin or their memory of her may impose upon them.

Let me stress yet again that, despite their demonstrably rebellious spirit, these narratives do sometimes betray a certain romantic attachment to Benin. This is no doubt a manifestation of the nostalgia felt by those emigrants who took "Benin" stories to their new places of abode. Bowra has made useful observations (albeit in a different context) on such an attachment on the part of a colony which "leaves home for some distant land and keeps touch with its past by glorifying it in legends" (1972:80). Hence we find Igwara in Ukwuani narratives principally defending his father, the Oba of Benin, and Benin's people. An Isoko tale entitled "The story of Odugo and his wife Ibakpolo," which is evidently a variant of the Agboghidi story, also tells of the hero Odugo (Ogie-Ugo, i.e. king of Ugo?) fighting in defence of the Oba but losing all restraint, until he is brought to grief by an army of red-uniformed children (Welch 1935:409–410).[21] However, even in such stories it is clear that, however deep the attachment felt for the homeland, there is usually a subtle comment against those who made life unlivable, whether in that homeland or in the new abode: usually the Oba and his war functionaries.

Of various other images from old Benin that have received negative treatment in the narrative traditions of its opponents, a particularly interesting one is the tooth-plucking Oba—that is, an Oba who every year or so demands one tooth from the mouth of a prominent man or leader of a "vassal" community for ritual sacrifice. A strange twist to this image has been recorded from the Ukwuani by Anene-Boyle in "The Narrative of Oba Nkpeze" (1979:75–84), in which the Oba is the Oba of Benin himself who, every year, must surrender a tooth to envoys from the town of Atu for an annual festival, until Igwara (= Aruanran) puts an end to the obnoxious order. In other traditions, however, the finger is pointed squarely at Benin. Akegwure discusses one such tale from the Isoko:

> The Omofobhon epic treats the theme of an Oba who would send a band of warriors to "pluck" the tooth of a particular man to him annually. This tooth he would offer to his personal god as festival offering. This continued for many years until the just God gave this man a hero child Omofobhon who avenged his father's shame by confronting and defeating each successive band of warriors and heroes sent against him by the Oba (1978:4).

On October 13, 1980 I collected a very similar story from Mr. Ojiudu Okeze at Igbuzo (see chapter 2); in this case, the ensuing war culminates in the killing of the Oba and the enthronement of his erstwhile victim as the new Oba of Benin! In the Isoko and Igbuzo versions of the tooth-plucking story we have, it would seem, a symbolization of the tributes Benin periodically exacted from these communities and the revolutionary spirit whereby they sought to throw off forever the yoke of subordination hanging round their necks.

History and the Folk Imagination

The variety of evidence so far examined seems to indicate that, in a good many cases, the oral traditions of communities within this region—insofar as they recall Benin whether directly or indirectly—have been employed to highlight one aspect or the other of their painful relations with the kingdom. Admittedly, in these tales, Benin may not always be identified as a culprit and may indeed be treated with some sympathy. But, even in such cases, a careful analysis will show that the accusing finger is being pointed at Benin, albeit obliquely, and that the story does hold up for castigation an evil, set well within the time when Benin had a dominant influence over the life of the community. For instance, in the Ukwuani story of Oba Nkpeze, it seems clear we have an inversion—motivated whether by politics or by art, we cannot really tell—of the system whereby Benin annually imposed tributes that hurt these people to their eye-teeth.[22] Or it may be the inversion was psychologically motivated: the Ukwuani would like to see Benin visited, even for one moment, with the sort of cruelty it practised on other communities!

Did the Ukwuani borrow that tale from their neighbors (e.g., the Isoko) or their ethnic kin (e.g., the Igbuzo) before making that inversion? This question touches the heart of limitations to our present knowledge of the cultural history of this region. Earlier in this chapter, I have done little more than corroborate both oral and written evidence in establishing the political eminence of Benin over her neighbors. I started by identifying, again following both forms of evidence, a wide range of cultural similarities between Benin and these communities. But until we can establish by other methods "which peoples are older than which or who drove whom in what direction" (Alagoa 1966:282), it would be difficult if not pointless to press any diffusionist claims on these narrative traditions.

In fact, we have to be careful what approaches we adopt in constructing our empiricist histories, and the perspectives from which we assemble our information. I suspect that part of the trouble with the Benin Scheme came from the fact that its labors were centered to a disproportionate degree on Benin, apparently with the aid of influential figures like Egharevba. However, in comparing the evidence of Egharevba and any of the traditions from outside Benin on any historical event—like the Benin-Ubulu war—we soon find that one people's history is another people's fantasy. For instance, in his history of Benin kings, Egharevba seems to have left little room for military failure on the part of any of them. But one strongly suspects that Ehengbuda, who, according to Egharevba, died in a boat accident "on his way to Eko (Lagos) to visit the colony founded by his father" (1968:33), may have in fact suffered a defeat—given the warmongering fever of that era—and died in the process.[23]

The same goes for the evidence from the oral traditions of Benin's rivals. None of them would be expected to tell stories which put them in an inferior position to Benin even though we know that, in terms of sheer organization at least, Benin stood a better chance of winning any military confrontation with them. Since, given the painful memory of their experiences, very few of them had reason to love Benin, the more fantastic the claims they make, the happier they will be to have surmounted, psychologically at least, those "inaccessible barriers" (Todorov 1975:158)[24] that Benin by its very might and status constituted to their self-realization as well as peace. Benin is evoked as a backdrop even in animal tales without human participants (Ben-Amos 1975:15, Okpewho 1983:66), and perhaps there is no greater proof than this of its pervasive influence. But it is mostly in tales of confrontation, set within the context of war and other tests of physical and supernatural strength, that Benin's opponents have steadily sought to turn the tables against a bogey that loomed so large in their lives.

On the whole, these tales define a terrain of hegemonist stresses that scholarship and policy have not always treaded with care. For the rest of this study, I will be examining some tales from my fieldwork to see ways in which one Nigerian subgroup—the west-Niger Igbo of the present-day Delta State —try to represent themselves vis-à-vis Benin in their mythology, and the message of such acts of self-determination for nations that have failed to attend to them.

The Hunter Who Became a King: Heroism and Social History

2

The present chapter will be built around a story told me in October 1980 by Mr. Ojiudu Okeze of Igbuzo (Ibusa), about a war of resistance against an Oba of Benin's imposition of tributary rights on the town. I have found the story interesting both for the historical claims it seems to make and for its development of the heroic figures on whom the championship of the cause of resistance is made to rest.

Before I go any further, perhaps it is necessary for me to defend the two concepts—history and heroism—which constitute the central focus of this chapter but resound in varying degrees throughout the rest of the book. Historians, especially of "Third World" societies, have pretty much won their fight to treat testimonies from oral culture as valid material for historical reconstruction. By benefiting from recent trends in the study of oral *performance*, scholars like Barber (1991), Vail and White (1991), and Tonkin (1992) have advanced the frontiers won by Dike (1956), Vansina (1961), Ogot (1967), and others in establishing the value of oral traditions as coded representations of the past. I must admit, however, that as an oral *literary* scholar, I collected Ojiudu's story under circumstances considerably unlike those in which most professional *historians* gather their own testimonies. Fully encouraged to exercise his artistic genius as best he could—including the use of musical instruments—Ojiudu has gone on to tell a story dressed for the most part in what would strike even the likes of Jan Vansina as the encumbering baggage of "myth." I have no desire, of course, to rekindle the fires of controversy between various schools of thought on the analysis of oral texts.[1] But I am impressed by the degree to which Ojiudu's story—or any other in this study, for that matter—respects, even as it subverts, the criteria set by the most conservative philosophers of history.

I will defer discussion of various positions regarding historicity and truth until later on in the present chapter. However, in addressing the historical claims the focal text appears to make, I will at least examine, however briefly, some of the basic positions taken on the subject by one such conservative scholar.

Collingwood, in his studies, has gone to considerable length in recommending what counts as historical evidence and subject and the sorts of intellectual or imaginative conditions enabling historical composition. In the first place, the relevance of Collingwood's thinking on the subject is severely limited by his Eurocentric bias, whereby he—rather like Hegel before and fellow Oxonian Trevor-Roper after him—credits Europe and no other nation outside the European world with a sense of history (1993:14, 22, 90). And yet there is little in his theorizing on history that would be judged totally alien to non-European thought at least as revealed in the oral traditions of the societies represented in this study. With regard to the proper subjects of historical thought, on which Collingwood has a considerable amount to say (1993:302–315), there will be abundant evidence in the narratives cited in this study that the communities in question have reasonably vivid memories of their historical relations with Benin, in matters concerning political strife and especially warfare (which represent for Collingwood the essence of "purposive action") as well as moral values (e.g. the proper conduct of the rulership).

A particularly interesting aspect of Collingwood's philosophy of history has to do with the relations between the past and the present, wherein may be found a kind of holistic intelligence that might be considered a fundamental virtue of historical thought. Earlier in his reflections on the subject, he says rather pointedly: "The past does not exist and cannot be perceived. . . . We come to know the past, not immediately, but by interpreting evidence" (1965:136). Over time, he seems to have come to a more subtle understanding of these relationships, and now the past "is not something that has finished happening"; it is reenactable, so that thanks to the present we are able to see the truth of history (1993:xxxviii).[2] However, on the whole Collingwood has shown a sufficient understanding of the bonds between events in the past and their ramifications in contemporary life to propose— against thinkers such as Spengler, Spencer, Santayana, and others—that "the historical past, unlike the natural past, is a living past, kept alive by the act of historical thinking" (1993:226).

Nothing here essentially contradicts the substance as well as the spirit of the traditions to be examined later in this study. Indeed, as several studies of traditional African culture have tried to point out (Abraham 1962, Mbiti

1969, and especially Soyinka 1976), the past makes sense only in the light of the present. For Africans who have an almost religious faith in the continuity between past, present, and future, no account of the past would make sense that did not reckon with the dynamics of present life, including the anxieties as well as aspirations of the people and the ideologies embraced in safeguarding their interests now and for all time.

Does this argue a narrow, parochial appreciation of the import of their localized experience? Not at all. Even when filtered through the idiosyncratic genius of a single narrator, the collective memory is characteristically inclined to set its lights on a wider universe, especially because it has been called to being by the people's need to defend their stakes and their values against the outside world of inimical interests. The ecumenical vision of these so-called "local narratives" is also evidenced by the proverbs with which the accounts are frequently seasoned: they serve the purpose of putting a historical event or personality within the larger scheme of human life, in the hope that the right lessons are drawn by whoever hears them for proper conduct in the future. When, therefore, Collingwood argues that "it is just the universality of an event or character that makes it a proper and possible object of historical study" (1993:303), he acknowledges in effect the power of these accounts to transport us beyond the local conditions in which they are situated to an ethical field wherein physical reality achieves its full meaning only within the context of a people's hopes and aspirations. Here history and culture (in the broadest sense) are indissolubly linked and—if we may borrow a technical idiom—an objective rational enquiry (*historia*) into a people's past is of necessity held in some balance by a subjective imaginary (*fabula*) that bears the full charge of the people's well-considered interest and time-hallowed outlook. Bietenholz clinches the point when he proposes that "elements of *fabula* occur in every facet of historical thinking" (1994:396).[3]

The idea of the subjective imaginary brings me to the sort of mind that conceives history. As I argued toward the end of the last chapter, every historian—whether literate like Egharevba of Benin or illiterate like Simayi of Ubulu-Uno, in their differing accounts of the war between their peoples —is in a fundamental sense subject to the view of reality embraced by his society and especially to the political interest underlying this. The philosopher of history is not that much better: else why does Collingwood so readily deny all the world outside Europe a sense of history? Collingwood is, however, quite on the mark when he acknowledges the subjectiveness of historical thought in resisting all bondage to antecedent authority, or its eclecticism in deciding which of a body of material to utilize in weaving what seems the best possible tapestry of events (1965:138–139, 1993:235–236, 245). The strength of the traditions around which this study is built is that their narrators have put a more than average premium on the *poetic* value of the details they have chosen to highlight in their accounts of their people's historical relations with Benin.

Collingwood runs into a particularly interesting problem when he begins to investigate the differences between the artistic and the historical imagination. The raw material of history is *evidence*, which for the historian "must be something here and now perceptible to him." And yet this evidence, Collingwood tells us, "is evidence only when someone contemplates it historically. Otherwise it is merely perceived fact, historically dumb" (1993:247). Whatever Collingwood might mean by *historical* contemplation, contemplation by its very nature involves some amount of interpolation or extrapolation that lifts the material in question from the level of general consensus to that in which it is subject to varying degrees of disposition or prejudice. And when that material is intimately bound with a people's nationalist and other aspirations—no less in the war between Benin and the Ubulu than in the ones between the Germans and the Western allies—we can understand why the lines between the aims, if not exactly the processes, of the historian and the artist may be a little blurred.

No less problematic is the concept of heroism which is linked with the nationalist spirit revealed in these traditions. Despite the level of curiosity and interest aroused by the growing vogue of publications on heroic literature, the heroic image has always attracted as much antagonism as admiration especially among Western audiences. Homer's Achilles captured the imagination of many an artist and intellectual in classical antiquity; but in the changing political as well as cultural fortunes of a world dominated first by Greece and later by Rome and Christian Europe, that image—as Katherine King has ably demonstrated (1987)—increasingly lost its appeal. In our own era, the ravages of global confrontation have made the hero as ugly as the causes he has been set up to defend; thus films like *Patton* and *Apocalypse Now* have endeavored to show up the grotesque illusions and demonic will of figures living well outside the humane outlook of civil society.

Two books in particular may be considered representative of the reduced estimation of heroism. In his interesting study *The Hero in History* (1943), Sidney Hook investigates two contending claims as to how history is made or progress achieved: is it by self-appointed leaders (heroes) who guide their nations' affairs along a path dictated by them, or by certain social forces that necessitate the emergence of personalities who provide timely leadership and thus propel the nation in an inevitable direction? Hook's verdict is that, whatever the merits of either claim, the interests of society today are much better served by a "democratic philosophy" that guarantees everyone free access to the decision-making process than by a system that entrusts the available options "to an event-making man, or to an uncontrolled elite."

Peter Tatham's *The Makings of Maleness* (1992) is directed at questioning the assumptions on which the social construction of maleness or masculinity were founded. This work of analytical psychology attempts to erase the differences between the sexes by seeing the genders as corresponding and complementary qualities—rather like the *yang* and *yin* of Chinese thought —that make up the human entity. Highlighting the ugly aspects of heroism and the essential loneliness of the heroic personality, Tatham argues that there really is a heroic *potential* in us all, male or female, that may be gainfully developed toward the emergence of so many "strong egos," thus offering society a wealth of democratic alternatives.

It would be naive to contend the wisdom of these counsels, especially in view of the obduracy with which the tyrants of the "Third World"—the site of the traditions examined in this book—continue to enforce their will against their peoples' search for democratic choices. Still, a close reading of the narratives will reveal they are fundamentally informed by the same spirit of self-assertion that propels the contemporary struggles for liberation from tyrannical rule. In fact, the narratives achieve their full significance in the context of the continued assault on freedom in these nations, and may be said to have continued to linger in the collective memory precisely because the factors inspiring the will to resist are still very much in place. Although a few of these narratives have names of attested historical figures, more often the hero is unnamed, so that (s)he serves the symbolic purpose of broadly representing the urge in every one of us, man or woman, to shed the shackles that constrain our quest for personal, cultural, political, or other form of self-realization.

The days, then, of heroism in the style projected by these tales of the oral tradition—when *men* spoke only with the point of the machete, as Simayi proudly declares in one of his heroic tales (Okpewho 1990:127)—may very well be over. But by the same logic of "presentism" underlying Collingwood's conception of the historical imagination, Ojiudu's story below, as well as all others around which this study is built, should be read against both the people's historical memories of the power of Benin and their contemporary discomfort under the structures of coercion inhibiting their lives.

Heroism among the Western Igbo

In his excellent and pace-setting study of the Anioma or west-Niger Igbo, Don Ohadike presents a picture of societies descended mostly from the Nri-Igbo stock, a people known for their itinerant professionalism and a culture marked by a certain aversion to all but defensive violence. West-Niger Igbo societies had a stable system of "peace weeks" (devoted to the veneration of divinities guaranteeing subsistence) during which they not only eschewed all harsh conduct but were, unfortunately, open to the well-timed assaults of war-mongering outsiders (1994:33–38). Ohadike contrasts these western Igbo peoples with some other Igbo communities east of the Niger (such as Ohafia, Abiriba, Abam, and Edda) where brigandage was the norm, and the practice of head-hunting was upheld as a stepping-stone to social prestige among men in the prime of youth. Ohadike makes the interesting point that this practice of head-hunting developed in response to the aggressive commercialism of the Aro-Igbo. The Aro, as middlemen in the growth of the Atlantic slave trade, encouraged young men among the Abam, Edda, Ohafia, and Abiriba to organize slaving raids on neighboring communities, thus inspiring among them a penchant for aggression and a code of conduct that required the young warrior to show proof of triumph (in the form of human heads). Nevertheless, Ohadike tends to follow several Igbo authorities in concluding that the Igbo are naturally averse to the shedding of blood, especially the blood of close kin, so that there are traditional rites designed to cleanse anyone who has committed any kind of killing (even of wild animals) and thus protect them from being damned by the tutelary spirits of their victims.

Any differences between the western and eastern Igbo in the practice of aggression or heroic daring can only be a question of degree, because the western Igbo narrators I have recorded tend to speak with considerable pride of the days when men *were* men and, to borrow a phrase from Ohadike, "combined patriotism with brigandage" (1994:34). If the more peaceable, Nri-descended western Igbo were not so easily under Aro influence, they at any rate caught on fast enough to the heroic ethic for which their eastern kin were reputed.

Perhaps the defense of hearth and home, or even defense of the community at large, was the earliest inspiration to heroic conduct. If that is the case, we may be sure that, in their long history of coping with the territorial hazards involved in settling themselves this side of the Niger and later of fending off one imperial power after another, the western Igbo have had their fair share of heroic action. I fondly recall one of the songs my mother used to sing in Asaba as she laundered our clothes on Saturdays. Originally sung to lament a war leader who died fighting on despite the massive decimation of his troops, it is performed these days mostly by female song groups on a variety of social occasions, but especially funeral ceremonies:

> Ojea, o-ho, Ojea
> Ojea, nene-kee n' ogu anaa
> Mmili amaa ahu-o, kpem' akwa?
> Ojea, nene-kee n' ogu anaa

Ojea, o-ho, Ojea
Ojea, nene-kee n' ogu anaa
Oku adu ugbo, kpem' odu ugba?
Ojea, nene-kee n' ogu anaa

Ojea, alas, Ojea
Ojea, behold, the fight is over
Would rain soak the body and spare the clothes?
Ojea, behold, the fight is over

Ojea, alas, Ojea
Ojea, behold the fight is over
Would fire raze the farm and spare the fence?
Ojea, behold, the fight is over.[4]

The reference to fire in the second stanza may suggest Ojea led the forces of the community in one of those wars in which Asaba was torched by the enemy, such as the one between Benin and Asaba (Ohadike 1988:122), or one of several confrontations between Asaba and the forces of British colonial occupation (Ohadike 1991:68–76). Ojea may thus be said to have been engaged in an altruistic duty, a hero fighting in defense of his nation against external forces of imperial domination. And yet the western Igbo were hardly free of the self-serving commercialism that inspired the head-hunters east of the Niger to go on slave-raiding campaigns. They may not have been in the service of the Aro middlemen, but the phenomenon of the evil commerce brought out the worst in the adventurous youth quite as much as it did in their eastern kin. Again, I recall a snatch of heroic song popular in Asaba during my early youth, possibly dating from the slave-raiding days, but lamenting the abolition of the practice:

Osiyoje, osiyoje, osiyoje-o?
Unu ma n' odika abu Oyibo
Anyi anwulu Igbo ge-elelie o!

What happened, what happened, oh what happened?
Do you know, but for the white man
We would have captured and sold off the Igbo![5]

The two images presented by the songs I have cited above are in a fundamental way indicative of the major strands of heroic personality to be found across a wide range of heroic narratives, both among the western Igbo and elsewhere. Indeed, we could go on to say that the nature of oral heroic literature is ultimately bound up with the discernible qualities of the heroic figures around whom the events of the narratives are built.

There has been a respectable corpus of scholarship on the subject both in an archetypalist light (von Hahn 1876, Raglan 1936, Bowra 1952, Rank 1959, de Vries 1963, Campbell 1972, and others) and from a more or less African perspective (Sidibe 1959, Biebuyck and Mateene 1969, Biebuyck 1978, Bird et al. 1974, Bird and Kendall 1980, Okpewho 1979, Johnson 1986). In my own cited contribution, I have defined the oral epic or heroic narrative as "fundamentally a tale about the fantastic deeds of a person or persons endowed with something more than human might and operating in something larger than the normal human context and it is of significance in portraying some stage of the cultural or political development of a people" (34). In my analysis of the heroic personality (80–134), I have tried to highlight those extraordinary qualities of the hero that give him peculiar claims to the attention of artist and audience alike and constitute the determining parameters of the heroic myth. Toward the end of that chapter, however, in my effort to understand the cultural relevance of such superhuman figures to the world of ordinary people, it became clear to me that in many cases what we have in the heroic personality is a complex mythic symbol of "the cooperative will existing side by side with single-minded arrogance." Such a symbol perhaps helps society to resolve the conflict of values imposed upon it by certain contingencies of its cultural history. "Society," I have suggested, "does welcome honor and distinction and has the highest admiration for a man who surmounts all odds to see that his people survive. But it is also aware that the person who accomplishes such feats is not like the rest of his fellows and should be feared" (131).

In my continuing investigation of heroic traditions of the western Igbo, there have been cases in which one might attempt a clear line between public-spirited heroism and heightened self-glorification. But there are also cases in which the line is so faint that value judgments become hard to make. Even in the song of Ojea cited above, would it be unreasonable to suggest that, in pressing on with the fight when it is clear he is so hopelessly outnumbered, he has been driven more by a blind urge for personal glory than by an honest sense of patriotic duty?

Ojiudu's narrative, cited fully below, will give us an opportunity to observe the point where private interest ends and public service begins. But let us do a quick sampling of tales from this region and the forms of categorization they suggest to the casual eye. To begin with, we may speak of *private heroism* in respect of stories in which the obvious principal aim of the protagonist is to show how much more powerful he is than everyone else in the society. He is a strongman, a terror, and in many instances an egotist or loner with little concern for the lives or interests of other people; he puts his strength to the service only of his own whims and self-gratification.

At Igbuzo in December 1977, Mr. Christopher Ojiudu Okeze told me the story of a certain Opia Nwammemee, a strongman who took pride in dis-possessing other men of their belongings and even of their wives. At Oni-cha-Ugbo in September 1981, Mr. Odogwu Okwuashi Nwaniani told me the story of just such a man; but the interesting thing about the latter character is that he was a prince—son of the paramount ruler of the town—who nevertheless chose to live on the outside, at the entrance to the town, where he was well placed to intercept unsuspecting travelers and visitors. He got away with anything he did, of course, both because of his extraordinary might and because of his privileged status in the community.

By far the most remarkable of the accounts narrated by Odogwu along these lines—usually short but arresting anecdotes—were of the legendary Omezi of Onicha-Ugbo, who was not really a loner but was no less given to acts of brazen arrogance. On one occasion, he had owed someone some money. When the man visited Omezi to demand payment of the debt, Omezi asked members of his household to build a fire. When the fire was crackling with red heat, Omezi called his creditor to come over and have a look. In the full gaze of the man, Omezi thrust his own hand into the fire and held it steadily while it burned; the frightened creditor abandoned the debt and took to his heels, imagining what Omezi would do to him if he would do so much to himself!

On another occasion, as Omezi was on his way to the village of Ubulu-Uku, eight stalwarts jumped out of the bush and blocked his path, threaten-ing to put an end to his life. He simply burst out laughing, declaring that God had at last answered his urgent prayers. While his assailants were looking, Omezi brought out a machete, placed one of his fingers against a tree and cut it off: the eight men turned and fled, frightened at the thought of what a man who cut off his own finger might do to his enemies!

Omezi was actually going to Ubulu-Uku to recover the debt of a cow owed his father by some persons there. Taking his gun and his machete, he had told his family, "You will see my feet going, but you will not see them coming," leaving them wondering what he might mean. On finally getting to Ubulu, he announced his mission to the debtors, telling them also what he had promised his relatives. To avoid his wrath, the debtors lost no time in procuring a cow. Again he reminded them what he had pledged his family, that they would see his feet going but not coming. To stress the point, he drew his gun and machete. The poor debtors took his persistence and menace to mean he wasn't quite impressed by the size of the payment, so they consulted among themselves and produced a second cow. When they thought all was set to go, he bawled at them, "Didn't you hear what I promised my people, or do you want me to walk home to them on my feet?" It was then the full meaning of his words got home to them. So, while some of them dragged the two cows to Onicha-Ugbo, others had to bear him on their heads. Even when they arrived at his compound, they were forced to slaughter a goat to him before he would consent to set his feet on the ground!

The prime focus of private heroism is on the hero's personal ego, but the last anecdote on Omezi indicates some potential of communal interest even in the conduct of such a personality. We may thus speak of *public heroism,* in the sense that the hero places his strength and other endowments at the service of others. Such a heroism might be seen not so much in terms of an antithesis as of an extension of the private kind.

As Omezi's mission to Ubulu-Uku suggests, the more immediate beneficiaries of the public hero's activities are his ego, his family, his friends, and other such limited circle. In chapter 1, I gave the instance of the Ukwuani giant Igwara who, dangerous individualist though he frequently is, nevertheless undertakes to defend his brother's wife (Oyibo) against her seducer, Okalimadu, whom he kills in a fierce battle, although he proceeds to turn Oyibo into an anthill because he suspects her (an exceptionally charming woman) as a possible source of future troubles for the family (Anene-Boyle 1979:90–93).[6]

In September 1981, Charles Simayi of Ubulu-Uno told me a story of the defense of a family's honor by two brothers. A poor elderly man of the village of Akwukwu is insulted in council by a younger colleague, who calls the older man irresponsible simply because he has no children of his own. The old man ambles home, lamenting his lot, and is overheard by his stalwart nephews, who demand the full details of their uncle's experience. Stung to the quick, the young men set out and systematically annihilate the offender and his entire family. There is a sad saying, sung repeatedly as a refrain accompanying the tale, that "the childless man never goes to a meeting." The heroic revenge carried out by the old man's nephews does the double service of defending their family's honor as well as offering protection to those who are only unfortunate victims of a natural disability.

The menace of wife-snatching also appears to be a favorite motif of much heroic lore. Besides the Opia Nwammemee career cited above from Ojiudu Okeze, Simayi had in October 1980 told me the story of the hero Meeme (Okpewho 1990a). Onukwu Agbada, one of the privy councillors to the Obi (king) of Ogwashi-Uku, loses his wife to a seducer from Abba by name Odogwu. When Onukwu seems incapable of taking the initiative to rescue his wife, his fellow councillor Meeme undertakes to do the job, scorning Onukwu as a despicable coward.[7] Single-handed, Meeme goes to Abba, terrorizes both the ruling council and the entire population of the town, rescues Onukwu's wife, kills her seducer Odogwu, and takes home with him the latter's head and some livestock, to be used in performing the annual rites of the Obi of Ogwashi-Uku. In Meeme's adventure we can again feel the thrust of the hero's personal ego; in fact, Meeme has undertaken the rescue mission to validate the boast he makes to Onukwu in council:

> I will tell you I am greater than you.
> We are all titled men, but I am greater than you.

But it is equally clear that Meeme sees the abduction of a titled man's wife both as an affront to the institution of marriage and as an insult to the community at large. He has thus put his overbounding self-assurance at the service of his peers and his people.

Meeme's heroism illustrates clearly enough the continuities between the private and public categories of that virtue, but it also projects public heroism as the highest level of duty and the best guarantee of a community's survival. No doubt this is what gives stories like Ezemu's defense of himself and his people (the Ubulu) against the formidable power of Benin a more than average measure of poetic afflatus, as well as an extraordinary level of appeal for indigenous audiences. While everyone respects those who can survive, on their own terms, the daunting threats to life in a world where might is right, there is much greater admiration for, and comfort in, those who put their extraordinary qualities on the line so that the less well-endowed masses are protected from the reckless abuse of power by those who have such a superabundance of it.

Do we now wonder why elements of the fantastic, with which many of these tales of confrontation with Benin are liberally tinged, are treated more as an article of faith than as dubious indices of a national identity?

Ojiudu's Story

The following story of the hunter who became an Oba (king of Benin) represents a fairly widespread motif from the Benin cycle—the tooth-plucking Oba—in which, as I indicated in chapter 1, the king demands a tooth or set of teeth from a prominent man or leader of a (subject) community for periodic rituals. These tales of tooth-plucking would seem, as I have suggested, to be the canonization of a pattern whereby Benin imposed itself upon these communities in intensely disturbing ways; they are of value mainly as reification of a psychological triumph—if not exactly as record of a historical victory—over a bogey that loomed so long and large over people's lives. At any rate, Ojiudu's story provides us a unique opportunity to assess the various levels of recognition accorded to figures who have traditionally assumed the challenge of championing their people's historic struggles for survival.

The story was recorded at Igbuzo (Ibusa) at about 9:00 P.M. on October 13, 1980 on the premises of my brother-in-law and field collaborator, Patrick Ibe Arinze, at St Thomas' College. Besides the performer Ojiudu and his accompanist, James Okoojii,[8] there was an audience of about one dozen people, including Arinze, his wife Kate Nwaka (my sister), their children Ngozi and Linda, their nurse Adobi, Ignatius Osadebe (Arinze's friend), myself, and some neighbors. The performance of this tale lasted 16 minutes and 54 seconds.

Of particular interest is the music that accompanied this and other tales recorded that night. Some of Arinze's neighbors were young men teaching at St Thomas' for their National Youth Service Corps (NYSC) duty and living in the apartment directly facing his. Before the session of tale performances, these young men had been playing popular (disco) music on their cassette deck, rather loud for our purposes. Although we had persuaded them to reduce the volume of their music for the sake of our recording, and although they listened to some of our sessions with faint interest (being non-Igbo speakers), their disco music was still fairly audible to us outside. To counteract the interference, our performers, Ojiudu and Okoojii, turned their instruments (the *opanda* box-harp for Ojiudu and a metal gong *agogo* for Okoojii) somewhat loud. The development was no more auspicious for my recording, as the vocal text would be severely distorted and pose considerable problems at transcription. I had to persuade the two gentlemen to move a little further away from the tape-recorder and to reduce the volume of their music.

But Ojiudu's musical temper was not to be controlled. In the 1950s and 1960s he had led semiprofessional groups playing parts of Northern Nigeria and later back home in Igbuzo. In the 1950s, in fact, so influential was his *opanda* music, so revolutionary and antiestablishment (*Opanda ama n' oyibo di,* "Opanda doesn't know [i.e. care] that the white man exists," was one of his favorite airs), that many youths took to it rather than go to school or seek regular employment, a development that on occasion got Ojiudu into trouble with the colonial government. Storytelling was for him, therefore, more than an exercise in words: it was a *musical* performance, and he was hardly going to be outdone by a bunch of youngsters playing the white man's music. The frequent musical flourishes in Ojiudu's tale—longer, on the whole, than in the performances of the other narrators I have recorded—are clearly an assertion of professional pride by a man who has had occasion in the past to defend it.[9]

But perhaps they serve a purpose that may be considered just as intrinsic to the content of the tale. As a close examination of the tale reveals, there are two segments to it, with a discernible hiatus between them. Now, I happen to have another record of Ojiudu telling the first segment (the seriocomic experience of the hunter with his women) as an independent tale. Is it at all possible that, in this atmosphere of confrontation between him and the meddlesome young corpsmen, Ojiudu has been driven to complicate a (superficially) lighthearted tale of gender rivalry with the memory of his people's historical confrontation with Benin? The answer may lie in how well the two segments of the story fit.

Ojiudu: This very one I'm going to tell is about how people come to be man and wife.
(*5-second music flourish*)
A man once went and had a child—a son, it was.
Since he was born, he [son] never married a wife:
If he lived with a woman, and she cooked a late meal, he would kill her.
5   While he lived
He took a first wife, went to the bush.
He said to her, "You see this food you are about to cook?"
She said, "Yes."
He said to her, "I'm going to the bush.
If you ever cook this food, and don't finish before I return, I'll kill you." His wife told him, "Go to your bush. I'll finish the cooking early."
(*4-second music flourish*)
10   When he returned from that bush, only the stew remained on the fire.
He asked her, "Where's the food?" She told him, "I've finished pounding the meal, and only the stew remains."
He took his machete and cut her head right off!
(*Side comments; 5-second music flourish*)
HE WAS A REAL STALWART, THAT MAN.
AFTER A WHILE, ONE WOMAN SAID SHE WAS GOING TO MARRY THIS MAN.
15   They told her, "Haven't you heard what's happening
That whoever cooks a late meal, he kills her?"
She told them she was going there.
(*6-second music flourish*)
She went right to his house, and told him, "I've come to your house." "What for?" he asked her. "To marry you," she said.
"What!" he told her, "Haven't you heard what I said:
That whoever cooks a late meal in my house will be killed?"
20   "I will marry you," she replied.
"Isn't it cooking early [that you want]?"
(*3-second music flourish*)
At daybreak, the man said he was going to the hunting bush.
She told him, "Go ahead."
She started cooking.

<table>
<tr><td>25</td><td></td><td>This time, she was only pounding the meal when he returned.
She began to plead, saying, "Please, my lord:
It didn't take me long to get up and start cooking early.
I didn't know that it . . . that you would return so soon."
    He told her, "You knew that was my rule": took his
    machete and cut off her head.
    (Low exclamations)</td></tr>
<tr><td></td><td>Okoojii:</td><td>She and the meal she was pounding lay sprawling.
    (3-second music flourish)</td></tr>
<tr><td>30</td><td>Ojiudu:</td><td>The next daybreak, he prepared for the bush, and set off.
Back from the bush, he roasted some corn.
Having eaten the corn, he lay down awhile.
Then it happened that a certain young [woman] called her
    mother at home and told her she was going to marry
    this man.
Her mother told her,
"What! Haven't you heard what's raging?"</td></tr>
<tr><td>35</td><td></td><td>She said she was going.
She got ready.
Getting to the man's house, she saw him lying down, and
    shook—roused him.[10]
The man asked, "Who are you?" "It's me," she said.
    (3-second music flourish)
He opened the door.</td></tr>
<tr><td>40</td><td></td><td>He said, "What's your name?"
She said, "Er, er, Do-gooder."[11]
"You are Do-gooder?" he asked. "Yes," she replied.
    "M-hm," he said.
"You sit down.
What brings you here?" "I've come to marry you," she said.</td></tr>
<tr><td>45</td><td></td><td>"Haven't you heard what's raging?" said he. "Of course,"
    she said. "I heard it before I came.
Isn't it that whoever cooks late will be killed?" He said, "Yes."
    (Laughter and side comments, to 6-second music flourish)
EARLY THE NEXT MORNING, he said to her, "I'm off
    to the bush. You will cook, won't you?" She said,
    "Of course, I'll cook."
    (4-second music flourish)
THAT FOOD . . . as soon as he'd left, the woman got . . .
    went off
Brought out her broom, swept the house</td></tr>
<tr><td>50</td><td></td><td>Made the bed.
    (Laughter)[12]
Went to sleep, and dozed off.
WHEN THE MAN RETURNED FROM THE BUSH
Saying, "Where has she gone? Why is this area so calm?"
She told him, "Do come in here where I'm lying—</td></tr>
<tr><td>55</td><td>Arinze:</td><td>For the food is done!</td></tr>
</table>

Ojiudu:	For one side of my leg is hurting me."

      (*Laughter*)

"How does it hurt you?" asked the man. She said, "Put it in
    where that hole is."

      (*Laughter*)

When he had put it in, she told him, "Work it!"

      (*Laughter*)

He worked it.

60   *Okoojii*:   "SHAKE IT."

    Ojiudu: "Shake it," she told him. The man was shaking it.[13]

When he had done shaking, he got off.

She said she was hurting on one side of her hip.

OUR MAN SAID TO HER, "CAN YOU BEAR TO EAT AT
    ALL?" SHE SAID, "I CAN, IF YOU'LL COOK."

65   The man got up, sliced up some yam jagwo-jagwo-jagwo
      [i.e., hurriedly], threw it in the pot

Put it on the fire.

  Arinze: The man had to do the cooking! (*Laughs*)

  Ojiudu: Our man had to do the cooking.

When the yam was done, he pounded it

70   Saying to his wife, "Can you bear to eat it?" She said, "I can, if
      you put it into my mouth."

The man washed his hands. When he cut a piece, dipped it in
    the stew, and put it in her mouth, the woman swallowed.

When she had swallowed and swallowed and had her fill, she
    asked him to eat his own, and he ate his own.

As soon as he had eaten, she said, "My leg is hurting.
    You have to work it again.

      (*Laughter*)

If you don't work it soon enough, I may pass away from you."

75   The man said, "Come on, turn around."

      (*Laughter, amid 4-second music flourish*)

Injected his remedy into her leg!

WHEN HE GOT OUT OF THAT, THE WOMAN SAID TO
    HIM, "MY LORD," and he said, "Yes?"

She said, "Will you go to the bush?" He said he was going
    to the bush.

"Be sure to go early," she said.

80   "My leg may get better

So I may be able to cook some food."

He said, "All right."

Off he went to the bush.

Getting there, he killed two antelopes.

85   On his return, he saw two pieces of wood placed by the
      fireplace:

She had set no fire to them.

He said, "Why, had you started making the fire?" She said,
    "No sooner had I struck the fire than the pain started."

Okoojii:		Didn't I tell you?
		(*Laughter, amid 3-second music flourish*)
Ojiudu:		He said, "Has the pain started again?" She said, "Yes."
		(*Laughter*)
90		He said, "Really?
		So if I do that same thing—" She said, "If you do it as you did
		it before, it [the pain] will surely stop."
		(*Laughter and side comments*)
		Our lady had already stretched out on her back!
		The man set to work.
		When he had gone through and come out, the woman said,
		"I'm well now.
95		Wait, let me see if I can manage to make the fire."
		He said, "Lie down and let me make it, lest the pain return."
Okpewho:		Hear, hear! He is now the wife.
Arinze:		Yes.
Ojiudu:		So they made the fire. Having made it, they cooked a meal
		and ate.
100		When they had eaten the meal, the man told her, "From
		today onwards, I don't want you near the fire."
Okoojii:		Didn't I tell you?
Arinze:		That he would now do the cooking?
Ojiudu:		That he would be cooking.
		This was the rule the man observed, when his wife became
		pregnant, and delivered two males, in one go!
105 *Okpewho:*		Hear, hear!
Okoojii:		A child is the pride of life.
		(*7-second music flourish*)
Ojiudu:		BY THE TIME SHE AWOKE, THOSE TWO MALES SHE
		HAD DELIVERED WERE ALREADY GROWING.
		(*4-second music flourish*)
		Well, they were growing.
		While this was going on—isn't it on the day a tale is
		conceived that it's born?[14]
110 *Okoojii:*		Right![15]
		(*Hums of approval*)
Ojiudu:		The Oba sent a message
		To this hunter, saying, "My sons will visit you tomorrow:
		It's with your teeth I'll worship at my shrine."
		(*5-second music flourish*)
		The hunter agreed.
115		They entered his home, took his gun
		And left.
		At break of day, they entered
		And told him to lie down: he lay down
		And they pulled out four of his teeth.[16]
		(*6-second music flourish*)
120		FROM WHERE THEY WERE SITTING, HIS SONS ASKED

HIM, "FATHER, WHAT HAS HAPPENED TO YOUR
TEETH?" "Keep on growing," he told them.
"You don't know anything yet."
His sons said, "All right," kept their eyes open,
    and took it all in.
Then came one day, and one of the sons said, "Father, if you
    don't tell me what happened to you, I won't put up
    with it.
What is that crowd outside?"

125   He said, "That crowd outside is, they've come to cut . . . the
    Oba will perform the new yam festival tomorrow
And they've come to pay me a visit."

Okoojii: That they have come to pluck his teeth.
Ojiudu: "It's tomorrow they'll cut . . . pluck . . . today, this very
    evening you're looking at, they will pluck my teeth, for
    the Oba will conduct the new yam festival tomorrow."[17]
"That's not true," said [the boy].

130   "Go and make me a machete, so I may hold on to it to keep
    myself under control."
"All right," said [his father]. A smith of the spirit world—[18]
He issued instructions to the smith.
He went and brought out a certain rod, the smith did
Put his chisel to it, split it right down.

135   Brought it out
Asked [the hunter], "Can you handle it?" He said he could.
He handed it to his son when he got home.
His son told him the machete was too small.
    (Okoojii groans wistfully)
Went to a stone behind his father's house

140   Placed [the machete] on it
Sharpened its edges
Laid it in the dust.
After a while, he felt nervous.[19] After feeling thus for some
    time, he brought out some potash
Rubbed it on the sides of the machete

145   Sprinkled some salt on its surface
Saying, "Today is the day I'm going to fight this battle, not
    any other day. Let those emissaries come."
    (6-second music flourish)
WHILE WE WERE SAYING ALL THIS, WORD CAME THAT
    THE OBA'S MEN WERE ON THEIR WAY.

Okoojii: Again?
Ojiudu: Ha, you haven't heard anything yet.[20]
    (8-second music flourish)

150   AFTER A WHILE, RIGHT WHERE HIS FATHER WAS, HE
    ASKED HIS FATHER, "WHAT'S THAT RAGING OVER
    THERE?" HIS FATHER TOLD HIM, "THAT'S . . .
    IT'S THOSE MEN COMING.

It's not tomorrow they're coming: it's today. As I sit here
        they are . . . they have already arrived."
    "All right," said [the boy]. "Let them come."
    Grabbed his machete
    Stood right there, while those stalwarts marched on.
155 He drew that machete out
    And as he walked up
    He saw a whole crowd [of them].
    Set his machete to work on their heads
    Killed nine stalwarts, leaving three; he told them, those three
        men, "Go home, and tell whoever sent you
160 That it wasn't a good day."
    Those three stalwarts left, and on arrival told the king,[21]
        "Where we're coming from, there's sorrow in store for
        your subjects."
    "Alas," said the king, "the things I've seen! Just those two
        children?" [The man] told him, "ONE OF THEM
        DIDN'T EVEN COME OUT."

Okoojii: Only one was doing all this!
        (*Laughter and side comments*)
Okpewho: Suppose it was both of them?
165 It would have been a catastrophe![22]
Ojiudu: "Only one person?" asked the king. *He* [the emissary] *said,*
        "*Only one person was there.*[23]
        The other one didn't even come out, didn't even know if
        anything was going on."
Okpewho: (*Laughing*) Unconcerned!
Okoojii: Perhaps that one was the champion.
170 Ojiudu: That was the one who said, "You go ahead: how many men
        are there—
Okpewho: Hm—hear, hear!
Ojiudu: —That I should come out?
        You go ahead and fight that battle: that's not . . . that's not
        the kind I'll fight. How many men are there?"[24]
        (*Laughter*)
    AT DAYBREAK, THE OBA MADE A PROCLAMATION,
        TELLING THE BENIN NATION TO COME OUT, for
        his guards would no longer go [on that mission].
175 The Benin nation joined in the preparations, as whoever
        came out fell in line: those with guns, those with arrows,
        those with machetes.
    He [younger son] told his brother, "They say the Bini are on
        their way." He [the other] told his brother, "Now the
        time has come for me to come out!"
Okpewho: Hear, hear!
Ojiudu: Grabbed his machete
    Placed it on a stone
180 Got it thoroughly sharpened

	Shaved his beard with it.
Arinze:	(*Laughing*) To test its sharpness.
Ojiudu:	"All right," he said.
Okoojii:	Then he treated it with salt.
185 *Ojiudu*:	Went outside to take a look, and saw a whole throng of stalwarts

Pitch-black,[25] human beings though they were.

"Aha," he said, "this is the best thing God could have done for me.

My father's sorrows are over."

When he came to the open square and saw the crowd
. . . throng of men out there

190 He told his father to come out.

(*3-second music flourish*)

THEY [the Bini] HARDLY KNEW THAT THERE WAS
SOMEONE ON THAT RO . . . ROAD FROM WHICH
THEY HAD COME.

SUDDENLY, ONE OF THE INVADERS SAID TO HIS MEN,
"DO YOU SEE WHAT'S RAGING BEHIND?" WHEN
THEY LOOKED BEHIND, THEY SAW THAT BOY
MOVING IN WITH A MACHETE AS THOUGH HE
WAS MOWING GRASS: IT WAS ACTUALLY HUMAN
HEADS HE WAS MOWING DOWN.

Okpewho: What!

(*Low laughter*)

From behind?

195 *Ojiudu*: He was advancing from the direction of the Oba's palace,
cutting down men like palm fruits.

(*5-second music flourish*)

Those in front, each man in his turn begged him, "Please."
But as they begged "Please, please, please"—no, that
was now out of the question

For those men had now reached the entrance

And sneaked into the house.[26]

(*7-second music flourish, at increased tempo*)

A stampede ensued.

200 (*Chant*) Ikpitili, iyawum

Ikpitili, iyawum

Ikpitili, (*Chorus*) iyawum

Ikpitili, (*Chorus*) iyawum

Ikpitili, (*Chorus*) iyawum

205 Ikpitili, (*Chorus*) iyawum

Ikpitili, (*Chorus*) iyawum

Ikpitili, (*Chorus*) iyawum

That was his machete mowing at . . . at the legs of those men.

Okpewho: What!

210 *Okoojii*: Men were dropping!

(*9-second music flourish*)

Ojiudu:	HIS FATHER HAD ALREADY COME OUT THERE, SAYING, "WOE, WOE!" CALLING HIS SONS	

Ojiudu: HIS FATHER HAD ALREADY COME OUT THERE, SAYING,
"WOE, WOE!" CALLING HIS SONS
WAILING, MOANING
WHENEVER HE CALLED OUT HE HEARD FROM THE
MACHETE, "NO WAY!"[27]
By the time the [fleeing soldiers] got to the palace, telling
the Oba the mission was now beyond them, [the twins]
had overtaken them into the Oba's courtyard.

215   The cock had crowed as they got to the courtyard, leaving
those men thoroughly confused. They [the twins]
entered the Oba's palace, only to find him trying
. . . trying to make his way up the ceiling.
The younger one asked him where he [thought he] was
going
Laid his machete to his . . . leg . . . haunches

Okoojii: As he was escaping.

Ojiudu: Cutting his two legs to the ground.

220 *Okpewho*: Cutting down the Oba's legs?

Ojiudu: Cutting off his legs. Cut off his head and brought it over to
his father, saying, "Hold it in your hand and let's go."
He [the twin] took off.
Walked right on into the house and . . . into the Oba's palace.
He told [his father] to sit on the throne, took . . .
brought the Oba's ornaments and hung them round
his [father's] neck
Asking the Bini nation to turn their faces towards his
father's house.

Okoojii: For his father was now king.

225 *Ojiudu*: He ascended [the throne].
      (*Interruptions*)
The entire Bini nation thronged to his father's premises.
So it was that his father became king.
That was the end of the war.
      (*Interruptions*)
Eh?

230 *Okoojii*: Yes.

Audience: Welcome!

Before we examine the structural fit of this story, we may want to observe how some of the heroic qualities revealed therein resemble elements of the heroic personality discernible in heroic traditions elsewhere. A particularly interesting feature of the misogynist hunter's behavior is his impatience or anger at the women who fail to do his will. Nagy has, I think, demonstrated convincingly enough the significance of anger in the composition of the heroic personality (1979:73–74) and the role of wanton violence—what he calls "the dark and latent side of the epic hero" (158)—in lending forceful-ness and effectiveness to the heroic character of these traditions.[28]

The hunter's two sons are driven, in their defense of their father, by no less anger at the dishonor brought to him from the horrors visited on him year after year before their very eyes.[29] But other aspects of their heroism are just as interesting. The narrator's statement, that it is "on the day a tale is conceived that it is born" (109), is of course a formula frequently used for abbreviating the plot of the tale; here it is equally useful in indicating the speedy, precocious development for which heroes are known in several traditions (Okpewho 1979:89–91). Much like Sunjata among the Mandinka or Ozidi among the Ijo, the hero finds the weapon made by no less a demiurge than "a smith of the spirit world" "too small" for him (130, 138). And we see the height of the hero's arrogant self-assurance when the senior of the twins leaves the junior to deal with the imperial guards all by himself—nine soldiers are not that much of a challenge for him!—but is immensely delighted at having his hands full when he is told that the entire army of Benin are on their way (166–187).[30]

Do these continuities in heroic composition support a unity of plot between the two segments of this story? To some extent, yes. For while it is true that the first episode of the tale—about how a stubborn misogynist is finally brought to heel by a woman no less tough than he—can comfortably stand on its own, the second segment can hardly exist without indications as to how the two boys came into heroic life. There is also a qualitative growth in the heroic image presented here that does justify the complication of the seriocomic tale about the domestication of a misogynist hunter. The first segment of the story yields to the second in such a way as to proclaim the beauty of numbers over the limitations of the solitary life: by the collectivist logic of traditional African life, the chances of the Igbuzo nation triumphing over the menacing power of Benin are better ensured by the combined strength of two men (the twins) than by the singular power of one.

The conversion of the hunter from a lonely misogynist to a family man thus facilitates the development of the heroic image in the story from a private to a more broadly based or public outlook. It is certainly arguable that our narrator, given his declared intent of showing "how people get to be man and wife," has endeavored to place marital harmony, with all its attendant pleasures and benefits, above the peculiar obsessions of celibate life; that the triumph of the woman is meant as a denunciation of the macho pretenses of private heroism; and ultimately that the tale's charged atmosphere—of a brutish and formidable man being brought to heel by an equally tough and determined woman, of the union of one kind of force with another—is the most fitting way of introducing the equally formidable twin heroes who crown their family and their nation with glory.

To be sure, there is ample poetry in the oral tradition's celebration of the singular hero who stands his ground in a world of abundant danger. We may recall the glorification of various antisocial, even anarchic heroes like the

Onikoyi in the hunters' poetry *ijala* of the Yoruba (Babalola 1966:124–129). Such reckless terrorism was condoned, even applauded, as the inevitable way to survive in those precarious days when nation-states were in the infancy of formation, and the machinery of social control had not been fully formed or recognized. In the present story, however, the canvas widens to encompass the threat to a family's honor if not a nation's survival, necessitating a commensurate growth from private to public-spirited heroism. Our narrator may well have been driven, in the threat posed by obtrusive foreign music to his professional pride, to raise a tale of gender rivalry to the level of a nationalist war. That in itself goes to show that, in the final analysis, the oral tradition reserves the highest honor for those who put their exceptional powers at the service more of collective security than of self-gratification. In subsequent chapters, we shall have occasion to examine more fully the stress in this culture between the individual and the group.

Hunter, Hero, and Society

What does all this have to do with the life of a hunter: why is the private, self-serving machismo of a hunter made the pivot of a tale of nationalist glory? A limited explanation may lie in the personal circumstances of our narrator Ojiudu Okeze. In his earlier days, he had combined the practice of carpentry with the less stable vocation of a semiprofessional music man in Northern Nigeria. On returning to his home-town, Igbuzo, he had done some more music-making; but as he grew older, and his variety of music got steadily out of vogue, he took refuge in the more traditional modes of subsistence, farming and hunting (mostly by trapping).

Despite this personal interest, however, hunters' tales do constitute something of a distinct tale type across the continent of Africa and perhaps in various societies of the so-called Third World as well. Part of the appeal of these tales may lie in the heroic mystique of the singular figure venturing into the fearful domain of wild animals and supernatural figures that inhabit the gray zones of the human imagination. Whatever the case might be, such a tradition should provide us a backdrop against which to observe the qualities and significance of the hunter in our tale.[31]

We may well begin with the not-so-attractive qualities of Ojiudu's hunter and examine why he behaves the way he does in the tale. He is a fiercely private man, who has no craving for company except such as would serve his personal needs, in this case a cook. In opting for a solitary existence, Ojiudu's hunter is very much like his fellows in the trade who, even though they belong to a guild and on occasion go out hunting in groups, are much better known for cutting their own paths and facing their challenges alone.

In his discussion of Yoruba hunters, Ajuwon describes them as "marginal men" who "live solitary lives" as they confront the dangerous game of the wilds (1982:29). Since "the hunter expects to spend long periods in solitary pursuit of game," he must cultivate self-reliance and self-sufficiency by taking to the bush everything he needs for survival; however, this self-reliance is a sacrifice he makes for the benefit of his society, which needs the game that he brings home (1989:176–182).

The hunter in Ojiudu's story comes home every day expecting to enjoy the food cooked by dutiful women. But for his survival in the dangerous world of the wilds he depends far more, really, on metaphysical resources with which every hunter endeavors to arm himself. Most heroic traditions relating to hunters portray them as men fully equipped with charms. In their study of heroes among the Mande (Mandinka) of Mali, Bird and Kendall point out that they devote a great part of their early career to procuring the means (*dalilu*) for controlling the spiritual agencies (*nyama*) inherent in the natural objects (men, animals, etc.) contingent upon their profession; hence we are told by Seydou Camara, the hunters' bard, that

No man becomes a hunter if he has no good talismans.
You don't become a hunter if you have no knowledge of the occult. (Bird 1974:90)

The same is evidently true even among the west-Niger Igbo: thus in his tale of the war between Benin and the Ubulu, Simayi shows how the Ubulu leader Ezemu, himself a hunter, confronts the Benin army with a mere band of seven hunters armed to the teeth with charms and nothing else (Okpewho 1992:196–197).[32]

His attachment to potent charms accounts, to a considerable extent, for the hunter's isolation and especially for his heavily circumscribed relationship with women. "Fearing relationships," to borrow from Latham, the hunter as hero "distances himself from others" and is "not much related to women or wives" (1992:13). It is not that hunters never get married: the hunter in Ojiudu's story is prepared, after all, to tolerate the possibility. But the relationship is, for a start, severely constrained by a deep-seated unwillingness to share the most intimate secrets of his life—not least those relating to his mystical powers—with the woman. So attached are these hunters, in fact, to their charmed profession that their relationship with their women often ends tragically, so that—like figures in similar occupations such as war—they would rather have the calling than the companion.

This ambivalence inherent in hunters and warriors becoming attached to women has been properly articulated by Walter Burkert in his discussion of the killer instinct in the traditional man of action. Although he agrees that the heroic life is marked by powerful drives such as may be found in equal measure in sex and aggression and is thus a key factor in the development of human society (1983:19, 59), Burkert is nonetheless convinced that the renunciation of love and the sexual impulse is essential for the preservation and advancement of heroic energies in hunting as in war, often demanding—as in Ojiudu's story—the sacrifice of the female. "Hunting and war," argues Burkert, "are sanctioned by social custom as tests of manhood, and they take precedence over courtship and marriage. Man declines to love in order to kill: this is most graphically demonstrated in the ritual slaughter of 'the virgin,' the potential source of a happy union and of disruptive conflict within the group" (64).

Consequently, in heroic myth the union of the man of action and a woman marks the termination of the heroic life, and quite often this is accomplished by a woman who is herself endowed with some extraordinary qualities and commensurate goodwill. In the Kambili epic, the hunter-hero could hardly have destroyed Cekura the baneful lionman, and saved his community without the support of Kumba, herself mystically aided by Bari, the hunters' sorcerer; their wedding brings his heroic destiny to a fitting close (Bird 1974). Nor could the Gambian Kiila la Mammadu have possibly put an end to the huge beast, Sii Baa, ravaging his people, without the aid of the mystically fortified Manding (Innes and Sidibe 1990). In Ojiudu's story, the hunter is cured of his misogyny by a woman who announces herself as "Omemma," a do-gooder.

A sexist reading of her name might render it as "Pleaser," on the ground that the woman achieves her transformation of the man purely by virtue of her sexuality. But there is a peculiar element in the disposition that she brings to her relationship with the man. It is not that she demonstrates any more stubborn determination to marry him than the earlier women who lost their lives, but that, rather than make the fatal mistake of beginning to cook a meal she may not complete, she proceeds to put the man's house in some decent order (lines 49–50). This peculiar twist in conduct might suggest an underlying confidence in her innate powers; at any rate, it portends a stabilizing, indeed a civilizing influence on a man whose life has so far been marked by a wild, unruly disposition.[33]

The victory of the lady over the hunter also makes a useful general case about the restoration of humane instincts to society by matching the overweening male with the more even-tempered female. A useful contribution of recent studies of Mande heroic traditions has been to recognize the stress between a manly urge toward self-assertion in an individualistic, isolationist sense (*fadenya*) and a more levelheaded instinct for a collective social unit rooted in an orientation toward the mother-figure (*badenya*) (Bird and Kendall 1980, Johnson 1986:42–45). The hunter's earlier aversion to females, in Ojiudu's narrative, certainly suggests an irrational machismo which is salvaged by the wit (the occasional "laughter" gives considerable

notice of Ojiudu's histrionic skill in representing the woman's adroit manipulation of the hunter's crude sensations) as well as sexual power of his
victor. This is a somewhat generous credit, coming from a patriarchal culture; in chapter 4 we shall examine the gender issues underlying such a
representation.

The hunter, then, is being prepared by the beneficent lady for a more
cultivated role, that of rescuing his community (with his two sons) and
settling it under a properly constituted civic authority. That a hunter is made
to assume such a role tells us two things at least. One, whereas in Benin
culture the monarchy is hereditary and therefore remains in the hands of a
privileged circle, in the republican culture of the west-Niger Igbo—as in
Igboland generally—anyone, whatever the ranks from which he or she
comes, has the chance to assume the mantle of leadership: we shall be
discussing the differences between the Igbo and the Bini in the next two
chapters.

A second point made by the elevation of the hunter reflects the familiar
rivalry between various interest groups about their place within the social
structure. A rather interesting hunters' chant from the Akan of Ghana
defends the profession's interests against those of the political leadership:

> Is the chief greater than the hunter?
>   Arrogance! Hunter? Arrogance!
> The pair of beautiful things on your feet,
> The sandals that you wear,
> How did it all happen?
> It is the hunter that killed the duyker:
> The sandals are made of the hide of the duyker.
>
> Does the chief say he is greater than the hunter?
>   Arrogance! Hunter? Arrogance!
> The noisy train that leads you away,
> The drums that precede you,
> The hunter killed the elephant,
> The drum head is the ear of the elephant.
> Does the chief say he is greater than the hunter?
>   Arrogance! Hunter? Arrogance! (Nketia 1963:43)

The republican Igbuzo society probably has no such tradition whereby one
group wrestles with a complex over another group, but it seems to share with
various other societies a celebration of hunters as culture heroes, taking the
term in the sense in which Tegnaeus identifies those responsible for bringing the benefits of culture or civilization to a people (1950:9–12, 179)—
although they do not have to be connected to the divine world in ways that
Tegnaeus seems to recommend.

Of those African societies in which hunters have enjoyed much reputation as culture heroes, the Mande and Yoruba groups in West Africa provide perhaps the best documentary evidence of what may be called a "hunting culture." With respect to the Mande (or Mandinka, Mandingo, as they are called elsewhere), Youssouf Cisse has given (1964) a classic picture of the role played by hunters and hunters' associations (*donso-ton*) in the emergence and growth of the great medieval empire of Mali—especially the prominence accorded the Traore (Toure, Taraware) clan, later joined by the Kone, Kamara, Keita (Sunjata's line), Konate, and other families or clans in the consolidation and expansion of the empire through military conquest. The striking thing about these contributions by various groups is that hunters have been a key factor, in the development of societies, in collapsing ethnic and other cultural boundaries toward the emergence of "a workable supraorganic unit" or nation as we understand it today (Bird 1972:276–277, Levtzion 1973:57). As society faced increasing challenges in the course of its development, it relied upon hunters to defend it against wild animals (Innes and Sidibe 1990) as well as invading forces (Levtzion 1973:58). And because of their close association with forest flora and fauna, hunters have played a conspicuous role not only in the augmentation of food supply (especially meat) for their societies but also in the exploitation of the botanical and medical wisdom contained in plants (Bird 1972:276–278, Levtzion 1973:56–57).[34]

Yoruba society has been no less generous in putting hunters in the vanguard of cultural history, enshrined to a considerable degree in the mythology of Ogun, the god who is fabled to have cleared the communication road between divinities and humans, the tutelary deity of those who use iron in their crafts (hunters, smiths, warriors, woodworkers, and so on), and the refuge of the oppressed. "Even across tribal frontiers," Judith Gleason tells us, "all hunters are brothers" (1987:157). This role of hunters in defining the spatial universe is attested by African scholars like Ojo, who describes hunters as "the explorers of the nation, who in the process of their work widened the bounds of the land and brought back news of strange lands and places," and as makers of "the footpaths followed first by farmers and next by traders. Many modern roads followed the tracks of these surveyors of the nation" (1966:40). Not only are hunters credited as founders of new settlements (Babalola 1989:149), but in disseminating common traditions across communities through which they travel as they hunt, they aid the emergence of a Yoruba national consciousness (Ajuwon 1989:174). Hunters also get credit for the development of Yoruba medicinal science (Ojo 1966:40, Fadipe 1970:251, Ajuwon 1982:29), for the defense of their communities in times of war and other crises (Ojo 1966:40, Fadipe 1970:251, Ajuwon 1989:184), and as instruments of social justice in their revolt even against contemporary forces of oppression (Ajuwon 1989:187).[35]

In his story of a hunter who facilitates (through his sons) the revolt against the high-handedness of Benin, the resistance of its imperial forces, and the appropriation of the monarchy, our narrator is very much in accord with traditions which project the hunter as a prime factor in the development of social or cultural history. As indicated above, Ojiudu's personal interest as part-hunter may have something to do with the structural engineering of the story. But it is clear that, despite the secondary place now occupied by hunters in Igbuzo traditional economy, they still enjoy a cherished niche in the collective memory kept alive in the reconstitutive art of storytelling.[36]

Ojiudu's image of the hunter is not without support in other oral evidence. In one of the testimonies collected by Ohadike on the origins of Igbuzo, we are told of one of the town's founders, Umejei: "He was a hero and a great hunter" (1988:129). There are at least two insights contained in this claim. First, the use of the epithet *great* indicates that despite the vagaries of economic history, there is some regard accorded to the craft of hunting in the Igbuzo scale of values; coming from someone who should have a dependable sense of Igbuzo's history—the testimony was collected by Ohadike from an L.N. Ashikodi, a "Senior Civil Servant"—the description seems to capture some nostalgic memory of a dying legacy or a cherished profession. A second insight is suggested by the obvious connections between hunter and founding ancestor, and prompts us to raise the following question: to what extent is Ojiudu's story—of a hunter and his twin sons championing their people's resistance of Benin and adopting its monarchical polity—a stylized memory, or a "historical contemplation" perhaps in some sense of Collingwood's understanding of the term?[37]

Historical Claims

At the end of Ojiudu's narrative performance, Arinze and I held the following discussion with him and his accompanist:

Okpewho:	This hunter you told us about—where was he from?
Ojiudu:	The one I told about?
Okpewho:	Yes.
Ojiudu:	What! The man I told about was from Imiidi.[38]
Arinze:	Ehn, an Igbuzo man?
Ojiudu:	Yes, from our Imiidi, in Igbuzo.
Arinze:	Really?
Ojiudu:	Yes, that's . . . the one . . . connected with the giant's ladder.[39]
Arinze:	Really?
Ojiudu:	Do you think it's the world we're in now that we're talking

	about? You know, in the past, you'd be seeing a lot of things of unusual proportions.
Okoojii:	That giant's ladder on the road to Imiidi.
Ojiudu:	That giant's ladder on the road to Imiidi. Wasn't that where Okomma Ogbodogbo[40] fought that great battle of his? There are quite a few relics there.
Arinze:	Really?
Ojiudu:	The charm they planted there, it was for that war they planted it.
Okpewho:	So that man [i.e., hunter] finally became Oba?
Ojiudu:	He became Oba.
Okpewho:	Oba of Benin?
Ojiudu:	Oba of Benin.
Okpewho:	Went all the way from Igbuzo to become Oba of Benin?
Ojiudu:	He says "to become Oba of Benin"—don't you know that big mango tree there, the mango tree on the road to Imiidi?
Okpewho:	M-hm.
Ojiudu:	You know who planted it?
Okpewho:	No.
Ojiudu:	(*Chuckles*) Don't you know—do you know Onicha-Ugbo?
Okpewho:	I know Onicha-Ugbo.
Ojiudu:	You know Onicha-Ukwuu?
Okpewho:	Ehen.
Ojiudu:	Ehn?
Okpewho:	I know it.
Ojiudu:	Do you know that those people and Benin were very close by—
Okpewho:	Really?
Ojiudu:	And lived here previously?
Arinze:	But it was from Benin that those people escaped.
Okpewho:	The Benin empire!
Ojiudu:	It was from those parts that they came, relocating here.
Okoojii:	Frantically, like dogs.
Ojiudu:	The wars dispersed titled men, capped and uncapped:[41] everyone went wherever he could find.
Okoojii:	The Benin wars.
Okpewho:	Yes.
Ojiudu:	Wasn't it—
Okoojii:	Umuwai.
Ojiudu:	Abubu-Ugo, Ohee Abubu-Ugo:
Okpewho:	M-hm.
Ojiudu:	Ohene Abubu-Ugo. Isn't it over there, covered up at our place?
Okpewho:	Hm?
Ojiudu:	That shrine, if you swore by it, anyone who swore by it, if (s)he's guilty of the crime, will not see the next daybreak.
Okpewho:	Hm!
Arinze:	In the past, or nowadays?

Ojiudu: Till tomorrow. (*6-second pause*). Till this very night, Igbuzo
              (people) still seek for it at my place.
Okpewho: Well, then. Thank you, sir.
Ojiudu: Life to you.

It is clear, then, that Ojiudu sees his story of the hunter and his sons as a
testimony of his people's historical fortunes. However, to put the key images
of his texts in a broader context, let us consult the various sources of
evidence assembled by both Onwuejeogwu and Ohadike (themselves native
sons of the town) so as to achieve as near a compromise account of Igbuzo
traditional history as possible. The cautious tone of my last statement is
guided both by divergences (great and small) between various oral testimonies and especially the sensitivities inherent in Igbuzo social organization,
which will become apparent as the following account unfolds.[42]

Two lines of settlement have been recognized in all accounts of Igbuzo
origins. One is the Nshi or Nri line, formed by those who migrated to the
town from the ancient Nri civilization, east of the Niger; the other is the Isu
line, formed by emigrants from an undetermined one of several towns, also
east of the Niger, so named. The difficulty in presenting Igbuzo history
stems partly from divergent claims as to which line of migration arrived
there first and partly from both sides often using the same format for
recording not only the reason but also the method of migration. Beidelman
drew attention many years ago to such similarities in the structure of oral
testimonies among various Tanzanian groups (1970), and although we may
grant that whatever drives people to leave their homes must be something
fairly serious, one suspects a possible tendency in these accounts to adopt
the most dramatic mode of presentation.

The following is, *roughly*, how the Nshi segment traces its presence in
Igbuzo society. One of the sons (some claim Edini, others Odaigbo) of Eze
(king) Agu-Ukwu of Nri commits murder in the course of a fight over a
woman. By custom this is punishable by death; but since a king cannot stand
to see his own son put to death before his eyes, he gives the offender the
option of exile, which the latter accepts. Perhaps out of true brotherly
concern, the one son offers to accompany the other on the exile, and their
father the king gives each a medicine pot—the Nri are recognized as the
foremost ritualists of Igbo land[43]—on the stipulation that the bearer should
settle down wherever his pot *accidentally* falls. Though inlanders, the brothers and their retinue somehow manage to cross the Niger and continue to
walk. Edini's medicine pot falls at a site now called Ani Udo (i.e., land of
peace), and he and his followers clear up the bush and settle there; the ward
occupied by Edini's descendants is today called Ogboli. Odaigbo moves on
with his group; his own pot drops some seven miles away, and they clear up
their settlement there, erecting a rather large hall with the name Ogwa Nshi

Ukwu (i.e., the big meeting-place of Nshi or Nri people), later contracted to present-day Ogwashi-Uku.

The Isu version of Igbuzo origins runs roughly parallel to this. Umejei, the son of an Eze of Isu, had an adulterous wife. One day Umejei caught her in the act with her lover, and in the fight that ensued Umejei killed the man. Rather than have Umejei executed, in accordance with custom, the king sent him away in exile, accompanied by his sister Omoha and her husband as well as many friends and relatives, each with a pot of medicine on his or her head and under the injunction to settle down wherever the pot fell. Of those whose pots fell soon after they crossed over the Niger, Omoha (who had borne Umejei's pot) settled down with her brother and husband at a spot called Omeze, a nuclear site of present-day Igbuzo. A skilled hunter, one day Umejei came across two brothers, Ogboli and Odaigbo, amid the forest searching for a place to settle; he apportioned a place to Ogboli (who seemed the gentler of the two brothers) close to him, but assigned Odaigbo a location much further off.[44]

The Isu colonists in time outgrew their Nri counterparts—in proportion, no doubt, to their original numbers—and consequently account for many more wards today in Igbuzo. At first, relations between the two groups and their descendants were smooth. As the Nri were the best-reputed ritual specialists among the Igbo, the Isu were content to accord them the privilege of carrying out the major ritual functions of the conjoint community, including the conferment of traditional titles. In time, however, stresses in their relations forced the Isu to withdraw these privileges. One of the causes was the killing of a Nri ritualist—considered an abomination at the time— by an Isu-Igbuzo man; the other was the more recent (1936) land dispute between Igbuzo and Ogwashi-Uku, in which the Nri-Igbuzo of Ogboli sided with the latter (their ancestral brothers). From that point, the Igbuzo decided to be responsible for their own ritual functions, so that even today the two segments of the town conduct their title-taking rituals separately.

A significant factor of Igbuzo history was the appointment of a paramount ruler (*Obi*) for a traditionally republican folk. Among other accounts, it has been said that this came about in the course of a confrontation with Benin. Forces of the latter had been scouring the various communities in the area in pursuit of the king of the Ubulu who had killed his wife Adesua, a Benin princess. A man by name Ezechi led the Igbuzo in their redoubt and victory over Benin, in gratitude for which the town crowned him *Eze ofu ani*—i.e., king of a united land, no doubt the union of the Isu and Nri segments of Igbuzo.[45] Ezechi was, however, the victim of a most meddlesome wife, who continually forced her presence on the king's meetings and dominated the proceedings, until one day a councillor was commissioned to defile her with pornographic language. Ezechi left not only the council but the town in disgrace, taking his family with him to settle in a town many miles away called Ejime (Twins). Generations later, one of his descendants became entranced and, under that influence, ran a frenzied race from Ejime to Igbuzo; although he had never been to the town previously, he concluded his race at the very spot where Ezechi had lived. But the effect of Ezechi's banishment was that for a very long time—that is, until 1995 when Professor Louis Nwoboshi resumed the mantle of paramountcy—the people of Igbuzo renounced the institution of kingship and reverted to the republican traditions of their founders.[46]

If we take these various bits of evidence together—Ojiudu's story, our post-performance discussion, and the composite history of Igbuzo as contained in the testimonies just cited—it is clear that our narrator's imagination, however much freedom it may have allowed itself, is reasonably well set on the historical fortunes of Igbuzo society. To start with, the image of the hunter is an invocation of the occupational backgrounds of the town's founding folk, whether we give pride of place to Edini of Nri or to Umejei of Isu. Ojiudu is himself an Isu-Igbuzo man; in identifying the hunter in the tale with the man from Imiidi (an Isu-Igbuzo ward), he may be indicating which way his sympathies lie in the question of origins.

I think we would be justified in seeing the feminine image in Ojiudu's story as a possible transformation of the figure of Umejei's sister in the account of Isu-Igbuzo origins. Omoha is, of course, Umejei's sister, not his wife in the accounts; but the restorative role of the mother of the twins in Ojiudu's story may be seen in some structural equivalence with Omoha's benevolence in bearing Umejei's pot during their migration to the new abode. Omoha is, herself, credited with being the mother of three sons who become founders of three of the wards in present-day Igbuzo; at best, though, we can only see a parallel symbolism between her and our hunter's wife.

An equally interesting image in Ojiudu's story relates to the trophies triumphantly claimed by the twins in their victory over the Benin forces: the head of the Oba and the ornaments that adorn his neck (lines 221–222), as well as the Oba's throne. No doubt, these are all emblems of authority of a roughly equivalent order to icons we encounter in both the post-narrative discussion and the testimonies collected by Ohadike: the cutlass dropped by the fleeing Oba and wielded by Ezechi as the emblem legitimizing his claim to kingship (Ohadike's testimonies), and the old shrine at Umuwai which continues to serve as the authenticating test for oaths taken by Igbuzo citizens in various matters. In positioning Benin within the vicinity of Igbuzo, our narrator operates within the same mythic geography wherein the Oba of Benin is accounted (in Ohadike's testimonies) to have led the punitive expedition in pursuit of his uxoricidal son-in-law. The relevance of emblems of authority in Ojiudu's as in other sources of evidence (we may, in fact, include those mango trees Ojiudu refers to in the postnarrative discussion) is in giving a stamp of validation to his people's heroic confrontation of Benin.

A final dominant image in Ojiudu's story is of the hunter's twin sons. There appears to be a refraction of images somewhere between the twins born to the hunter and his wife in Ojiudu's story on the one hand and, on the other hand, the village Ejime (Twins)—in Ohadike's testimonies—to which the first paramount ruler of Igbuzo is exiled following the coup that terminates the monarchy. Within this (median) zone of refraction is located the scenario of the war with Benin, which is championed on the one hand by the hunter and his sons and on the other by Ezechi. But we may be equally justified in seeing the twin image, in terms at least of its origination from the hunter image, as an attempt by Ojiudu to reconcile the competing claims between the Isu and Nri elements over the foundation of their town. Seen in this light, Ojiudu's story becomes a mythmaker's disinterested act of wish-fulfillment within the context of his people's search for a viable solution to problems of unification that have plagued them since the dawn of their history.[47]

At the end of his performance, Ojiudu looks to his coadjutor and friend James Okoojii for endorsement, and gets it (lines 229–230). There are at least three ways in which we may address that interlocution. Seen against his battle with those corpsmen trying to ruin his performance with their disco music, Ojiudu's question may signify an urge to be reassured that the two men have given as good a proof of their virtuosity as they have been known to do all too often in the past. Ojiudu may also have been anxious to know that he has given an accurate representation of the fortunes of his people as far as the accepted facts of their history go. When I sought him out and declared my interest in hearing stories he might want to tell me, he suddenly realized he no longer had the instrument he used to accompany his stories with, and so set about fashioning one; obviously he had not given these narrative performances for some time, so his question to Okoojii possibly indicates a desire to be assured that he has got his facts right.

A third possibility may be connected with the delicate political ground on which any account of Igbuzo history might be seen to tread. If my experience in recording other storytellers like Simayi of Ubulu-Uno is any indication,[48] Ojiudu might have very good reason to mind that he didn't put his foot in his mouth in discussing matters that had taken fellow citizens to court on many an occasion. His caution is evident enough in the somewhat clipped, tentative responses he gives now and then to our queries during the postnarrative discussion. But perhaps we should see, in his seriocomic portrait of the domestication of the misogynist hunter, a master-stroke of metaphoric treatment of the sensitive facts of social history. It is entirely possible that Ojiudu had Ezechi at the back of his mind in his portrait of the misogynist hunter; but, although he comes close to naming names in the postnarrative discussion, it is clear that even there he has been no less chary about committing himself than he was in the narrative performance. For him it is enough that, in the combined heroism of the hunter and the twins, the essential components of Igbuzo's problematic history—the professional identity of the founders of the conjoint community, the fashioning of the town's collective integrity in the crucible of foreign war, the double-edged fate of the experimentation with a monarchical polity—are brought to light in an imaginative format that projects one citizen's honest hopes for the realization of a truly harmonized society.

To that extent, Ojiudu's story is less a celebration of a putative victory over Benin than a creative exegesis of Igbuzo's troubled history. There are, of course, ample reasons why Benin provides a convenient setting for this exegesis. From the point of view of myth, it has encoded itself, in the collective memory of its neighbors and rivals, as "the embodiment of all that is distant and mysterious, the empire of improbable happenings that together with the world of spirits help to explain the events of their own lives" (Clark-Bekederemo 1991:xvii); so, whatever its historical backgrounds, Ojiudu's tale of confrontation with Benin comes automatically invested with everything that appeals to the aesthetic yearnings of his captive audience. This element is in turn augmented by certain contextual structures that highlight the conflictual nature of the events that Ojiudu here narrates. On the larger national plane, the criminal insensitivity of the Nigerian military dictatorship lends credibility not only to the high-handed attitude of the hunter toward his women but also to the imperious will of Benin. On the more localized level of the performance context, the intransigence of those youth corpsmen playing their disco music posed a challenge to our narrator's professional pride, engendering in him no less a will to resist than the political factors just cited.

The invocation of Benin is therefore well founded on several grounds; the story may indeed be seen primarily as standard fare in the western Igbo anti-Benin traditions. But our analysis has drawn attention to the presence of narrative images that suggest the pressure of local political factors on Ojiudu's imagination. His story starts off with a developmental portrait of figures who wear the mantle of defense of the national interest, and ends by drawing attention to the most delicate issue in the people's political history. To be sure, he has not presented a linear record of that history. He has simply chosen seminal images and moments from his people's chequered engagement with social and political reality and woven a metaphoric fabric that respects the sensitivities called into play in the course of that engagement. Whether we view the postperformance discussion as a parallel attempt to evoke experiences more coherently presented in the main story, or consider it as some kind of subtext to that story, it is evident from both kinds of statements that our narrator has chosen the path of metaphoric *contemplation* (to cite Collingwood) because a realistic approach to Igbuzo history would not only be less interesting to his audience but might touch some sensitive nerves.[49]

Perhaps we needed the postnarrative discussion to put those sensitivities into proper relief after all. As indicated above, the tragicomic story of the subjugation of a wife-killing hunter could exist independently of the nationalist account of Igbuzo's triumph over Benin. But the discussion following Ojiudu's story has helped us to see the hidden nuances of that story a little more clearly and saved us from treating both parts thereof as—to borrow from Lévi-Strauss's analysis of the bonds between myth and history—"disconnected stories . . . put one after the other without any clear relationship between them" (1979:34). Ojiudu's tale is history, though not exactly in the sense in which philosophers of history (not excluding historians who have come to oral tradition with biases inspired by literate culture) understand the term.[50] As we saw above, in terms of spirit and objectives oral history has striking affinities with its literate counterpart. But it adopts a somewhat different strategy to achieve those objectives precisely because it exists in a considerably different cultural climate, in which context makes more than a little difference not only to event but indeed to the narrative of it: the latter, as I have suggested, may have been influenced both by the culture of military dictatorship on the one hand and, on the other, by the conduct of those youth corpsmen around our narrator. Considering the sensitivities with which Ojiudu would appear to be wrestling, we would appreciate his effort better if we consulted the insight achieved by a scholar like Scheub from his detailed explorations of oral narratology: "Oral history is not the aligning of images in linear modes, but the fragmentation of lineal images and their recasting in new configurations and contexts" (1985:2).

Male Manqué: Divinity, Authority, and the Individual

3

We need to be reminded that, although the narrators' principal concern in these tales is with problems closer to their own lives, there is a kernel of memory of some old trauma trapped somewhere within their psyche, which continues to express itself in images (however casual) of the terrible Oba. Take the image of the Oba ordering the pulling of an old man's teeth, or, as we shall see in the next chapter, the summary execution of various persons. It is not without reason, given the extraordinary powers over life and death enjoyed by the Oba and even extended to principal functionaries like the *ezomo* (Bradbury 1973:253), that such icons of terror have been emblazoned in the memories of communities which either had to flee Benin or lived constantly under the pale of its influence.

In many instances, such images simply provide a loose frame within which the more seminal concerns of culture or society are explored. However, in a tale I collected from Mr. James Okoojii of Igbuzo, the order of execution occupies a crucial position: since it comes at the end of the story, as a punishment for an obvious social menace, I believe it should be treated with the seriousness it deserves. The tale also foregrounds some aspects of the ethical and religious traditions of the narrator's culture that need to be explored before the role of the Oba can be fully appreciated.

Okoojii's tale is about a young man, born without a penis, who wins the Oba's daughter as his wife, but has to correct his sex before the marriage can be consummated. In his effort to correct the defect, the young man resorts not to physiological medicine but to a mystical journey back to the prenatal sources of his personality. Here, we are dealing with a phenomenon which anthropologists have recorded from various West African peoples: the belief that our life on earth basically follows the choice our protoself made before the supreme divinity at the moment of creation.

In his investigations into the belief systems of the Tallensi of Ghana, coupled with comparative readings of work done by fellow anthropologists in this region of Africa, Meyer Fortes (1983, 1987) has provided a fairly neat formulation of what it means to be an *individual* and a *person* in a situation where regard for ancestors and lineal obligations constitute the principal basis upon which social life may be defined. Roughly stated, after we have been created by God, the soul is asked, in the presence of its guardian spirit, to choose the sort of life it wishes to live on earth: it may wish to be a very wealthy person, or one blessed with many and successful children, or one endowed with tremendous powers, and so on. This pre-chosen destiny, what Fortes calls a "pre-natal vow," guides us through life, determining our career as *individuals*. "At the level of doctrine," says Fortes, this principle "postulates a supernatural or mystical determinacy in human affairs such that the whole course—or at least significant parts—of each individual's life is set, if not minutely pre-ordained, by pre-natal allocation, prescription or commitment" (1987:145).

However, according to Fortes, the individual does not exist in a vacuum. He or she is part of a network of relationships spanning both the temporal and spiritual realms of existence. As such, one is considered a *person* primarily by virtue of the fit between one's individual (prenatal) commitment and his/her obligations to the lineage to which one belongs. In other words, it is accepted that there is, within each family, an over-arching Destiny that has diffused through its succession of ancestors and stands surety for the individual destinies of its constituent members. In such a situation, one attains full personhood only by performing the socially accepted roles through life and eventually becoming, upon death, part and parcel of that line of ancestors from which one has benefited and which will guide the destinies of future members of the lineage. This principle is, in the final analysis, designed to account for the role of the individual within the structure of communalistic African life, in which "familial and lineage status is an inescapable determinant of personhood at every stage. The person emerges through the dialectic interplay of individual and social structure" (265).

The choice made by the protoself before it is incarnated into the world, its "prenatal destiny," is seen as an Oedipal choice partly because of the quality of the irrevocable in it, partly from the absence of the element of consciousness in the whole exercise—understandably, since it is made before the attainment of knowledge of the self—and partly because of the implication of ancestral or family ties within it. But what happens when, in full, conscious, adult life, the person discovers that the lofty expectations of the choice made in the protolife are not realized, and failure attends every undertaking made here on earth? Relying on his own fieldwork and work done by other scholars like Melville Herskovits in Dahomey (present-day Republic of Benin), Fortes has found that there are ritual processes, facilitated by a diviner, for exorcizing such cases of bad destiny (1983:8, 16; Horton 1961:111).[1]

So much for the larger picture. Now let us see how these guiding principles are illustrated by representative cases within the cultures defined by the Benin cycle, and particularly what conclusions the narrative dramas force upon us.

"Ehi" and the Divine King

In his studies of Benin culture, Bradbury has sketched a rather impressive picture of the mystical dimensions of the human personality which agrees in many key respects with what Fortes has revealed from the Tallensi evidence. Guided to a large extent by Bradbury's pioneering researches, later scholars have fleshed out this picture by locating the personality of the Oba within the complex of Benin social and religious outlook. Since Okoojii's tale, which will form the main focus of attention in this chapter, is set in the mythical realm of Benin, it is perhaps necessary to present this picture so as to show in what ways Okoojii's tale coopts the image of the Benin monarchy in its affirmation of the outlook or expectations of the narrator's culture.

In his treatment of Bini concepts of the personality, Bradbury (1957:57–58, 1973:251–282) has identified three elements so central to this idea that cults have been established around them. One is the *ehi* or the person's spiritual counterpart which, as in the Tallensi case, is seen as responsible for the destiny or lot that the protoself chooses before God and subsequently lives out on earth. One is said to "*hi* well" when one leads a successful life but to have a "bad *ehi*" when one turns out to be a social failure. How can an *ehi* be bad? It is tempting to read this to mean that the protoself has made a bad choice in "heaven," but there is really no reason why, even despite the preconscious circumstances of the prenatal event, anyone would "choose" a bad lot in life. The choice is blind not so much in terms of a total ignorance of the difference between what is desirable and what is disastrous as of the protoself not knowing the full implications of the commitment; after all, we also learn that when one's soul is later reincarnated in one's family, the *ehi* now carefully avoids the earlier lot as a problematic one.

The *ehi* is constantly sacrificed to, either in gratitude for successes or for guidance in rather difficult circumstances. Why is the *ehi* consulted in hard times? According to the Bini, the *ehi* remains in heaven to supervise the fortunes and protect the spiritual interests of the incarnated person. And here Bradbury provides a rather revealing key. "Close as a man and his *ehi* are they are yet thought of as being independent agents and so there is a possibility of conflict between them. *Ehi* must, therefore, be propitiated in much the same way as other supernatural entities and failure to do this results in trouble" (1973:273).

The other elements of this metaphysical system, around which cults have also been built, are the head (*uhumwu*) and hand (*obo*), conceived no doubt to account for the degree of initiative and resourcefulness shown by the incarnated person in realizing the full potential of the lot s/he has chosen. The head is seen as the seat of "fortune" or "luck," so that a person for whom things have gone well is said to have a "good head." There would appear to be a slight confusion here. On the one hand, to the extent that one's career on earth was predetermined by one's prenatal destiny, there is little place for fortuity "in the Benin view of human fortunes" (Bradbury 1973:271). On the other hand, the Bini evidently accept that the good things of life cannot be realized without the active pursuit of them by those to whom they have been allotted. So they may have concluded that, since the head is the seat of all human faculties (thought, judgment, and will, as well as the various senses), it "represents the purposive, sentient aspect of the human person-ality" (272) and is thus responsible for coordinating, with conscious care, everything needed to realize the preconscious commitment made by the protoself. Hence sacrifices are made to the head, the supreme one being the annual ritual (*igue*) held in honor of the head of the Oba who has guided the fortunes of the Benin nation through the previous year.[2]

The hand takes some of the credit for this purposive agency. It is recog-nized as "the seat of the power of accomplishing things" (Bradbury 1957:58) and as "a more positive symbol of wealth and social achievement than either the *Ehi* or the Head" (1973:264). The hand in question is, of course, the *right* hand: traditional society discourages the use of the left hand as an attribute more suited to beasts like the leopard than to humans.[3] In traditional Benin, special recognition is accorded to the dexterity of three professions in accomplishing feats of particular relevance to the survival as well as the prestige of the society: war, hunting, and smithery.[4] Since these professions utilize iron in their works, it is understandable that in their religious worship they pay due court to the two figures to whom their careers are beholden: the Oba and Ogun, god of iron. "In many houses the shrines of *Oba* and *Ogun* are adjacent to each other" (Bradbury 1973:265).

A key icon in this worship is a cylindrical object known as the *ikegobo* or "shrine of the hand," on which is represented key elements of the pro-fessional's career or success. "Smiths and carvers," Bradbury tells us, "have *ikegobo* on which are depicted hammers, tongs, adzes, and other tools of their trade" (*ibid.*), while war leaders are wont to represent on theirs indices of their military triumphs: Bradbury has given us (252–270) an insightful ethnographic portrait of the bronze *ikegobo* of Ezomo Ehenua—at that time in the keeping of Ezomo Omoruyi, eighth in succession to Ehenua—depicting a scene from a war he conducted in the reign of Oba Akenzua I (eighteenth century).

Now what if, despite this combined effort of the head and the hand in the pursuit of the fortune predetermined by the *ehi*, a person turns out a failure in life? It is an interesting facet of Bini belief that, while credit for success is frequently given to the head and the hand, blame for failure is invariably shifted to the *ehi* since it is an inscrutable agency—the hidden hand, as it were—beyond the conscious control of the striving individual. Yet by reason of this independent status, the *ehi* is by and large open to be approached to set things right, so that a person suffering a particularly adverse fortune may offer prayers and sacrifices, no doubt in consultation with a diviner, to his/her *ehi* "asking it to intervene" (Bradbury 1973:263).

But in what sense does the *ehi* intervene or set things right? In describing the concept of the hand among the Bini in the context of a predetermined destiny, Bradbury rightly suggests it "implies personal responsibility and self-reliance in a highly competitive and relatively individualistic society" (1973:265). Those last three words are significant because they indicate the constraints, inherent in the structures of Benin life, which in a subtle way color their perception of the metaphysical apparatus directing their fortunes.

Three stories which Bradbury goes on to publish (1973:271–282) from his ethnographic work give us some insight into these subtle constraints. The first, titled "Use,"[5] is about a farmer who never realizes any harvest from his labors. He prays God to turn his luck, and for once the crops grow; but when he goes to harvest them he finds they have been devoured by wild pigs. So he follows the trail of the pigs, and they lead him through the depths of a stream to the palace of God. There he is made to listen to a conversation between God and his *ehi*, in a separate chamber, in which the latter berates the farmer for pursuing a career different from the one he had chosen at creation—trapping. God emerges to advise the farmer to do as his *ehi* has said. When the farmer proceeds to lay traps in the ground, he strikes a pot of beads "of the most precious kind . . . Use sold them and became by far the richest of men. From that day to this people have always said 'If you do not do what your *ehi* has told you, you cannot prosper.'"

The second story, titled "Ai s'agbon hi,"[6] is of two brothers, the older an abjectly poor farmer for whom no one has the least regard, and the younger so rich—with a superabundance of wives, slaves, and farmland—that his word is law. Overcome by envy, the older brother goes to a master herbalist to plot the death of the younger. The herbalist makes him procure the ingredients of the charm and put them in a calabash vial, telling him to rub this on the stomachs of any two pregnant women he meets as a way of testing the efficacy of the charm. When the man rubs the vial on the belly of the first woman, he sees through her a child tricked out as a peasant; through the belly of a second woman he sees a child fully accoutred as a chief and in ceremonial procession amid a crowd of attendants. The two visions bring the man fully to realize that one's lot is decided in spirit-land before existence on earth. He returns the vial with sincere apologies to the herbalist, who then tells him how to make peace with his younger brother. Taking his implements, he goes early to the younger one's farm to cultivate yams for him. The latter is moved by the gesture, celebrates the accord with a sumptuous feast, and rewards the elder with a large apportionment of wives, slaves, clothes, and attendants as well as a position of honor and privilege in the estate.

The final story is about three brothers who are allowed to choose their own names. The eldest elects to be called Ogiso-will-enrich-me (*Ogiso-gha-fe-mwe*), the second Other-people-will-enrich-me (*Eree-gha-fe-mwe*), and the youngest Ehi-will-enrich-me (*Ehi-gha-fe-mwe*). The first regularly takes gifts to the Ogiso[7] in hopes of being handsomely rewarded; the next does favors to other people, convinced they will provide for him in his hour of need; but the third prays daily to his *ehi*. One day the third brother finds some spirits playing in the forest, and accepts their invitation to join them. When he complains of hunger, they send him home with a yam. On getting home he finds his parents dead and his brothers dancing in funeral ceremony. Not having a partner, he moves off apace and builds a shelter, but laments he has no fire to roast his yam with. Whereupon he hears a voice from inside the yam saying, "The-slave-of-the-Oba-is-not-negligible is in here." When he cuts open the yam, a surfeit of wealth in property and people fills the place.

Ehi-will-enrich-me is not blessed with child, and consults Obiro the diviner who, on making a spiritual journey on his behalf, returns with a promise from the consultant's *ehi* that he will find a girl by a plantain tree who will bear him a child. When he later visits the tree, a hollow plantain falls between his legs. Around the same spot he finds a basket lined with cloth, on which are placed a half-plantain, a yam, and some hair, and is advised by the spirits to take these home. When he gets home he tries to peel the hollow plantain, intending even to roast it, but out steps a young woman from it; he begins to cut up the half-plantain and the yam, and out tumble a welter of riches; then when he takes the cloth from the basket, his whole house is filled with money and now looks "like the Oba's palace."

Jealous of his wealth, his brothers proceed to live up to their names. The first takes gifts to the Ogiso, but the latter threatens to have him executed if he finds him again in the palace. The next gives out everything he has to other people, and they kill him when he has nothing left to give. Finally the Ogiso, becoming uncomfortable that some upstart is wealthier than he, declares a contest for counting their riches; whichever of them loses will have all his relations killed. Ehi-will-enrich-me wins the contest, but the Ogiso goes back on his word. Whereupon heaven and earth threaten to convulse the nation, forcing the Ogiso to capitulate. "Ehi-will-enrich-me became the Oba, and Ogiso became his sword-bearer."

The three stories are clearly synoptic in affirming the stability of our choice of fate and the value of keeping faith with this choice. In the first story, Use's fate is not altered when he seeks to "set it right"; he is simply reminded of the choice that he initially made, and begins to prosper only when he returns to the chosen career. Bradbury considers it a "somewhat naive little tale" (1973:276), apparently because Use becomes rich not exactly from trapping animals but by chancing upon a pot of beads buried in the spot where he tries to lay his traps; but the luck is perhaps a symbolic way of showing Use as "striking gold" when he finally gets down to his true profession.

The humble submission enjoined in the first story—with Use's *ehi* berating him for straying outside the preappointed path—is recreated in the second story in the humble submission of the older brother to the good graces of the younger. There is indeed some comical touch in the picture of the older brother, striding ever so cheerfully and confidently to play midwife with the vial of herbs, convinced he has in his hands the instrument that will rid him of his bothersome younger brother, only to be gazing at an all too vivid revelation that he is simply the victim of an order that was established well before he was born into the world. As in the first story, there is a happy ending with the older brother being received into the pomp and privilege of the younger's estate; but the point is firmly made that happiness comes only if we abide unquestioningly by a preset commitment.

The third story is obviously intended to establish that the *ehi* should be cultivated as a more dependable guide through life than our fellow humans or even leaders whose credentials may not be altogether healthy. But here we encounter certain elements which make clearer to us the peculiar character of the machinery within which the Benin conception of immutable destiny is set. For, in a rather subtle way, this story like the others maneuvers symbols of the image or authority of the Oba into a critical point in its development, so that the monarchy is shown as intrinsic or central to the spiritual order of Benin reality.

Take the pot of beads which brings Use his wealth in the first story. Although these beads are highly valued in Benin (as in many other African societies) and often indicate a high degree of social standing, "the most precious kind" belong without question to the Oba, some of whose ceremonial attires are made predominantly of them. At any rate, the image of the most precious beads conjures at once the pomp of royalty. It is perhaps arguable that, in his anxiety to pay some court to—to salute, as it were—the circumstances of the Oba, the narrator of this tale has ended up presenting Use less as a successful trapper than as a lucky finder of precious jewels buried in the earth!

In the second story the image of the monarchy is seen in the circumstances of the younger brother, whose word is law and whom no doubt the elder sees figured as a child in the womb of the second pregnant woman, all decked out in ceremonial apparel, with "people supporting his arms, attendants in front of him, and others at the back. He was in the middle of them and behind him stretched a long procession." These emblems of pomp and power are of course used by various state officials like the *iyase*, the *ezomo*, and the *iyOba* (queen mother), but they possess them only by the monarch's grace.

The emblems are just as evident in the final story, where the figure of the monarchy is most directly presented. At the height of his material success, the house of Ehi-will-enrich-me looks, we are told, "like the Oba's palace." But more than anything, this story seems to dramatize the triumph (moral and otherwise) of the institution of Oba over that of Ogiso, the ascendancy of the second over the first dynasty of the Benin kingdom.

Although the Ogiso dynasty started off auspiciously with the wise and benevolent administration of the earliest rulers, notably Igodo and Ere, it lost its credit with the Bini people due to a long run of misrule in the latter part of the period, culminating in the disreputable reign of Owodo, who "did not die a king because he was tabooed for maladministration, more especially his ordering of the execution of a pregnant woman, an abomination to the Binis" (Ebohon 1972:1–2; cf. Egharevba 1968:1–3).[8] In the mythology, whether of Benin or of the peoples within its sphere of cultural and political influence, the Ogisos have not fared very well either. The capriciousness and reckless urge for blood-letting credited to the Ogiso in our third tale above is, as Bradbury has suggested (1973:281, note 19), amply borne out in Benin oral traditions. One tale in particular—the story of Uzi—tells of a founder-Ogiso who "was ruthless. All acts of wrongdoing were punished by death. Not only the offender suffered, all members of his family—paternal and maternal—were also killed." So blind was he in his ruthlessness that, simply because one of his children sang a song that displeased him, he summoned all his people before him and invited the child to repeat the song, determined that after the repetition he would kill the child's mother "his wife Uzi and all her relatives." But God intervened to substitute the child's offensive song with an innocuous one, whereupon the people, alarmed by their ruler's abominable design, "killed the Ogiso and destroyed his relatives—both paternal and maternal," thus precipitating the termination of that dynasty (Adedeji 1989:71–73).

The consensus regarding the overthrow of the Ogisos of the first dynasty and the establishment of the second with the new title of Oba seems to be that, after a brief interregnum under a distinguished commoner, Evian, the Bini sent for and received—from the Oni (king) of Ife in Yorubaland— prince Oranmiyan to establish a new kingdom; this new dynasty eventually took off with Eweka I, Oranmiyan's son by a Bini woman, as the first Oba.[9] Ife was, of course, governed by a divine kingship, not without military history but given more to the arts of peace through religious institutions and the plastic arts. But it would appear that, early enough in its history, the new Benin dynasty set itself a grand project of territorial expansion rooted, for a start, in the consolidation of a power base in Benin itself.

This consolidation evidently began with the very first Oba, Eweka I who, beset by severe power rivalries among functionaries inherited from the Ogiso period, organized them into a council of state (*Uzama Nihiron*) to establish some sense of order in the new polity, relocating the palace to a farther site to remove himself physically from their cloying shadow. The councillors continued to assert themselves against the new rulership, until Oba Ewedo (thirteenth century) was forced to make changes in the organizational structure of the state: in the end, the Oba emerged in supreme control, and the respective cadres of authority were subordinated to the monarchy, holding their powers and privileges only by his grace.

Conflicts between the monarchy and these functionaries continued for many generations, including the famous rebellion led by the Iyase in the seventeenth century, which ended in his defeat and the further entrenchment of the Oba's preeminence (Ryder 1969:5–21). As we saw above in chapter 1, these power struggles were one of the major causes of migration of several groups of citizens from Benin to the outlying communities, and firmly established the fabled reputation of Benin as the land of anger (*ile ibinu*)[10] and terror.

A significant factor of these developments in the history of the new monarchy is the use to which Benin put the legacies it may have inherited from Ife—in the arts and religion—toward the consolidation of the position of the Oba. Clearly, the Bini must have had their own traditions in these areas before their contact with the Yoruba: for instance, Egharevba (1968:1) credits Ere, the second Ogiso, as founder of the guild of wood and ivory craftsmen (the Onwina and Igbesamwan) responsible for making numerous items and emblems that grace the king's political and ritual offices. But sometime in the fourteenth century, during the reign of Oba Oguola, the technique of brass-casting, by the *cire perdu* or lost-wax technique, was introduced to the Benin royal court by an Ife brass worker named Igueghae, sent by the Oni of Ife (Dark 1975:10, 46; Fagg 1978:14, 39; Hull 1981:9).[11]

The use of brass became a watershed in the relations between the monarchy and the rest of the realm, because it was clearly a more precious and more durable medium of artistic representation, available to the more affluent and powerful like the Oba rather than to the rank and file (see Frazer and Cole 1972:203). Paula Ben-Amos has made a significant point about the relative values of wood and brass in Benin artistic traditions. She thinks that, since wood is a "natural product intimately related to the life cycle of growth and decay . . . it is the most appropriate material to represent the cyclical nature of Edo [Benin] social and religious life." Brass, on the other hand, mirrors the flux and temporality of monarchical history and, since it never rusts, is perhaps best suited for preserving the accomplishments of each king and thus enshrining the nation's history (1983:14–16), "which is, above all, the saga of kings" (13).

All this may be true, but the premium put on brass should also be seen in the context of the power dynamics of the time. To curb the powers of the *Uzama Nihiron*, Oba Ewedo, Oguola's immediate predecessor, had created a council of *palace* chiefs (headed by the Ezomo) essentially as a counterweight to the power of the former body. Since the days of Oguola, only the Oba, the Ezomo, and the Queen Mother were allowed the use of brass in representations of cult objects like the *ikegobo* (Vogel 1974:10) and the head; all other citizens, even the craftsmen who played such a key role in the cultural life of the monarchy and the nation, were restricted to using wood and terra-cotta for corresponding purposes (see Dean 1983:36). It was simply one solid way of establishing who was in charge, and indeed ensured that the history of the nation would be enshrined in human memory more securely through the superior iconography of the royalty than of the lesser elements of the society.[12]

The use of brass is particularly relevant to the centrality claimed for the king in the religious life of the Benin nation. Many of the "bronze" heads found in museums across the world today are, as I have said, icons of successive ancestors of the Oba and were (as they still are) pivotal in the worship of the king's head at the annual *igue* festival (Fagg 1978:23, Schaefer 1983:78). It is indeed revealing to what extent the monarchy has imposed itself upon the traditional gerontocracy and the theology inspired by it. Talbot has recorded (1926:554–555) that the village gerontocracy, typical of Edo society, is absent in Benin. It is not surprising therefore that the traditional spirit cult, in which the figures hallowed by this system are enshrined, "has been overshadowed at Benin by the spectacular cult of the Oba's ancestors . . . based on a belief that the well-being of the people depends directly on the Oba's life force or spiritual energy" (Fagg 1978:34).[13]

That the Oba is a divine king, equal indeed to a god, is amply demonstrated by a myth about how "the great Oba Ewuare (about 1450) went down to the shore and wrestled with Olokun, god of the sea (and of wealth), and won his [coral] beads from him" (Fagg 1978: 27). Equally eloquent are the various appellations with which the Oba is reguarly saluted, as recorded by Ebohon (1979), such as *Olaye, Ogiegbon ogedegun,* "The king and god on earth that owns the world" (43) and *Oba n'Osa,* "A king that is god to his subjects" (45).[14] Being divine, the Oba does not die: "To the Binis, the Oba of Benin is like a god and he is, [upon his demise], not addressed as if he were mortal. For this reason, several figurative expressions were used to convey his sickness, passing away, internment and burial—Emwinekhua. It is an abomination to think or say that he is dead, for THE OBA OF BENIN NEVER DIES" (48).

The implication of the Oba's divinity is evidently that he is superior to the fortunes of mortal men and indeed is in effective control of the destiny of his citizens. This is partly suggested by the concept of the "bird of disaster" in Benin iconography, which is said to be a record of a historical event.

> When the warrior Oba Esigye [*sic*] went forth to war against the Ata of Idah in about 1515, this bird of ill omen (sometimes identified with the ibis), made such deprecatory noises overhead that the soothsayers warned the Oba to call off the expedition, since he would certainly be defeated. But Esigye refused to turn back and ordered that the bird should be killed. He went on to win a great victory against the Ata, and decreed that figures of the bird should be cast in bronze and beaten with metal rods in his presence as a part of court ceremonial in commemoration of the event (Fagg 1978:28).

If the Oba is superior to the forces of divine agency, he is clearly not far from overarching the fortunes of his subjects. We can now appreciate the force of the subject-phrase in those words heard by Ehi-will-enrich-me, in our third story above, from inside the yam given him by his spirit playmates: "The-slave-of-the-Oba-is-not-negligible is in here." The idea of slave assumes its meaning not simply in the practice of human subjugation but in the deeper submission of the total personality—physical and spiritual—of the average subject to the divine kingship of the Oba. In old Benin, the Oba had total control over the life and death of his subjects. "One of the most important meanings of the human sacrifice, for which Benin became notorious, lay in its capacity to demonstrate the sole right of the Oba to take human life. He was addressed as *Omo* 'Child' to distinguish him from all other men, who, in relation to him, were *evien,* 'slaves'" (Bradbury 1973:75; cf. Ben-Amos 1976:246). The concept of the irreversible destiny in Benin achieves its full meaning, therefore, in the context of an order that imposed severe constraints on the liberty of the average citizen. No doubt this justifies Bradbury's caution in qualifying Benin as a *relatively* individual-istic society (1973:265).

"Ehi-will-enrich-me" is not fully a standard choice of destiny story, be-cause we are not told—as we are in "Use" and "Ai s'agbon hi"—what choice the hero made before he came into the world. The story is primarily an illustration of the wisdom in cultivating one's guardian spirit, who protects one's interests in the divine order. Later on in the story, however, we are told that he is not blessed with child, and so consults the master-diviner Obiro for help; on the basis of this, his *ehi* offers him a young girl whom he finds in a hollow plantain, a sexual symbol—as Bradbury has rightly noted (1973:282)—which promises the fulfilment of his desire for a child.[15]

Now let us examine closely the modes of entry into the divine world represented in the three stories. In the first story, Use follows the trail of wild pigs into a stream; they are obviously divine agents, for on diving into the river (the standard mythical boundary between the human and spiritual worlds) he ends up "at the palace of Osanobua [God]." He sees God, but, since no human being is allowed to see his/her *ehi* (Bradbury 1973:275, note 6), he is sequestered in a room while God holds consultations with his *ehi* that he is allowed to hear. Thereafter God returns to speed him on his way back to earth.

In the second and third stories the consultation with destiny is done through diviners. In the second story, the farmer is given a medicinal vial with which, looking through the womb of a pregnant woman, he sees his alter ego tricked out with the tools of his trade. In the third story, it is the diviner who undertakes to make the journey for Ehi-will-enrich-me. He actually "died on the spot and decomposed," only to reappear later—dressed with a mortar for a cap and a pestle for a walking-stick—and deliver to Ehi-will-enrich-me the message from his *ehi.*

The interesting thing about these latter appeals to destiny is that the consultants remain earth-bound and so have no opportunity to actually encounter their *ehi*: what the farmer in the second tale sees is his *choice*, not the guardian spirit that helped him make it. Although he actually goes up to "heaven," Use, in the first tale, does not see his *ehi*, because as a human being he should not. Now that is strange, because in entering into the spiritual world he can hardly be seen as a human being in the normal sense of the term. If there is any conclusion which these mythical scenarios urge upon us, therefore, it is that in traditional culture the Bini are usually as constrained in their metaphysical circumstances as in their relations with the monarchy. If the theory that religion is an opium of the people ever needed an illustration from traditional mythology, the fate of these three characters in the land of the divine king surely offers a classic one.

Before moving on to discuss the evidence from the west-Niger Igbo, let us look briefly at cognate material from the Ijo of the Niger delta, whose relations with Benin are fairly well attested. The Ijo border the southwestern flank of the old Benin kingdom. To reach Ijo country from Benin, you pass through Ughoton (Gwatto in the old colonial nomenclature) on present-day Siluko Road to the marshes of the Benin River, a distance of less than fifty miles. However, as with most things shrouded by time and the vagaries of the oral tradition, we cannot be absolutely sure in which direction the formative influences have gone between the two peoples. Jacob Egharevba confidently includes the Ijo (Ijaw) among the subject peoples of the old Benin empire (1966:11, 1968:80). Alagoa (1972), as we saw in chapter 1, does have it that the Mein clan of the Ijo was founded by a certain Mein who led a colony out of Benin as a result of internal wars—though this does not necessarily mean that he was Bini—and settled in various parts of the creeks. His descendants formed settlements in other parts of the region and, once established, returned to Benin to receive from the Oba sanctions of authority as king (*pere*) of their territories; one of these kings was a certain Mgbile. Yet another colony, of the Tarakiri Ijo, was led by a certain Ondo, who had "lived at Benin, but left with his three sons because the Oba seized private lands and levied heavy taxes."

Alagoa also mentions stresses in the relations between the Mein and Tarakiri clans of the Ijo, leading to wars, but we can assume that as members of the same ethnic family they have long shared cultural bonds. Some of these are at least suggested by the evidence of masks and masking traditions found among the Bini. The stylized masks of the *Ododoa* and *Igbile* cults—with images of aquatic reptiles emanating from various parts of the head (Fagg 1978:34–37; Preston 1981:69; Gallagher 1983:22)—are of possible Ijo origin; their names suspiciously echo those of the colonists Ondo and Mgbile. Fagg suggests that the Igbile cult, some of whose masks were captured from dancers who joined Benin soldiers resisting the British punitive expedition of 1897, "came to the Bini by way of the Ilaje Yoruba," formed by an Ijo group that has long lived with eastern Yoruba elements on the Atlantic coast.[16]

However, in whichever way the influences may have flowed, and whatever role Benin may have played in legitimizing the monarchies of various Ijo groups, the Ijo are essentially a republican people with figurehead monarchies hardly recognized as divine kings in the sense we have been discussing the phenomenon among the Bini. If it is true their forebears left Benin in those days of kingly high-handedness and sheer terror, it is unlikely they would permit a restitution of a way of life they had fled so desperately from.

Something of this free-spiritedness of a republican society is reflected in their mythology. I once did a detailed analysis of an Ijo creation myth in which a character returns to God to demand a change of destiny because life has left her rather unhappy with the one she had chosen (Okpewho 1983:137–152). Here are the salient details of the story. After God—Woyengi ("our Mother")—has created human beings out of mud and breathed life into them, she asks them to choose what kind of life they wish to lead on earth. Among one group of these humans are two women, one of whom chooses to have many successful children while the other (Ogboinba) chooses to have unequaled powers. The two elect to live in the same town.

They both finally marry, and while her friend continues to have children who do well, Ogboinba grows in powers (with which she helps her society) but never has a child. Finally, out of frustration, she decides to return to Woyengi to ask for a change of destiny. On her way, she is offered hospitality by various figures—humans, animals, even divinities—each of whom she challenges to a fight and systematically destroys; she is later persuaded to revive some, but insists on adding the powers of all of them to hers until she is overloaded with her baggage of powers. She finally confronts God and challenges her to a fight. But all God does is command the return of all powers she has seized to their former owners, and Ogboinba, thoroughly weakened, is driven by fear and shame to hide in the eyes of a pregnant woman she meets on the way. Woyengi, who has decreed that pregnant women should never be harmed, decides to spare Ogboinba. "But Ogboinba remained in hiding and is still in hiding not only in the eyes of pregnant women but in the eyes of men and children as well. So the person that looks out at you when you look into somebody's eyes is Ogboinba."[17]

One interesting thing about Ogboinba's mission, which says something about Ijo notions of destiny not unlike what we learnt from our three Bini texts, is that one of her hosts—the forest king Isembi—warns her to abandon her quest, for no one ever sees Woyengi alive. It is interesting because it confirms the point I made about the presence of Use in the divine court: at that point, he is far less a human than a spiritual entity, so his being denied a meeting with his *ehi* should be explained not so much by the Bini concept that one cannot see one's guardian spirit as by the limits imposed upon individual self-realization within the structures of Bini life. Although Use is allowed to return to the world as a human being—and his humility certainly serves him well—Ogboinba continues to exist only as an attenuated essence, a disembodied symbol employed to point a moral about the dangers of overreaching oneself especially in the quest for, or use of, earthly resources like power.

It is significant, nevertheless, that the Ijo imagination can conceive of an encounter with the supreme divinity; the moral about indiscretion is taken, but the point is that the Ijo do believe that destiny can be revised. In his studies of Kalabari Ijo belief systems, Robin Horton (1961, 1962) shows that people who have been afflicted by particularly adverse fortunes can consult the services of diviners, who will usually recommend certain phatic and dramatic processes that will enable them to revoke their prenatal destinies and so turn their lives around. The Ogboinba myth does not show her consulting a diviner, partly perhaps because she has too much belief in her own mystical powers and partly because the mythmaker may have found the direct approach far more heroic—as well as dramatically attractive—than her going through an intermediary. She does not exactly succeed, but in her bravado she exemplifies a republican, self-assertive individualism that sets much store by taking one's fortunes, as it were, in one's own hands.

Okoojii's Story

The story I collected from James Okoojii of Igbuzo on the night of October 13, 1980 makes the same point in a plot that combines elements in our Benin texts with the spirit of Ogboinba's adventure. It is important to stress at this point that, although the Igbo (as we shall demonstrate later in this chapter) are a fiercely individualistic people, they are no more tolerant of the sort of overweening self-assertion revealed by Ogboinba. Chinua Achebe relates the interesting story about the wrestler who, having beaten every contender on earth, carries his challenge to the spirit world, where again he defeats every spirit in sight. But he refuses to leave because he is convinced that the fabled land of spirits can do better than the opponents they have presented him. At which point his *chi*—guardian spirit, the Igbo equivalent of the Bini *ehi*—appears. "The wrestler laughs at this miserable-looking contender," we are told, "and moves forward contemptuously to knock him down, whereupon the other lifts him clear off the ground with his little finger and smashes him to death" (1975:163).

Against this background, let us examine the behavior of the strongman in the following tale. And because the tale has been set in the mythical land of Benin, we shall see what relations there might be between the Igbo culture in which this story has been told and the sort of outlook we have presented of old Benin.

Okoojii:	Ehn . . . it[18] took off, saw a true marvel.[19]
	(*Music begins*: *3-second flourish*)
	It took off, saw a true marvel
	And landed on God.[20]
	He was creating young men and collecting them
5	Creating young women and gathering them.
	After being created
	The young women were leaving for the world, the young men were leaving for the world.
Okeze:	You won't be able to strike it.
Okoojii:	What?

10	*Okeze*:	The gong—you're unable to strike it!
	Okoojii:	No.
		Ah, let him handle it (*hands the gong to Arinze*)
		So we can make progress.
		The young men were leaving for the world.
15		Shortly after,

One young . . . one [young man] so handsome—you would
      be looking at him till your cooking was done:
One young woman
Kept looking at him, saying, "There goes my husband!"
"What?" God asked her. "There goes my husband," she said.
20   That boy: *God had created him, but had not given him a penis.*[21]
He was neither female, nor was he male.
Those he had been created with had . . . moved on
So he got angry, asking God, "What's the delay?
Finish your creating, and let me go." [God] told him,
      "If you're leav—restless, then go off restless."
25   That boy took one look
And left for the world.
The young woman who had chosen him
Turned out to be the Oba's child
Turned out to be a princess.
30   While that child was carrying on
His mother and father, his parents
After he was born, on seeing how he was
Seven nights after his birth, they died:
His mother dead, his father dead.
35   An old woman picked him up
Brought him home, cleaned him up
Made him all right.
One look down his legs—he was neither male, nor female.
He was just—vacant:[22] he used his anus for urinating.
40   The woman nodded, saying, "So this is what I've found?"
That boy was growing
The princess was growing, the one who had chosen him back
      yonder.
Not long after
As he came of age, that boy looked at himself, and said,
      "Oh, now what have I come to?"
45   He called his old mother, and she said, "Yes?"
He said he was going to act male
And go about like a male.
On seeing young men, he would be so happy.
He tied on a stretch of cloth
50   Picked up his thumb-piano, playing it as he strolled:
A smashing young man—you would be looking at him till
      your cooking was done!
As he had his outing on that day
He walked on, and passed in front of the Oba's palace.

		Young boys trailed after him, so handsome was he.
55		They followed him about.
		SHORTLY AFTER, THE PRINCESS, ON LOWERING HER EYES, SAW SOMEONE OF RADIANT CHARM, playing the guitar he had on him.
	Okpewho:	Hm!
	Okoojii:	She ran indoors, and called her father
		Saying that was her husband out there.
60	Okpewho:	That she had found herself a husband! (Laughs)
	Okeze:	That's right!
	Okoojii:	Her father said, "What?" She said she had found a husband.
	Arinze:	Hey!
	Okoojii:	Well, her father asked them to call that boy.
65		When they had called him over, her father took a good look and said, "Well, so be it.
		Boy, you're in luck
		For you're going to marry my child here.
		LEAD HIM RIGHT AWAY," HE TOLD THEM. "HE'S NOW MARRIED."
		They led that boy away, right up to his mother's house.
70		They asked him for his father, and he told them he didn't have a father, because—well, here was his mother:
		He only had a mother.
		Benin agreed with him.
		They left that [girl] with him.
	Arinze:	The princess?
75	Okoojii:	The princess.
	Arinze:	Just because he was handsome?
	Okoojii:	QUITE HANDSOME:
		THE GIRL WAS PRETTY, TOO.
		They both sat for a while—
80		TO DO THAT THING a man and woman do, they couldn't.[23]
		For about two months, three months, four months
		They hadn't had intercourse.
		So, one day
		In that enclosure—bathroom, where they had their baths
85		The palmwine tapper had climbed up
		Where he tapped his palmwine
		On lowering his eyes, and looking
	Okpewho:	The palmwine tapper told what he saw?
	Okoojii:	The man who'd been given a wife had no—he was neither male, nor was he female.
90		Tapper landed his leg on the rope kachii,[24] snapping the rope
		Tumbling from the heights
		And dashing his head to the ground kai!
	Arinze:	To his death?
	Okoojii:	Dragged up his head, as he made his way to the Oba of Benin's palace to tell a lie.[25]
95	Okeze:	What a pity!

Okoojii:	Ambled off, right up to the Oba of Benin's palace.
	Saluted the Oba, and he answered.
	He told the Oba, "The man you have given a wife is neither male nor female.
	They are both there [idle]."
100 *Okeze*:	"What?" said the Oba.
Okoojii:	"WHAT?" SAID THE OBA.
	"If I am lying," said [the tapper], "let me be executed."
	As soon as day had broken, a proclamation was issued[26] throughout Benin
	Telling the nation:The Oba wished to ascertain what he . . . what he had heard.
105	This was no longer [*the rest of the line is not clear*].
	The proclamation was issued all around:
	A week and two days from then
	Starting from such and such a place, the entire realm of Benin was going to . . . to go naked.
Arinze:	Hm, just to get that boy!
110 *Okoojii*:	Just to get that boy!
	That boy had been out strolling, playing his guitar as he went, and winced:
	His body went cold.
	(*General ululation*)
	Shortly after
	He went and told his mother.
115	His mother said she had heard:
	"EVEN IF I WERE A CORPSE[27]
	I raised you."
	She called the boy, and he answered, "Yes?"
	"Are you capable of going to war?" she asked.
	"Wherever you send me, I'll go," he replied.
120	That old woman went off and . . . cut out a piece [of iron]
	Smelted it.
	He flung the piece kpai kpai kpai kpai kpai: it broke.
	He told her that blade wasn't strong enough.
	The old woman shuddered
125	Saying, "This child of mine is for real: the boy is capable of going to war."
	She pulled out . . . pulled out another one
	Smelted a piece, smelted a mighty thing
	Which turned out a cutlass.
Arinze:	Was that what the "piece"[28] was—a cutlass?
130 *Okoojii*:	It was from the piece she smelted it: one bar
	That's what she used in smelting the cutlass.
	After smelting, she lifted it up to him, and told him to fling it.
	THAT BOY FLUNG THE CUTLASS, and the cutlass caught fire,
	Saying, "God, here's fire: tafufufu, tafufufu!"[29]

135	"Don't worry," she told him. "You'll go to war."
	That boy . . . having got ready
	HIS MOTHER GOT UP, picked up her broad-knife[30]
	And laid it by his wife's head, saying, "The broad knife only
	lies on one side.
	Man, here's your talisman:[31]
140	When you have walked right up to the eye of the thicket on
	the outskirts, thrust your head in there
	So you will end up back yonder
	And confront those who left you naked."[32]
	"All right," he said.

Okeze: [*Says something to Arinze about the gong the latter is striking: not clear*]

145	Okoojii:	Upon that night
		That boy got ready.
		As soon as they had had supper, he left.
		Walked right up to the eye of the thicket, on the outskirts
		Peered in like this
150		Thrust his head in, and found himself back yonder.[33]
		Behold, the gateman!
		On taking a close look
		OUR MAN DREW OUT HIS CUTLASS:
		Gateman, here's fire: tafufufu, tafufufu!
155		Gateman, here's fire! *Chorus:* Tafufufu, tafufufu!
		Gateman, here's fire! *Chorus:* Tafufufu, tafufufu!
		What!
		The gateman said to him, "Sorry!
		Weren't we here when you were passing along:
160		Did you tell me you—that you didn't have such a thing?"
		"Why don't you—" said [the young man], "the people
		you send along, why don't you take a look at . . .
		at their groins?
		(*Okpewho laughs*)
		Yet you ignored me as I passed."
		Gateman, here's fire! *Chorus:* Tafufufu, tafufufu!
		"Sorry, my son," said [the gateman]—
165	Arinze:	Who is this gateman?
	Okoojii:	The gateman is the man guarding the boundary between
		spirits and humans.
	Okpewho:	Right!
		Once you go past him, you enter the abode of the spirits.
	Okoojii:	Once you go past him a little, you've jumped in—
		you're now in spiritland
170		You're now in God's abode.
		"Sorry," said [the gateman].
		"Let's have the kolanut you have on you."
		He produced the kolanut, and gave to him.
		"May you find your way home,"[34] he said.
175		"May you get what you are looking for.

Safe journey."
"All right," said [the young man], and put his sword
　　　back in his hip
So he might properly move in back-yonder.
How far could he go, when:
180　　　　　　What! my *chi*, here's fire: tafufufu, tafufufu!
　　Arinze: Even his *chi* [guardian spirit]?
　　Okoojii: 　My *chi*, here's fire! *Chorus*: Tafufufu, tafufufu!
　　　　　　What! my *chi*, here's fire! *Chorus*: Tafufufu, tafufufu!
　　　　　　The fire from the cutlass was blazing
185　　　　　That whole village had come out—
　　　　　　His *chi*'s village:
　　　　　　He'd set the cutlass-fire all over the place
　　　　　　The cutlass fire the boy had come to war with.
　　Okpewho: What!—
190　*Okoojii*: "Sorry, sorry, sorry, sorry!" they pleaded. "What's the matter?
　　　　　　　What's the matter?"
　　Okpewho: —That he would use in lopping off heads!
　　Okoojii: That he would use in lopping off heads!
　　　　　　[They] said, "What's the matter? What's the matter?"
　　　　　　"Sorry."
195　*Okpewho*: "What's the problem?"
　　Okoojii: "When I was going out here," he said, "my *chi*, didn't you see
　　　　　　　that I . . . that I had no penis?
　　　　　　That I . . . that I was neither female, nor was I male, yet you
　　　　　　　ignored me as I passed.
　　　　　　Really, you've embarrassed me."
　　　　　　His *chi* said, "Sorry.
200　　　　　WHAT YOU'RE LOOKING FOR, YOU'LL GET IT:
　　　　　　　Let's have the kolanuts you have on you."
　　　　　　He brought out kolanuts, and gave to [his *chi*].
　　　　　　"Life to you," said [his *chi*]. "God be gracious to you.
　　　　　　　May you get what you're going for.
　　　　　　Go forth, my child. It's me, your *chi*."
　　　　　　He drew in his blade
205　　　　　And left.
　　　　　　How far could he go, when he saw God well ensconced
　　　　　　Smiling at him, a little amused
　　　　　　Saying, "Here comes that youngster.
　　　　　　Well! Didn't he get fussy
210　　　　　Saying he was in a hurry to leave?
　　　　　　Now, he has surely seen what he was looking for."
　　　　　　ON GETTING CLOSER, AND LIFTING HIS EYES LIKE
　　　　　　　THIS, HE SAW GOD LOOKING AT HIM.
　　　　　　Drawing out his blade:[35]
　　　　　　　God, here's fire! *Chorus*: Tafufufu, tafufufu!
215　　　　　God, here's fire! *Chorus*: Tafufufu, tafufufu!
　　　　　　Say, God, here's fire! *Chorus*: Tafufufu, tafufufu!

Say, God, here's fire! *Chorus*: Tafufufu, tafufufu!
God said to him, "What's the matter now?"

Arinze: But isn't he afraid—what!

220 Okoojii: "Aren't you afraid—don't you know I created you?"[36]

Okpewho: "I, who created you?"

Okoojii: "I am the God."

"So?" said [the young man].
"Was that why you let me walk off naked, to my shame?"

225   Say, God, here's fire! *Chorus*: Tafufufu, tafufufu!
So [God] said to him, "Sorry, sorry, sorry!"
Called . . . the keepers of his work tools
Telling them, "Come—that boy must have met woes
where he has been.
DO, BRING ME A COUPLE OF BREADFRUIT SEEDS
over here."

230   So they brought out a couple of breadfruit seeds.

Arinze: Meaning testicles?

Okoojii: He dropped them in, and they became his testicles.
(Arinze and Okpewho laugh)

Okpewho: Breadfruit!

Okoojii: TURNING AROUND, HE [God]

235   Called his servant, saying, "Do, bring me a stick of plantain."

Arinze: Oh? Oh?

Okoojii: He gave him a stick of plantain.

Arinze: That was for penis?

Okpewho: What? What?

240 Okoojii: He took that stick of plantain and stuck it on
Then asked [the servant] to bring over that stone.
He put down that stone
AND DASHED THE PLANTAIN AGAINST IT [the stone]
to a resounding choei!
Splitting the stone into two pieces.

245   He [God] told [the young man], "This would kill someone
So you won't go with it."[37]
He asked [his servant] to bring him a lump of chalk
from over there.
(Okpewho laughs)

Arinze: To bring him what?

Okoojii: A lump of chalk—

250   The kind of chalk they make like this *(demonstrates)*.[38]

Arinze: Yes!

Okoojii: He asked him to bring it. He brought the chalk to [God],
who then stuck it on [the young man].
He slapped on the chalk, and it bent, slapped on it again,
and it bent.
He told [the young man], "This is what you will take with you
to the human world.

255   If you took that other one, well . . . and hit someone with it,

it . . . just as this stone is now, well . . . it would kill
someone."

Arinze: It would cut them all up!
                 (Okpewho laughs)
Okoojii: "So, go on home, and safe journey.
                 May you find your way home."
                 THAT BOY WAS STILL ASLEEP,[39]
260   Under that spell laid on him.
Okpewho: Right!
Okoojii: He still hadn't stirred.
                 On coming down, a-a-and re-emerging—
Okpewho: That was his spirit moving.
265 Okoojii: On coming out, returning from spiritland
                 Back to the human world
                 On that night
                 He laid down his blade.
                 TURNING HIS WIFE AROUND, he laid that thing [penis]
                     on her kachii[40]
270   Driving it deep inside. The prin—his wife lumbered around,
                     saying, "What now?
                 So such a thing was here all along, and you ignored me?"
Okpewho: And you kept quiet!
Okoojii: "And I nearly died from shame?"
                 [Her man] said, "Well, you're a princess
275   And I am a poor man's child.
                 I was afraid
                 Lest I be rough with you, and your father quarrel with me—"
Arinze: And come to quarrel with him!
Okoojii: "And I'd be ashamed.
280   Since things have turned out like this, well
                 It's all a matter of good fortune, then."
                 So they both fell asleep: at that, the first cock crowed.
Okpewho: He slept with her?
Okoojii: He slept with her!
                 (Laughter)
285   At the first cock-crow, before the break of dawn, at about
                     six o'clock
                 A proclamation had been sounded in Benin.
Okpewho: The time has come.
Okoojii: Saying the time had come:
                 As previously proclaimed, they should all come and strip
                     themselves naked.
290   They said that was how it was.
                 "AT FOUR O'CLOCK, everyone should clear out . . .
                     and make their way to the Oba's palace
                 And come strip themselves naked."
                 All preparations made, everyone arrived.
                 As everyone came to the front of the Oba's palace

295		They took off their clothes.
	Arinze:	The Oba already knew whom he was looking for.
	Okoojii:	He already knew whom he was looking for.
		(*Laughter*)
		Everyone coming over to the courtyard would say,
		"There he is! There he is!
		That's he over there!"
300		After a while
		That boy stomped in.[41]
		His wife came up, stripped herself, and there was a loud
		uproar.
		HER HUSBAND TURNED AROUND, TURNED AROUND,
		TURNED AROUND, TURNED AROUND:
		Lifted his eyes, looked at the Oba
305		Looked down his [own] feet
		Nodded to [the Oba], saying, "Yes, indeed!" There was a loud
		uproar, saying he was about to cry. AS HE TOOK OFF
		HIS CLOTHES, HIS THING SWUNG ABOUT.
	Okpewho:	Hear, hear!
		Nodded its assent!
	Okoojii:	With his left hand, he swung that thing to its full length, then
		pulling it up, showed it round to the Benin nation
310	*Okpewho*:	You see! (*Laughs*)
	Arinze:	So where was the palmwine tapper?
	Okoojii:	Saying the day [of reckoning] was here.
	Arinze:	So where was the palmwine tapper?
	Okpewho:	The palmwine tapper had gone wet in his arse!
315	*Okoojii*:	THE GUARDS HAD TURNED AROUND
		Asking the Oba, "How now?" The Oba told them, "Why are
		you looking at me?"[42]
	Arinze:	[*Comment not clear*]
	Okoojii:	*Wait awhile, I'm coming.*[43]
		"PEOPLE OF BENIN, GREETINGS!"
320		They cheered him on.
		He said to them, "Whoever . . . whoever climbs up
		Should never reveal everything he sees up there.
		He should reveal some, but leave some."
	Arinze:	Correct!
325	*Okoojii*:	"At nightfall," he said, "take him away and execute him."
		I dashed off from there at top speed. That's why the
		palmwine tapper doesn't tell everything he sees up
		there.
	Arinze:	After what he's been through!
	Okoojii:	My friend, thank you.[44]
	Okeze:	Thank you! Welcome!

This narrative image of a man without a penis bears some interesting comparison with a figure recorded in Benin plastic arts. Philip Dark (1983) has drawn attention to a plaque in the Fine Arts Museum of San Francisco showing a young naked Benin male with chased pubis but no penis. There is some controversy about this oddity—in light of the frequent representation in Benin art of the genitalia on naked male figures—thus prompting reference to a story about Prince Odogbo, who was later to be called Oba Ohuan (early seventeenth century), reported by Egharevba. Briefly, he was so effeminately handsome in his early youth that he was thought to be a girl. To erase that impression his father, Oba Ehengbuda, caused the young prince and his attendants to walk naked from Uselu (where every heir apparent to the Benin throne lived in bachelor quarters) to Benin City. "Thus Odogbo was shown publicly to be a young man" (1968:33–34).

The young man in Okoojii's story, however, is a pauper, not a prince. If the story in any way suggests a strained memory of the old Benin rumor that has lingered in the mythic imagination of the emigrants, then it should matter that the image of the young man has been transferred from the privileged environment of the royal court to the subaltern circumstances of the old lady who aids the infiltration of the closed world of power.

An equally close connection between our story and Edo culture may be seen in a story Daniel Ben-Amos collected many years ago and cites (1975:46–47) in his discussion of the major musical instruments—a box-harp *akpata* and thumb-piano *asologun*—used for storytelling in Benin. Briefly, a young man is warned by a diviner against three things: putting on tribal marks, getting circumcised, and playing the *akpata*. He ignores all three injunctions. Upon being circumcised, his penis turns out to be very small, and he is exposed to public ridicule. In shame and embarrassment, he takes up playing the *akpata* just to relieve his sorrows, but when in his frustration he tries to hang himself, God comes down to dissuade him and enlarge his penis. Overcome with joy, the young man takes off his cloth and parades his normalized penis for all to see.

One thing at least unites these three characters with penile problems, and that is the emphasis placed by traditional society on normal sex as a prerequisite for procreation. The story of Prince Odogbo has a special significance in the anxiety of his father not only to erase the embarrassment brought upon royalty by rumors about the prince's sex but to forestall any problems that such rumors may pose for the heir apparent's chances of succession to the throne. Primogeniture wars were a standard feature of Benin monarchical history, and Oba Ehengbuda may well have been anxious not only to nip the issue in the bud but to assure his people that, in the hands of their future king, the Eweka dynasty was guaranteed a healthy continuity.

With regard to the young men in Okoojii's story and the one reported by Ben-Amos, the issue of sexuality and procreation is complicated by their condition of liminality. In his study of these musical instruments used in storytelling and other kinds of performance, Ben-Amos identifies them—the *akpata* in particular—as icons of marginality and exclusion in Benin monarchical culture. On the one hand, two figures in the dynasty, first the rebel prince Aruanran in the reign of Oba Esigie and later the heartless and unpopular Oba Ewuakpe, are known to have played the *akpata* in the tragic moments of their lives. Although various heirs apparent, even Obas and chiefs, are known to have played the instrument (as an exorcism, perhaps, of a historical trauma), instrumentalists are as a rule excluded from courtly circles and even from the titled organizations of the realm.[45] On the other hand, because they play their instruments far into the night as they entertain clients, the instrumentalists are said to invade the domain of extra-human forces like witches and "spirits of the night," who often constitute their elusive audiences. Although they try to keep these forces at bay by recourse to certain protective charms, their very contact with them puts them effectively outside the margins of normal society.

The instrument played by the young man in Okoojii's story is, like the *asologun*, the thumb-piano (Igbo *ubo*), and his marginality to the circles of power is clear enough from his connection with the liminal old lady who infiltrates the realms of authority in the interests of a just social order. Although she is endowed with extraordinary mystical powers which she summons to the young man's advantage, the temptation to see her as a "witch" like the sinister forces skirting the peripheries of normal society is offset by the salutary uses to which she puts her skills. The reaction of the old lady to the report brought home by the young man—about the Oba's decree that everyone should go naked—is particularly interesting: "EVEN IF I WERE A CORPSE," she tells him, "I raised you" (lines 116–117). It could, of course, be seen as a bold assertion of the efficacy of the resources she is about to fortify the boy with in his metaphysical journey. But there is an underlying tone of offended subaltern sensibility in those emphatic words: I may not count for much here, but I am as good as your mother and I will not let them rob you of what belongs to you.

The subaltern revolt is equally represented by the music. It may be proscribed from Benin court circles, but beyond the world defined by the monarchy it hardly carries this negative image,[46] for despite it the Oba is persuaded to give his daughter to the young man. In his booklet, *Marriage of the Princesses of Benin*, Egharevba tells us that in the old days these princesses were given in marriage "to the high ranking titled chiefs of the first and second classes and the Uzama and the Eghaevbo only"; although in more recent times the tradition has been modified "to extend the Royal grace and honour to the ordinary men" (1962:9), even today a player of musical instruments like the *akpata* and *asologun* would have a very poor chance indeed of being considered for the "honor." For the music man in Okoojii's Igbuzo story to so infiltrate the court of the Oba of Benin as to win the hand of the princess in marriage—destiny or no destiny—is a high mark of subaltern revolt against the exclusionary world of authoritarian power, and could only come from outside Benin.

Before we interrogate the young man's entry into the spiritual world of his destiny, perhaps we should examine the psychological factors which dispose him to "act male" and, like his counterparts in Benin, seek "psychological therapy" in music (Ben-Amos 1975:45). It is probably not out of place to trace our man's condition to the site of his disrupted creation. In the story we are told that he is so anxious to go to the world that he walks away impatiently while God is still at work on him. This is admittedly a dramatic moment, but should be considered along with the contiguous scene in which he is so desperately desired by the young woman (who ends up as a Benin princess) that she instantly chooses him as her husband in the world.

In examining the level of consciousness or individual agency involved in the choice of destiny among the Tallensi, Fortes is led to contemplate the possibility of seeing "the evil Predestiny as a projected representation of perhaps feared and self-recriminatory impulses" (1987:168). Although the young man in our story is shown as impatiently opting out of the processes that would make him a full male, it would not be farfetched to see him not as a stubborn architect of his own doom but as a hapless victim of either of two factors: the forceful ego of the princess (she practically imposes her desire for the young man on her father, the king!), or his protoself's fear of the circumstances into which it is being drawn. One part of it is excited by the prospect of going to the world, but the other—and hidden—part is not so sure that it can live up to the *kind* of world it is being pulled into. When the young man becomes old enough to realize what he has brought upon himself, so to speak, it is too late (line 44), but it is not until his condition has been corrected that his temporal self admits to the princess (lines 274–279) the fears that dogged his protoself.[47]

Okoojii's story may be considered closer to the "Ehi-will-enrich-me" story than to any of the other destiny stories we have considered so far, in the sense that there was no open declaration or acknowledgment of a specific choice. But it reveals something of an interrupted process for which, as we have seen, the young man may not be held entirely responsible. It is not without reason, therefore, that the old woman in arming him for his journey back to "heaven" puts the blame for his condition on the forces responsible for creating him and sending him on to the world (line 142). She is sensible and auspicious enough to include in his provisions an item (kolanuts) which helps him to observe due cultural processes and so avoid the sort of unmitigated insolence Ogboinba shows even toward God (Woyengi).[48] But it is clear the young man's journey turns out well more because the super-natural forces accept some of the blame for his condition, and apologize for it (lines 164, 190, 226), than because he is well equipped to confront them.

"Chi" and the King in Every Man

But confront them he does, and here he demonstrates more the sort of aggressive individualism we found in Ogboinba than the submissiveness of an Use. Our hero's aggressiveness is perhaps explainable as a combination of a fierce sense of wrong and his being raised by a woman with rather extraordinary powers. But he is clearly also a product of a republican culture far less tolerant of superior authority than the figures we encountered in Bradbury's Benin tales. Let us now look closely at the Igbo concept of the individual and its relation to the structures that provide some context for its self-realization.

In their investigations of this subject in Benin and Tallensi societies, Bradbury and Fortes respectively have provided a viable model by locating the individual within the immediate structure of family relations. In subject-ing the Igbo evidence to this model, we begin to find considerable similari-ties between these cultures but would do well to defer our investigation of these similarities until we have quite concluded our study. We shall, in fact, center our discussion around the two emblems used especially by Bradbury in his studies of Bini personality: the portable shrine, or "shrine of the hand" (*ikenga* among the Igbo, *ikegobo* among the Bini), and the guardian spirit or spiritual half of the human personality (*chi* for the Igbo, *ehi* for the Bini).

Among the Igbo, the *ikenga* stands both as an index of manhood and a link with protective forces. As an index of manhood, it is the icon that both enshrines a man's personal achievement in fields of manly endeavor (like hunting and warfare) and represents that personal deity to which he prays for protection and guidance as he undertakes his mission. In the latter sense, it has often been seen as a plastic figuration of the guardian spirit, *chi*: hence Jeffreys concludes from the evidence of some of his informants "that the sky gods allot to a man a fate or destiny and that the [*ikenga*] is the means by which you ascertain what is your destiny or fate. Having discovered it the [*ikenga*] must be treated with due regard so that it is not closed or lost" (1954:34). Boston corroborates this idea when he suggests the "*ikenga*, like any other spirit, may indicate through a diviner that it requires attention, and a man who is suffering from misfortune in his normal pursuits is likely to be advised that his *ikenga* can restore the situation" (1977:77).

Basically, the *ikenga* is an icon celebrating the power (*ike*) of the right hand as revealed through physical exertion. It is a wooden figure carved in the form of a man, sometimes standing and sometimes seated; from his head spring two horns of a ram; on his left hand he holds some symbol of success or victory (the standard object seems to be a human head), while on the right he wields the instrument by which he has achieved it, often a knife or machete (some modernized versions show a gun).[49] The preponderance of the human skull in the tradition of *ikenga*-making would appear to lend credence to the view that the icon "was formerly associated with the practice of head-hunting" (Jeffreys 1954:27; cf. Meek 1937:39). Whatever its backgrounds might be, we have in the *ikenga* the principle that Bradbury has identified in the Bini philosophy of the self: that the human being—the male being the model in these traditional cultures—is responsible for fashioning or realizing his place in this world. In this, he must rely on the strength of his [right] arm, but he should also acknowledge that his success depends in a fundamental sense on his being able to maintain an auspicious relationship with those spiritual forces charged with protecting his interests and ensuring that his undertakings turn out right; the *ikenga* is the medium for achieving this necessary balance between a belief in the might of his [right] arm and his obligations to the overarching power of the protective spirits.

The significance of this icon becomes clearer as we set it within the context of the individual's relations with his family and the wider society. In the topography of the traditional household, the master of the house kept a shrine which contained emblems personal to himself (*ikenga*) and to his ancestors (*ofo*, a staff of jural authority which the Bini call *ukhure*). Achebe tells us in his description of his hero's compound:

> Near his barn was a small house, the "medicine house" or shrine where Okonkwo kept the wooden symbols of his personal god and of his ancestral spirits. He worshipped them with sacrifices of kola nut, food and palm-wine, and offered prayers to them on behalf of himself, his three wives and eight children. (1958:10)

When Okonkwo, forced to relocate to his maternal home as a result of an accidental manslaughter, builds a new homestead, he takes care to reinstal "his personal god and the symbols of his departed fathers" (91).

The close connection shown here between personal and ancestral interests is clearly a token of the communal ethic in traditional society: some of Jeffreys's informants have gone so far as to state that the *ikenga* represents the ancestors (1954:31). Basden tells us that the *ikenga* "is the first god sought by a young man at the beginning of his career" (1921:219), and certainly it is understood that, if the young man is to succeed in life, he must cultivate the spiritual forces contingent upon his personality, including the ancestors. But the principle guiding the disposition of the *ikenga* shows equally

clearly the order of relations between the individual and the wider authority. For despite the collocation of personal and ancestral emblems in the
domestic topography, it is understood by everyone that the two entities are
essentially separate from one another. This point is brought starkly home
when a man's *ikenga* is destroyed as soon as he dies (Arinze 1970:16): his
career is ended, and with it the icon that enshrined his singularity as an
individual. Boston has expressed rather neatly the implications of this practice for the relations between the individual and the wider social structure
within the context of the philosophy of the self, especially among the Igbo:

> The classic *ikenga* is individually owned and forms a visible record of its
> owner's social achievements. When a man dies, but before his burial, his
> friends arrive, take up his *ikenga* and recount his exploits and achieve-
> ments in a funeral lament. In the final stage of the funeral ceremonies the
> *ikenga* is split in two and discarded. The *ikenga* is called into being by the
> need to differentiate between those qualities which the individual owes to
> the collective wisdom and experience of his lineage and those talents
> which he has developed within himself. In principle therefore it ceases to
> exist when its owner dies, and is snuffed out with the vitality that gave the
> man his power to create. In practice *ikenga* are not always destroyed thus,
> but survive to become incorporated into the ancestral cult. But the formal
> rule that the carving should be split and thrown away shows how strongly
> the carving is linked with the idea of individual development and attain-
> ment rather than with the nexus of qualities that the Igbo attribute to
> lineage membership. (1977:84)

As I have pointed out above, the situation is fundamentally the same
among the Bini; as Bradbury tells us, a man's *ikegobo* is usually buried with his
corpse for, as the Bini say, "You cannot leave your Hand behind" (1973:268).
Here, however, lies a subtle difference. The burial of the *ikegobo* with the
corpse implies some continuity between the individual and the affinal
group; the dead man is expected to join the company of the ancestors, and
the bond of collectivity by which he is defined in temporal life persists in the
spiritual realm as his *ikegobo* takes its place among those of his progenitors
in the ancestral earth. The Igbo respect the logic of ancestry, of course; but
the physical destruction of the dead man's *ikenga* is a clear separation of the
individual's singular identity from whatever he owes to the collectivity.

The Igbo would be the last, indeed, to deny there was anything capricious
in the individualism credited to them. The caprice is evident even in the
principle underlying the making of the *ikenga* icon. The figure, as I have
said, is understood by the Igbo to be the instrument guaranteeing a balance
between a man's belief in his personal powers and his subordination to
superior spiritual forces. But even here, the man seems to take responsibility
for setting the terms of his relationship with this medium. Jeffreys has

recorded evidence from informants who told him that they would destroy or do away with their *ikenga* if it failed to bring them any satisfactory results: "If a man's efforts continually meet with no reward that man's regard for his [*ikenga*] wanes until he cuts it in two and gets another" (1954:26, 33).

If, therefore, among the Igbo man *makes* his own *ikenga* or at least calls it into being, then he is in essence responsible—to some degree, at any rate—for setting the terms of his destiny. Indeed, there is sufficient ethnographic evidence that the Igbo see the *ikenga* as a plastic representation of the spiritual surety of one's prenatal destiny, *chi*. Besides Jeffreys's evidence already cited above, Chinua Achebe points to "such tantalizing speculations as what happens to a person's chi when the person dies and its [the chi's] shrine is destroyed" (1975:160). Onwuejeogwu obviously refers to an emblem equivalent to the *ikenga* when he discusses the rites of emergence of a paterfamilias among the Nri: "Every man on having his first child plants a ritual tree in the front of his house. This ritual tree *Ogbu chi* represents his *chi* and will be cut down the day he dies" (1981:33). And Chukwukere corroborates this view when he speaks of "a special tree (e.g., *ogbu, ogilisi, oha*) planted in one's own compound" and other emblems used as shrines protecting a man's *chi* and ensuring the welfare of his household; at the owner's death, "the shrine is destroyed" (1983:525).

What is *chi*? There has been a great deal of controversy around this element of Igbo cosmology, arising largely from connections drawn between it and the Igbo word for the supreme divinity *Chukwu* (i.e., *chi ukwu*, the latter word meaning "big" or "great"), usually translated as "God" as in the Christian concept. The controversy has often been traced to the coming of Christianity to Igboland and its influence on indigenous theological concepts. In seeking to convey the idea of the supreme figure responsible for creating the world and everything in it, the Christian evangelists used a word very much out of the Igbo vocabulary: *Chineke*, which for them meant the spirit (*chi*) who creates (*na eke*). Students of Igbo culture and society such as Green (1964:52) and Achebe (1975:159–175) have pointed to the recognition by the Igbo of two separate entities, *chi* (spirit) and *eke* (lot, portion), in the composition of personhood,[50] and have stressed that the concept of an overarching creator-figure is dubious or alien to Igbo traditional thought; the word *Chukwu* is itself suspected to have been a concept imposed on the Igbo by the Aro subgroup as one of the devices whereby they sought to impose their economic ascendancy over all Igboland (Chukwukere 1983:528).

Although some notable scholars appear to be subject to these foreign influences in their treatment of the subject,[51] it is at least generally recognized that *chi* is the spirit which helps the protoself negotiate a prenatal destiny before the supreme divinity; it either remains in the spiritual world to ensure the individual's welfare as (s)he acts out his/her choice or accompanies him/her to the world as some kind of protective spirit-double. Whatever the case may be, the fundamental principle of the *chi* is that it is so individual to its owner as to be incapable of replication even under the best of conditions: thus the Igbo say, *Ofu nne na-amu, ma ofu Chi adi eke,* meaning that even those born of the same mother—including twins!— will have different destinies (Arinze 1970:116; Achebe 1975:166).

The idea of a spiritual "double" or parallel to the human personality is significant, for in the final analysis it implies that the two entities are separate although supposed to be working in concert. The separation, even the potential for conflict, is evident enough in the Bini story of Use, where the fellow is chided by his *ehi* for living contrary to his prenatal commitment. However, whereas in the monarchical culture in which he operates Use is not sufficiently empowered to assert his wishes, the republican culture of Okoojii's Igbo protagonist has instilled "the god in every man" (Chukwukere 1983) to the point that the individual is emboldened to act with a considerable sense of independence.

This independence can indeed be so strong that, if we read aright the import of certain Igbo sayings, some precedence appears to be given rather to the individual than to his guardian spirit in the determination of his fortunes in life. The question of which of these is superior to the other is not exactly clear: traditional thought is notoriously ambivalent, as the predicament of Okonkwo in Achebe's *Things Fall Apart* bears out. Although he emerges as a man laboring under an uncompromising sense of self, it is sufficiently clear that he epitomizes a culture of fierce self-esteem, now run foul of the superior *physical* might of the new dispensation. His earlier good fortune is adequately explained by the acknowledged Igbo understanding of such phenomena. Luck? "That was not luck," reflects the narrator. "At the most one could say that his *chi* or personal god was good. But the Ibo people have a proverb that when a man says yes his *chi* says yes also. Okonkwo said yes very strongly; so his *chi* agreed. And not only his *chi* but his clan too, because it judged a man by the work of his hands" (1958:19).

Later, of course, as Okonkwo's overweening temper gets the better of him and his affairs gravely decline, we learn that he has grossly misread the principle of life as enshrined in that old saw. "The saying of the elders," he is led to conclude, "is not true—that if a man said yea his *chi* also affirmed. Here was a man whose *chi* said nay despite his own affirmation" (92). But the very fact that he can point an accusing finger on his personal god for the evil turn in his affairs puts a certain adversarial touch to their relations, a touch we see vividly dramatized in Okoojii's story in the accusatory tone of the old woman's words as she prepares her ward for his journey to "confront those who left you naked" (142). Igbo religion or ritual does allow that an unfortunate destiny may be corrected in a future life (Achebe 1975:167) or that, with the aid of prescribed phatic and other rites, the ill hands of fate can be reversed even within the same life (Chukwukere 1983:526). What we have in Okoojii's story, however, is a vivid illustration of a potential contained within a fiercely republican outlook somewhat ill at ease with constraining structures. In Benin monarchical culture, the principle of *ehi* keeps the individual subordinated to the supernal authority not only of divinity but of its temporal personification in the Oba: put differently, threatening God is as good as threatening the Oba who is his representative on earth, and this is simply unthinkable to the average citizen in Benin.

The situation is radically different among the Igbo, and here we may safely invoke their political sensibilities in corroboration of their religious outlook. Although, as we saw in chapter 1, a number of riverine and west-Niger Igbo claim their forebears migrated from Benin, the major sources on Igbo history and culture (Basden 1938, Uchendu 1965, Nzimiro 1972, Afigbo 1972 and 1981, Henderson 1972, Isichei 1976, Echeruo 1979, Onwuejeogwu 1981, Ohadike 1994, among others) are firmly agreed the Igbo have a fiercely republican temper; their societies, even those modeled after the Benin monarchy (such as Onitsha, Ossomari, Issele-Uku), have been governed on far more democratic principles than may have been possible in Benin.

In his book, aptly titled *The King in Every Man*, Henderson tells us of Onitsha society: "The culture patterns which most distinguish the Onitsha [Igbo] as a people were those religious beliefs and values that exalted 'individuality'—the set of ideas that placed high positive value on the human individual per se, ideas stressing one's autonomous capacity to realise whatever his personal potentialities might be" (1972:521). In this culture, therefore, the concept of *chi* unites the king in every man with the god in every man to ignite a spark of unbounded freedom that occasionally craves to be kept in check.[52]

The Oba in the Story

Against this background, the image of the king in Okoojii's tale deserves a careful look. When we first meet him, he reacts with characteristic imperiousness and summary ruling to the situation presented by his daughter: a bold declaration of intent to marry the young pauper (59, 62). I say "bold" because Arinze's exclamation (63) captures not simply the precipitacy of the girl's decision but the risk she is taking in virtually forcing her wishes upon her father the king, contrary to tradition. The next thing we know, the king asks that the young man be summoned forthwith, and announces to him that he is in luck as the husband of the princess. Without allowing the young man any moment to savor his "luck" the king, apparently piqued by the suddenness of the whole business and anxious to be rid of the unaccountable fellow, orders the young man to be led away instantly (68). Later, when the palmwine tapper informs the king that his son-in-law is sexless, the latter reacts—understandably, we may grant—with the same sense of outrage (101) with which he earlier received his daughter's marital intent.

Further into the story, when the young man makes his mystical journey to the spiritual kingdom to correct his prenatal defect, there is a noticeable reversal of attitudes. There, he is the one who acts imperious and aggressive before the spirits, including God himself; but his behavior is redeemed by the token of proper ritual conduct he carries with him (the kolanut), so he is treated with deference and accorded his wishes. Throughout this episode the diction of the spiritual figures—both the young man's *chi* and God himself—is marked by studied courtesy and indulgence, in contrast to the imperious diction of the Oba.[53]

In the final episode of the story, we return to the imperious Oba who, true to his reputation, sanctions the execution of the palmwine tapper. Here, however, the order of execution is to some extent redeemed partly by the auspicious moments that led thereto—the restoration of the young man's sexuality, facilitating marital bliss between him and the princess and the public vindication of his manhood, to the obvious relief of the king—and especially by the fact that it was the tapper who offered to be executed should his information be proved false. The order of execution is, in the final analysis, presented as a well-merited punishment for deviant behavior. In framing the tapper's crime in the form of a decree against such misconduct (321–322), the Oba is presented both as a wise judge and as the author of a proverb that is very much part of the moral code of contemporary society. Indeed we might say that, in punishing the flippant tapper and facilitating the vindication of the young man's honor, the Oba has established in the temporal order the same harmonious state of affairs that God brought about in the spiritual order by restoring normal sexuality to the young man. This reformed image of the Oba as divine king may thus be represented in a schema that posits him as the earthly counterpart of the supraterrestrial God in the reciprocal fortunes of the young man and the palmwine tapper (see figure 1).

In that diagram, the supraterrestrial zone is both the locus of superior or privileged awareness and the abode of the superintending divinities: at the physical level, it is the height from which the tapper gains his privileged insight into the young man's flawed sex, while at the metaphysical level it is the site of the acts of creation and prenatal choice.[54] The terrestrial zone is the earth of raw reality, superintended by the Oba, who wields summary powers.[55]

Equally significant in this schema are the two lateral axes representing the fortunes of the two parallel figures in the story (the young man and the tapper), as well as the intervening space through which they cross from

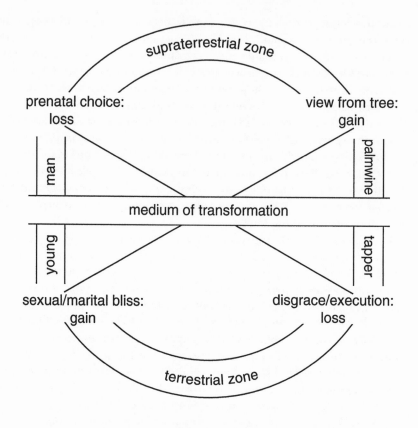

Figure 1

one zone of existence to another and experience two different kinds of transformation. The attribution of "loss" or "gain" to these characters in the supraterrestrial zone represents only the initial situation of the narrative drama. We know, for instance, that the young man's loss is made good when God finally gives him a penis; but the result of his journey back to heaven is validated only in the marital bliss that he enjoys with his wife back on earth. It is significant however that, in the parallel representation of these two characters, they are shown to make their journeys with the same impetuousness although they are headed in opposite directions. The young man's impertinence in heaven is indulged only because, as the spiritual forces themselves admit, he has indeed been wronged. The palmwine tapper is driven by equal haste—notice the narrator's brilliant description of the poor man's near-suicidal anxiety to report his discovery to the Oba (90–94). But his cause is unjust, and ultimately earns him the death he swore upon himself; the medium of transformation holds true for both characters because each experiences some measure of transition from physical existence.

But why does Okoojii give the Oba such a positive role in this story: sharing with God a harmonious circle of complementary roles, whereby the monarch bestows upon his world a just order equivalent to the compensation the creator awards to a violated human essence? Is there not something contradictory in putting the robe of justice on a figure whose bloody record is a standard ingredient of the traditions? We know the Edo salute their Oba as "the son of the wise judge and peace maker who combined wisdom and wealth with long life" (Ebohon 1979:45); could our Igbo narrator be validating such an image, against the grain of his people's historical experience of Benin? These questions undoubtedly mirror the complexities involved in a people's construction of their identity through the tales they tell. In a recent examination of the institution of kingship as reflected in the Igbo oral narrative tradition, Azuonye (1995) offers some ideas that might help us comprehend the paradox of a killer king as just judge.

The focus of Azuonye's paper is a proverb which mirrors the republican ethos of the Igbo people: *Igbo enwe eze,* "The Igbo have no kings." Azuonye carefully analyzes the political organization of Igbo life to uncover the principles which dictate that the *eze* "occupies, not the apex of a hierarchical social order (as is suggested by the title, *Igwe,* which implies 'the one with the gods who dwell in the sky'), but the center or heart of a closely woven social system (as suggested by the title *Obi,* which implies 'the one who occupies or represents the center'), surrounded by an inner council of *nze* or minor *eze,* with the populace occupying the outer fringes of the circle but operating within the same egalitarian and republican order in which the possibility of movement into and out of the inner circles or the center itself is never foreclosed". Contrasting what he calls "the ideal type of *eze* cherished by Igbo culture and various categories of deviant or alien *eze* apparently imposed by outside powers or modelled on the kingship institutions of proximate kingdoms and empires, notably the ancient Edo kingdom of Benin which is commonly described in the tales as *Iduu,*" Azuonye draws attention to the "combatively denigrative image of *Iduu* (the Benin kingdom) and its kings (*Oba Iduu* or *Oba n'Iduu*) in many Igbo folktales. The tales . . . suggest that the Igbo would have nothing to do with monarchical power of the kind associated with the Benin kings, be it in the form in which it is exercised in the Benin kingdom itself and in Igbo and other vassal kingdoms under Benin dominion, or in the form in which it exists in those Igbo communities which have at one time or another established themselves as kingdoms modelled on the Benin kingdom. In this sense, the saying *Igbo enwe eze* would seem to represent a traditionalist rejection of the power and influence of imported types of *eze* in favour of the people's own democratic institutions" (68–69).

So why does the Oba in Okoojii's tale enjoy, as our schema suggests, a fairly privileged representation as the counterpart on earth of the heavenly god who dispenses just deserts? The answer should be sought not so much in the well-worn characterization of the Igbo polity as "being acephalous, and containing no machinery for the authoritative settlement of disputes" (Boston 1977:22)—the traditional council of elders took care of such business—as in the tendency of these Igbo tales to engage in wishful fantasies about what Azuonye has called the "ideal type" of king. Azuonye cites a speculation by Achebe—compatible with the facts of Igbuzo history discussed in chapter 2—"that the Igbo had previously had kings and through a bad experience somewhere in their history had decided they were either not going to have kings again or were going to severely limit their power" (70).

It may be that a memory of the old days when they had kings has been permanently engraved in the Igbo *mythologique*, or that, particularly for communities like the west-Niger Igbo which have long lived within Benin's pale of influence, there is a splendor in the Benin style which continues to induce what Azuonye sees as "a deep-seated Igbo admiration for royalty" (78). At any rate, the image of the killer king as just (or divinely inspired) judge would appear to be a mythic compromise between the horror which the old Benin conjures in the mind of its old rivals and their vision of the proper qualities of an ideal ruler of the people.[56]

The Old Woman on the Outskirts: Myth, Gender, and Power

4

One of the very key figures of James Okoojii's story in the previous chapter is an old woman who helps a young man turn his fate around and, by marrying the Oba's daughter, win a favored place within the world of monarchical power. I intend, in this chapter, to investigate the position given to this woman—on the outskirts of the community, well outside the world of organized authority—by presenting two other stories of women like her and examining what relations they bear to the structures of power within those societies. Since these stories have the old kingdom of Benin as their point of reference as well as setting, we may well assume that, whether the story has to do with correction of a defective destiny or with some other social or spiritual imperative, the presence of the Oba in it has some bearing with power relations at one level or another.

Let me hasten to point out that, in the oral traditions of the west-Niger Igbo, women are given a variety of roles which often invite us to take an ethical view of their behavior, about as much as we are inclined to do with male characters. Some of these tales have to do with women who exercise mystical powers; women who wallow in abject poverty but possess the knowledge or power that will benefit whoever treats them with consideration; spirit women who, as *femmes fatales*, visit the world of humans to teach severe object-lessons, especially to men who let their lust get the better of their good sense; women in polygynous homes who are not on the best of terms and who take their animosities out as much on one another as on one another's children; and so on.

When I was a boy in the village, such tales were especially prominent in women's narrative performances; chapter 5 will have a female narrator telling one of them. But men have also always told stories with women characters in them. In this chapter we have two stories recorded from two male narrators in two distinct villages—the recordings are separated by an interval of thirteen years—but which are united by the same theme of marginalization of women from the circles of power in their societies that we saw in Okoojii's story. In these tales, the figure of a helpful old woman[1] provides us with useful perspectives for understanding how a people endeavor to cope with fears of inevitable power by countervailing it with the subtle designs of the powerless. One tale is set inside the Benin nation; in the other, a man from a community within Benin's pale of influence infiltrates the royal court with the same purpose of correcting a wrong. Whatever the case may be, there would appear to be some political factors underpinning the representation of marginalized old women in the world defined by both tales.

The Tales and Their Telling

The first tale was recorded from Charles Simayi of Ubulu-Uno on the same night that he told the story of the war between his people, the Ubulu, and Benin (see above, pages 17–18).

Simayi:	Yes . . . my tale takes off and captures a pauper
	Captures . . . (*false start; music corrected*).
	Er, my tale captures the Oba, captures his wives.
	One of these wives was a pauper
5	With not a single belonging.
	The [Oba's] wives, they bore him females upon females
	There was no male, no one to succeed the Oba.
	The Oba went to a medicineman
	Asking him to please make him a charm:
10	For how could an Oba be without a son—would a woman become king?
	That was long ago, not nowadays.
	Er . . . the medicineman came
	Telling him, "Find me a single seed of alligator pepper
	And pound a mortar-full of yam meal."
15	They sliced up yams into a pot:
	A deep-bottomed pot[2]—tossed whole tubers of yam into it.
	Young men held down that mortarful of yam meal.
	[The medicineman] told [the Oba], "Call your wives."
	The medicineman proceeded to bury that single seed of alligator pepper deep down in the mortar
20	Used in pounding the yam meal,

Mixing up the meal thoroughly.
The meal was portioned out.
They ate the meal
The Oba's wives lining up to take their shares.
25   Sharing continued up to . . . where the pauper was
                tucked away in the house—that poor one
That had nothing, had no cloth.
She would not come out.
By the time she got there, her mates had scrambled up the meal
And now . . . gathered up the particles in the mortar
30   For her as her share
Whether she ate or not.
Took a bite, and spat it out
Saying, "Eh-hen!"[3]
She asked one [co-wife] if there was a pepper in her share,
                and she said no, there was no pepper.
35   She asked another if there was a pepper in her morsels, and
                she said no. "I'm done for," she said.
"In this mortarful of meal consumed by my mates, how did I
                alone find pepper in my morsel? My mouth is peppery."
First Percussionist: Her mates told her, "Don't interfere."
Simayi: One of them told her, "Whatever you found is your problem."
                (*Laughter*)
The pauper . . . er . . . er . . . this pauper did not menstruate
                any longer, and became pregnant.
40   When she was about to . . . deliver her child
When she fell into labor
Those co-wives surrounded her
Snatched up the child, threw it into the river
And placed some trash by her loins.
45 *First Percussionist*:   But the earth was protecting her.
Simayi: They summoned the Oba, "Come and execute her.
                She has done an abomination: your wife has borne trash!"
What! The Oba was shocked
Saying, "So the medicineman has played me a trick?"
50   The co-wives had tossed [the child] into the river.
The river took the pauper's child and carried it along
Carried it on to a certain old [woman].
"Stop!" she commanded. "The wounded cow does not refuse
                the [aid of the] poor."
The old woman placed her calabash tray
55   Picked up the pauper's child.
On seeing the child dragging along, in the water, an umbilical
                cord that had not been cut
She caught hold of the cord, and cut it.
Old women of the spirit world are not the same as old women
                among the Enuani.
Picked up the child and took it home.

60		Took a look at it and said, "Pity! The Oba has been hoodwinked.
		I will take you home."
		Grabbed the child, cut off its head
		Chopped [the child] into bits, set a pot on the boil
		Threw the child into it.
65		The pot heated up
		She . . . took up a grinding stone, ground the child thoroughly
		(*coughs*)
		Took out its heart from the cooking pot
		Picked up the stone, dashed it against the surface of the
		heart *gbai!*
		On looking up, she saw the child approaching her—
70	*Spectator*:	What a man!
	Simayi:	Coming in from the outside.
	First Percussionist:	Which means that one man surpasses another,
		father!
	Simayi:	"I can . . . I can handle your training" [said the old woman.]
		Went to fetch a hunter of the spirit world
75		Said she would use all available resources to train this child,
		for his journey was a long one.
		A spirit-world hunter with his gun never bats an eye, nor does
		his gun miss anything.
		His gun misses the earth, it still gets the earth.
		[The old woman] took one of her charms
		Set the child down, and charmed him to that spot, to stop
		him from struggling.
80		Told the hunter to come over
		And shoot the child.
		The hunter said, "You mean . . . ?" She said, "Shoot him,
		I tell you."
		Man, the hunter licked [his mouth], pulled back
85		Took backward steps, hunter-style, levelled up, aimed at the
		child's chest
		And went *Dakwalalalam!*
		The hunter pulled back the gun, his gunpowder scattered
		The gun broke.
		(*Laughter*)
	Spectator:	Man surpasses man!
90	*First Percussionist*:	A superior is indeed a superior!
	Simayi:	She told the hunter he wasn't quite fired up yet.
		Loaded a cartridge into the hunter's gun-barrel
	Mr. Osadebe:	Life's journey! Hm!
	Simayi:	A lazy man never fights a war.
95		Told him, "Aim your gun, and shoot him, I tell you!"
		He levelled his gun at the child's chest.
		The two shots, this big, that were in that gun
		Went *Gbawalalalalam!*
		She told him to point the gun down.

100 He pointed it down, the two shots dropped out
They didn't touch the child in the least—
Spectator I: Hey!
Spectator II: What! He'd been truly boiled!
First Percussionist: What did I tell you?
105 *Simayi*:   The child was relaxed, for nothing had touched him.
First Percussionist: One man surpasses another, indeed!
Simayi: She then told [the child], "You'll . . . you'll have to go.
When you arrive . . ." She took up a bow
Strung the bow, using a thread—rather in the form of a
spindle for spinning wool.
110 *First Percussionist*:   And a mere stick-arrow!
Simayi: And carved him an arrow
Setting it to the bow—no fletches on the arrow:
Merely split a strip of wood in two and gave it to him—
you know what a woman's arrow looks like.
First Percussionist: A woman's business never amounts to anything!
115 *Simayi*:   Told him, "Go to the Oba's compound and play."
That boy took off
And getting there found his mates at play. They thought he
was a neighborhood boy, not knowing he was from
spirit-land.
First Percussionist: A terrible spirit-child, that!
Simayi: "Look at the miserable bow he has!" they said.
120 They set themselves to shoot arrows, and claim a prize—
the sort of thing we of the older generation did.
They set up a post, and positioned an orange thus
So that whoever shot it
Would clear them out of their prize.
At the end of the competition, whoever failed to shoot
[the orange] would be given seven lashes.
125 *First Percussionist*:   Father, his arrow would get it!
Simayi: That pauper's child from spirit-land took up his stick-arrow
They told him, "Move further: you, move further, move
further"—putting him down
So he wouldn't get the point.
Spectator: Right!
130 *First Percussionist (to Second)*:   Keep striking.
Simayi: Taking his position, he aimed his arrow: it went *vuuu!* right at
the orange *chogai!*[4] spinning it round and round.
(*Exclamations*)
Shouts arose, "Ah-hah!"
Spectator: Whose child would this be!
(*Laughter*)
Simayi: They decided to do wrestling.
135 They laid aside their bows, deciding now to wrestle—
wherever did this boy come from?
(*Laughter*)

First Percussionist: Send him away!
Simayi: He was encircled
But that boy slipped out, breaking the encirclement.
The one who encircled him offered him [a hand].
140   As he took the hand, the other made a throw, only to see
the pauper's son coming from yonder:
Ha-hah!
(*Laughter and exclamations*)
All right.
[The other] tried another style. He lifted up the pauper's son
—No! The pauper's son grabbed him by the back—
First Percussionist: Back is where you grab the calabash!
145 *Simayi*:   Spun him round, caught him—What! That caused an uproar,
for [the other] was the champion wrestler of them all.
But that's all right. What!
Where did this child come from?
Soon after, it had gone beyond play.
When he had played and played a little more at the Oba's
compound, information was sent to the Oba, reporting
that a certain child had come around
150   That he was behaving mysteriously
That he was troublesome, and he was disruptive.
What! The Oba ordered them to behead him:
How could a little child be disruptive—whose child was he?
They said they didn't know.
155   Soon after, the Oba then asked them to bring him, so he
could see him.
They took him right up.
The Oba took a good look at him, told them to take him to
the backyard.
They took him to the backyard.
The Oba and his son had been deadlocked in the house:
160   Blood had spoken to him
So he told them to take him to the backyard.
The [Oba's] advisers went to interrogate him
He said he was the Oba's son
That the old woman told him he was the Oba's son, that he
should go to this compound and play.
165   The Oba told him to go home where he came from; he
needed some time.
He went home. On getting home and telling his mother [the
old woman] how his playing had gone, she told him,
"You're going home."
Her earlier charming of him was merely a preamble.
Gave him a bath, thrust his head into a pot.
The third day—
170   A tale is born the same day it's conceived.[5]
They brought the pot and held him suddenly by the neck:

She lifted the boy—right to the Oba's palace *shojim*
    [instantly]!
The Oba held consultations.
He told them to go and cook

175   For he would like to eat food from the Oba's wives—that was
      the boy talking—
So they should go and cook.
The Oba's wives set about cooking.
The one who . . . his mother had nothing at all for stew.
Went to the rubbish heap in the premises, saw a dead rat
    killed by a trap

180   Picked up the dead rat, roasted it
Cooked some okra.
You could hear the Oba's [other] wives chopping up okra:
"*Olokoto kpam kpam kpalala kpam kpam kpalala olokoto puu puu
    yoo yoo:*[6] when he eats, let him say I am his mother."
    (*Exclamations*)
"All right," they said.

185   They began to set out their dishes.
Ugbi![7] Those who cooked antelopes, those who cooked
    anteaters, those who cooked grasscutters—
    (*Laughter*)
Those who had slaughtered pork—

Spectator: So they would impress him!

First Percussionist: Even slaughtered oxen!

190 *Simayi*: They set out their dishes in a file, inviting the pauper's son
    to eat.
The pauper's son would open a dish and throw sand into it.
    (*Laughter*)
The pauper's son would open a dish and throw sand into it.
Walked on *tiii*, got to the last one, the final one
And saw a broth that had been cooked with a dead rat:

195   The okra was now smelling *wani wani wani*,[8] it was not done.
The pauper's son bent down, cut a morsel into his mouth—
    (*Shouts of approval*)
Mother's food is gold, oh!
    Chorus: Mother's food is gold, oh!
Ah-ha!

200   *Chorus*:   Mother's food is gold, oh!
Oh, oh, oh!
    Chorus: Mother's food is gold, oh!
Oh, I agree!
    Chorus: Mother's food is gold, oh!

205   Yo, yo, yo!
    Chorus: Mother's food is gold, oh!
Oh, oh!
    Chorus: Mother's food is gold, oh!
She may cook anything and everything!

210	*Chorus*:	Mother's food is gold, oh!
		She may cook anything and everything!
	Chorus:	Mother's food is gold, oh!
		Oh, yo, yo!
	Chorus:	Mother's food is gold, oh!
215		The pauper's son picked up the food and ate.
		"What!" they said. "What! What! What! What! What!"
	First Percussionist:	Who told him? Blood!
	Simayi:	The Oba took him away—
		(*Side talk*)
		The Oba took him away—attention, please!
220		The Oba took him away
		Gave him a house of his own
		Where he now lived
		And assembled seven young brides in one day
		For him to wed, so he would have sons as soon as possible.
225		That was where I left them and returned.
	Audience:	Hear, hear!
	Okpewho:	Welcome!
	Simayi:	Welcome, my dear!

I shall be doing a cultural analysis of this and the second tale shortly. For the moment, I intend to give some attention to certain technical aspects of this performance that appealed to us on that night. Simayi's narrative performances are not usually marked by the sort of ebullience we find in storytellers who see themselves primarily as performers. Although he often employs histrionic devices like movements of various parts of the body to indicate attitude (e.g., lines 191–192) or give an idea of extent (e.g., line 193), and although he frequently relishes the humorous flavor of the odd detail or episode, he is far more inclined to see his story as a body of information—in a somewhat historical sense—to be treated with the seriousness it deserves: many a time, in fact, his countenance remains totally unperturbed while the audience rock with laughter at something he has said or done in the narration!

But there is an undeniable artistic touch and intent to some of the descriptions of scenes and events in this encounter. The portrait of the mistreated wife in this story is clearly intended to set her apart from the other wives of the Oba who scheme against her. She is so poor she has no cloth to shield herself with, and so insecure she slouches away in an obscure corner of the palace, moving so timorously that, by the time she comes over to take her share of the yam meal ordered by the palace diviner-physician, all she can find are left-over particles at the bottom of the mortar used in pounding the meal (25–31). This contrast between the poor wife and the others is pressed even more delicately in the kinds of effort made by them to prepare a meal to be tasted by the hero (177–196). Also, the scene in which the Oba and the wonder-child confront each other face to face (157–161) has been told with due suggestiveness and a careful sense of foreboding. From this, we can quite vividly picture the Oba and the young boy caught in a "deadlock" as the natural bonds of kinship tug between father and son and they experience a subtle moment of recognition.

Whatever may be the standard allegorical implications to be drawn from this tale, it has been told by a narrator with a deep feeling for the historical and cultural sources out of which his people's sense of themselves have been woven. These sources include the complex interplay of forces that have pitted the Ubulu people against the powerful kingdom of Benin and have consequently defined for them a whole network of ideas about right and wrong, the sensible modesty of those who have little and the tragic arrogance of those who have everything, the responsibilities of those who have power toward those over whom they exercise it, and so on. As a member of his community's inner councils and one who has played executive roles on behalf of its paramount chief (*obi*), Simayi is in a privileged position to set the images of his tales within this complex network of ideas.

No less privileged is Okafor Nwambuonwo of Idumuje-Uno, the narrator of our second tale, who introduces himself to us as the "Ozoma" of his village (18). The title announces right away the influence of Benin over this community (see note 9 below). The following tale was collected from Chief Nwambuonwo on Monday, November 30, 1993:

	Okafor:	Gentlemen, you are welcome.
	Audience:	Thank you!
	Okafor:	The kind of tale I've chosen to narrate
		To tell you
5		[Is] how Oye was captured
		And taken to Benin
		At a time when human beings were used for sacrifices.
		Oye had borne a diviner
		And borne a smith
10		And borne a thief
		And borne a carver, an artist.
		Oye their mother was captured
		(*Percussion begins*)
		And taken to Benin.
		I'll tell you how it came about
15		That she was brought back home.
		You are welcome.
	Accompanist:	Thank you!
	Okafor:	The man telling you all this is Okafor . . .
		Nwambuonwo, the Ozoma of Idumuje-Uno.
		I'm known throughout Nigeria as Okafor Odagwue.[9]
		(*4-second pause*)

20   So, my story begins.
Upon a time
They [i.e. emissaries from Benin] came along
Walked on and on
And landed in Aniocha.[10]
25   The first person they pounced on was Oye.
They grabbed her
And took her to Benin.
    (5-second pause)
When they got to Benin
They took her into the palace of the Oba
30   And his brother the Ogiso.[11]
They shaved her head clean
And pushed her into a chamber [okwule].
What the people of old called okwule, is now called
    "my room."
So she stayed there.
35   They [i.e. Aniocha people] searched for Oye
And searched on and on:
THE NEW YAM FESTIVAL APPROACHED, *and still Oye had
    not been found.*
Whereupon her son the thief offered to go and look for her,
    and having found her to bring her home.
Thief took off
40   And traveled right to Benin
Then started searching for Oye.
Whoever he stole, though human, was not his mother.
Whoever he saw, be she a woman, he would steal her, take a
    good look at her, but she wasn't his mother.
Whoever he saw, be she a woman, he stole her, took one good
    look at her, but she wasn't his mother.
45   *After some time, he came to his wits' end, and left.*
When he entered his house, and they asked him, "What
    about our mother?" *he said he couldn't find her.*
OH?!
(Laughs) They burst out laughing. *(Arinze laughs)*
NEXT TO VOLUNTEER WAS THE CARVER, saying he was
    going to bring home their mother.
50   The artist took off
Went on and on, right up to Benin.[12]
He found a spot and set up shop—a carving-house, as they
    used to call it
In the olden days.
    (5-second pause)
He started carving things:
55   He carved mortars deep
He carved mortars small
He carved trays

He carved pestles long
He carved pestles small.
60   WOMEN OF BENIN CAME TO BUY FROM HIM.
Whoever came, he took a good look at her, but she wasn't his
        mother.
This would come to buy, he'd look at her: not his mother.
That would come to buy, he'd look at her: not his mother.
He hung on for about three weeks, never saw his mother.
65   So he left.
Getting home, he told them he couldn't find his mother.
HO?! (*General laughter and exclamation*)
THEY LAUGHED OUT!

Spectator: What an experience!
70   *Okafor*:   WHAT!
Spectator: A fly looking for a fart will surely find it!
Okafor: AMAZING!
They were like, "Really!"
THE SMITH SAID HE WAS GOING, that he would find her
        and bring her home.
75   *Drummer*:   Smith that molds life!
Okafor: The smith set out
Went on and on, right up to Benin.
        (*6-second pause*)
The smith set up his smithery.
        (*4-second pause*)
The smith set to molding:
80   He made door-locks
He made needles
He made sieves
He made knives
He made everything smiths usually make, and women came
        over to buy them.
85   Whoever came to buy, he took a good look at her face,
        but it wasn't his mother's face.
This would come to buy, he'd look at her:
        not his mother's face.
The smith hung on for about four weeks, *didn't see his mother.*
The smith left. Getting into the house, he was asked about
        their mother, and said he couldn't find her.
WHAT!
        (*General laughter*)
90   Alas!
Spectator: He's brought her home indeed!
Okafor: They exclaimed:
"So our mother is lost!"
THE DIVINER SAID, "REALLY?
95   I am diviner extraordinary, and I'm going to bring home our
        mother."

Spectator:	The diviner is the seeker-finder!	
Okafor:	*They said, "Really?*	
	You'll go to Benin?" "Yes," he said. "You're the youngest of us," they told him. "How can you accomplish what we couldn't?"	
	"That's all right," he said. "I'll go anyway."	
100	(*6-second pause*)	
	THE DIVINER TOOK OFF!	
	(*4-second pause*)	
	MY MUSIC HAS CHANGED!	
	(*Drum joins percussion, as pace of music grows in an 8-second flourish*)	
	The diviner has taken off, the diviner has taken off!	
	Chorus:	Let's see if he's gone to find
105		Let's see if he's gone to find
		Let's see if he's gone to find
		Let's see if he's gone to find
	Okafor:	He's off!
	Chorus:	Let's see if he's gone to find!
110	*Okafor*:	He's off!
	Chorus:	Let's see if he's gone to find!
	Okafor:	He's off!
	Chorus:	Let's see if he's gone to find!
	Okafor:	He's off!
115	*Chorus*:	Let's see if he's gone to find!
	[*Drum sounds stand in for Okafor*]	
	Chorus:	Let's see if he's gone to find!
	Okafor:	Let's see, oh!
	Chorus:	Let's see if he's gone to find!
120	*Okafor*:	Let's see, oh!
	Chorus:	Let's see if he's gone to find!
	Okafor:	Let's see, oh!
	Chorus:	Let's see if he's gone to find!
	Okafor:	Let's see, oh!
125	*Chorus*:	Let's see if he's gone to find!
	Okafor:	Let's see, oh!
	Chorus:	Let's see if he's gone to find!
130	*Okafor*:	Oh, oh, oh, oh, Oye, my mother!
	Chorus:	Let's see if he's gone to find!
	Okafor:	Oye, my mother!
	Chorus:	Let's see if he's gone to find!
	Okafor:	Oye, my mother, ay!
135	*Chorus*:	Let's see if he's gone to find!
	Okafor:	Oye, my mother!
	Chorus:	Let's see if he's gone to find!
	Okafor:	When you hear this, come on out!
	Chorus:	Let's see if he's gone to find!
140	*Okafor*:	Oye, oh, oh!

	Chorus:	Let's see if he's gone to find!
	Okafor:	Oye, oh!
	Chorus:	Let's see if he's gone to find!
	Okafor:	Oye, my mother, oh!
145	*Chorus*:	Let's see if he's gone to find!
	Okafor:	Oye, oh!
	Chorus:	Let's see if he's gone to find!
	Okafor:	Oye, oh!
	Chorus:	Let's see if he's gone to find!
150	*Okafor*:	Oye, oh, oh, oh, oh, oh!
	Chorus:	Let's see if he's gone to find!

(*3-second music flourish*)

SO, HE TOOK OFF
And went on till he got to Benin.
ON GOING PAST IKPOBA [HILL][13]

155   And raising his eyes, from atop that oilbean tree (*gesturing*)
He jumped into a house
And saw an old woman.
He said to her, "Greetings, mother!" She asked him, "Man,
    where have you come from?"
He said he had journeyed from Aniocha.

160   "WHAT'S YOUR MISSION? Aren't you afraid?"[14] He said no,
    that he was a diviner.
    (*3-second drum flourish*)
"Really?" she said.
"WHAT'S WRONG WITH YOU?"
He said he had decided to come to Benin to ply his
    diviner's trade.
    (*3-second pause*)
"IF YOU REALLY HOPE TO WORK AS DIVINER IN
    BENIN," SHE SAID,

165   "YOU MUST SWEEP AWAY THIS PILE OF ASH BY WHICH
    I'VE SLEPT FOR THE LAST THREE YEARS."
    (*Drum emphasis*)
Ah . . . the diviner took up the broom
And fell to sweeping the ash
Swept it right to the bush
PAINTED UP THE HOUSE!

170   The woman took a good look at him, *and told him he was in
    truth a diviner.*
"You know what you'll do?" she asked him. "No," he said.
"First you must tell my fortune," she said,
"Since you're a diviner [*the rest of the line uncertain.*]"
DOWN TO BUSINESS!
    (*Drum emphasis*)

175	*Drummer*:	It's with his staff he does his talking!
	Okafor:	Hardly the fault of Okafor Odagwue!

    (*5-second pause*)

HE DASHED IT (i.e. staff) TO THE FLOOR, TO A
   RESOUNDING GBAI!
He saluted the old woman
And asked her, "You know what I'll do?" "No," she said.
   (*5-second pause*)
180 HE SAID THAT BEFORE HIS VISIT WAS OVER, HE
   PLANNED TO GO OVER TO THE OBA AND
   TELL HIS FORTUNE!
   (*Drum emphasis*)
"Really?" she asked. "Yes," he said.

Drummer: Has he gone to find?
Okafor: "But what's wrong with you?" she said.
   "What's the matter? What could have driven you, a diviner,
    from your home?"
185 He said he was searching for his mother.
   (*3-second pause. Okafor chuckles*)
The old woman burst out laughing.
"You know what you'll do?" she asked him. "No," he said.
   (*5-second pause. Drum emphasis*)

Drummer: Has he gone to find?
   (*Okafor chuckles. 20-second drum flourish*)
Okafor: "YOU'RE GOING TO THE OBA'S?" "Yes," he said.
   "All right," she said.
   (*4-second pause*)
190 "When you've gone on right to the Oba's palace," she said,
"The earth in his entire compound is paved with stone.
The first thing the Oba will tell you," she said,
"He'll tell you to pierce your lance in the earth
And if the lance pierces the earth, he'll know you're indeed
   a diviner
195 But if it fails to pierce the earth, you're finished:
That's the end of your mission."
"Really?" asked the diviner. "Yes," she said.
"What you'll do is this:
Once you get to the Oba's palace
200 If he tells you to stab your lance in the earth
STAB IT DOWN RIGHT CLOSE TO HIS PERSON
HE'LL LOOK AT YOU WITH ALL SHOCK AND CHAGRIN:
AS SOON AS HE LIFTS HIS FOOT, STAB IT RIGHT THERE
   WHENCE HIS FOOT WAS RAISED
For that spot is ordinary earth.
   (*Drum emphasis*)
205 *Drummer*: Has he gone to find?
Okafor: Certainly!
   Behold the seeker-finder: he's off!
   Chorus: Behold the seeker-finder!
   Okafor: He's off!
210   *Chorus*:   Behold the seeker-finder!

	Okafor:	He's off!
	Chorus:	Behold the seeker-finder!
	Okafor:	Oh, oh!
	Chorus:	Behold the seeker-finder!
215	*Okafor*:	He's off, he's off!
	Chorus:	Behold the seeker-finder!
	Okafor:	He's off, oh, oh!
	Chorus:	Behold the seeker-finder!
	Okafor:	He's off, oh!
220	*Chorus*:	Behold the seeker-finder!
	Okafor:	He's off, oh, oh, oh!
	Chorus:	Behold the seeker-finder!
	Okafor:	He's off, oh!
	Chorus:	Behold the seeker-finder!
225	*Okafor*:	Oh, he's off!
	Chorus:	Behold the seeker-finder!
	Okafor:	Spell never bound the seeker-finder!
	Chorus:	Behold the seeker-finder!
	Okafor:	Oh, oh, oh!
230	*Chorus*:	Behold the seeker-finder!
	Okafor:	Friends, the diviner is off, oh!
	Chorus:	Behold the seeker-finder!
	Okafor:	He's off, oh!
	Chorus:	Behold the seeker-finder!
235	*Okafor*:	He's off, oh!
	Chorus:	Behold the seeker-finder!
	Okafor:	Oh, oh!
	Chorus:	Behold the seeker-finder!
	Okafor:	Behold, oh!
240	*Chorus*:	Behold the seeker-finder!
	Okafor:	He's risen, oh!
	Chorus:	Behold the seeker-finder!

Okafor: He'd brought it down!
"Really!" [said the Oba]
245 THE LANCE SET FIRMLY IN THE EARTH
The Oba said to him, "Truly, you're a shaman!
Well, divine for me, and let me see."
"All right," he said.
HE LANDED HIS TACKLE ON THE GROUND, WITH A
    RESOUNDING GBAI!
250 And burst out laughing.
Hailing the Oba, "Death that kills on life's sweetest day!"[15]
SAYING, "DID YOU ASK ME TO DIVINE FOR YOU?"
    He said, "Yes."
HE SAID, "ONE OF THE WOMEN YOU HAVE HERE
Is about to destroy your household.
    (*4-second verbal pause*)
255 She has a clean-shaven head

Is light of skin
Is inside a chamber.
Have her brought here—"
Drummer: That's right!
260 *Okafor*: "So we'd have her buried at Ikpoba.
I'll do to her what you had in mind."
"Really!" the Oba said to him.
The Oba turned around
And asked his guards, "Did you hear what he said?"
They answered, "Yes."
265   HE SAID, "WELL, GO AND FETCH the captive slated for
execution.
FETCH HER at once.
Didn't the diviner say she would destroy my household?
Go and fetch her."
They went into the palace, and brought out . . . Oye."
(3-second music flourish, with loud applause)
"SIT HER ON THE FLOOR!" HE [diviner] SAID. They sat
her on the floor.
270   Little did Oye know she was being handed over to her son.
"Hey, woman: didn't you aim to ruin the Oba's household
That, upon your execution, the palace would be destroyed?
Well, you won't be killed here:
It's to Ikpoba we're taking you for that."
275 *Drummer*: That's right!
Okafor: HE SAID TO THE OBA, "SELECT THOSE OF YOUR
GUARDS who do the executions: QUICKLY!
AND BRING OUT ONE RAM
ONE ROOSTER
(3-second verbal pause)
A POT OF PALM-KERNEL OIL
280 A POT OF PALM-NUT OIL
A PIECE OF CALICO CLOTH.
MAN! They went into the house and brought out what the
Oba . . . what he [diviner] had asked: quickly!
He told the guards, "Don't stand there looking: tap her on
the head!
Move!"
285 HE PICKED UP HIS BAG—I mean the diviner
UNPIERCED HIS LANCE
COLLECTED ALL HIS EFFICACIES
He told them to follow him to . . . bury her at Ikpoba.
AT ONCE! They took her off to bury her.
290 THE OBA HAD SLATED HER FOR HIS NEW YAM FESTIVAL!
(Drum emphasis)
Drummer: Has he gone to find?
Okafor: Mm, behold the seeker-finder!
Chorus: Behold the seeker-finder!

	Okafor:	Behold, oh!
295	*Chorus*:	Behold the seeker-finder!
	Okafor:	Behold, oh!
	Chorus:	Behold the seeker-finder!
	Okafor:	Behold, oh!
	Chorus:	Behold the seeker-finder!
300	*Okafor*:	Behold, oh!
	Chorus:	Behold the seeker-finder!
	Okafor:	Behold: Move!
	Chorus:	Behold the seeker-finder!
	Okafor:	On the double!
305	*Chorus*:	Behold the seeker-finder!
	Okafor:	Come on, let's go!
	Chorus:	Behold the seeker-finder!
	Okafor:	Come on, let's go!
	Chorus:	Behold the seeker-finder!
310	*Okafor*:	Come on, let's go!
	Chorus:	Behold the seeker-finder!
	Okafor:	Come on, let's go!
	Chorus:	Behold the seeker-finder!
	Okafor:	Come on, let's go!
315	*Chorus*:	Behold the seeker-finder!
	Okafor:	Move!
	Chorus:	Behold the seeker-finder!
	Okafor:	THEY GOT TO IKPOBA
	Chorus:	Behold the seeker-finder!
320	*Okafor*:	AT ONCE
	Chorus:	Behold the seeker-finder!
	Okafor:	HE TOLD THEM TO START DIGGING THE EARTH
	Chorus:	Behold the seeker-finder!
	Okafor:	They dug the earth, oh!
325	*Chorus*:	Behold the seeker-finder!
	Okafor:	They dug the earth, oh!
	Chorus:	Behold the seeker-finder!
	Okafor:	They dug the earth, oh!
	Chorus:	Behold the seeker-finder!
330	*Okafor*:	He said, "Turn your backs!"
	Chorus:	Behold the seeker-finder!
	Okafor:	"You men of Benin"
	Chorus:	Behold the seeker-finder!
	Okafor:	He commenced, oh!
335	*Chorus*:	Behold the seeker-finder, oh!

They all turned their backs to him.
HE CUT OFF THE RAM'S HEAD
And turned it towards the earth
He picked up his staff[16]
340   He jangled it at Oye's head

And said, "You, woman
Had a mind to ruin the Oba's household?"
HE TOLD THE GUARDS, and all who had come with him:
    "TURN YOUR BACKS!" They turned their backs.
He told them, "Farewell to your homes. QUICK, GO HOME!

345   Anyone who looks back will be killed along with the woman.
COME ON!" They all gave him their backs: LET'S HAVE A
    FULL HAND OF APPLAUSE!
    (*Loud applause*)
They all gave him their backs: keteketeketeketekete![17]
WHEN HE LOOKED, they had run far.
He called, "Oye,

350   Oye, my mother!"
Oye raised her eyes and looked at him. "Don't you recognize
    me?" he asked.
She told him, "Man, I don't recognize you."
"I AM YOUR SON, THE DIVINER," HE SAID,
COME TO RESCUE YOU!"

355   Oye, Oye, I've got you
               Oye, oh, I've got you
               Oye, oh, my mother, I've got you
               Greetings, oh!
    Chorus: Oye, oh, oh

360   Oye, oh, I've got you
               Oye, oh, I've got you
               Greetings, oh!
GIVE A FULL HAND OF APPLAUSE AT SEEING HIS
    MOTHER!
    (*Loud applause*)
    Okafor: Oye, oh—

365   *Chorus:*   Greetings!
    General chorus: Oye, oh, greetings!
               Oye, oh, greetings!
               Oye, oh, greetings!
               Oye, oh, greetings!

370   Oye, oh, greetings!
    (*Drum emphasis*)
               Oye, oh, greetings!
               Oye, oh, greetings!
               Oye, oh, greetings!
               Oye, oh, greetings!

375   *Okafor:*   Oye, oh—
    Chorus: Oh, ho, ho
               Oh, ho, ho
               Oh, ho, ho
               Greetings!

380   He took his mother on and on into the house
AND CALLED THE CARVER

(*Percussion emphasis*)
Saying, "Look, mother is home!"
He called the thief
Saying, "Thanks for all your collecting!
385   Look, mother is home!"
THEN HE CALLED THE SMITH
Smith, the Facilitator,[18] saying, "Look, mother is home!"
Whereupon the smith hailed him, "Diviner, Minister to the
    Sun!"[19] and he replied, "Yes!"
"You are the Seeker-finder!" said the smith:
390   THAT WAS HOW DIVINERS CAME TO BE GREETED
    "OGBUEBUNU ACHO-AFU!"
                    Oye, oh
                    Oh, ho, ho
                    Oh, Oye, oh
                    Oye bore the diviner and the smith
395   Greetings, oh!
        Chorus: Oh
                    Oh, ho, ho
                    Oh, ho, ho
                    Oh, ho, ho
400   Greetings, oh————!

From a technical point of view, it is clear that this is a considerably different tale from Simayi's tale, and this is largely because Okafor and Simayi have somewhat different temperaments and dispositions as narrators. As a man holding such a highly placed title in his village as the *ozoma*, Okafor may be considered to be as deeply informed about the cultural history and the traditional values of his people as Simayi is, and to be taking just as much of a serious view of the content and implications of his tale. But a narrator like him who has, by his own account, participated in state-organized narrative competitions clearly would take his role as performer far more seriously than Simayi, who has never practiced his art at such a public level. We are therefore not surprised at the high level of formal structuring that we see in Okafor's tale.

For instance, there is a considerably higher degree of the lyrical impulse here. Simayi of course sings songs in his tales. In situations where any of his characters has to make a seminal point with a song, he employs a song for the purpose. But, on the whole, he puts so much premium on the informational or educative purpose of his tales that he narrates them almost entirely in the form of conversational speech punctuated with illustrative proverbs at appropriate intervals, using a song either as a recessional tune or to mark the climactic point of the tale, as in his story cited above. One major reason for this concentration on the narrative text is that, although he plays various instruments competently, Simayi more often leaves the job to his accompanists. But Okafor played an instrument in every one of the tales so far recorded from him. In the above tale, he played one of the accompanying gongs, working his shoulders frequently to the choreography of the music and thereby lending forceful dramatic impact to the narration.

Under the circumstances, we can understand why songs are sung on five different occasions in Okafor's tale[20] and why the tale reveals such a high degree of repetitive form. The songs are rendered long mostly by a repetition of the same ideas under the compelling throb of the music, indicating, as often in traditional storytelling events, that there is quite as much interest shown in the music as in the tale proper—a point further confirmed by the narrator's using a charged song in place of a description of the actual process whereby the diviner pierces the ground under the Oba's feet (207–242). The repetitive form is equally evident in the parallelisms by which Okafor relates various events and actions, such as Oye's delivery of her children (8–11) and the formulaic structure framing the careers of the first three brothers in Benin and their failure to bring home their mother (Thief, 39–48; Artist, 50–68; Smith, 76–89).

But perhaps there is a deeper reason for the strong musical sentiment in Okafor's tale. Okafor happens to be the president of the club of diviner-physicians in his village as well as a widely consulted practitioner of the trade.[21] The prominent position given to the diviner-physician in his tale may thus be put down to professional sympathy if not bias. The tempo and volume of the accompanying music certainly rises ("MY MUSIC HAS CHANGED!" line 101) as the diviner-physician arrives to save a hopeless situation, and we can justly say that the high lyrical impulse evident in the tale may in a fundamental sense be seen as a celebration of a professional ancestor or culture hero who used his wits to thwart the famed terror of Benin.

The Image of Benin

A close look, then, at both tales will reveal that in their different ways the narrators and their communities are endeavoring to define themselves, their values, and their traditions against the background of their encounters with Benin.[22] Simayi paints the picture of a Benin monarch consulting the conventional tradomedical wisdom of the realm in his anxiety that one of his wives bear him a successor to the throne and in the context of a conspiracy by most of these wives against the one on whom fortune has smiled.[23]

Although Simayi's tale contains several motifs which may be judged the general patrimony of folktale traditions across the world, certain details within it arguably mirror his people's long-held memories of Benin domination as well as traditions which they have shared with Benin over time. For a start, the reputation of the Oba as an insensitive tyrant is very much in place here. The ease with which the scheming wives recommend execution of the poor wife they accuse of having "borne trash" (46–47) readily suggests the capricious ease with which the Oba uses that mode of punishment against his subjects. The Oba certainly bears this out by the haste with which he orders the execution of the young boy reported to be "behaving mysteriously" and to be "troublesome" and "disruptive" (150–152).

The seed of alligator pepper which the palace diviner buries in the yam meal is an interesting symbol. This article generally supports the kolanut as traditional offering to a guest. Although one should not take the mystical business of this diviner too lightly, I find no evidence of that item's use as a reproductive catalyst, and it may well have been intended by the narrator as a purely symbolic element: separated from its usual convivial union with the kolanut, it emerges here as the agent of rupture in a polygynous union which is as much a factor of the narrator's as of Benin culture.

Equally enlightening, perhaps, is the scene at the end of the story where the Oba, happy at last to have won an heir, apportions the young man "a house of his own"[24] and quickly procures him "seven maiden brides in one day / For him to wed, so he would have sons as soon as possible" (223–224). The interesting thing about this episode is that the Oba shows a more zealous desire for a successor than is suggested by the standard reputation of these rulers. It would be anathema, of course, for the king to die without having a male to succeed him: Benin happens to be a hereditary monarchy ruled—at least since the injunction against female rule dating from the disqualification of Princess Edeleyo in the fifteenth century (Egharevba 1968:76)—only by males. But there is some evidence that succession was, perhaps in the earlier periods, often a stressful affair, because the heir apparent tended to be anxious to take over from his father before the latter had actually died and consequently brought about a tragic struggle between father and son for the throne (Ekeh 1978). In the overzealous reception of an heir apparent by this particular Oba, the narrator would seem to be offering an especially happy prospect of a harmonious succession: for him this is the way things should be, whether in the heartless realm of Benin or in any other rulership.

This humane regard for the proper order of things perhaps explains why our tale, admittedly set in the cheerless history of relations between the narrator's people and Benin, seems more concerned with exemplifying certain virtues than with castigating the Benin monarchy. Here, the rivalry between the Oba's wives mainly provides the context within which the narrator explores ideas that constitute the bedrock of a civilized moral code. The triumph of justice over exploitative privilege is here represented by the woeful failure of women using unfair advantage against the least favored among them; the independent laments by the Oba (49) and the old woman (60) against trickery certainly demonstrate how seriously the narrator views the incidence of foul play in human relations. The poor and helpless may yet win against the rich and favored: the poor, raggedy ward of a marginal old woman stands tall and triumphant over princes who mock his inadequate resources, while the poor woman who has nothing to wear but her shame and her humility turns out to be the mother of the young man destined to rule the land and everything it holds. The song that marks the climax of this story aptly celebrates the unequaled blessings of a mother's nourishment.[25] Nothing can be more touching than the immediate attraction that the boy feels for his mother's food, miserable though its composition; the song that concludes Simayi's story makes the story every bit a celebration of mother-son empathy as much as a representation of power relations in the monarchical world. Finally, in the subtle contest of wills between the young man and the Oba, during which the vibes of kinship flow between father and son, we see the fearless resolution of the ordinary citizen fully matched against the menace of the powerful ruler.

   This last point rings a certain republican note within the overwhelmingly monarchical environment of the tale, and may well be the major political case that the narrator and his community here make against the overarching power of Benin. Indeed, the image of a young man raised at the outskirts of the domain becoming poised to succeed to the fabled monarchy is as much a symbol of subaltern wish-fulfillment as of a stress between two political systems. Like most Igbo-speaking peoples in south-central Nigeria, the Ubulu are really a republican polity although—again, like many of their neighbors—they have, over time, borrowed various elements of Benin political and social institutions (Ohadike 1994:24). It is therefore doubtful that, in real terms, attaining to the fabled royalty of Benin, with all the negative image attached to it, would suit the temperament of the average Ubulu person, including the narrator. The accession of the young man from the outskirts to the position of heir apparent, especially under the harmonious conditions that mark the end of the tale, may therefore be the narrator's final harmonizing brush-stroke in his representation of a just social and political order, in Benin as much as anywhere else.

   Although we have remarked the differences in artistic style and temperament between Okafor Odagwue and Charles Simayi, a close look at our second tale reveals that Okafor and Simayi share very much the same concerns in respect of their tales' representation of ethical and political issues. As in Simayi's tale, the Oba is not spared his reputation for capricious slaughter. The diviner salutes the Oba with a eulogy that evokes this reputation—"Death that kills on life's sweetest day," 251—which, as we saw in

Christopher Ojiudu Okeze of Igbuzo

Charles Simayi of Ubulu-Uno

Okafor Nwambuonwo Odagwue of Idumuje-Uno

Christy Mmaduaburochi Arinze, with brother-in-law
Patrick Arinze, who recorded her.

chapter 2, is standard salute for the monarch. The events of the story are set during the period of the new yam festival, when noncitizens of Benin are said to be unsafe as they may end up as sacrificial victims in official rituals held to solemnize the event. It was evidently for that purpose that the Oba's emissaries had gone on a raid into non-Bini country and Oye had ended up in their net: the Oba admits that much (265). The old woman in whose house the diviner lands is thus genuinely amazed at his boldness in visiting Benin at such an inauspicious period, when he could be happily plying his trade in his native land (183–184).

The appearance of the diviner in the Oba's palace raises an interesting point about relations between Benin and especially the Igbo-speaking communities with whom it was constantly at war. Although there was not very much love lost between the two peoples, the Igbo provided certain services in which they were reputed to be experts and which were found crucial to the survival of the Benin monarchy. History records that, among the Igbo who migrated from the east to the west of the River Niger (about the tenth century A.D.) in search of fertile land, many were ritual specialists from the famed Nri civilization who traveled from one community to another offering their services. The Benin monarchy, constantly under the disruptive influence of internecine conflicts fought as much with mystical as with military weapons, was very much in need of the services of these Igbo experts and often welcomed them into the palace even while their communities were under threat from the imperial forces.[26]

It is to this sense of security, this concern for stability in the realm, that the diviner in our story appeals most, and this perhaps tells us as much about Okafor Odagwue's as about Simayi's real stake in telling his story. Despite the painful history of relations between his people and Benin, the narrator is really less interested in invoking the horrors of the past (which are hardly dwelt upon in any of these tales) than in highlighting the sterling virtues—some, at least—upon which their ethical conventions have been founded. The stability of hearth and home is clearly one of them, and although the standard image of the Benin monarchy in these western Igbo narratives is as the seat of chilling terror, it is frequently used largely as the setting for the valorization of an ethical system. Although nationalistic pride encourages the narrators in presenting their communities as having defeated Benin and even humbled the Oba, the Oba is shown in many respects to have acted with some of the wisdom or at least expediency becoming of a ruler of his people. Thus in these tales, despite flashes of the capricious anger and imperial high-handedness codified by a long tradition into his image, he listens carefully to the injunctions of ritualists in whose hands he has had reason many a time to entrust the welfare of his person and the realm.[27]

It is this concern for an ethical system, this sense of his people's cultural traditions, that has encouraged Okafor in giving prominence in his tale to certain virtues over and above the menace of Benin. One of these may be seen in the success of the youngest of four brothers (the diviner) where his elders (the thief, the artist, and the smith) have failed: note the elders' surprise at the youngster's boldness in tackling a task that proved too much for them (97–98). In a political culture built, as we saw above, as much on a system of age-grades—that is, a gerontocracy—as of titled men, the point is obviously being made here that the success of an endeavor requires due recognition of the capabilities and merits of everyone, however low they may rank in a pecking order.

Particularly remarkable is the behavior of the young diviner in this story, especially toward the old woman from whose house he launches his infiltration of the Oba's palace. Here he is a model of civility, courtesy, and above all the patient, suffering humility that ensures triumph in any endeavor. Surprising the old woman in her hovel, he greets her nevertheless with such gentle disposition that her shock is considerably mitigated (158). And when she requests him—in a test that is as much of his character as of his strength—to sweep away a three-year-old pile of dirt, he satisfies the woman well beyond the terms of the trial (164–169).

"Patience wins the angler his meal," goes a popular saying among the Western Igbo of our tale,[28] and we may well take this as the allegorical point made by the young man's behavior. But in this tale we are not talking about just any young man. Here the narrator has used the conduct of the diviner to point out one of the central qualifications for membership of his guild. We might in fact say that, in a fundamental sense, the tale is designed as a portrait of what it takes to be a diviner in this society. This point is suggested by several factors in the story. First is the privileged position given to the diviner vis-à-vis his brothers, coming in the end, when everything seems lost, to solve a problem that has frustrated the others. Second is the gain in dramatic representation that may be observed as we move from the humdrum, repetitive format of his elders' failures to the self-assertive brio with which the diviner executes the tasks that he undertakes both in the old woman's residence and in the Oba's palace: notice especially his imputation that as a shaman he knows no fear (160).

By far the most striking factor, however, is the way the narrator and his accompanists punctuate their performance throughout by stressing the sterling quality of the diviner as the one who seeks and finds. We see this, for instance, in the drummer's persistently seeking—in the tense episodes of the middle portion of the tale—to be assured that our diviner is living up to that charge (182, 185, 205, 291). Also, on three occasions the narrator and his group perform the song about the diviner as seeker-finder. Finally, the narrator concludes the tale, just before he and his group do the recessional, by giving us a few etiological lessons on the role and image of diviners (389–390). We may therefore safely say that, whatever lessons may be drawn from the story about the qualities recognized by the general society as central to their ethical system, the story, told by a diviner, makes a special case about the essential qualifications for membership in the guild of diviners, no doubt in defense of the profession against detractors or against those within it who may have lost sight of what are expected of them.[29]

In these stories, then, Benin serves essentially as a mythic backdrop for the exemplification of an ethical system recognized by the narrator's society or by the special interest within it that the narrator is obligated to defend. And yet, although the fabled terrors of Benin are not given special prominence and the stories, at least to the extent that they are climaxed by tunes that celebrate motherhood, evince a tender regard for the timeless virtues on which a society's ethical system is built, we see in each story a structure of oppositions that somehow advertise the conflictual environment within which the ethical system has been fashioned and perhaps continues to be tested.

To begin with, in both tales, there is some recognition by the narrators of the divergences between present-day society and some legendary past within which the events are subsumed. Thus Simayi tells us (11) that, in the world of his tale, it was inconceivable for a woman to be a ruler, as seems to be the practice today—apparently with his mind on countries like Britain but possibly also on the vogue of prominent females in contemporary Nigerian sociopolitical life. Okafor Odagwue, who has performed in more cosmopolitan settings and so has a broader sense of cultural as well as temporal differences, recalls the old days in Benin when human beings were the standard victims in ritual sacrifices conducted by the state (7); he also draws distinctions between what his Western-educated fellows today call "my room" and what traditional society would characterize as an inner chamber, *okwule* (33), as well as between conceptions of a sculptor's workshop "in the olden days" and in present-day society (52–53).

Other oppositions are just as revealing. No doubt, the fabled splendor that was Benin inevitably impressed itself upon the mythic imagination by way of contrast with less fortunate states of being. In Simayi's tale, for instance, there is hardly doubt in our minds that, as the youngster leaves the old woman's home on the outbacks for the grounds of the Oba's palace, he has made a qualitative move in terms both of material comfort and of the power and authority for which he has been carefully prepared. The image of power certainly expresses itself in several polyvalent clusters within the tale: whether in the contest of skills between this marginal boy and his playmates in the central world of the palace; in the battle of wills between the mighty king and the nameless boy whose paternity has become a point at issue between the two; in the conspiracy between the Oba's other wives as a privileged team and the boy's natural mother pitted against them, alone and without even a shred of cloth to shield her; in the contrast which Simayi frequently draws between the relative potencies of mystical ("spirit") and temporal forces (58, 74–77, 117–118); or in the notices which various members of the audience take, as they assimilate the images of confrontation presented in the tale, of inequalities in power between human beings (70–72, 89–90, 106, etc.).

These polarities are no less prominent in Okafor's tale. Here as in Simayi's tale, the contrast in material circumstances between the old woman and the Oba is vividly demonstrated as we move from a hovel beset with a three-year-pile of ashes (a clear symbol of exhaustion) to a palace marked by pomp and activity as guards move briskly in the performance of duties. Note also the change in the circumstances of the diviner, who moves from taking orders in the old woman's hovel to giving them in the Oba's palace. The power relations between the Oba and the diviner are especially notable. Although the latter conducts himself with caution, civility, and above all cunning, there is clearly a subtle contest of powers between him and his host. The one is a monarch who coerces by force of his all too visible power, the other a mystic who does his own "talking," as a spectator rightly observes (175), with a charmed staff. There is perhaps a subtle irony in the fact that the latter finally wins his control over the former by an act which physically threatens the Oba's person (200–204, 245–246).

Conflict is thus the backcloth against which these mythmakers represent the ethical standards of their societies. As we have observed, this representation does not always involve a wholesale evocation of the physical horrors and actual military contests that (as we saw in chapter 1) characterizes most overtly historical accounts. But to the extent that Benin continues to be the context in which this conflict is played, it remains for us to take a close look at that character in our tales who facilitates the conflict by masterminding the hero's assault on the Oba's palace.

The Old Woman on the Outskirts

Who is this figure, and why does the myth frequently place her in a liminal state?[30]

We should first dispose of certain misapprehensions to which this character is liable to lend herself. As someone well past the age of vitality, she may be thought to have been relegated to the margins by her family or a society that has no more use for her. It would, however, be generally true to say that, in most African societies, the elderly are treated with more than a little respect, as perhaps befitting those on the threshold of joining the company of ancestors. They are not cast out from the family circle, unless they have revealed questionable traits of character or perpetrated unspeakable acts that automatically disqualify them from continuing to enjoy the fellowship of decent folk. On such considerations, they are often tagged *witches* and dismissed from the wholesome fold of the townsfolk. But the old women in the above tales can hardly be seen in such terms, because in each case they have done nothing but facilitate the establishment of a just social order, whether in preserving life, or in restoring persons to positions from which they have been wrongly driven, and especially in helping children *re*-cognize the sweetness of motherhood.

We may as well tackle the metaphorical implications of the location of the old women. In Simayi's tale, we are told that the conspiring co-wives toss their poor companion's newborn baby into a river, which carries it quite a ways until it is picked up by an old woman. In most Nigerian communities, rivers usually mark the boundaries of a community's territory, well outside the inhabited areas of the town; the implication is that the old woman lives in this liminal region, evidently in the bush bordering the river. In Okafor's tale, the location of the old woman in the environs of Ikpoba Hill (on the outskirts of Benin)—as well as the evocation of the image of an oil-bean tree (154–155)—certainly conjures the picture of someone well outside the center of human habitation.

This positioning of the old women immediately invokes the dichotomy between "bush" and "town" which has informed various kinds of interpretation, and we have to be careful which of these works for the situation in hand. Cosentino's characterization of the bush as "the home of the un-human and anti-human" and the realm of "ambiguous and dangerous characters" (1982:25) is certainly not acceptable for the old women of our tales, whose mystical powers are employed for the restitution of social harmony. Much more to the point is Jackson's examination of the complementary roles of bush spirits (*nyenne*) and old women in restoring deprived/outcast orphan children to their proper positions in town: under the circumstances, "the wilderness or the 'back yard' . . . is the source, in ritual and in narratives alike, of the compensatory powers which can be tapped to redress injustices, protect life, and restore harmony" (1982:259–260).

But what are these old women of our tales doing on the fringes of society, on the outside looking in? It seems relatively clear, from the hints given by our narrators, that these women surely know something of the goings-on in the palace, are rather well-informed of the intrigues that characterize such a closely guarded world. In Simayi's tale we are told the old woman took a look at the floating child and said, "Pity! The Oba has been hoodwinked" (61). Even without any physical indications as to where the child has floated from, she can tell the source of its unhappy fate. She puts the child through the most severe trials in preparation for his return to the palace because she knows very well the sort of future that awaits him there.[31] In Okafor Oda-gwue's tale, the old woman breaks into laughter the moment the young diviner confesses he is really in Benin to look for his mother (186). There may be no special wisdom involved here, for everyone in Benin would know that this was the period of the *ague* festival, when non-Bini were statutorily procured as victims for the Oba's ritual sacrifice. But when she goes on to give the diviner detailed clues on how to survive the test the Oba will set him (190–204), she reveals very much an insider's wisdom. So what is this woman, who has evidently been privy to the world of the court, doing here on the outside of organized society and constituted authority?

We may permit ourselves to begin our investigation of this figure by looking to Benin traditions: after all, each of these conflicts is set in Benin. There may be justification enough in seeing the liminal old woman as a symbol of the disempowered female in Benin monarchical circles, now come to haunt the system by promoting all manner of assault against it. Mba summons evidence from two historians of Benin, Egharevba and Ryder, to the effect that there were women rulers in the first dynasty of the Benin monarchy (1982:16). How strong this evidence is may not be very clear. But the statement by the same Egharevba, that women were proscribed from the throne ever since Edeleyo, the daughter of the fifteenth-century Oba Ewu-are, was disqualified on grounds of "a feminine indisposition" (evidently prolonged menstruation) lends some support to the claim that women did once rule. Ever since the second dynasty, however, feminine rule has become thoroughly out of the question. In the reign of Oba Esigie (sixteenth century), the marginalization of women in Benin monarchical circles was taken one significant step further. For he initiated the practice whereby, three years after the accesion of a new Oba, his mother was removed from the palace and ensconced in glorified exile as the Iyoba (Queen Mother) of Uselu, a long way from the palace, with functions and powers that were terminated when the British brought Benin into colonial rule (Egharevba 1968:75). Mba further provides a detailed analysis of Benin society, prior to the consolidation of British rule, that reveals a total marginalization of women in most spheres of Benin life (1982:15–20).[32]

In Benin, therefore, women have long had an axe to grind with their traditions; in invoking Benin, these tales of the Western Igbo may seem to some observers to be perpetuating a tradition of revolt against monarchical authority transmitted through the diffusion of tales.

But is it not possible to argue, as we did in chapter 2, that these tales derive their inspiration from issues closer to contemporary cultural or political history than from a memory of a distant trauma? People formulate ideas, more than ideas people. Although ideas leave their impress upon people, the latter would be inclined to perpetuate those ideas only if, as psychologists have pointed out, they were fundamentally predisposed to harbor them.[33] Even then, the ideas are reformulated in the light of the new context into which they have been relocated. For our two narrators, the most plausible reason that their tales have continued to appeal to their communal audiences is that they evoke images and ideas that have a relevance for them within the context of contemporary life or at least of a more cognate cultural history. There is ample evidence, in fact, that in the traditions of the Igbo "culture area"—a phrase evoked by Afigbo (1981) and Onwuejeogwu (1981)—women played a more central role in the lives of their societies than may have been the case in Benin and so had more reason to be aggrieved when that role was severely curtailed if not summarily erased.

The sources for this may indeed be sought in the differences between the political traditions of the two peoples. Benin, as far as historical evidence goes, has always had a centralized government under a political ruler (ogiso, Oba). The evidence seems to suggest that the rulership has been predominantly male, and the record of these rulers makes it difficult to characterize Benin as traditionally a democratic polity.

On the other hand the Igbo, as we saw in chapter 3, have traditionally been ruled by republican instincts and structures, and their societies, even those modeled after the Benin-type monarchy, have been organized along more democratic lines than may have been the case in Benin.[34] Indeed, several studies that have taken a closer look at sociopolitical life among precolonial Igbo have shown that, despite pristine traditions of patriarchal rulership among them, there existed a firm structure of dual-sex organization on several levels that conferred very few special privileges on males.

Nzimiro, writing of his native Oguta east of the Niger, tells us that their women "have their own organisation which parallels that of the men" and "a council of female elders equivalent to that of the Ndichie college of the men's organisation" (1972:76). A similar situation may be found in traditional Onitsha on the eastern banks of the river, whose last Omu (*Queen* in the sense of being roughly equivalent in authority to the Obi or king) Nwagboka participated in signing a treaty with the British Queen Victoria. In his detailed evolutionary analysis of this intensely republican community, whose life has traditionally centered around its vast economic enterprise (Onitsha has perhaps the largest indigenous market in all of black Africa), Henderson tells us of the queen and her organization:

> The queen and her councillors each pay the king annual tribute, but they are not under his command in market affairs. Indeed, the queen is re-

garded as the king's equal in some ways; her palace can serve as a sanctu-
ary to anyone who has incurred his wrath, and she may actually compete
with him in splendor. She is regarded as greater than his chiefs, and
through her prominence in trade she can mobilize the power of Onitsha
women. Her decision-making capacity in community affairs is quite substantial (1972:313).

An equally eloquent picture has been painted by female scholars. Margaret Green, one of two female investigators commissioned by the British
colonial establishment to study Igbo women who gave them so much trouble
during the Women's War—often condescendingly called the Aba Riots
(1929–31)—published a book (1964) that leaves us in no doubt about the
forceful centrality of the women of Umueke Agbaja in domestic and religious life and in kinship relations (1964:171–172, 206, 232).

The picture has become considerably sharper in more recent feminist
scholarship. In her researches on women's participation in Igbo life especially west of the Niger, Okonjo exposes what she calls a "dual-sex political
system" (1976), or "a political system with bisexual functional roles" (1981),
in which women played roles that were in fundamental ways equivalent to
those of men despite the paramountcy guaranteed by more recent tradition
for the latter. Prominent among these was the position of the *omu*, who was
(as in Onitsha) the community's grand matron and who, with her council of
women, superintended crucial aspects of the community's economic, ritual,
and ethical life and generally provided a counterweight to the patriarchal
political authority. Other functionaries included the *otu umuada* or association of daughters (females native to the village) and *otu inyemedi* or association of wives (married to village males in the exogamous system), each of
which again had distinct roles that could never be countermanded by male
authority.[35] In Amadiume's study (1987) of Nnobi (east of the Niger), we
have perhaps the most authoritative analysis by a native daughter of the ways
in which her people's culture is permeated at all levels—mythical, ritual,
social, economic, and political—by a studied balance of gender roles and
the ideological implications of this balance in the social construction of
identity.

One admirable aspect of these female studies, one in fact that brings an
interesting pattern of light and shade to this discourse, is the honesty with
which the scholars admit the constraints to female power, whether inherent
in the internal dynamics of the culture or imposed upon it from outside.
Nearly every one of the studies concludes somewhat ruefully by pointing out
the ways in which the colonial intrusion into traditional African life terminated the privileges guaranteed women in the old dispensation; the Victorian morality that guided colonial policy simply could not condone the
liberal participation of women in various spheres of colonial life. And yet, a

careful reading of these analyses soon reveals that colonial policy only put official fiat on prejudices enshrined in traditional culture.

The incidence may be seen, for a start, in Margaret Green's study of Umueke Agbaja which, while revealing the significant ways in which women play parallel roles with their men in society, notes nevertheless their willing concession to male priority and "a sense of seemliness in women's behaviour which in normal circumstances demands a certain reserve on public occasions" (1964:169). We are also shown how the positions and deserts of women in their marital locations are in fundamental ways determined by the places their husbands occupy within the social structure (180–181), a situation which forces the women to touch psychological base with their natal homes as a safeguard: "The patriotism of birth took precedence, apparently, of that of marriage" (228).

The most revealing picture in these feminist studies comes, however, from Amadiume's analysis of the centrality of the female in Nnobi life and culture. Citing what she calls "contradictions in Nnobi gender ideologies" in the constitution of traditional authority, Amadiume explores the origin myths of her community and the processes whereby men have come to enjoy the prominence they have today. According to her, the founding deity of Nnobi was a female, Idemili, who, in submitting herself in marriage to "a less powerful god, Alo" (a hunter), acquiesced in her own domestication and subsequently facilitated the establishment of male supremacy in Nnobi ritual traditions. Amadiume goes on to cite three rituals that illustrate the imposition of patriarchal ideology over a traditional female essence. The result is that, although they continue to be accorded a great deal of respect and protection in the system, women have steadily lost the primacy initially enshrined in the origin myth and are today forbidden to play certain ritual roles, such as tending patrilineage shrines and breaking kola when a man is present (1987:99–114). We have thus not moved very far from the picture of willing self-submission that we saw in Green, graphically captured in one of the marriage songs from Nnobi cited by Amadiume:

> Be you as beautiful as a mermaid, the beauty
> of a woman is to have a husband.
> Be you one who has been to the land of white
> people, the beauty of a woman is to have a husband.
> If a woman does not marry, her beauty declines. . . .
>
> (1987:72)[36]

In exploring the implications of the Aba Women's War for the development of a feminist consciousness in contemporary activism, Judith van Allen has warned of the danger of women ending up "*where they have always been*: invisible, except when men for their own purposes personal or politi-

cal, look for female bodies" (1976:85). I have emphasized that phrase because it echoes Amadiume's honesty in recalling how far back in the traditions men have been taking advantage of women.

Indeed I believe that, in her study of female activism in Nigeria, Nina Mba
has plausibly exposed the limitations of that status and power which scholars
like Okonjo and Amadiume have credited to women in traditional Igbo
society. "They were excluded from male title and secret societies," she tells
us of their place in traditional hegemonic structures, "and while in some
areas they had their own societies, these had no political significance"
(1982:29). Of the institution of the *omu* ("queen") she reveals, by comparison with similar institutions in Yorubaland especially, that there was a less
than democratic process involved because the omu was invariably selected
only from specific lineages or patriclans and were in some instances used as
props for the selfish interests of an established oligarchy.

The exploitation of women becomes most glaring, however, in the colonial era. Amadiume has done a careful job of demonstrating the preeminence of women in Nnobi agricultural and economic life; so that even
though yam, the principal staple, was reputedly a *male* crop (as against
cocoyam, the *female* crop), "in reality the role played by men in yam production in the Igbo areas where less food was produced [as in erosion-racked
Nnobi] was minimal" (1987:29). The picture changes, however, as we move
from a subsistence economy to larger arenas of wealth, power, and privilege
defined by export commodities. With the termination of the Atlantic slave
trade and the promotion of alternative commodities like the oil palm, a
new enterpreneurial class emerged in many societies in southern Nigeria.
Women again found their berth in the new economy, but the following
statement by Nina Mba brings to light once again the same pattern of male
usurpation of female roles that we encountered elsewhere:

> Until the trade with Europe in palm produce from the early nineteenth
> century, the production of palm oil was carried out entirely by women,
> and was used principally for immediate household consumption. . . . The
> women were free to pick palm fruits wherever they found them. However,
> once palm produce became a major export, it came to be regarded as a
> man's product since it could be exchanged for men's goods, such as guns
> and spirit. . . . The ownership of palm produce was vested in the men
> landowners and their harvesting strictly regulated. The women still largely
> carried out the actual extraction of the oil and sold the oil in local
> markets, but the men took over the long-distance and external trade in
> palm oil. (1982:30)[37]

Despite all this, it is to the enduring credit of Igbo women that they have
persistently resisted the obstacles placed in the way of their full self-realiza-

tion and the usurpation of their cherished roles both in the tradition and since colonialism. This brings us round once again to the image of the old woman at the outskirts who makes her assault on the citadels of authority admittedly through the proxy heroism of wronged males.

Interesting insights from traditional society have emerged in the studies by Green and Amadiume. Agbaja women expressed a subtle revolt against male power demonstrated "when a male child was born by holding it upside down so that its head touched the ground or by putting a foot on its face to show their dominance" (Green 1964:176). Equally revealing is the tendency among married women to seize every opportunity they could of violating the taboos of modesty imposed upon them by their status. Green relates an event in which a band of village wives troop to exact a prescribed penalty on one of them found guilty of theft. In the security of numbers, and under the cover of night, they allow themselves the license of chanting ribald songs as they descend on the culprit, some of them stating unabashedly: "I am looking for somebody to fuck me!" or "The vagina is good to hold in the hand like a flute; only, there is no way of holding it in the hand."[38]

Amadiume relates an equally eye-opening incident in which a widowed young woman, not yet inherited (as permitted by custom) by another male in her late husband's family, allows herself to get drunk and to exclaim obscenities at her assembled relatives, accusing them of generally "failing in their conjugal and sexual responsibilities to her as a wife. She . . . claimed that she had not had sexual intercourse for years; her vagina was therefore getting rusty, and she was hungry for sex" (1987:61–62). In a conjugal morality designed (as has often been charged) to shelter male insecurity, these women could hardly suffer their constraints gladly!

Beyond these rites of insubordination in the domestic sphere, women have utilized an established machinery for resisting constituted traditional authority whenever they have felt their prerogatives trampled. We should again stress that the fierce republicanism characteristic of the Igbo is no less discernible in the women than in the men, and that in many cases women are likely to act with a more impenetrable obduracy than the men. Perhaps the most celebrated public illustration of this was the confrontation in Onitsha between Omu Nwagboka and the king, Obi Anazonwu, in the course of which the "queen," acting in the interest of Onitsha women, enjoined all of them to stop cooking for their husbands until the women's demands had been met by the Obi and his council. The boycott was so effective that the king and his men were forced to capitulate (Henderson 1972:525, Mba 1982:25–26).[39]

The high mark of women's public revolt against constituted authority in Igboland was, of course, the Women's War of 1929–31.[40] The interesting thing about this war is that, although it was touched off by colonial arrogance and high-handedness, it gave the women an occasion to vent a long-festering anger and frustration at the oppressive patriarchal structures under which they had for so long lived. For a while the coming of the British—especially bringing laws proscribing certain misogynist institutions—had offered women hopes of liberation from these structures. But when, under the "warrant chief" system, women saw ensconced in supreme authority several men of dubious repute among them, they could no longer contain themselves and undertook to visit on the government the same system of protest—"sitting on a man"—that had worked so well in traditional society. So determined were the women in their action that, despite the loss of many lives and the withdrawal of men who had joined them in the movement, they pressed on, crude weapons against superior firepower, until the government was forced to the negotiating table. In time, however, colonial power became an inescapable reality, enlisting native males in the progressive diminution of whatever powers and privileges traditional society had guaranteed the Igbo woman.

The figure of the liminal old lady—old only by virtue of a long tradition of abuse—may therefore be read as an imprint on the mythic imagination of irrepressible Igbo womanhood, forever haunting the margins of patriarchal power and determined that, even if women never regain the pride of place they once held in a balanced sociopolitical order, society should at least be spared the worst excesses of males in control of its destiny. Benin continues to be the setting for these tales, especially because, besides being the site and the agent of traumas enshrined in the collective memory, it provides a standard paradigm for repressive power, especially of mythical proportions. Still, it is just as arguable that these narrators are to some extent guided more by lessons of history closer to home than by memories of Benin that time, as well as the more pressing concerns of their daily lives, may have fairly frayed.

The Singer in the Tale:
Two Profiles

5

So far the words *culture* and *tradition* have been used rather frequently with a certain discursive license. We—by which I mean all of us concerned with investigating the customs and outlooks of peoples—have often assumed that these words convey some sense of a general pattern of conduct or system of usages, hallowed by time and habit, to be found across a society. Although on the whole we have outgrown the shortsightedness, even prejudice, that defined the concept of *tradition* in earlier social science, we still have a tendency to see it as a body of ideas that might be expressed with almost equal competence by a dependable cross section of a community.

If the above discussions of west-Niger Igbo tales of self-assertion have left that impression, one way to begin correcting it might be to ask the following question about the stories told in chapter 4 by Charles Simayi and Okafor Odagwue: assuming that my analysis of the image of marginalized women is correct, why should male narrators be trusted to harbor in their imagination the image of women who facilitate an infiltration or subversion of the well-guarded world of male authority? For although there are traces of what might seem to be sexist representation—for instance, in the picture painted by Simayi and his percussionist of the bow and arrows the old woman fashions for the little boy (lines 111–114)—on the whole the two tales take a positive view of womanhood, in terms of nurturing helpless youth to effective maturity as well as facilitating the establishment of a just ethical system.

The answer to the above question should be sought, to a good degree, in the circumstances within which our narrators grew up. Most traditional households are polygynous. If we recall, once again, the structure of such a household that Chinua Achebe has presented in *Things Fall Apart*, each wife has a separate quarters that she shares with her own children. Although as the children grow older the male ones get closer to their father to aid him in carrying out masculine duties, on the whole children grow up far more attached to their mothers than to their fathers, whose style of upbringing, especially in such a conflict-prone environment, often inspires more awe than love. It is against this background that we may best appreciate the ode to mother with which our two narrators bring their performances to a close. Both men are, as I pointed out, members of the ruling councils of their villages and may, on occasion, express certain hegemonist prejudices. But we can also allow that, if they are ever called upon to represent motherhood, there is a good chance that images of tender regard will be uppermost in their minds, unless of course something went very wrong somewhere along the way.

With the above in mind, I intend to devote this chapter to seeing ways in which biographical factors might be brought into an interrogation of these west-Niger tales of power and identity. There is, of course, already some respectable scholarship in this regard. Albert Lord has been in the forefront of interest in the place of individual performers within traditions that have shaped their art (1960, 1991, 1995). Other scholars like Richard Bauman have helped in promoting "the study of the individual performer, now beginning to replace the anonymous collectivity as the focus of folkloristic attention in explorations of the social base of folklore" (1986:78). Correspondingly, there has been a growth of interest in the investigation not only of artistic competence in contexts of performance (Bauman 1977, 1983; Ben-Amos 1971, 1977, 1993; Briggs 1988; etc.) but also in issues of power relations brought into play by the performative responsibility (Bauman and Briggs 1990; Briggs 1990; Briggs 1992; etc.).

In the present chapter, I would like to use the art of two narrators to explore the usefulness of certain aspects of our contemporary life in the interrogation of Benin, especially since they factor rather neatly into the logic of power relations in which any discourse on Benin is inevitably implicated. One of these is women's storytelling about that old kingdom. In chapter 4, I examined gender issues raised by stories told by two male narrators; here, it would be useful to see how women construct or represent their lives and their gender against the canvas of the monarchical world of old Benin.

Another issue to be examined is the role of Western literacy in these mythical representations. Perhaps no element of our cultural history is as indicative of the changes or adjustments to our perceptions of ourselves and our historical fortunes as the expanded idiom of discourse arising from our encounter with Western education and technology. What is the place of this new idiom in the mythology of self-determination inspired by Benin?

Some Theoretical Issues

Before we proceed any further, it might be well to address the theoretical hackles raised by the two issues just mentioned. In the last few decades, feminist scholarship has justly drawn attention to the marginalization and devaluation of the female (both as agent and as subject) in a long tradition of humanistic discourse pretending to be addressing fundamental problems about humankind when in fact the idiom had a firmly androcentric bias to it. In her lucid survey of feminist scholarship on the family, Linda Thompson (1992) has seen feminists as concerning themselves with research either *on* or *for* women: in other words, the effort has been directed either toward correcting the imbalance in our knowledge about the female side of the human equation or, perhaps more purposively, toward equipping women with the necessary tools for intellectual and other forms of empowerment.

Clearly, the lines have been sharply drawn in contemporary scholarship to the point where, as McKeganey and Bloor remind us rather painfully, "all knowledge is gendered" (1991:195, quoting Warren 1988). Although in any investigation we need, ideally, to "'deconstruct' gender and examine its interaction with a wider range of social variables" (197), quite evidently the pendulum is steadily swinging toward "a piquant reversal of patriarchal power relationships" (206) in various areas of intellectual endeavor. We need only look at the uncompromisingly gendered psychoanalysis of Luce Irigaray to see the way in which feminist scholars have moved beyond equalizing concessions to the entrenched patriarchal system—"What do women want to be equal to? Men? A wage? A public position? Equal to what?" she has queried (1991:32)—in order to construct a paradigm or an ethics (1993) that would reconstitute womanhood in its proper outlines, apart from the concerns of men.

Not all feminists have embraced this radical agenda to the degree that Irigaray has done, but in general there has been a strong effort to correct the gender misapprehensions in various areas of humanistic research. In an epochal study inspired in seminal ways by the women's liberation movement and edited by Rosaldo and Lamphere (1974), the contributors seek to establish the parameters of what may be identified as the peculiarly female contribution to human organization at many levels and—especially in Chodorow's very illuminating study (43–64)—sketch out the characteristics of the female personality often against the grain of the kinds of psychoanalytic conventions Irigaray has tried to question. In ethnography and folklore studies, there has been some consistency not only in denouncing the institutionalized androcentrism of especially male scholars but in identifying the ways in which women's interests and techniques (as informants, artists, etc.) are distinct from those of men.

Scholars like Claire Farrer (1975), Marta Weigle (1978, 1989), and Jordan and Kalcik (1985) denounce the ways in which traditional American folklore scholarship has not only defined certain stereotypes about the proper domains of women's culture (e.g., the home, birthing) but also subordinated and devalued female expressive forms in relation to discursive categories recognized for men: "story" for men, "gossip" for women; and so on. To project a peculiarly feminine outlook, therefore, Susan Kalcik proceeds to demonstrate how women's personal narratives are different from men's in being structured in a manner that parallels the rhythm of most women's lives in a domestic context characterized by multiple chores and engagements (1975). Carol Mitchell argues some basic differences in the joking devices of women and men (1985). From their respective researches, Yocom (1985), McKeganey and Bloor (1991), and Langelier and Peterson (1992) establish that we get better ethnographic results when women informants and artists have women rather than men as interviewers or audiences: only women can be safely trusted to appreciate the sentiments and experiences that their kind convey in their personal and other narratives.

Speaking of narratives, a particularly telling difference has been argued between men and women in their circumstances and styles. Perhaps because patriarchal society puts men in control of the public sphere, where the key decisions governing life are made and defended, while women are left to the more mundane arena of domestic life, the performative techniques of the two sexes reveal some key divergences. A gathering of men is more often than not a site for a contest of egos, so that their narratives are inevitably marked by a tone of self-projection of a more or less combative kind, in which everyone is so intent on pressing home a point that there is little patience for other interests: which partially, at least, explains the self-serving hyperbolism of heroic lore.

By contrast, in the more modest environment of the home in which they operate, women are more attuned to the mundane arts of conversation and compromise and are just as likely to subordinate their subjective personalities as the men are to project theirs. In their various ways, scholars such as Kalcik (1975:8), Yocom (1985:52), and Langellier and Peterson (1992:164, 168–172) make the point that women's storytelling is marked essentially by patient attentiveness and an interactive, collaborative, nonexclusive, and nonindividualistic conversational style where the exchange of ideas is far more important than the urge to press a point.[1]

These concerns have found resonance in feminist scholarship relating to African social instutions and folklore. In a volume of essays she edited over three decades ago, Denise Paulme (1963) argues for a gynocentric approach to the study of African culture and society; although the evidence is limited to the francophone nations, it is a work more of the type characterized by Thompson (1992) as research *on* women. A few years ago, Omolara Ogundipe-Leslie and Carole Boyce Davies guest-edited an issue of *Research in African Literatures* (1994) devoted to the topic of "Women as Oral Artists." Scholars like Finnegan (1970) and myself (1992) were especially taken to task—with some justification, perhaps—for giving little attention to women as oral artists. On the whole the volume aimed, in a similar spirit to Paulme's, "for a less unbalanced equation in terms of gender as far as the discourses of orature are concerned" (1994:2).[2]

The contributions contained in that volume and elsewhere in African oral literary study are fundamentally in agreement with Euro-American studies that, as we saw above, have tried to argue for a peculiarly female psychology and perspective on culture and society. Of particular interest is the study by Sekoni (33–46) which, among other things, endeavors to read the Yoruba tradition of trickster narratives—in his view, a phenomenon dominated by women—against the dynamics of the marketplace, a sphere equally controlled by women. The following analysis interestingly echoes the insights yielded by the Euro-American scholars cited above on the nature of the feminine imagination:

> The dynamics of interaction in Yoruba markets can be characterized as dialogic, defined by exchange and interchange of signs as means of constructing reality. Yoruba market dynamics can be described semiotically as a two-way flow of signs between two individuals serving simultaneously as sender and receiver of signs. Bargaining and haggling over the price of a commodity between vendor and buyer depicts metasemiotically that the value of meaning of any such phenomenon is open to negotiation by the human subjects that value and revalue such phenomena. As is obvious in the literature of Yoruba marketing, the price (value) of a good is never fixed. . . . Unlike myths or legends, performed largely by official spokesmen of the culture's hegemonic group in a public space and mostly during calendarized rituals and festivals, trickster tales are narrated in the privacy of homes mostly by grandmothers, elderly aunts, and mothers, and occasionally by grandfathers and elderly men. The predominance of women as narrators of trickster tales that are outside the purview of direct and indirect censorship often provides opportunities for women to encode their perception of social life in the codes that best illustrate their aesthetic of social processes. The primary thesis of this study is that Yoruba women . . . produce an aesthetic code that ritualizes and narrativizes a non-dualistic, unitive, or incorporative imagination that is reminiscent of the culture of perpetual negotiation and reversal of roles between ad-

dresser and addressee, between the protagonist and antagonist, or the dominator and the dominated in complex trickster tales characterized elsewhere as metatales or trickster tale qua trickster tale (see Sekoni [1994b]) (1994a:34, 37).

Finally, in her study of female *griots* in contemporary Malian society, Lucy Duran contrasts them with their better known male counterparts. Whereas the latter were traditionally bound to ruling houses to which their lofty historical narratives and praises were consecrated, the former "create a sense of history and tradition without excluding members of the audience who do not belong to noble lineages" (1995:201).

The argument about the role of literacy in a fundamentally oral-noetic culture leads us in a slightly different direction, although it involves issues of empowerment every bit as sensitive as the struggles that women have had to wage in their interests. The stresses between orality and literacy have been the subject of much intellectual interest, especially in the light of debates first about the compatibility of the two modes of cognition, then about the superiority of one over the other. On the basis of researches carried out under the guidance of Milman Parry, first into the mode of composition and recording of the Homeric epics and subsequently into the nature of oral narrative composition in contemporary Serbo-Croatia, Albert Lord came to the conclusion that the coming of writing to an oral culture inevitably spells dangers for oral composition because "the two techniques are . . . contradictory and mutually exclusive" (1960:129). A cognitionist like Eric Havelock (1963, 1976, 1982) has gone on to suggest that the introduction of the Greek alphabet was a unique achievement, because it facilitated a level of visual coding and analysis that paved the way for the practice of abstract and scientific thought in a way that scripts previously fashioned in the ancient Near East could never have done. The effect of such deductions has been to draw a line between what has been seen as the paratactic nature of oral composition and thought and the neat precision of literate processes, so much so that Walter Ong, somewhat echoing Albert Lord, has suggested that the phrase "oral literature" is a contradiction in terms (1982:10–15).[3]

Understandably, these arguments have been brought to bear on the African field, where there has been much interest in the study of oral traditions as well as sociological implications of the encounter between societies guided by that mode of communication and Western culture built predominantly on literacy. Perhaps the most significant contributions to the orality/literacy debate with respect to the so-called Third World has been made by Jack Goody, a longtime student of African culture and society. But despite the sophistication of his analysis of this complex issue and his apparent defense of the quality of traditional culture, he often leaves one wondering where exactly he stands. In an early essay (1968), he seems to be thinking along the same lines as Havelock when he credits the individual in literate culture with a higher volume of wisdom than his/her counterpart in oral culture (57). In a later and more densely argued study, he is persuaded that literacy makes it easier for the individual to express himself or herself with objectivity and discernment, and thus to engage in an abstract level of reflection, more than might be possible in oral culture (1977:150–151).

It might be safe to say that, on the whole, Goody's views on these matters would have gained somewhat from careful comparisons of representative texts which, I suggest, would have brought him to see that literacy exists as an *additional* (not a *substitutive*) resource no less in the oral cultures of Africa than he has found in Western society (1968:68).[4] Besides, his heavy reliance on sociological variables for monitoring changes occurring in Ghana (1987:144–147) raises questions about the "divide" he has argued between oral (traditional) and literate (technological) cultures. As often in these developmental studies, there is a tendency to lament the movement of populations from the rural communities to the urban centers, ignoring the frequent return of the migrants (whether permanent or periodic) with ideas and symbols that help either to collapse the cultural line between the country and the city or, even more forcefully, to strengthen the indigenes' pride in their native traditions. It is such lopsided views of change and other dynamics of social life that cause critics like Ruth Finnegan, armed with a keener insight into representative texts, to accuse Goody of promoting notions of the Great Divide between two kinds of mentality by ignoring the frequent overlap between their modes of expression (Finnegan 1988:120).

I have drawn attention to the above issues because, although I am not going to be concerned in this chapter with contending or valorizing the prejudices they conjure, they find some resonance in the myths of self-affirmation that will engage our attention here. Before proceeding to a discussion of the stories and their narrators, however, I would like to say a few words in relation to the underrepresentation of female oral artists with which I and other scholars have been charged.

So far in my fieldwork, I have recorded texts from roughly seven narrators, two of whom are women: a maternal aunt in Asaba (1983:79–81), and a young woman named Adaeze Nwajei in Igbuzo (1995). It is true that, on the whole, I have collected far more tales from the male artists than the female, but that is due in large measure to sociological changes which have necessitated a concentration of interest by one group or the other in specific forms of folklore. When I was growing up in the village, women (mothers, aunts, other relatives, and neighbors) formed a major proportion of narrators—although men were not that much fewer—who told us tales in the moonlit compounds or open square.[5] But nowadays electric lights have somewhat replaced the moonlight in the compounds and squares, and electronic equipment has become the favorite source of relaxation and enlightenment for most youngsters: recall the disco music in chapter 2, above.

For these reasons, the women are no longer as much in the picture as they used to be. But there are other factors to be considered. Engaged as they deeply are in the entrepreneurial and other developmental endeavors of the postindependence economy (Ohadike 1994:177–210), women show somewhat less interest in the narrative roles they once played. Indeed, many women nowadays consider storytelling a rather idle activity, and if you went to a village enquiring for the best known narrators, you would be as likely to be pointed by women as by men to *male* ones, especially if you happened to show special interest in the kind of tales upon which this study has been built.

Women have, of course, continued to be very active in other areas of folklore they have traditionally prevailed in, such as semiprofessional orchestras that are engaged for performances on social occasions like weddings, title-taking festivities, burial ceremonies, child-naming celebrations, political rallies, and the inauguration of development projects. Somehow, in villages where I have recorded, they seem to have ceded the sphere of narration (especially of legends) to male artists. It is entirely possible that a female researcher would have had better luck than myself. But I feel strongly that female narrators would rather not come forth to tell stories unless specially induced, as were the two women I have referred to above.[6]

The Pauper Princess: A Modern Woman's Story?

Since relocating to the United States in 1991, I have kept touch with the field both by periodic visits home and especially through my brother-in-law, Patrick Arinze, who has joined me on courtesy calls to, and participated actively in tape-recording, artists for over two decades now. Following instructions from me which he has often adjusted imaginatively to suit the situation in hand, he has continued to record tales, discussions, and interviews with artists old and new, of which the following tale, collected on December 13, 1995 from his sister-in-law Christy Arinze, is among the most recent.

A couple of things may be noted before we get into the story and discussion of it. Although she is a prominent member of some of the women's orchestras that (as I mentioned above) perform on a variety of social occasions, Christy admitted she had not told a story of the kind we have here in a very long time. We can therefore understand why her imagination, framed by images of her immediate concerns and preoccupations, seems less committed to anything that may be vaguely identified as *tradition* than may be seen in the tales of narrators like Charles Simayi of Ubulu-Uno or Okafor Odagwue of Idumuje-Uno (see chapter 2 above), who are frequently consulted by field-workers.

The story itself was collected under conditions that had a mixed impact on it. Christy had been mourning a death in the family. Although the clarity of her voice is a testimony to her skill as a singer in her orchestras, the lingering hoarseness,[7] coupled with the occasional slippages in detail, equally testify to the fairly unstable circumstances in which she was recorded.

However, if the points made above about recent scholarship on female narrative performances are anything to go by, then the physical outlook of Christ's story is hardly uncharacteristic. For one thing, Patrick Arinze's frequent dialogic interventions are certainly well suited to the conversational format in which women's storytelling is most usefully set: a trader like Christy should be at considerable ease with the two-way banter between her and her interlocutor. It will also be observed that, now and then, children intrude upon the scene of performance and are put to some order. If we recall what Susan Kalcik said of women's narratives, that their structure "parallels the rhythm of many women's lives, filled as they are with small tasks and constant interruptions from children, husbands, telephones," and so on (1975:11), then it is clear there is nothing out of the ordinary in the atmosphere in which Christy told the following story.

	Christy:	My story took off
		Went to the palace of the king of Benin
		This king of Benin had . . . he had two wives
	Arinze:	Only two wives?
5	*Christy*:	Only two wives.
	Arinze:	Okay.
	Christy:	But one of them he despised greatly.
		So,[8] they both . . . went on
		To have girls, girls.[9]
10		None gave birth to . . . a male.
	Arinze:	Okay.
	Christy:	So, those children of theirs kept growing, and growing
		And growing.
	Spectator:[10]	Hurry up your narration.
15	*Arinze*:	No. Leave her alone.
	Christy:	They had grown up thoroughly well
		When, one day, a man
		Who was very rich, came in his car
		To look for a wife, in the king's palace, telling him,
		"I have come to marry . . . your daughter."

20   HE SAID TO HIM . . . [11]
                "Summon all the children in your house, so that I . . . may
                       choose the one I will—
                Those two [girls] came out
                And he said it was the despised wife's daughter that he liked.
     Arinze: Okay.
25   *Christy*: The king refused, asking him to marry the one that—
     Arinze: That he [king] favored!
     Christy: That he favored.
                       (*Arinze laughs*)
                The man refused
                Saying he wouldn't marry her, that he would rather marry
                       this [other] one, for she was the one he liked.
30   The king then said, "All right."
                The man went home, while the king pondered
                       THAT MATTER.
                He was baffled, he and his wife.
                That man later returned
                Telling the king he had arrived
35   That they had now brought the wine.[12]
                THE KING TOLD HIM HE WOULD MUCH RATHER
                       ADVISE HIM TO MARRY THIS ONE, FOR SHE
                       WAS MORE INTELLIGENT.
                [The man] said no, THAT THE ONE HE LIKED
                Was the one he would marry.
     Arinze: That's right!
40   *Christy*: The king agreed.
                The Benin nation assembled.
                The wine was presented.
                On completing the customs
                Of wedlock between husband and wife
45   They all went home.
                Whereupon one day
                The king and his wife discussed what they could do
                To kill that girl.
     Arinze: Oh, kill the girl?
50   *Christy*: Kill the girl.
     Arinze: Okay, and not the husband?
     Christy: No.
     Arinze: Not the one who came looking for her?
     Christy: No.
55   *Arinze*:   Okay.
     Christy: So they could kill that girl.
                So they said—
                The king said he wasn't quite sure.
                His wife said it was all right, she would go and ask one
                       medicineman.
60   *Arinze*:   Really!

Christy:	She went and asked the medicineman.
	The medicineman told her, "It's not really difficult.
	I'll prepare you a charm, you'll put it in her food,
	set it down for her
	And she'll eat it."

65   NOW, THE FOOD THEY WERE FEEDING HER WAS
      [THE KIND] HER MOTHER HAD DIED FROM:[13]
      it wasn't good food.
      For after they had finished eating
      Whatever was left over—

Arinze:	Really—they would give her?
Christy:	They would gather together

70   Having gathered the left-over food
      They would leave it for her
      Having left it for her, upon her return from the farm
      Or wherever they had sent her to
      She would go and take that left-over food, served in a
          broken plate and set down for her

75   And eat it.
      She would save a little of it
      And take it to . . .
      And take it to . . . a certain . . . man in poor health
      Resting against the . . .

80   He was resting his body against the . . . that king's palace.
      She would give him, and he would eat.
      That man, WHATEVER was said against that girl
      The man would report to . . .
      The man would report it to the . . .
          (*Fading tone, as Christy turns towards distraction*)

85   That man would report it to that . . . girl.

Arinze:	M-hm.
Christy:	As an informer

      He made the report to her.
      After a while

90   They [king and queen] said they would prepare a charm,
          and prepared that charm.
      That child was away to the farm.
      Upon [her] return from the farm
      That woman went ahead and WASHED THOROUGHLY
          A CHINA DISH

Arinze:	M-hm.
95 *Christy:*	In which she usually served food for her own child

      Then cooked . . . kneaded an excellent helping of meal
          (*Background voice warns a child doing some cutting*)
      And put that poison in it
      Then . . . set it down for that child, and covered it up.

Arinze:	M-hm.
100 *Christy:*	THAT GIRL HAVING RETURNED FROM THE FARM

Was called over by . . . that sick man[14]

	Arinze:	Okay.
	Christy:	Telling her, "You see that food they've set down for you?
	Arinze:	M-hm.
105	*Christy*:	Don't eat it: there's poison in it.
	Arinze:	Okay.
	Christy:	There's a charm in it: so don't eat it."

That girl was hungry:
She told him she was seriously hungry.

110   "I've warned you," he said. "Don't eat that food.

Arinze: Really!

Christy: Starve for today:
That won't kill you."
          (*3-second pause*)
She said to him, "*Well, how can I . . . go through with this?*
          (*A child cries in the background*)

115   I am extremely hungry."
"No," he said, "don't eat that food. Once you eat it,
You will . . . surely die."
          (*3-second pause*)
Where's that song for it, by the way?

Arinze: Ah, ehn—

120   Oba has poisoned it
          Oba has charmed it!

Christy: Right—he called her
And said:
          Don't eat, don't eat

125   *Chorus*:   Shamala
          Don't eat, don't eat
          Chorus: Shamala
          Oba has poisoned it
          Chorus: Shamala

130   Oba has charmed it
          Chorus: Shamala
          To kill you
          Chorus: Shamala
          And take away your belongings.

135   Pauper's child
          Chorus: Shamala
          Pauper's child
          Chorus: Shamala
          Don't eat, don't eat

140   *Chorus*:   Shamala
          Oba has poisoned it
          Chorus: Shamala
          Oba has charmed it
          Chorus: Shamala

145   To kill you

> *Chorus*:   Shamala
> And marry off your husband.
> The pauper's child said, "What!
> I must eat this food, for I'm hungry."
> *[Interruption: Arinze had accidentally switched on another*
> *recording at this point, but shut it off with an apology*
> *as soon as he realized his mistake]*

150 Again the man told her:
> Pauper's child
> *Chorus*:   Shamala
> Pauper's child
> *Chorus*:   Shamala
155 Don't eat, don't eat
> *Chorus*:   Shamala
> Oba has poisoned it
> *Chorus*:   Shamala
> Oba has charmed it
160 *Chorus*:   Shamala
> To kill you
> *Chorus*:   Shamala
> And marry off your husband.
> The pauper's child . . . meanwhile, the Oba and his wife
> were upstairs

165 *Arinze*:   M-hm.
Christy: Having fun
> And . . . rejoicing that the pauper's child—
Arinze: Had eaten that food.
Christy: That . . . she would eat that food.
170 *Arinze*:   Okay.
Christy: So the pauper's child let that food be
> And coming to one section
> Made a cut in the food, made another cut, dipped it in the
>   sauce: gathered them together (*claps her hands*), and
>   threw them (*snaps her fingers*) into . . . the bush.[15]
Arinze: They thought she had eaten it [the food].
175 *Christy*:   They thought she had eaten it.
>   (*Background noises*)
> SO, HER [queen's] CHILD RETURNED:
> Her child had gone to school
Arinze: The king's child?
Christy: The king's child.
180 *Arinze*:   The one they had asked . . . that man to marry?
Christy: That's the wife . . . child of the . . . favored mate.[16]
Arinze: Ehn, the one . . . they loved more.
Christy: The one they loved more.
Arinze: Yes.
185 *Christy*:   Then she said
> She was hungry.

ON LOOKING for her food, she could not find it
BUT FOUND HER DISH
Where they had—

190 *Arinze*:   Had left food for her.
   Christy: Where they had left it
That dish of hers, but that was where they usually set [food]
     for the despised woman's child.
SHE SAID, "WHO WAS IT THAT LEFT MY DISH HERE?"
On opening it—

195 *Arinze*:   She saw food.
   Christy: She saw food, saw sauce
And set about eating that food.
   Arinze: Oh, you see that!
   Christy: She finished eating that food
200   Then she died.
   Arinze: Okay.
   Christy: Then she died.
Then they went after the pauper's child
     (*claps hands to signify pursuit*)
Then he [sick man] called out to her:
205   Pauper's child
       Chorus: Shamala
       Pauper's child
       Chorus: Shamala
       Don't eat, don't eat
210   *Chorus*:   Shamala
       Oba has poisoned it
       Chorus: Shamala
       Oba has charmed it
       Chorus: Shamala
215   To kill you
       Chorus: Shamala
       And take away your belongings.
The pauper's child ran away
And ran to her husband's house.
220 She and her husband lived on together
And had children, upon children, upon children.
She and her husband were living . . . happily (*claps hands*)
When her father
Paid a visit to her daughter
225 That was when it dawned on him
That she was his child
HER FATHER'S WIFE, SHE BEGAN TO PROFESS
Telling her, "It was I who raised you"
   Arinze: Okay!
230 *Christy*:   "And gave you excellent food."
At that point, she sought to make peace.
That is why mistreating someone

Is a bad thing.
    Arinze: That child . . . those two children are quite similar.[17]
235 *Christy*:   It's all the same thing.
    Arinze: That's right: clap for that![18]
             (*Applause*)

I became reacquainted with the narrator during my visit home to Asaba in July 1996. I say *reacquainted* because I had known her in my early youth as a maternal cousin, and recalled with gratitude that she was one of a close circle of relatives who had attended my mother in her final hours. She was born Christiana Mmaduaburochi Okonkwo on December 19, 1939 to Okotubo Okonkwo of Umugbabi in Umuonaje quarters and to Anyamdio Okonkwo (nee Okobi) of Umuekwo in Umuaji quarters. Christy attended All Saints Anglican (Elementary) School but finished up at the Convent School, where she excelled as a track star. She had done two years of teacher training college in Igbuzo (Ibusa) when her progress was terminated by the Nigerian Civil War (1967–70). Now married as a second wife to Francis Chike Arinze of Umuezei quarters, a retired storekeeper of the old United Africa Company (UAC, itself a redesignation of the old colonial Royal Niger Company), she has lost six of nine children to sickle cell anemia; the surviving children, two males and a female, are employed. An enterprising trader, Christy has a stall in the two main markets at Asaba (Ogbe Olie and Ogbe Ogonogo) where she sells foodstuffs procured from neighboring communities such as Ugbolu and Illah in Delta State and Ogbaru in Anambra State. As a young girl, she was prominent in various song and dance groups and famed for her voice. At present, she belongs to several indigenous cultural (e.g., Otu Osodi-eli, wives of Umuezei men; Otu Chukwubuluzo II, an Asaba-wide women's club; Otu Aguba, which performs even outside the Delta State; and Otu Idegbani, under the tutelage of Omu [Grand Matron of Asaba] Ejime Obi-Elue) and church choral groups.

One of the first things to strike us in her story is the similarity it bears with Simayi's story that we encountered in chapter 4 above, specifically in terms of the conflictual nature of relations in the polygynous environment of the Benin royalty. As we observed in that chapter, such stories feature as much in the narrative traditions of Benin as of non-Bini peoples like the West-Niger Igbo.

However, while Christy's story would be considered on the whole a characteristic portrait of relations in the traditional polygyny, certain aspects of it bear witness to the narrator's personal interest or stake in the portraiture and to the general outlook of women of her generation on issues of gender or marital relations with which her society has continually wrestled. To begin with, I think it is interesting that the crisis in this story centers on female children, rather than on a male child as in the Simayi story we have just referred to. Although there is, to my knowledge, no study devoted specifically to this issue in African folklore, it is safe to suggest that stories in which females are the protagonists are more likely to feature in the narrative repertoire of women than of men.[19]

The foregrounding of female characters in women's narrative performances is perhaps not so hard to understand. Women are, of course, conscious of the primacy enjoyed by men in contemporary patriarchal society and are as anxious as their male counterparts to bear sons who would claim their own place in the society's power structure; this is particularly evident in stories relating to struggles within the monarchy. But there is little doubt that female children are closer to a mother's heart than male ones, a phenomenon that may be explained by psychological considerations. "The mother," Solange Falade tells us, "is always particularly happy to have a daughter. The little girl (unless she is given to some other member of the family) will live with her mother until she gets married, whereas a boy will not be with her for so long. The little girl will be breast-fed for 24 months (six months longer than a boy), which establishes an even closer link between mother and child" (1963:219). Christy herself has two males as against one female surviving from her many births. But her interest in this story is perhaps explained by psychological factors of the sort identified by Falade.

An equally interesting figure in Christy's story is the old man who hangs around the Oba's palace and eavesdrop on affairs within it, for the benefit of the pauper girl who treats him with kindness. In chapter 4 we saw women consigned to the margins of the patriarchal society. But there is a slight twist to the liminality of this figure. True, he is sick, incapacitated, and left at the mercy of the kindness of all and sundry. But he leans constantly on the palace walls, whose secrets he is very much privy to. This might suggest he retains a certain stake, at any rate a vestige of attachment to, the dominant authority in the land, and may be seen as representative of those beggared by the endemic struggles for a foothold in the structures of control therein. If, therefore, this figure may not be seen in the same relation to the power structure as the marginalized females—he is stationed near the walls of the palace, not on the outskirts of the community—is he then perhaps a feministic counterpoint to a motif constructed by a male imagination?

A particularly significant aspect of Christy's story is the polygynous structure credited to the royal household, and here the narrator's story shows somewhat of a departure from the norm established by traditions relating to Benin. These traditions invariably portray the Benin monarch as attended by an extensive harem, the product of the Oba's traditional privilege to claim as wife any female subject by simply laying his hand on her; indeed, any woman who accidentally touches the Oba automatically becomes his wife, unless he specifically disclaims her (Ebohon 1979:34). In crediting the

Oba in her story with only two wives—notice Arinze's surprise at this detail, and Christy's insistence on it (lines 4–5)—our narrator projects a familiar cultural outlook. In ordinary society as against the royal household, and certainly in the west-Igbo society to which Christy belongs, there are many more two-wife households than those with three or more wives. Although in present-day Nigerian society a far greater proportion of women disapprove than approve of polygyny—this is certainly clear from Okonjo's study of west-Igbo marital culture (1992)—it has equally been suggested that unions with two wives show a much lower rate of divorce than those with three or more wives (Gage-Brandon 1992). It is thus arguable that, in opting for two wives rather than an extensive harem for her Oba, our narrator, who is the second wife in a two-wife household, projects a stake in the stability which such a union seems to guarantee as against the insecurity entailed by a possible expansion of the marital fold.

As I have mentioned, Christy is the second of two wives in her household, a situation that evidently finds resonance in her story. We are not told the position occupied by the wife favored by the Oba, but the conflictual relations between the two wives is clearly an ever-present danger in ranking relationships within the polygyny, a situation vividly represented in Buchi Emecheta's *The Joys of Motherhood* (1979) set in Igbuzo, next-door neighbor to Christy's hometown Asaba. Having acquired a certain amount of Western education, where her senior mate in the marriage has none, Christy may well have little to fear about her fate in the union. That her co-wife is, unhappily, ill seems to guarantee her some pride of place as the mainstay, economic and otherwise, of the family. But we can hardly deny that, in insisting on crediting the Oba in her story with two wives rather than the conventional harem, Christy projects some psychological anxieties, whatever these might be, about polygynous relations of the sort in which she is involved.

Remi Clignet has had a considerable amount to say, in his study of the effects of modernity on traditional polygyny (1970), about these relations which has resonances for certain aspects of Christy's life and art. Power relations between wives in polygyny are to a fundamental degree dependent on the role played by the husband in the union (12, 152).[20] Of the various grounds of conflict between co-wives identified by Clignet, education is given considerable attention. On the one hand Clignet suggests, quite rightly, that the presence of education spells dangers for the traditional values recognized in the institution of polygyny (33), and I think his arguments may be taken to include relations which result when one wife in the union has some education and the other does not. Clignet also draws attention to certain expectations which parents in the polygyny have in encouraging "the participation of their offspring in educational enterprises" (160); obviously, the potential for conflict is enhanced when the children of the one wife are actively engaged in schooling and those of the other wife are not. Finally, Clignet recognizes the impact of a wife's economic independence on the relations between her and her partners in the polygynous union (46–48, 313–327).

We should be careful, of course, not to argue a one-on-one correspondence between these factors and the details of Christy's tale or even of her life history. Mythmaking is a notoriously eclectic activity, in which images are frequently deployed in refractive rather than reflective relations with the facts of a lived reality. To that extent, we should see Christy's images simply as signs intended to throw flashes on aspects of her life and outlook, in some cases tangentially rather than frontally. Nevertheless, there are enough of these signs to suggest that her story might be seen, in some respects at least, as an exercise in self-apprehension if not exactly self-justification.

Let us take a few instances. The role of the Oba in the story demonstrates the dangers facing a polygynous marriage when a husband, perhaps only too naturally, reveals a preference for one wife over another. It is clear from Christy's story that the preferred wife exerts considerable control over the behavior of the Oba, sometimes against his better judgment: for instance, we can clearly see that the favorite wife is the prime mover in the decision to devise a poison that would kill the daughter of the despised (deceased) wife, a decision with which the Oba is not exactly comfortable (lines 58–59). My enquiries about the known relations between Christy and the rest of her family reveal that there is considerable harmony between all concerned, even in the face of the stresses involved in the senior wife's poor health. But when one wife has as many as seven children, while the other has only three surviving from nine births—Christy's emphasis on the way the young woman and her husband are blessed with numerous children (line 221) is particularly touching—images of death might tend to impose unkind pressures on an otherwise harmonious mind. Christy's husband is, by all accounts, a good and decent partner and, perhaps more than the Oba in the story, unlikely to lend his thoughts (let alone support) to sinister moves against any unit of the family. But polygyny is inherently plagued by stresses and dispositions that are not always unitive, so that images of poisoning and death become, in myth, an amplification of certain fears which in reality are kept under affable control in the interest of harmonious relations.

The picture of one of the Oba's daughters being engaged in schooling shows this as a "modern" story, evidently reflective of our narrator's regard for the resource she has acquired, to some degree at least. True, it has been credited to a fairly negative character, whose rejection in favor of the poor girl involved in farmwork symbolizes the preference of honest traditional values over the sinister mentality of the "intelligent" elite (line 36). I have qualified the scholar as *fairly* negative, for although she is the daughter of an evil co-wife, her disposition in the story does not go beyond reclaiming the dish with which she has usually been served. Obviously our narrator wishes to contain the extent to which education may be construed as a negative factor. At any rate, the juxtaposition of education and rusticity in this modern story does give some notice of the social stresses underlying the movement from one dispensation to another and, to some extent, suggest the rewards that would attend the educated (marriage to a man of substance, for one) if the resource were pursued under the right conditions. Despite the unwholesome circumstances in which she finds herself, therefore, the scholar girl serves as no less a symbol of the lofty hopes which a mother, especially within the competitive context of a polygynous household, has for her child.

The image of the rich suitor—his car is one more token of the modernity of our story—carries a message of entrepreneurial success with which the economically resourceful Christy might be thought to identify. Incidentally, there is a vogue in present-day Nigeria, especially among the Igbo east of the Niger, whereby a young but barely educated businessman (often, a trader in motor spare parts) who may have been previously married to an equally homespun woman, invests in wedding a young graduate more for upward social mobility than for love. In urging the suitor to marry the scholar girl because she is "more intelligent" the Oba and his wife are being used to indicate the vogue. However, in making the suitor see through the sinister basis of the offer, our narrator seems to be suggesting that entrepreneurial success should be associated with nothing but honest virtues.

In many ways, therefore, Christy's story is a traditional story told from a modern, posttraditional sensibility, projected through parallax lenses so that we strain to glean, against the backdrop of the known facts of her life, the substance hidden on the obverse side of the flashed image.[21] Before we take leave of the story, perhaps we should give attention to one more token of its modernity, the use of English words with which the narrator here and there punctuates—indeed deconstructs—the indigenous idiom of discourse, as if to underline the fate of mores that she and many like her are constrained to uphold despite the stresses of contemporary existence.

We have noted above the position of various scholars on the nature of female narrativity, which is judged to reflect women's incorporative, nonexclusionary, unitive instincts as against the individualistic, self-projective imagination of male narrators. The camaraderie revealed in the exchanges between Christy and her interlocutor, who also happens to be her brother-in-law, is every whit as admirable as the dramatic counterpoise achieved thereby. But we should not forget that Arinze was a teacher, and Christy, who had tried to be one but for the civil war which curtailed her ambitions, is clearly aware of it. Whatever harmony they enjoy as in-laws, therefore, and whatever accommodation Christy evinces as a female involved in an exchange of social information or as a trader engaged in negotiative banter, we cannot ignore the fact that, as her interlocutor persistently goads her whether with concurrence or with interrogation, she somehow finds herself in the midst of a subtle imaginative ploy in which she is forced to defend her competence in English speech.[22]

In this story, therefore, the well-urged nonindividualism of the female imagination must be taken with some qualification. Like McKeganey and Bloor (1991:197), I am inclined to look beyond the logic of gender for insights into such dynamics of power as stories about Benin inevitably entail. It could be countered, of course, that it takes a man to make an aggressive individualist of a woman in a conversational situation. The point might be valid, though no less arguable. At any rate, I suggest it would be uncharitable in this case to deny Christy the success of that stroke of self-definition whereby she has woven her trials and her triumphs with the combined fabric of traditional lore and modern sensibility.

Odogwu: The Singer Also Writes

Of all the narrators I have had the good fortune of knowing in the course of my fieldwork among the western Igbo, I remember the late Odogwu Okwuashi Nwaniani of Onicha-Ugbo ("Albela," as he was popularly called by his townsfolk) with much fondness and respect. Those of us who grew up in the village will recall with some nostalgia a curious class of men who impressed us as erudite and who many a time captivated us with the wealth of their wisdom in a wide range of subjects. Some of them had seen service in foreign theaters of World War II and were now back to the old homestead, regaling us with exotic tales in equally outlandish idioms. Some others were home on retirement from service in the colonial administration or the businesses subtending it. With little else to do but farmwork, some of these men set up shop, especially near the local post office, as more or less licensed "letter-writers."

Whatever it was that led these men home from centers of culture beyond the narrow world of the village, they invariably impressed us as very learned men. This was partly because many of them spoke English with accents we were inclined to associate with white people. Partly also, we were struck by the ease with which others combined whatever they had absorbed from the world out there with the cherished elements of our traditions.

Odogwu was one such wit, and a great artist to boot. In his performances for my benefit, he so enthralled me that, when I was making plans to perform the "second burial"[23] of my mother in Asaba, I had little hesitation in seeing him and his group as the centerpiece of the entertainment slated for the final evening of events. Here is the letter I wrote to invite his services:

Department of English
University of Ibadan
Ibadan
31 October, 1981

Mr M. Odogwu Okwuashi
Idumudiagbo Quarters
P.O. Box 93
Onicha-Ugbo
Bendel State

Dear Mr Okwuashi:

You will remember me as the gentleman from Ibadan University whose father is Urhobo but whose mother is from Asaba; you will remember that sometime in early September I came with my brother-in-law and tape-recorded some stories from you and your group.

I just wanted to write to thank you very much once again for very kindly letting me collect such very interesting and valuable material from you. I think you are a very talented person who deserves greater encouragement than you seem to get at the moment. By this letter I want to reestablish contact with you so that, if the efforts I am making now towards giving people like you more encouragement materialize, I will let you know at the right time. I have applied to some agencies to help me in my research, and if my application makes any headway (though funds are rather tight these days), I will certainly make you benefit from whatever I get.

I do not know when I will come again, though if I get any funds I will come before Xmas. However, I intend to do the second burial of my mother at Asaba at Easter and I would like to invite you and your group to Asaba for the wake-keeping night and pay you better than I did last time. I'll let you know.

Best wishes to all your men and family.

Sincerely
(Signed)
Dr Isidore Okpewho

The only other one of my artists to whom I ever addressed a letter was Charles Simayi of Ubulu-Uno who, being illiterate, had to have the letter read for him. But Odogwu was different. . . .

Odogwu was born in 1927 (he cannot recall the exact day or month), to Aniani—hence he is often called Nwaniani, the son of Aniani—and Ekwu-toziam Okwuashi, both of Onicha-Ugbo; he clearly came from a polygynous household, since according to him he had over 70 brothers and over 100 sisters. His father worked as an accounts clerk in parts of northern Nigeria, but especially in Oturkpo (in the present Benue State) where most of the children including Odogwu were born.

Odogwu had the distinction of being one of the earliest citizens of Onicha-Ugbo to attain a secondary school education (in the 1940s), after which he worked as a clerk with various colonial establishments—most notably in the railways—in various parts of the North but mostly in Odega (also in present Benue State). He was very fluent in Hausa, the dominant language of the North, and was so well liked and respected both socially and professionally as to be nicknamed *akawo mai-gash*, Hausa for "clerk of no mean order." While in the North he married his two wives, who together bore him his eleven children (one six, the other five).

As with Christy, Odogwu's life and career were affected by the Nigerian civil disturbances of the 1960s. One of the major events leading to the civil war was a series of riots in northern Nigeria that claimed the lives of numerous Igbo-speaking peoples who, being tribesmen of the first military Head of State, General Aguiyi Ironsi, were easily linked by the Northerners with a power structure accused of trying to maintain a monopoly on political power. Odogwu barely escaped death by hiding in a dug-out well (*rigiam*) for seven days; his right leg had been clubbed and broken, and to the end of his life he walked with a limp. When he emerged from hiding, he made his way out of the North with the help of loyal northern friends, and settled for the rest of his life in his hometown.

At Onicha-Ugbo Odogwu tried various trades, though his major accomplishment was in leading a group of men in storytelling and song performances that gained them considerable renown both among the west-Niger Igbo and indeed across the state.[24] Of the players who accompanied him over the years, perhaps the best known, and the ones who have survived to give us the bulk of our information on him, are as follows: John Anumenechi, a quite affable albino, nicknamed "The Reverend" not only because his complexion gave him the look of a (white) Catholic priest but also because he tended to affect the somber comportment of one; Okonji Ogbechie, easily the oldest member of the group and nicknamed "Ababa Chico" both for his age (*Baba* is for *father*) and for the maturity he showed above the others; finally Sunday Okocha, the youngest member of Odogwu's group, was nicknamed "Sunny Time-keeper" because though illiterate he owned a wristwatch which he treated with jealous care and often showily consulted at the group's performances, as its self-appointed timekeeper.

Odogwu led his group to competitions at local cultural festivals held in places like Ogwashi-Uku (headquarters of the Aniocha Local Government Area, in which Onicha-Ugbo is situated) and Idumuje-Ugboko, a few miles north of Onicha-Ugbo,[25] as well as state-organized storytelling contests held in Benin City, then capital of Bendel State. At Benin he won a few first prizes with diplomas that he sometimes proudly displayed to visitors. In recognition of their proficiency and acclaim, the Obi (paramount chief) of Onicha-Ugbo and his council of elders had decided to take up official sponsorship of Odogwu and his group but for his death. That death may well be related to complications arising from grave injuries sustained in the 1966 riots. But, alas, Odogwu and his group were known to favor the cup quite liberally, though this scarcely impaired either their stamina—"It's our patron we're sorry for," he once said to me—or their skill. He was diagnosed with kidney complications in 1987 and taken to Kano for treatment, but died there sometime afterward. None of his relatives remembers the exact date of Odogwu's death in Kano any more than he did the date of his own birth, a sad irony for one about whose skills there was never any doubt.

Although he belonged to the club of traditional doctors (a profession that is frequently associated with the oral arts in many societies), and although he enjoyed the regard of the ruling council of his town, Odogwu was never one of its political elite. Of course, he performed the rituals required of adolescent males in the village (e.g., *ichi mmo*, entry into the mask-spirit cult) or members of the cult of doctors (*icha aka*, collecting of icons and washing of hands), but he never took any of the formal titles of the village, though he had family enough to assist him if he lacked the means. He simply never bothered to follow that trail, merely contenting himself with the reputation which, according to "The Reverend" and "Sunny Time-keeper," he enjoyed across Onicha-Ugbo: as a man of knowledge and worldly wisdom, a well-travelled man, an astute but kind manager of his men, an artist with superb and varied performative skills (vocal, dramatic, instrumental, etc.) who nevertheless sought first to highlight the talents of his accompanists; above all, a man of the people.[26]

Odogwu told me many stories, among them (as I mentioned in chapter 2 above) heroic portraits of some of the strongmen who flourished in his community in the days when might was right. Of the more extensive narratives I recorded from him, I would like to cite only two which might give us some insight into the man's personality and outlook. I can only present them in paraphrase, and here's why. Of the many artists I have recorded, Odogwu had a complex performance style whereby he moved very freely between the three major modes of vocal performance (speech, recitative, and song)[27] and wove his narration quite intricately through the equally patterned choral refrains of his accompanists. I intend to publish a full libretto of each of these tale performances in a forthcoming program. For our present purposes, I consider the texts a little too long and will therefore present here only so much of an outline of the tales as might reveal the internal dynamics between the artist and the logic of power defined by the Benin myth.

The first of the two stories is about three brothers and how they averted from themselves the Oba's fateful justice:[28]

The tale centers on the Oba of Benin, "Death that kills on life's sweetest day," and on a man with three children, all males. One of these sons was a wrestler by profession, and grew to be champion wrestler in the whole Benin nation. Another son was an expert in herbal medicine, a doctor. The third was what English-speakers would call a lawyer, or a thinker. These boys were quite young when they lost their parents. In all Benin, however good you were as a wrestler, the champion would throw you.

Then one year, the Oba summoned the wrestler to him. In those days, unlike nowadays, if you were summoned by the Oba, your people went into mourning, for they knew that was the end of you. The wrestler ignored all the wailing around him and made for the palace, presenting himself to the Oba. The Oba welcomed him.

"The reason I summoned you," said the Oba, "is simply this. Out there, you will find four cows, eight trunks of clothes, eight boxes of precious jewels, and eight of coral beads. All these are yours, if you will teach my eldest son how to wrestle."

The wrestler was relieved to learn he was not going to be killed after all, but before he took his leave of the Oba he made one request of him: that he be permitted to give the lessons in his home, since he never wrestled anywhere else. So it was agreed the prince would go to the wrestler's home for his lessons.

The first lessons were tough on the prince; the master wrestler spared him no pains, since he was charged to teach the prince his skills. For three years, wrestler and prince carried on their routine, until the prince became so versed in the art that, in the fourth year, he brought down the man whose back had never once touched the ground. The prince did this many more times, and became so self-confident as to challenge his master to a fight to the death: winner take life! The wrestler brought home to his brothers the painful news of his defeat, and of the appointed contest. Alarmed at his brother's predicament, the doctor set about preparing a charm the wrestler would apply just before the fight.

The next day the prince arrived; the fight commenced. He caught the wrestler in a grip and threw him; the wrestler foiled the throw. The prince tried once more, but was not quick enough for the champion, who snatched him up in the twinkle of an eye and smashed his brains against a stone, killing him instantly. The wrestler broke down in tears, for he knew his fate was sealed. He consulted his brother the doctor. The latter tried his most potent charms ("Some of them could even speak!"), but the prince was too far gone to be revived: he had "drunk the water of death."[29] There was now wailing by all and sundry, for everyone knew what the penalty would be: death, not simply for the brothers, but for their entire clan.

The wrestler now turned to the lawyer for help. The latter came, held his hand against the prince's breast, and said to the mourners, "Who told you he was dead: can't you see he is still breathing?" Picking up the prince's body, the brothers took it into their house. The thinker asked to be given time to think; retiring into his room, he racked his brains to the limits of calculation, and emerged with a plan which he now set to work. Going over to the palace, he enquired about the prince, and was told the latter had gone off since morning to wrestle, and hadn't yet returned. The visit gave the thinker the opportunity to stake out ("what you English-speakers call an ESTIMATION") the complex layout of the Oba's palace.

Back home, he worked with his brothers to construct a stretcher for carrying the prince's corpse to the palace, to which they set out in the dead of night. Armed with a charm (provided by the doctor) that ren-dered them invisible, as well as a halter to be used for the corpse, they scaled over the palace walls and landed the body right by the quarters of the Oba's first queen. The thinker knocked on the door and, identifying himself as the prince, ordered the queen to open the door at once so he could fuck her. Alarmed, the queen reminded him that the king his father was still alive. The thinker repeated the order, threatening to hang him-self if the queen would not come out.

"Go ahead and hang," replied the queen. "That's what will happen to you anyway."

Affecting the guttural tone of one whose throat was being stretched, the thinker addressed the queen one final time, "Queen, I'm hanging now." At that he tied the halter to the corpse's neck, and left it dangling by the queen's door. The three brothers returned to their home.

The burden of murder now rested on the queen. At first cock, the inmates of the palace got up to fetch water for the day and, on passing by the first queen's door, saw the prince's body hanging there. There was a loud uproar, and news of the event finally reached the Oba. "So, my dear," said the king, "the prince we had been looking for was all along with you? Now, tell us what happened between you and him. This is no longer a matter between you and me, but for the realm to decide."

The entire Benin nation assembled, and the queen was ordered to state her case. She saluted the king, and told how, in the dead of night, the prince had knocked on her door and ordered her to open so he could fuck her, saying he would hang himself if she didn't open. She had reminded the prince that the Oba was still alive, and refused to open the door, asking him to hang himself if he so pleased. After she had spoken, the *iyase*[30] said to her, "I have only one question to ask you before the decision is reached on what's to be done to you. Suppose you had allowed the prince to fuck you, who would have been responsible for procuring the articles to be used for cleansing you: was it you, or the Oba?"

The Oba lost no time in ordering the queen's execution, whereafter the two bodies were laid to rest.

"After three years, the equivalent of a week in spiritland," says Odogwu as he concludes the story, "the wrestler and his brothers sent word to me here in Onicha-Ugbo, asking me to please come over. So I went to the public square of Benin, where he told me what transpired between him and the prince in consequence of their boasting. I told him this was not something I alone should know about. Hence I have proceeded to tell the story to everyone, including an Urhobo man, whose mother hails from Asaba. Step on it, Nwokolo," says the artist to his son, who is swaying nearby to the music, "son of Odogwu of Onicha-Ugbo."

Amid the loud applause that greets the performance, Odogwu is hailed "Albela!"

In the discussion that followed this performance, I asked Odogwu why the queen should have been condemned for the prince's suicide; after all, she would have been held no less culpable had she opened her door willingly to be defiled. Odogwu defended the judgment partly on the grounds raised by the *iyase* (i.e., the abomination would have been expiated with articles to be provided by the Oba, owner of the realm and all it holds), but especially by acknowledging the ingenuity shown by the thinker-lawyer. In his exchanges with the queen, the "prince" had instigated her to challenge him to take his own life; that challenge, which is now considered the principal cause of the suicide, is upheld as a master-stroke of genius and the nemesis that visits the realm of insensitive justice.

Let us consider one more story from Odogwu before we can see to what extent his art is an exercise in self-affirmation. This story is about a young child who uses a combination of magic and ingenuity to counter the high-handedness of the Oba of Benin and to turn upon him the fatal designs he had woven for the child:

> Somewhere in the Benin nation, a man and his wife had their first child, a son. Every year, the Oba sacrificed a human being to usher in the New Yam festival: he would cut off the person's head, post it on a stake, and sprinkle on it particles of boiled yam. Before the rituals, a diviner would be consulted to find who would be used for the event.
>
> The first queen was anxious for a positive divination, for there were fears about the Oba's health. However, the diviner assured her things would turn out well; he had to say so, for it was a crime, punishable by death, to foretell ill-fortune for the Oba. The diviner fell to his divination but, try as he could, he was still searching for an answer when markets closed for the day. In his frustration, and with the Oba breathing down his neck, he pleaded desperately with his divining articles for a sign. At last the symbols revealed that the victim for that year was a young boy, his parents' first child, who was still crawling. How could a New Yam festival be held with a little child as sacrifice?
>
> Shortly after, a man walked in—stealthily, as gossips usually do—and

asked what was happening. On being told the message of the oracle, he disclosed he had recently visited a man and his wife who had just such a child. In no time at all, an order went out to the young parents: their child had been chosen as sacrifice for the year's New Yam festival! The woman broke down in tears: how could it be her lot, to lose her very first child? Shortly after, the little boy was taken away and sacrificed.

The couple resumed their lives, and were soon blessed with their second child: another boy. The following year, in due time, the oracle again picked on that child for the New Yam rituals; so too every male child, up to the sixth. At this point, the man's wife ordered her husband to go and kill the Oba, even if she had to lose her head over that! Why should the king, whose house was full of children, spare them all and sacrifice all six of her own: what crime had she committed? Her husband reminded her it was the king's prerogative to impose upon his subjects, and, if she thought that was too much for her to bear, they should flee the land. Which was what they decided to do: they fled into the forest, and settled there, where the woman had her seventh child, another male. Just as they were about to cut out the umbilical cord, a gourdlet dropped out of the woman's womb. The child ordered the gourdlet saved for him, for he would need it sometime!

A week after this, the man went to the town and invited his friends to celebrate the birth of his child. Amidst the drinking, one of the guests rose and called for the child to be brought forward for naming.[31] Before they could begin the rituals, the child declared that nobody but himself would choose a name for him! News of this wonder finally reached the Oba, and he wanted to know who was the precocious child. His hornblower reported that the child was brother to those six boys he had earlier sacrificed. Delighted, the Oba now looked forward to an even more delicious feast, not just a yam festival.

"Bring that child to me," he ordered. "Or, rather, let him grow until he has begun to walk."

Not long after, the boy had even begun to run, vowing to his parents that he desired no other occupation on earth than archery. So his father made him a bow and arrows. He shot the first arrow, and it landed in the Oba's palace. He engaged the Oba's children in the shooting game. Asked what his name was, he simply said "That Boy," for he did not want his real name publicized just yet.

They were at the game one day, when one of the princes took a better shot than he; he swore that could never happen to him, the "Child-wiser-than-the-Oba!" The prince asked him what he had just said, and he repeated his exact words, daring the prince to take the news to his father. That was the end of the game. At home, the Oba had settled down to eat his meal, and had a morsel in hand, when the prince told him of a certain boy in their archery games who said he was wiser than the Oba; the food dropped from the Oba's hand.

He quickly summoned his hornblower, who soon afterwards reported that those words were from the little boy who had talked in his infancy. Overjoyed, the king could not wait for a chance to engage the youngster in a contest of charms, to entertain his citizens. He summoned a gathering of the entire nation, informing them that a child born within the realm had claimed, as never before, that he was wiser than the Oba. The alarmed citizens demanded that the child be produced forthwith. An order quickly went out to the forest ordering the parents of the child, now only eight weeks old, to produce him right away. His mother cried, fearing she was doomed as usual to lose her child.

"Don't cry," said the boy. "I'll go over to the Oba: after all, the mouse eats, but so does the maggot."[32]

Armed with a girdle made for him by his mother, he took off to the palace, addressing the assembly even before he was invited to speak.

"Hail, your highness, Death that kills on life's sweetest day! I, Child-wiser-than-the-Oba, greet everyone."

The *iyase* asked him to repeat what he had just said, and he proclaimed his name with even greater audacity. The crowd called for the boy's execution, but the Oba, savoring the prospect of revenge, stayed the course awhile. He threw the child a challenge.

"Up there," said the Oba, pointing to a breadfruit tree, one of whose fruits had eight nuts, "is a fruit. I want you to tell me how many nuts it has, which one of them will mature and ripen first, and on what day it will fall. If you predict correctly, you will be spared. If not, you will lose your head."

The boy went to sleep, awoke, and pointed to the fruit in question, predicting it would fall two days after at first cock; if it didn't, the Oba should go ahead and kill him. The assembly was dismissed, and the child went home. But the Oba knew no rest. He ordered a bed built for him and posted under the breadfruit tree. Abandoning his house, he slept there every night, like a nightwatchman, waiting to see the fruit fall. Amid widespread alarm, at first cock on the predicted day, the breadfruit fell. The Oba exclaimed: to be worsted beyond his wildest fears, and by a mere boy! He picked up the breadfruit, and stuck a needle to hold the fruit together. He had the fruit put back up on the branch, duly surrounded by leaves, so that anyone who had not been there in the past few days could not tell there had been any activity there; yet the Oba had been sleeping there.

The Benin nation reassembled; the Child-wiser-than-the-Oba appeared. The Oba, with obvious agitation, asked him where the fallen breadfruit was. The boy lost no time in bringing down the breadfruit and presenting it to the Oba.

"A plague on you," swore the Oba, "you have done the unprecedented!"

"A plague on you," retorted the boy, "we have seen the unprecedented in your realm: what's a needle doing inside a breadfruit?"

"Go home," said the Oba. "You are an evil child!"

The child had saved his head, and returned home. A few days later, the Oba ordered him summoned again. He told the boy he was dying of thirst, and asked him to go to the river with a basket and fetch him water to drink. The boy agreed, but before he set out he dug an earthworks, asking the Oba to please take it in for him should the rain begin to fall.

"A plague on you," said the Oba. "How can the earth be moved?"

"A plague on you," replied the boy. "How can a basket hold water?"

"Go home," said the Oba. "You are an evil child!"

The boy had again shaved his head, and returned home. A few days later, the boy was recalled to the palace. The Oba told him his barbers had failed signally in shaving his head, and wanted the boy to do it right. The boy replied his mother had set him an inescapable task, which was to seed several corn-cobs; he would gladly shave the Oba if the latter would help him seed the cobs. The king agreed, and both fell to their tasks, each making a clean job of removal at the same time as the other.

"Ah," cried the Oba, on feeling his clean-shaven head, "you are a dead man: you should have left a clump of hair!"

"Ah," cried Child-wiser-than-the-Oba, "you are dead by my mother: you should have left some rows unseeded!"

"Put back some hair on my head," ordered the Oba.

"Put back some seed on my cobs," ordered the boy. As the child failed in his attempt, so did the Oba in his. Once again, the child had saved his head, and was let go.[33]

The Oba summoned the boy yet again another day. He told the boy that, since he was now an adult, he should report for work at the palace at first cock the next day. In preparation for the boy's visit, the Oba had a ram slaughtered; while some workers ground a superabundance of hot peppers (which sent the whole town sneezing), others set about washing bitter-leaves,[34] all this for the stew to be cooked for the boy. At first cock, after the cooking was over, the boy promptly arrived at the palace, to the Oba's surprise.

The Oba cut a morsel of yam meal, dipped it in the red-hot stew with a generous helping of the meat, and offered it to the boy. The boy asked to be allowed to take the dinner home, for since his birth he had never eaten anywhere else. The Oba let him take the entire pot of stew home, promising to see him again a week later. Back home, the boy committed the pot to his gourdlet for safekeeping. One week later, the Oba asked the boy to return the pot exactly as he had taken it, since he had done no work for which he deserved to be so lavishly entertained. The pot was piping hot as ever when the boy recovered it from the gourdlet and returned it to the Oba.

"A plague on you!" cried the Oba, ordering the boy to go away with the food, since a king should not look upon a meal more than a day old.

Not long after, the Oba summoned the boy to help him with a problem. There was a terror in his chambers that scared his wives from sleeping with him; he needed the boy to sleep over with him and rid the terror. Early the next day, the Oba ordered the palace guards to dig a trench seven spans deep at the palace gate, and set a mass of water on the boil; as soon as the boy got to the gate, they should knock him into the ditch, pour the scalding water in after him, and seal his doom. Meanwhile, the boy brought down his gourdlet, threw in two live coals of fire, slung it over his shoulder, and took his leave of his parents.[35] At the gate, he went past the guards without any difficulty,[36] entered into the Oba's chambers, and saluted him accordingly. Caught off his guard, the Oba asked the boy how he got there, and he confronted the Oba with the schemes the Oba had laid for him.

They crawled into bed, but sleep would come to neither of these strange bedfellows. Next, the Oba told the boy he was dying to smoke, and asked him to go over to the guards and fetch some fire. Taking his leave, the boy went over to his gourdlet and fetched one of the two coals of fire, and gave it to the Oba. When the Oba asked how he got the fire, the boy said he had found the guards fast asleep beside the trench and the boiling water, and simply helped himself to the fire. The Oba had his smoke, but hardly at ease. Going over to the palace guards, he was about to ask them why they let the boy cross them repeatedly, without killing him. In a panic the guards, thinking they had their quarry, pushed the Oba into the trench, poured the boiling water upon him, and sealed the trench with earth. From inside the room the boy rejoiced, "Ho, the king is gone!"

There is an old saying that whoever is found on the throne is the Oba. Early the next morning, the Child-wiser-than-the-Oba had a warm bath, dressed himself fittingly with apparel fetched from the Oba's trunks, and ensconced himself on the throne. One after another, the Oba's wives came to give their salutations, and the boy would reply accordingly. The Oba's children also came to greet their father. Last to come was the despised wife, with her seven-month baby in her arms. The baby took a long look at the Oba, and tears fell from his eyes. Shocked at his manners, the woman reminded the child that that was the king up there. To reassure him, she asked the "king" to offer the child a piece of yam; the "king" obliged, but the child recoiled from the gift, crying that the man on the throne did not look like his father.

When the despised wife took a good look, she discovered how right her baby was. She brought her equally careless co-wives to the shocking realization that the man they had paid homage to was a total stranger. A proclamation was issued, summoning the nation to an assembly. In preparation for the meeting, Child-wiser-than-the-Oba bathed and dressed himself afresh, and sat on the throne. When the *iyase* asked the first queen why she, contrary to tradition, had summoned the assembly, the queen cried that the man on the throne was unknown to them, and asked that the chief of palace guards be called to tell what could have happened the night before. The man recounted the instructions the Oba had issued them; they had carried their orders out accordingly, and if they doubted him they should go and check for themselves; as far as they were concerned, the man on the throne was the Oba.

The *iyase* gave His Highness his due salutations, and the latter returned his blessing; the other chiefs came one after another to pay their homage. Child-wiser-than-the-Oba was recognized as king, following the wisdom of the fathers that whoever sat on the throne was the Oba. The Child sent to the forest for his parents. When they arrived, he called for the *ogene*,[37] and asked the latter to bow to his father; as the *ogene* bent his head in salutation, he was decapitated at once, and his position was given to the king's father. The king called the grand matron (*omu*) of Benin, and asked her to bow to his mother; as the *omu* made her bow, she too was beheaded, and her title passed on to the king's mother. Child-wiser-than-the-Oba, along with his mother and father, ruled the land years without number.

"Just before he died," says Odogwu, concluding the story, "the king sent to Onicha-Ugbo and said to me, 'Come over, Odogwu Nwaniani!' So I went to the public square of Benin. He told me what happened between him and the Oba of Benin, and I said this was not a story for me alone: I would tell it to Urhobo people, and to Asaba people, and to Onicha-Ugbo, and to the whole world. That was my mission." Following the concluding airs, Odogwu is greeted thunderously with clapping and shouts of "Albela!"

In the postnarrative discussion, someone asked Odogwu on what impulse the Child took those live coals of fire with him in his gourdlet: how could he have known the Oba would need fire? The narrator responded by pointing to the logic of the Child's name, and to the infallible prescience of that guardian gourdlet; at any rate, he added, the Child might have been determined that, if he got to the end of his luck that night in his confrontation with the Oba, he would not hesitate to bring the whole palace down with him in flames.

One noteworthy element of Odogwu's narrative performances is the choral interludes with which he generously punctuated them. In the course of these, he took care to salute his accompanists as well as various members of the audience. Although this device could be found in the performances of other traditional artists, there was a particularly elegiac tone and mood to the airs that Odogwu sang at these points, especially in his acknowledgment to his sister Tina and other attending relatives that "Blood-kinship is not [i.e., is greater than] friendship," no doubt a variant of the saying "Blood is thicker than water." In these mournful airs we may doubtless hear echoes of Odogwu's tragic experiences and be persuaded that, in his acknowledgment of his kinsfolk, he is showing due gratitude for the sympathy and support the extended family must have given him when his career was cut short by the 1966 riots and he had to return to his native land.

We can therefore understand the significance of at least two details in these tales for the narrator. One of these is his vivid evocation of the natal/native home in the circumstances of various characters. The hero in the first story lets the Oba understand he is more comfortable teaching the prince to wrestle in his own home, not in the palace; in the second story, Child-wiser-than-the-Oba would rather take the baneful broth offered him by the Oba to his own home. Although there is an internal logic to these details, no one knows better than our traumatized narrator how much home means to us amid the dangers that threaten our lives. Another and even more apposite echo is the trench in which the Oba had sought to end the little boy's life. It could scarcely have failed to evoke for Odogwu the dug-out well where he landed with his broken leg in the midst of the 1966 riots. In the story, Odogwu describes that scene with due sense of moment, which obviously gains from his psychological response to the sign conjured by that deep hollow in the earth.

As we saw above, Odogwu's accompanists and townsfolk judged him a man of the people who, though blessed with superb artistic skills, took care to share the spotlight with his accompanists in their performances. Clearly the frequent salutes to them, and to the general audience, in the periodic choral interludes does bear witness to this populist concern. But the stories are even more strikingly marked by a certain radical temperament, best revealed by the antiauthoritarian implications of various statements. To begin with, the punch line of the periodic choral interludes in both tales is invariably "The cocoyam has become a porridge," a statement that puts the cocoyam on equal terms with the yam (king of crops among the Igbo) and thus symbolically denies the royalty any special claims over the general citizenry. This spirit is especially strong in the second story. Here the hero-child is not only determined that the worm is no less entitled than the mouse to enjoy pieces of food in the house—the metaphors have a curious resonance in the well-known claims, among various cadres of the Nigerian society, to a share in the "national cake"—but is quite defiant and discourteous towards the king. The epitome of this antimonarchism may perhaps be seen both in the sexual insult to the queen in the first story and in the death of the king in the second.

We have of course drawn attention, especially in chapters 2 to 4, to the characteristic republicanism of these (west-Niger) Igbo societies in relation to the absolute authority of imperial Benin. But if we compare an artist like Odogwu with another like Simayi, especially against the background of their personal circumstances, we will observe an added edge to the behavior of characters in Odogwu's tales. In the story of Ezemu told by Simayi, the war between the Ubulu and Benin ends in a civilized demarcation of boundaries between the two peoples; the Oba is of course humbled, but his rulership is not violated. Here Simayi, a titled man and close adviser of the *obi* (paramount ruler) of Ubulu-Uno, is inclined to respect the sanctity of the traditional authority in which he has a vested interest. But Odogwu, never having taken a traditional title in Onicha-Ugbo, was *ipso facto* outside the structures of political authority in his community, and so had reason enough to contend the superior postures of the political elite. In his tales, the Oba presents a good target for his egalitarian shots.

Although excluded from the traditional oligarchy, Odogwu put considerable premium on his unique position as one of the first generation of Western-educated citizens of Onicha-Ugbo and on the reputation he had earned for his clerical or literate skills. I think there is some significance to the position he claims for himself at the end of his two stories above, especially if again we compare them with the stories we have so far seen from Simayi (Okpewho 1990:127–135; 1992:183–191, 192–201; chapter 2 above). Simayi programmatically concludes his stories by casting himself as an (unobtrusive) observer who emerges from the scene of the events he has "witnessed" to tell us about them. This is equally true of nearly every other narrator I have so far recorded. In his stories, however, Odogwu occupies a more dignified position. It is the principal characters of his tales—rebels who rise from the rank and file to triumph against the high-handed monarchy—who invite his services as chronicler of their memorable experiences.

True to his populist instincts, Odogwu in these codas treats the tales not as privileged wisdom but as information available to all and sundry. There is, nonetheless, a subtle claim beneath the veneer of modesty. Odogwu, known far and wide for his skill with the pen, is being invited not simply to preserve these tales in the oral tradition but to invest them with relevance for the larger world, beyond the limited universe of his people. We may usefully compare Odogwu's image here with that of the writer's persona in Fagunwa's hunter tales, who is invited by the heroic hunter Akaraogun to preserve, for the benefit of the wider world, the wisdom of his extraordinary exploits.[38] Such is the position ultimately claimed by Odogwu, *akawo maigash* and wielder of much worldly wisdom, in his narrative codas. He may not be one of his society's political leadership, but he is known far and wide for an intelligence considered fit even to record the accomplishments of legendary potentates.

That Odogwu was very much at ease with Western culture and technology is here and there attested by the narratives. At the bottom of the scale, in this regard, is his occasional recourse to English words and phrases. Even the illiterate Simayi does it here and there, though the accuracy of Odogwu's pronunciation of the English words, and the aptitude as well as level of his usage, set him fairly apart from the likes of Simayi. His grasp of the subtle implicature of English words is perhaps best demonstrated by his repetitive use of the ideophone *foki-foki-foki-fo*, in the second story, to signify both the frothiness of the bitter-leaves being washed by the Oba's women and the sexual appeal of their act (which he demonstrated by a rhythmic jerking of the hip).

Also, unlike the general run of rural-based performers, he was not unfamiliar with the workings of the recording apparatus. He understood well enough, for instance, how disorienting it was for the tape to run out in the midst of development of a tale; so he had acquired sufficient presence of mind to maintain the flow of his performance while casting an occasional glance at me to be assured our exertions had not been in vain. That he understood the paratactic structure of oral narrativity was equally evident in the way he chose the right point at which to interject choral interludes to fill in the time that it took to turn or change the spool of tape. The narrator of *The Ozidi Saga* (Clark-Bekederemo 1991) was obviously ill at ease with the demands of the recording technology, as evidenced by his disoriented remarks at various points. The same could hardly be said of Odogwu who, when once I turned over a tape for him to continue his narration, helped to check for receptivity by announcing, "Testing, testing, testing; this is Odogwu Nwaniani of Onicha-Ugbo, Albela; testing, testing, testing."

The nickname "Albela" is itself evidence of our narrator's conscious appropriation of the icons of modern technology, in this case, the film industry. When big-screen film came to West Africa, especially to Nigeria, in the 1940s and 1950s, audiences were introduced to works that ran the gamut of the industry at the time: the silent cinema, Western romances, and so forth. It was in the 1950s that films from the Indian subcontinent began to invade the theaters; they immediately captured the imagination of movie-goers, for their high emphasis on music and dance appealed to popular tastes in entertainment. The sentimentality of themes in Indian cinema was not dissimilar to what the publics had seen in Western film, but the effeminate styles of dancing seen in the male actors was a rather new element which struck the curiosity of many people. Odogwu, whose performances were marked by a high level of histrionics, was in his element when he danced to the airs played by his accompanists and especially when he dramatized the swaying motions of female characters. One of the best-known Indian films of that era was titled *Albela* (after the principal character's name), and it was from this that Odogwu acquired the nickname by which he became much better known.[39]

It should be stressed that Odogwu did not think any the less of his people's traditional culture simply because he put his understanding of Western culture and technology to effective use. I believe that his ample use of proverbs and other structural and stylistic resources of the western Igbo storytelling tradition[40] bears witness to his regard for and commitment to that tradition. His adoption of Western or other culture and technology should thus be seen not in substitutive but in additive terms, in the sense that his exposure to life beyond the local universe of his native land had disposed him to seek a wider frame of reference for his tales. He was very much a man of the times, a citizen of postcolonial Nigeria whose tales bore considerable witness to the trials and traumas of its social history.

I was delighted when I got his response to my letter. It was written in rather fine calligraphy, in the characteristic officialese of the colonial service, and with a touch of piety which reflects the current vogue of evangel-

ism that Nigerians have embraced as a salve for contemporary social problems. Here is what he said:

> From M.O. Okwuashi
> Idumudiagbo Qtr., Box 93
> Onicha-Ugbo
> 27/11/81

> Dear Dr Okpewho,
> This is just to assure of your present health and that of all in your family.
> With hope things are normal I say thanks be to God.
> Your letter dated 31st Oct. 81 was received with many thanks and the
> contents therein were gone through. We are very grateful for your remem-
> bering us for the little we did, and we hope that the Almighty God shall
> help you & us so that your promise shall be fulfilled.
> You shall get us at home any time [you] reach our town.
> We await with jubilation for the time of the ceremony of your late
> mother, because that will give us [the] chance to demonstrate to the gen-
> eral public in another town.
> We pray that God shall guide you and us in all our undertakings. Con-
> vey our warm greetings to your Brother in Law.
> Awaiting for a favourable reply.

> Yrs truly
> (Signed)
> For the Group.

A populist to the last, he had signed "for the group."

My application for a research grant from Ibadan University to continue
my fieldwork was not successful, so I did not return to Onicha-Ugbo or
elsewhere in the region for a long time. In 1984, with a little more money
in my hands, I revisited Odogwu, hoping to redeem my promise to invite
him and his group to my mother's funeral rites in Asaba, which I finally
performed around Easter. Unfortunately, I was told he had gone to the
North,[41] for unspecified reasons. I never saw him again. But I will always
remember him fondly and respectfully, because for me he occupies a special
place in the company of artists I have had the good fortune of knowing and
working with.

A Mythology of the Self

Why have I chosen to see these artists in their art? I am not at all claiming
that in every instance they are the original creators of the tales that they tell.
When I asked Odogwu, in the course of our general discussion in 1981, how
he and his group set about building their repertoire of songs and tales, he

told me the repertoire grew largely by each member contributing bits and pieces of material he may have stumbled upon in his visits to other places; they would incorporate these new elements into their usual format of performances, and do it so intricately that their audiences would have no idea of the sources of the constituent materials. It is entirely possible, for instance, that Odogwu had picked up some of his material in the course of the cultural festivals he participated in now and then, even as far away as Benin. But they ultimately became his own because, to the extent that as leader of the group he was the main arbiter of its textual choices, he gave them the imprint of his insight and outlook on life.

Let us take an example. The closest variant I have found to Odogwu's tale of the three brothers and the Oba is the story of "Okodan" in Sidahome's *Stories of the Benin Empire* (1964:16–26). Briefly, of three brothers, one is a farmer, another a hunter, and the third a shiftless fellow who simply loves fighting. He invariably wins, and one day encounters the Oba's eldest son who, though beaten, refuses to give up, until the fighter loses his patience and knocks him dead with a club. Afraid he will lose his life for the crime, he devises a scheme for passing the burden of the murder on others. He starts with his brothers, who have been trying to force him to get a regular job by refusing to give him of their food. He hides the prince's body in a bush, and tricks the hunter into shooting the body and assuming responsibility for the murder; he promises to help the hunter out of his trouble in exchange for some game. Next, he hides the body in the farmer's barn, where the latter, suspecting it to be a yam thief, knocks it "dead"; again, for an offer of yams, the fighter removes the prince's body safely from the barn. At night, the Oba throws his bedroom doors open for a draft of fresh air, when he observes a head peeping through one of the doors; suspecting a burglar, he quietly grabs a bronze image by his bed and brings it down on the head, only to discover on close look that he has "killed" his own son. The prince was the heir apparent, popular with the people, and his father could easily be accused of deliberately murdering him (possibly to defer succession).[42] The fighter later emerges to rid the king of his trouble, by skillfully dressing the corpse to leave the impression that the prince died from illness; he is rewarded with the rulership of his town, a vassal to Benin.

Despite the divergences, the similarities between this—one of Sidahome's "Benin stories as told in Ishanland"—and Odogwu's story are sufficiently striking: three brothers, one of them a wrestler/fighter; wrestling with a prince, who proves persistent; wrestler kills the prince, and conceals the body; prince's body ends up in the palace, foisted upon royalty; the killer wins not only his freedom but indeed a kingdom.

Sidahome does not source his stories, so we do not know who told this one. But a glaring weakness of that story is in the cunning credited the fighter. He is presented to us far less as a fight artist than as a nuisance in a less than harmonious home. Although he did not really mean to kill the prince with his club, his cavalier wielding of the weapon shows him as something of a bungler. So where does he get the ingenuity with which he foists the corpse so methodically on one person after another, right up to the Oba?

Odogwu's handling of the theme is somewhat more convincing. The wrestler is too disoriented to plan the disposal of the body so methodically, so the job is entrusted to the more resourceful thinker, the "lawyer." And herein lies Odogwu's personal touch, one which gives us a glimpse of his personal stake in the story. A good share of the ingenuity shown in disposing of the prince is supplied by the traditional doctor; fair enough, for Odogwu was one himself. But the greater share of the responsibility in this task is borne by the intellectual: in using the term *lawyer* for this character, Odogwu seems to put special value on the resource (Western education) which puts him above the average storyteller. It might be argued, of course, that his was a display put up more to impress us university folk with our "sophisticated" tackle. But there was no doubt that he set much store by his achievement not only as one of the earliest citizens in his town to obtain modern (Western) education but as one who distinguished himself in his career as a clerk.

His use of a "lawyer" may thus be judged an idiosyncratic twist to this "traditional" tale. He may not have been the first to tell it in this way, nor even to have used an intellectually inclined character to solve the problem. That he did use such a character reveals a disposition reflective of his background or his circumstances.

In their respective ways, therefore, the stories we have examined in this chapter reflect some effort at self-apprehension on the part of their narrators. There is no doubt that, in every practical sense, the stories are taken from a larger storehouse of motifs and themes available either to the narrators' societies or to the human universe, but in choosing certain details rather than others they have effectively used the tales as what Clifford has called "reinforcing allegories of identity" (1988:104). They have not violated tradition; they have only refashioned it in the light of their experiences and dispositions.

The Benin myth becomes a fruitful site for this exercise in self-affirmation, for it is essentially framed by situations and images of power and dominance that inspire self-consciousness as much in individuals as in communities. Benin looms large in the mythic imagination, and somehow the individuals who tell stories of it are forced to match their impulses with its themes quite as much as the communities which once faced its menace are driven to contend its claims over them. The correlations I have tried to draw in this chapter between works and lives are intended to show that individuals are just as anxious as communities to make sense of themselves and to defend their stakes even if this will entail adjusting the details of convention (e.g., an Oba with two wives rather than an extensive harem; a "lawyer" who argues that a man is alive when he is stone dead) or the idiom of its construction (the self-conscious use of English words by both narrators, and especially Odogwu's double-edged play on the sound *foki-foki-fo*).

Myth, Empire, and Self-Determination

'Tis done—but yesterday,
The palaces of crowned kings;
And now a chaos of hard clay:
Sleeping on the abyss.
Without a surge.

'Tis Benin, Oh! Benin—the might of yore,
A fair red City;
Crowned with ancient majesty:
Gracefully reclining,
Down the slopes of Oguola fame.

That City I oft remember,
With gallant sons all in array;
Rising in clouded majesty:
Such graceful grandeur clothed the City,
Of Benin—with radiant spendour.

'Tis done—but yesterday,
The palaces of crowned kings;
And now a chaos of hard clay:
Sleeping on the abyss,
Without a surge.
    (Moru Yesufu-Giwa, "Once Fair City")[1]

I had presented the original version of chapter 1 of this book in a seminar at the University of Ibadan, Nigeria. One of the questions asked me at the end of my presentation came from a colleague engaged in an aspect of Benin studies. "Why," he said, "is it always assumed that Benin was the prime influence on the culture of its region: why couldn't the influence have moved in the other direction?" I was to discover later that my colleague hailed from the village of Udo which, as we saw in chapters 1 and 3 above, had been embattled with the Benin kingdom in the early days of its consolidation. Udo has, of course, been part of greater Benin for so long that its citizens would have little hesitation now in considering themselves bona fide Bini, or at least "Edo." But we can understand why, in a discussion of the kingdom's history, the old antagonisms buried so deeply in the collective psyche might be roused again. My colleague's question remains valid in any event, but the impulse behind it bespeaks a subdued sense of pride.

That subdued empathy is certainly evident in the above poem by Yesufu-Giwa, which is particularly remarkable for the pattern of contrasts on which it has been constructed. In practically every stanza, the poet endeavors to balance the lofty glory of Benin with a sense of its collapse, to undercut its achievement with a subtle suggestion of something sinister. Thus, in stanza one, the beauty of an ordered structure (*palaces*) is offset with the horror of total disorganization (*chaos*), a sense of elevation (*crowned*) with a sense of total decline (*abyss*). In stanza two, the phrase *fair red* may at first suggest the geological appeal of the city (Benin has red soil); but it may well have been intended also as a subtle oxymoron suggesting the kingdom's reputation for acts of blood. A similar intention may be read in *clouded majesty* (stanza three). It very likely conjures either the glory of the imperial army as it advances on an enemy, or the grandeur that attends the Oba of Benin at the annual ceremony for honoring his ancestors (*igue*), during which he is decked in his most elaborate regal finery and attended by a princely coterie (*sons*) of palace and town officials, as well as a large crowd of citizens singing his praises; a goodly cloud of dust usually attends the occasion. But *clouded* may also suggest something sinister, in this case the secrecy in which many of the rites conducted by this all-powerful monarchy are reputed to be shrouded.

Such ambivalence is by no means ungrounded. I have been unable to ascertain who Yesufu-Giwa is, but from his name he is obviously from a northern Edo community, possibly from the Owan or Etsako area, in the present Edo State. Coming from a region that felt the heavy hand of Benin nearly as much as the area on which this study has concentrated—the west-Niger Igbo—Yesufu-Giwa has understandably written his poem with a touch of subdued celebration. But he was also evidently a nationalist student in the United Kingdom in those pan-Africanist days when the struggle for the liberation of African nations from colonial rule was being hotly waged in the foreign media. Images of old glory from Africa's past were very much part of the arsenal for that struggle, and Yesufu-Giwa had little difficulty in lending his voice to the cause of nationalist self-determination. Hence, although we can glean his people's historical resentment of Benin between his lines, the image of the kingdom that he presents here still manages to be positive.

Influence of Benin on Others

Any sincere assessment of Benin should, indeed, begin with acknowledgment of its immense achievement. It is perhaps not out of place to wonder if, amidst the overwhelming evidence of horror in the myths of rival communities, Benin's humanistic qualities may not have been ignored. In chapter 3 we saw an Oba playing the role of "wise judge"; although the penalty he pronounces may not easily qualify as a humane one, he is nonetheless represented as delivering his verdict after a due process of verification. In other tales, indeed, he is portrayed as no less just a judge than any community would wish to see amongst them.

An interesting perspective on the Benin monarch is provided by one of the plates in William Fagg's *Divine Kingship in Africa* (1978:8, plate 2). The picture shows the late "Oba Akenzua II seated in front of the altar of his father, Eweka II, at the annual ceremony of propitiating his spirit [*igue*]." The point of interest in this picture is the Oba's posture. The regalia worn by him is the most elaborate Obas of Benin ever wear, as heavy as the ceremony is grave, but Akenzua hardly loses sight of his role as head of his family as well as his people. He is surrounded by attendants and about a dozen of the youngest of his children from the traditional harem. It would appear there are difficulties in getting one of these children conveniently settled near the Oba, and though one of the attendants or adolescent children is trying to sort out the problem, the Oba himself takes an interest in the matter and even lends a hand to help out.

The picture records a rather humane moment in the midst of a ceremony demanding the most solemn instincts on the Oba's part. It is of interest to us because it reminds us starkly enough that Obas are, after all, flesh and blood personalities like the rest of us, with families whom they care about, and neither primarily the ghoulish embodiments of fetish nor the insensitive destroyers of human life that we find both in subaltern legend and especially in official reports by which the British sought to justify their best-laid exploitative schemes. These schemes have been exposed by numerous scholars both African and non-African,[2] and in any case have failed to erase the appellation *great* that the kingdom has been given by generations of observers. Akenzua II's image in the aforementioned portrait is significant because it brings to our attention the humane intelligence to which that greatness must, to some extent, be due.[3]

Part of that greatness lies in the political organization that a small city-state was able to achieve on the basis of an antecedent model judged inadequate within the power dynamics of the period. Conventional scholarly wisdom seems agreed that the Benin nation rose from the ashes of a dynasty that continued to be consumed by the fire of internal conflict until the people rose to snuff it out for good. Upon the fall of the *Ogiso* kings of Igodomigodo, the people sought help from the Oni of Ife, who thereupon sent his son Oranmiyan to set their nation back on the path of proper government. The Yoruba ruler found the people too contentious for his disposition, and returned to the land of his fathers, but not before doing two things: one, rechristening the nation as the land of anger—"ile ibinu," to be corrupted by an early ruler as "Ubini" and further anglicized as Benin—and two, siring a son who as Eweka I was to inaugurate the second dynasty of *Oba* kings.

Whatever structures Oranmiyan may have laid down have been lost to memory. But he was clearly the child of a theocratic system and outlook— not, we may be sure, akin to the temperament that gave rise to the warlike states of Oyo and Ekiti. History is not much clearer on how soon after its establishment the new dynasty found itself pressed to hold its own against the already well-heeled polity of Udo. But the stage seemed set for a fight to the finish between a reorganized kingdom and a nation not so willing to yield its pride of place. In incorporating the losers into the new kingdom, the Benin rulers proceeded to weaken Udo's traditional aristocracy (*Uzama Nihiron*) with a system that sought a mildly democratic balance between a civic authority (*Eghaevbo n'Ogbe*) and a palace bureaucracy (*Eghaevbo n'Ore*) beholden first and foremost to the monarchy.

In time, the elaborate political structure that resulted therefrom was graced with the due appurtenances of pomp as well as power, with an imposing ring of titles that became the envy and the model for communities far and near, which must have watched the evolving scene with growing interest. Opinion is of course divided, as in much else lying in the undocu- mented past, as to the real influence of Benin on these communities. But the blatant adoption, especially by Igbo communities bordering both banks of the Niger, of Benin ceremonialism at various levels of ritual and political life bears witness to a phenomenon observed by Hobsbaum and Ranger: the emergence of neo-traditions in those situations where an imposing polity so captivated other societies with the physical appeal of pomp that they came to influence "the ceremonial centre rather than the political or cultural center" of the latter (1983:244)—especially when, as I tried to show in chapters 2 and 3 above, the political and cultural traditions of the imitators are basically distinct from those of their models.[4]

Benin never abjured the arts of worship, whatever relations these bore with the spirit of Oranmiyan's rule. But it must have become clear that, in the growing conflictual climate, its needs were much better served by the arts of war. An early step taken in this regard was a transformation of the artistic medium. Although archaeological evidence has turned up metal ornaments at Udo, the bias of historical evidence is on the early use of wood and ivory, which gave way soon enough to iron and bronze, not only for the making of ceremonial implements but for the equipage of an increasingly well-organized military force (Blackmun 1983:86). So intent was the new kingdom on being unrivaled that it availed itself of the best craftsmen in the business. Legend, again, has it that the first such artist articled to the second dynasty—"Igueghae," hardly a Yoruba name—came with his metal-ware from Ife, in the company of Prince Oranmiyan. Whatever relation the work of Igueghae and his followers bore to the artistic standards of the period, it was enough to raise Benin's level of achievement to a point where it not only became the model of creativity for peoples from whom it had ostensibly learnt the trade—the Yoruba (Ojo 1975)—but controlled no longer a kingdom (originally, a collectivity of small villages) but an empire embracing several outlying communities of the old Guinea coast (Barnes and Ben-Amos 1989:39–51), in many instances consolidating its position through intermarriage with these subject peoples (Akintoye 1971:29).

The exact dynamics of empire are, however, not so easy to identify. In the unstable political relations between various subgroups in Nigeria, it has become increasingly difficult to determine to what extent Benin may be said to have built anything like a stable empire over communities within her region. A case in point was the Agbor Patriotic Union's protest in 1939 to the colonial administration against Chief Egharevba's claim, in the first edition (1934) of his *Short History of Benin*, that Agbor was a Benin colony whose internal problems and disputes were regularly referred to it for settlement. "Benin originated from Agbor," countered the Union; "Ekas [i.e., people of Agbor] have never been subjugated by Binis or other tribes. Binis were fewer and weaker. Before 1897 Benin influence never went further than Ugo. Ekas harassed Benin with successful wars which led them (i.e. the Bini) to dig the trench around them."[5] As we have seen often enough in this study, hardly any of the communities in Benin's presumed sphere of influence has admitted that it ever lost a war with Benin.

The argument about empire becomes particularly difficult to sustain because, unlike most imperial powers in history, Benin appears to have operated more on the basis of sporadic strikes—to extort a tribute, to round up slaves for sale to Europeans,[6] or to avenge an affront—than on a policy of extended occupation. Even in instances where it may have imposed on a subject people a paramount ruler who would conceivably promote Benin interests, as in one of the accounts I recorded at Igbuzo (Okpewho 1983:62–63), the experiment hardly lasted long enough to have been of any use to Benin: the people soon rose to rid themselves of the shackles imposed on them. In light of this, one is inclined to conclude that Benin may have gained more than it could claim to have given to other peoples. The possibility rests on the fact that Benin seemed to be so busy trying to amass power and resources that it was prepared to incorporate from other peoples whatever it could use from their cultural armory. The readiness with which Benin allied itself with Ife for the development of artistic skills and later utilized Portuguese mercenaries in campaigns suggests that it could have had similar recourse to those neighboring peoples it claims to have subdued had the need arisen. I shall devote the next few pages to probing the complex interconnections between Benin and the Igbo as yielded by evidence from the oral traditions.[7]

Influence of Others on Benin

In his analysis of the relations between these two peoples, Afigbo is inclined, like most Igbo scholars, to see the Igbo west of the Niger as descendants of immigrants from the east whose fortunes ran foul of Benin's expansionist agenda: in the course of their history, they allowed their native instincts, political and cultural, to bow to the impact of Benin's manifest successes in social and political engineering. "This impact is seen most in the rise of village chieftaincies and monarchies all over the western Igbo area. It is seen in the regalia of these chiefs, in their court ceremonials, in some features of their title system as in the claims that many of these institutions came from Benin" (1981:19).

A notable icon of Benin ceremonial influence is the sword of office (*ada*), which various old rivals—even inveterate ones like Ubulu-Uku—continue to receive from the Oba of Benin on the installation of their paramount rulers (Bradbury 1973:258). I should hope that the analysis made, in chapters 3 and 4 above, of the basic individualism and republicanism of the Igbo would convince us that the sorts of influence Afigbo refers to above are only a superficial ceremonial garb over the fundamental outlook of the Igbo. But perhaps the most problematic issue in the discussion of Benin-Igbo relations is the movement of groups of migrants eastward in their flight from the forces of Benin. It doesn't seem quite clear whether this flight was prompted by internal rivalries within the Benin aristocracy—forcing the most notable of these migrants, Chima, to escape imminent reprisals by fleeing the city with his close associates and kin—or whether Benin's frequent raids into communities east of the kingdom drove their citizens steadily on until many of them found themselves across the Niger where their forebears may have originally hailed from. The latter hypothesis at least suggests that sometime in the indeterminate past the Igbo, whose area of concentration is the region east of the Niger, must have shared with the kingdom of Benin territorial and perhaps social space, and indeed that the Igbo might well have established themselves as a power of some stature that Benin obviously saw as an obstacle to its rise to preeminence within the immediate geographical zone (west of the Niger).

Part of the evidence that has been adduced to promote the claim of early Igbo presence and ascendancy in the zone of Benin influence has come from archaeology. In 1959 Thurstan Shaw, a British archaeologist working under the invitation of Nigeria's Department of Antiquities and attached to Ibadan University, was able to unearth a hoard of artifacts buried in three sites within Igbo-Ukwu, in the heart of the ancient Igbo civilization of Nri. Among these artifacts were a variety of ritual implements cast in bronze by *cire perdu* or lost-wax technique; using radiocarbon 14 tests, Shaw was able to establish the ninth century A.D. as the probable date of these objects (Shaw 1970). There has been some controversy over the validity of this date, notably by Babatunde Lawal, who has argued that the inclusion of pieces of textile and other items of a more recent history would suggest a considerably later date—possibly after the fifteenth century—for the objects (Lawal 1973).[8] On the whole, however, the artistic genius of the Igbo-Ukwu bronzes has been defended by art historians like Ekpo Eyo, who has described them as "indigenous manufactures . . . unparalleled in Africa" (1977:92) and as providing "the first evidence of the artistic use of copper alloys in the whole of Black Africa" (72).

For our purposes, the crucial issue in the discovery of these Igbo-Ukwu bronzes is their relationship to other evidence of metal use elsewhere in West Africa, especially in Benin and Ife. An initial aspect of this relationship has to do with the nature of the medium used by the Igbo-Ukwu craftsmen as against those used by craftsmen elsewhere. Eyo suggests that "while the people of Ife and Benin made their works out of either pure copper or brass, and only a small percentage out of bronze, Igbo Ukwu works are mostly of bronze" (94). Bronze is, of course, an alloy made partly from copper; so, how did the Igbo-Ukwu workers get that material in an area that is not known to contain viable deposits of its ore? The debate has more recently been advanced by a group of native Igbo and foreign archaeologists, working in collaboration with Thurstan Shaw, who discovered traces of early indigenous production of bronze from lead-zinc-copper deposits in the Benue rift ("right on Igbo-Ukwu's doorstep"), an enterprise evidently terminated by colonialism which encouraged importation of copper (Chikwendu et al. 1989).[9]

The precedence of the Igbo over Ife and Benin artists in the use of copper/bronze no doubt suggests the possible influence of the Igbo on the latter peoples. Take, for instance, the evidence of facial scarification on casted heads from the three cultures. Although Eyo considers the Igbo-Ukwu marks (*ichi*) "indigenous to the region" (1877:94), they are rather similar to the ones found on Ife bronze heads, leading us to suspect possible influences. We will recall that in his play *Moremi*, about the foundations of Ife society, the Yoruba playwright Duro Ladipo presents the land as originally occupied by a group of autochthonous "Igbo" people, later brought into collision with some Yoruba migrants. Although Ladipo went on to respond—to inevitable questions about these "Igbo" people—that the word is simply Yoruba for *bush* (implying *primitive*) and that the language of that group was indeterminate, in most of his known productions of the play he made the "Igbo" characters speak in some dialect of the Igbo language. This may have been intended for dramatic effect, but it is arguable also as a product of a historical mind-set.

If elements of Igbo culture cannot be decisively shown to have infiltrated Yorubaland so early in the history of intergroup relations in Nigeria, there is at least some evidence of their privileged presence within the core of Benin culture. One of the significant pieces of evidence about Benin-Igbo relations relates to the ritual ascendancy of the old Nri civilization—which was served by the craft of bronzecasting—over various peoples in the regions east and west of the Niger, including Benin. Nri ritual experts, backed in no small degree by the mystical awe achieved through the use of metal and other icons of culture, were in the business of making far-ranging travels (called *mbia*) to foreign communities, making available to these their wisdom especially in matters of ritual (medical, divinatory, ceremonial, and otherwise) and sometimes settling among their hosts for extended periods of time.

With special reference to Nri relations with Benin, some early British colonial authorities have reported Nri claims that the land of Benin was subject to them and that the Nri king or *Eze Nri* "crowned the Kings of Benin and generally presided over all the religious observances of surrounding peoples."[10] Being descended of immigrants from Nri society, professionalists from the west-Niger Igbo apparently inherited the skills for which their forebears were famed. In chapter 4 above, we saw how a young doctor from this region offered his services to the Oba of Benin in his effort to rescue his captive mother from the palace. We also have the account, cited by the Benin scholar Osemwegie Ebohon, of how a medical expert named Ogbonmwan,[11] from Ogwashi-Uku (an Nri-descended community), was detained by Oba Akenzua I as his ritual specialist, and subsequently appointed first *Iyase*, then—following a dispute—*Ologbosere* (1972:84–86).

Another community to establish some presence within Benin's zone of influence were the Aro, who used religion for more devious ends. These people, in the area around the Cross River, were essentially middlemen in the slave trading between the Igbo hinterland and the Atlantic coastline. Advertising themselves as keepers of a great oracle called "Chukwu" or the Great God—also called *Ibini Ukpabi*, or "Long Juju" by the British—they held all citizens in the hinterland communities captive to this medium, by which they were able to round up slaves with relative ease, using force only when any resisted their religious tactics.[12]

Although the Aro operated in the broad land mass east of the Niger, they are known to have made inroads into areas within the Niger Delta where

Benin also operated in its slaving expeditions. How far the Aro may have ventured into territory effectively ruled by the Benin kingdom can only be conjectured. But one account at least has it that Chima, who is generally held to have fled Benin with his followers following a quarrel with the Benin monarchy and so "founded" some of the communities east of Benin, even up to Onitsha across the Niger, was a sixteenth-century Aro man who had established in Benin a branch of the Aro religio-commercial enterprise. He had in fact been appointed by the Oba as his personal ritualist and ultimately to an office in the kingdom, enjoying such intimacy with Benin life that when he departed the land, he had influenced their culture and traditions quite as much as he had been influenced by them (cited in Afigbo 1987:171–174).

Amid these claims and counterclaims by parallel strands of Igbo oral tradition, it is not very easy—nor indeed is it that necessary—to decide which aspects of Igbo cultural influence on Benin should be credited to either of these two Igbo movements. However, despite the imposing stature of Egharevba's nationalist history of Benin, one cannot help feeling that the Igbo may have left some imprints on Benin culture from generations of conflict and interaction between them. Consider, for example, one aspect of Benin religious life treated by Bradbury which we discussed in chapter 3 above: the emblem for the cult of the hand, called *ikenga* by the Igbo and *ikegobo* by the Bini. In his typology of figures in this genre Bradbury, while holding that Benin does not evince the concept of the "ram-headed god" claimed by Jeffreys as intrinsic to the Igbo type, nevertheless suspects there are "some grounds for supposing that the peg on *ikegobo* may be derived from an original pair of horns" (1973:267n): that is, a possible Igbo influence?

The influence is even more arguable from the etymology which Bradbury tries to assign to the word. After citing possibilities raised by Melzian with the two constituent segments of the word *ikegobo* (*ikega* and *obo*), Bradbury tells us:

> A case can be made out for deriving the word *ikega* from two roots, *ik-* and *ga* both implying circularity. *Ga* means "to surround" and is found in *lega*, "to move round." *Ik-* appears in such words as *ika* and *ikele*, a circular bead necklace, *ikagha*, bridle, and *ikoro*, a broad brass or ivory armlet. There is, therefore, a faint possibility that *ikega* originally meant "wristlet" (*ikegobo* would mean "something that goes round the arm") and, by association, the wrist itself. Every *ikegobo* in use should have a cowry circlet round it and when the owner dies this may be buried with him instead of the whole object. I would not, however, press this etymology or an Edo origin for the word. One of Jeffreys's informants (1954, p. 30) gives what appears to be a more satisfactory etymology. (1973:262n)

The etymology offered by Jeffreys's Igbo informant (Egbuniwe) is certainly more helpful: "*Ikenga* comes from the two words *Ike* = strength and *nga* = to succeed." I accept the first root, but am rather hesitant about the second. Earlier, I gave the root *ga-* as indicating movement or distance covered (chapter 3, note 27), and I suspect the same holds true for the etymology of *ikenga*, which I suggest breaks down into *ike* (strength) and *nga* (i.e., the effort involved in making a move: an endeavor, enterprise). The two concepts of *endeavor* and *success* are, of course, not so widely separated from each other, and are indeed closely linked. What all this means, however, is that the Igbo etymology comes much closer than the Edo (Bini) in capturing the essence of the concept symbolized by the word; if we should trace the direction of cultural influence in this regard, we would more defensibly move from the Igbo to the Edo.

Equally revealing are the correspondences between the speech forms of various units in this sector of the Kwa language family. There have been some respectable configurations by linguists like Ben Elugbe on the structures of what has been called the "Edoid" group of languages (1973, 1979). But if the sorts of evidence adduced above on possible Igbo-Benin relations are of any value, then Afigbo is entirely justified in questioning the validity of Egharevba's derivation of the cosmology and nomenclature for the four days of the Benin week: "*Eken* (the east), *Orie* (the west), *Okuo* (the north) and *Aho* (the south)" (1968:82)—corresponding to the Igbo *Eke, Orie, Nkwo,* and *Afo.* For if market days are, like much else in the cultural lives of peoples between whom we find striking linguistic correspondences, in seminal ways determined by religious orientations, then there is a chance that Benin owes more to the religious ascendancies of the Nri and the Aro than its champions are inclined to concede.

As fortune would have it, however, in the struggle for prominence between these groups, especially in the days when the traffic in slaves put more emphasis on might than on other means of control, the balance of power lay in the hands of those who took its demands more seriously than others. In explaining the decline of Nri, Angulu Onwuejeogwu, its best known ethnographer, comments that its culture "remained relatively stagnant after it had reached its climax. The political and ritual philosophy was constant: homicide was sin against the Earthforce (Ana) and this debarred the development of militarism. . . . In the face of militant cultures like that of the Benin, Igala and later on the Abam and the British, the hegemony simply recoiled like a snail into its shell and this is one of the reasons it eluded earlier observers" (1972a:50). Nor did the Aro fare much better. Theirs was really a commercial enterprise relying more on religious awe than on military organization to advance their goals; it was only when religious awe failed to influence their opponents that they relied on main force provided by professional head-hunters (from the Ohafia, Abam, Edda, and other groups) over whom they had no control (Dike 1956:39). This was hardly any match for the very determined military machine of Benin.

Yet one thing is equally certain, and this is that Igbo influence within the region in which Benin may be said to have flexed her military and other muscles—especially west of the Niger—is by no means negligible. Indeed, to the extent that one could speak of empires, I believe it would be fair to say that until British colonial presence put paid to various forms of local exertion in the areas east and west of the Niger, there were at least three empires in varying states of health: the military empire of Benin, the commercial empire of the Aro, and the cultural empire of the Nri. The last of these, energized by achievements in metalcraft and metaphysics, definitely made a strong impression on Jeffreys who, in investigating it during the 1930s, commented that he was "witnessing the last stages of the decay and breakup of what must have been at one time a large empire" (Afigbo 1981:62). The descendants of such a people have seen reason, now and then, to feel proud that they are different from, if not superior to, other peoples and that their cherished institutions have sustained them through the vicissitudes of history. Why should we deny a community the privilege of being *splendide mendax*—of engaging in what Anthony Appiah has called "the ennobling lie" (1992:175)—about its merits, especially when these have been steadily undermined by testimonies and histories accorded the stamp of official approval?

Nation, Narration, and Self-Determination

For though the scholars engaged in the Scheme for the Study of Benin History and Culture seem to have taken care to weigh the various bits of evidence available to them, it is no secret that the work of Jacob Egharevba formed the master-text against which they read pieces of ethnographic and other material. There is a sad irony, however, undergirding the history of the Benin Scheme which has everything to do with the hegemonic implications of relations not only between Benin and its neighbors (as enshrined in the myths under study) but also between the larger Nigerian nation and its constituent communities. The Scheme, as I pointed out above in chapter 1, was instituted by Kenneth Dike, an Igbo man, who in true professional objectivity (as well as nationalist spirit) saw in its program the prospects of valuable reassessment of the achievement of a great Nigerian or African empire, rather poorly served by official colonial histories. Hardly had the Scheme's labors begun to bear fruit when Nigeria was plunged into a bloody civil conflict, beginning with the massacre of hundreds of Igbo people first in northern Nigeria and, when the crisis developed into a civil war, in the western part of the country as well. Dike, already politically embattled with certain elements at the University of Ibadan, of which he was the Vice-Chancellor, felt quite unsafe in the generally hostile climate, and escaped with the rest of his ethnic kin to his home east of the Niger.

In the jingoistic environment of secessionist Biafra, Dike had little room to pursue the freedom of thought he had worked hard to promote as a scholar and academic administrator; so it came as no surprise that, even before the war was over, he had accepted a position as Mellon Professor of History at Harvard. But his experiences had left some sore feelings in him. In the meantime, the Scheme he had founded had practically fallen to pieces. Bradbury had fallen ill and returned to England (1961), dying in 1969 while the civil war was still raging; Alan Ryder may have returned to England very soon after the war ended; the rest of the glorious team found their own separate ways. In time, of course, publications from the Scheme's work began to appear sporadically. But the spirit that galvanized it was no longer there, and the coordinative labors envisaged for the disparate disciplinary insights yielded by the various scholars failed to take off. When Dike himself resumed scholarly research in America, thoughts of the Benin Scheme were pretty much behind him. Although the subject of Aro entrepreneurial history had been part of the material for his great classic study (1956), and Dike had indeed taken some steps toward advancing it in his last days at Ibadan, I think it would be fair to say that by this time Dike had lost enough of his nationalist zeal to give closer attention to an area of more or less ethnic interest to him.[13]

"The problem of the twentieth century," W.E.B. DuBois once said, "is the problem of the color-line" (1995:54). Adam Kuper is just as discerning in a more recent statement: "In the 1990s, we will find ourselves increasingly preoccupied with ethnicity" (1994:545). As we approach the end of the twentieth century, it has become clear that these two propositions are sorely in need of time extensions, for the problems they highlight are in no hurry to go away. Indeed, it requires no special sagacity to observe that those issues are so ingrained in the condition of humanity that we were better advised to see them as dispositions to be channeled to advantage than as demons to be exorcised. For wherever human beings share common interests and space, they will be disposed to ensure that their respective stakes in these are at least recognized: constructing myths is simply a way of giving form to the desire to safeguard your stakes in the context—which may on occasion be conflictual—of contiguous stakes. A nation is either blessed or doomed by the degree to which it is willing or able to pay serious attention to this natural urge for self-determination among its constituent subgroups and to channel the resultant stresses to political profit.

Needless to say, the concept of "nation" conjures different images to different schools of political philosophy. Two, at least, have commanded our attention in the last few decades. On the one hand there are thinkers of a more or less postmodernist temper who, dismayed by instabilities in the geopolitical scene and the doubts these have cast on our accustomed certainties, are inclined to dismiss the lines traditionally used in demarcating peoples as more or less convenient fictions. Benedict Anderson (1983) defines the nation as an "imagined political community" (15) in which, among a vast agglomeration of people most of whom hardly know each other, fiction so steadily overtakes reality as to create a "remarkable confidence of community in anonymity" (40). Hobsbawm and Ranger also see "nation" as a "comparatively recent historical innovation" characterized by such "exercises in social engineering" as the assumption of a defining space and the invention of validating traditions (1983:13). In his brilliant analysis of the judicial hearings over claims brought by the Mashpee Wampanoag Indians of Cape Cod, Massachusetts on 16,000 acres of tribal land, James Clifford throws light on the fluidity of cultural identities on which the plaintiffs based their ill-starred case (1988:277–346).

Similar qualifications have been made by scholars working specifically on the world of Africans, whether in their native continent or in the western Atlantic. Mudimbe has no doubt made a plausible case in drawing attention to the shades of interest and enterprise that facilitated the "invention" of Africa both in more recent geopolitics (1988) and in classical antiquity (1994). Appiah warns that tribal identities are too subject to "economic and political exigencies" for us to indulge essentialist notions of place:

> Every human identity is constructed, historical; every one has its share of false presuppositions, of the errors and inaccuracies that courtesy calls "myth," religion "heresy," and science "magic." Invented histories, invented biologies, invented cultural affinities come with every identity; each is a kind of role that has to be scripted, structured by conventions of narrative to which the world never quite manages to conform. (1992:174)

Gilroy (1993) would have a "Black Atlantic" world that should cut its ties with an African antecedence and the racial particularism that this entailed. His is a cultural project in which "an image of the authentic folk as custodians of an essentially invariant, anti-historical notion of black particularity to which they alone somehow maintain privileged access" (91) is replaced by "fractal patterns of cultural and political affiliation" (88) that more fittingly reflect the fluid universe of peoples who have little stake in the convenient fiction of a nation-state.

Gilroy's position is best understood as an anguished cry *de profundis*—foreshadowed by his earlier *There Ain't No Black in the Union Jack* (1991)—by a subject whose cultural identity and contributions have gone unacknowl-edged and who would sooner drift freely in a floating isle than be bonded to an inhospitable land. But an isle even of self-elected *déracinés* is still a home, and for me this somehow weakens the antiessentialist argument of the inventionists.

A second school of political philosophy, distrustful of "all the cultur-ological talk about 'imagined communities'" (Kuper 1994:551), has ac-knowledged the self-validating fictions by which communities have sought to press their claims in the competitive climate of the postcolonial polity. This school of thought has given some attention to the modes of social engineering whereby ethnic groups have sought to adjust to one another in plural societies. Although there is increasing literature on the matter of ethnicity from the "melting pots" of the West to more recent trouble spots like Bosnia-Herzegovina, the subject has often been the focus of scholarly interest on the multiethnic societies of the "Third World" and their troubled efforts at nation-building. Here, it has been accepted that ethnicity is an inherent dynamic in the emergence of social and political attitudes among groups divided by language and the attendant cultural history. In his com-parative analysis of interethnic situations in Trinidad and Mauritius, Erikson sees ethnicity as "the single most important criterion for collective social distinctions in daily life; ethnic distinctions are rooted in perceptions of differences between lifestyles" whereby the *others* "represent lifestyles and values which are regarded as undesirable" (1991:139). The burden of such positions, and their relevance for our understanding of Benin relations with her rivals as mirrored in the tales studied above, will become clearer as we explore sample recent studies of the political implications of ethnicity in postcolonial societies like Nigeria.

There have been many studies of ethnic conflict in African societies, but the most relevant for our purposes are those that examine the dilemma that has emerged in the contemporary polity since colonialism, namely: how to reconcile the contending claims of the constituent ethnicities on the one hand, and on the other to secure the commitment of these units to the growth of a united nation. The emergence of ethnicity in Africa has been traced by Peter Ekeh (1975, 1990) to the role of colonialism in aggravating the inherent potentials for conflict between traditional kinship structures.[14] According to Ekeh, each ethnic group had its own traditional codes of morality which provided a stabilizing focus for its members; on the other hand, the nation created out of a collectivity of various ethnic groups was run along disinterested or amoral lines. Consequently, there has emerged within the nation two separate publics—the *state*, representing the central structure of government, and *society*, representing the sum total of the constituent ethnicities within the nation—with interests and expectations that desperately need to be reconciled with one another in the interest of the survival of the nation.

The solution that has generally been devised to harmonize these conflicting interests is a federal system of government, which has sought, with varying degrees of success, to reconcile the centrifugal and the centripetal tendencies within the nation: on the one hand, ensuring that the needs and expectations of the constituent units of the nation are adequately met while, on the other, exercising a sufficiently firm control at the center to guarantee that every unit recognizes that the sovereignty of the nation surpasses all other needs. Here, then, is the crux of the problem. Which of these two needs should be placed *first*: in other words, if present-day African nations, with their basically multiethnic structures, are not to remain forever in danger of total collapse, should their emphasis in governance be put first on consolidating their constituent units and ensuring that they are satisfied to a relatively equal degree, or on consolidating the center to ensure that the nation is never held to ransom by any one or group of these constituent units?

The problem is by no means an easy one to resolve, and has been resposible to no small degree for the catastrophes—not the least of which is civil war—that have befallen many independent African nations. The reason for this is that, from the very dawn of independence and even before it, they were drawn into a nexus of global obligations—pan-African politics, membership in world organizations, with the attendant economic and other commitments, etc.—that forced their attention more on external relations than on internal responsibilities. The result of this was that these nations spent an inordinate proportion of time and resources on erecting those organs (ministries, corporations, etc.) that would fit them more properly for functioning in a global community than for being a stable community at home.

The implications of this extroverted vision are particularly evident in the inert implementation of the federal machinery of government, seen especially in the effort to concentrate power at the *center*. Under the colonial administration, this arrangement was intended partly to protect the key functionaries, who were mostly Europeans, from too-direct contact with the vast majority of the subject population (in the rural communities), but partly also to secure a central clearinghouse for the wealth of the nation, which was colonialism's essential quarry.[15] Upon inheriting this centralized structure from the colonists, the indigenous African leadership found the privileges it conferred on them too attractive to give up, and were somewhat disinclined to make any substantial changes. Consequently, there has been an unfortunate concentration of physical development at the federal capital, due largely to the leadership's selfish interest in "extending its functions at the center and its capacity to influence the course of events at the periphery" (Rothchild and Olorunsola 1983:5). In Nigeria, where the creation of an increasing number of states should technically bring the government closer to the people, there have been occasions in which the states have been locked in constitutional battles with the federal government; to protect their selfish centralist interests, "federal government political executives and officials . . . always seem to try to interpret the constitution in such a way as to favor the federal government" (Elaigwu and Olorunsola 1983:292).

The creation of more and more states may seem to be bringing the government closer to the masses in the rural communities, but it has hardly mitigated the centripetal tendencies in policy and behavior. Elaigwu and Olorunsola have particularly observed the "political rashes" resulting from this policy. In the intensely multiethnic structure of Nigeria, each state becomes a microcosm of the larger nation; the state capital becomes the new "center" of controls, against whose background the various communities now resolve themselves into "'new majorities' and 'new minorities'" (1983:288). As in the federal capital, state executives arrogate to themselves—again, largely for personal and class interests—the zealous duty of protecting the powers of the state against the often legitimate expectations of local government councils. And again, as in the federal capital, there is a concentration of development projects at the state capital, with the accompanying drift of manpower from the villages to the capital, where everyone has been led to believe all hopes of self-realization lie.[16]

The answer to the question which we posed earlier on seems clear. Although it would be naive of anyone to assume that the problems of managing a multiethnic nation could be easily solved by one bold stroke of constitutional fiat—the periodic revision of the Nigerian federal constitution serves a notable warning—it is evident that the needs of the pluralistic structure imposed on the erstwhile colony were better met by a reversal of priorities. The foreigners who ran the colony created a centralized structure that enabled them to hoard the colony's wealth from a convenient base. The indigenous leaders of the nation that emerged from the colony should be sensible enough to disengage themselves from the old exploitative agenda and realize they are beholden not to some outside metropolis but to the constituent units of their nation, from which the wealth is derived. The gross imbalance that has been pointed out by Elaigwu and Olorunsola in revenue allocation in Nigeria between the federal government on the one hand and the state and local governments on the other (1983:294) should be reversed in such a way as to set aside far more money for the periphery than for the center(s). A nation can achieve greatness and stability only to the degree to which its constituent units feel satisfied enough to be committed to those goals.

The solution to the perpetual imbalance and eruptions in the political structure of a multiethnic nation like Nigeria may thus lie in creating a level playing field for its constituent units. Admittedly, delimiting these units may not be easy. It would be unwise to use ethnicity as a guide, as some political scientists (e.g., Nnoli 1994:22) are inclined to do, for there is likely to be much imbalance in size that might invite comparison and thus animosity. Rather, the country should be structured into roughly equal local government units (or counties) determined more along *communitarian* than on ethnic lines: i.e., in terms of units with a demonstrable history of cultural affiliation or ancestral ties. Such a principle has been useful, for instance, in separating the west-Niger Igbo into some four local government areas— Oshimili, Aniocha, Ndokwa, and Ika—and may have guided the division of the rest of the country as well.[17]

A proper devolution of powers to these local governments or counties will entail the elimination of "states" which, as we saw above, merely multiplied the centripetal effect of the federal authority, in the process creating more parasites on the national revenue. With the states gone, the revenue allocation formula should be revised so that a considerably larger portion is shared between the local governments—on a mutually agreed formula— than is allocated to the federal treasury. The point here is that the federal government should be seen more as an overseer of the even development of the constituent units of the federation than as a landlord arbitrarily superintending the use of national space, violating the liberties of his tenants at will,[18] and draining their pockets for rent which is insufficiently ploughed back into the improvement of their conditions.

Yet this reduced role of the federal government is not meant to destroy a sense of national purpose among citizens in their respective units. There will, of course, continue to be certain central organs transcending the powers of the local governments, such as the security forces, the supreme court, agencies for the exploitation of natural resources, construction of transnational highways, and provision of other key services that will give some uniformity to the image of the country as a nation. There should also continue to be those agencies or ministries that enable it to meet its obligations as a member of an international community. And with proper planning, there should be enough disposition of federal offices across the various sectors of the country to give them a sense of a national presence. But these efforts will have to be tailored, in budgetary terms, to fit the change of emphasis in the developmental initiatives from the center to the periphery where the constituent communities of the nation live and which provides the bulk of the nation's revenue.

I have spoken above of *sectors*. Here I have in mind the fact that, given the unwieldy number of local government areas or counties into which Nigeria will inevitably be subdivided, there is need for a partitioning of the collectivity into roughly equal zones (say, four) for the election of a national leader and the council of ministers. In this, the country must needs bid goodbye to the old kinds of nationwide electioneering inherited from Western nations and settle for two expediences that would respond better to the sensitivities of an intensely pluralistic society: a total absence of political parties, and a rotational presidency such as has been advocated in recent constitutional parleys. The exact mechanisms for implementing these choices, which are all too obvious given Nigeria's historical experience, need not delay us here. Suffice it to say that in them there is a better chance than ever before of giving each group the satisfaction that its identity is recognized and that it has just as much stake in the governance of the country as any other group.[19]

Will the Subaltern Please Speak Up?

These factors—recognition of identity, and equality in the political playing field—are clearly the guiding concerns in the tales of self-assertion I have examined in this study, whether those in which communities project their more republican outlooks against the menace of authoritarian structures, or those in which individuals are determined that their integrity and their merits be recognized. They are just as important for an understanding of the political psychology that brought the Scheme for the Study of Benin History and Culture into existence. In the euphoria of independence, Nigeria was so eager to look good in the eyes of the world that she embraced the outward trappings of greatness, without realizing she was encouraging the preponderance of some groups of her people over others, thus enabling the full growth of the seeds of intergroup conflict that had quietly germinated in the years of colonial rule. Ajayi points to one such measure in the federation's early life: "Regional governments sponsored research into the culture of dominant ethnic groups" (1990:19). Worthy as the Benin Scheme was as an effort by an African nation to begin exploring the true facts of her history, we can now see that in this, as in other aspects of her policy, Nigeria did not listen enough to the different voices within her that clamored for equal attention. Her postindependence performance has so far leaned too heavily on a hegemonic program—all too eagerly embraced by the military leadership, an unfortunate aberration—scripted in the theatre of colonial and global politics.

The tales on which this study has been built remind us that there is an undercurrent, if not a groundswell, of self-assertion that continues to resist the hegemonist pressures imposed upon communities that cherish their identities too dearly to see them sacrificed at the altar of grandiloquent but ill-advised agendas. It is particularly irksome to these communities to discover that the traditions of their erstwhile adversaries are privileged over theirs by a third force (the colonial administration, the federal government) pretending to impose an impartial order, then turning around to ally with the communities' adversaries.[20] In the literate traditions of Nigeria, the swift rejoinder of the Agbor Patriotic Union to Egharevba's hegemonist account of Agbor-Benin relations, and later revisionist exegeses by Igbo historians like Afigbo, may be seen as acts of self-assertion that have benefited from the wide publicity offered by the mass media. The oral tradition has not been quite so lucky, but the tales discussed in this book are proof enough that there are *alter*-native traditions not so eager to tolerate what Gayatri Spivak calls "the violence of imperialist epistemic, social, and disciplinary inscription" (1988:285) that projects like the Benin Scheme may tend—perhaps unwittingly—to promote. In other words—to borrow a thought from Jean-François Lyotard—none of these communities would wish to see its traditions debased to the position of "local narratives" while the story of Benin was privileged with the status of a "master-narrative" in the construction of a national political identity.[21]

Nigeria has been used as our main point of reference in this epilogue only because it is the political geography within which the tales under study are set. There is no doubt, however, that the phenomenon of empire mirrored by the tales is not at all unique to this corner of the world. Africa, for one, is replete with "heroic epics" and other traditions of domination upheld by those anxious to demonstrate that the continent has as proud a political history as anything that might be found in European and Asiatic traditions. The feats of Sunjata Keita, Askia Mohammed, Samory Toure, Uthman dan Fodio, Shaka the Zulu, and other figures are loudly proclaimed (even by people from communities brutally overrun by these warmongers), all in pursuit of validating claims to cultural and political integrity. Today the nationalist's zeal has drastically cooled, as the nation pays the bloody price of its misguided suppression of *other* voices within its plurality in its eagerness to look good in the eyes of the world.[22]

The same may be said for other zones of sectional conflict across the world—Eastern Europe, the British Isles, even the Americas—that have long prided themselves in having outgrown the sorts of "primitive" outlook characteristic of "tribal" peoples. For some of these societies the self-delusion has gone too far to be reversed. For the rest, it is not too late to admit that "the oppressed *can* know and speak for themselves" (Spivak 1988:279), and that true peace will come only when they are allowed to tell those stories that have for too long been hidden or muted. After all, as my narrator Odogwu Okwuashi of Onicha-Ugbo would say, "The mouse eats, but so does the maggot."[23]

Notes

1. For some insights into the relationships between the two disciplines, see Lewis 1968, and especially Beidelman 1970 and Pender-Cudlip 1972 on the study of African oral traditions.

2. Bradbury did collect and publish actual narratives (1973:271–282). But, in both his editorial and analytic treatment of these tales we can see the functionalist biases once again at play and the aestheticist interest eloquently absent.

3. See Bradbury 1973:253–254. "That the Ezomo should have a casting of such size and complexity," Bradbury tells us, "is in itself remarkable and this is recognized in the story that it was made secretly" (253).

4. This region was established in 1963 as the Midwestern Region of Nigeria by the government of the First Republic under Abubakar Tafawa Balewa. In 1966, its name was simply changed to "Midwest State" in a delimitation carried out by the military administration of General Yakubu Gowon. In 1972 it was again rechristened "Bendel State"—after its old (colonial) constituent provinces, Benin and Delta—but in 1992 was broken into two (Edo and Delta states), following a string of agitations by various communities essentially clamoring to be separated from ties with Benin. The west-Niger Igbo and the (western) Ijo are located in the Delta State.

5. In his privately printed *Fusion of Tribes* (1966), the Benin historian Jacob Egharevba made some remarkable claims about the extent of "the Benin empire," which according to him extended as far southeast as to the "Idiobo [Diobu] of Port Harcourt" and to "Eko (Lagos) in the West"; "the Gas [of] Accra left in 1300" (10–11). There is no doubt that, as in Shaka's *mfecane*, several peoples were displaced from their communities in the course of military campaigns under various Benin kings, and may have spread news of Benin's might far and wide. But claims about the actual geographical coverage of the "empire" seem to have been grossly exaggerated. The actions of certain countries west of Nigeria in naming themselves or their institutions "Benin" are more likely tokens of mythic wish fulfillment than of historical reality.

6. There is some gratuitous benevolence in the following statement by Evinma Ogieiriaixi: "In all my publications, I have consistently maintained that

the term *edo* does not exclude the speech-forms of the people of the so-called '*edo* Group of Languages' who live outside the Benin divisions of Midwestern Nigeria (now Bendel State). Accordingly, *edo* for me is not synonymous with *Idu* (Bini). The latter to me, is a variant of *edo*, just as Esan, Ora, Urhobo, Isoko, etc. are variants of *edo*" (1974:10).

7. Nontitled men, we will recall, do not enjoy very much respect in the Igbo society of Chinua Achebe's *Things Fall Apart* (1962). Okonkwo's idle father, Unoka, is ridiculed as an *agbala*, which literally means "woman" (10). In one scene, Okonkwo, we are told, brusquely dismisses a nontitled man who criticizes him in their village assembly by simply telling the man, "This meeting is for men" (19)! It will become clear, as this study progresses, that Benin society was originally organized on the basis of the village structure before an overarching monarchical system came to be superimposed upon it.

8. The kings of the first dynasty were called *ogiso*. After several generations of misrule, this dynasty was overthrown in a popular revolt. There was a brief interregnum, during which the people appealed to the Oni of Ife (among the Yoruba) to help them solve their constitutional impasse. The Oni sent them Prince Oranmiyan, who came down to Benin with a retinue of chiefs and other functionaries to set the Benin nation in proper political order. Oranmiyan soon lost his patience with the Bini (whom he found unusually quarrelsome) and returned to Ife. But he had managed to father a son with a local woman; the son, named Eweka (the First), inaugurated a new dynasty of rulers (with the title *oba*) which, despite intermittent crises, has continued to rule Benin to this day.

9. Since the late fifteenth century, when the Europeans first came to Benin for trade and other business, the monarchy has led the outreach to the world outside Benin. Egharevba reports (1968:27–28) that Oba Esigie sent one of his priests as ambassador to Portugal; he also quotes a letter (dated 20 October 1516) by a Portuguese missionary to the King of Portugal which reports, inter alia, that Esigie "ordered his son and two of his greatest noblemen . . . to become Christians, and built a church in Benin. They learnt how to read and did it very well." The present Oba, Erediauwa I, is a Cambridge University graduate and has held some of the highest administrative offices in Nigeria. The present Asagba of Asaba, Obi Chike Edozien, a world-renowned medical scientist, has been Dean of the School of Medicine at the University of Ibadan, Nigeria and subsequently held distinguished professorships at Massachusetts Institute of Technology and the University of North Carolina, Chapel Hill. The present Adakaji of Abraka, Ovie Luke Ejohwomu, a graduate of the University of Nigeria, Nsukka, was a top administrator in the civil service of the Delta State.

10. On Mgbile's journey to Benin to be ordained as *pere*, see Edoh 1979:2–3. Further on the search for legitimacy, Edoh says: "Any Ijaw Pere (king) at that time who did not go on a chieftaincy pilgrimage to Benin City was regarded as inferior and generally nicknamed juju priest. . . . Conditions to be satisfied before becoming Pere, my father told me, were difficult. Among them was the producing of a child while in Benin by a Benin woman."

11. Dike, who has investigated the oral traditions of this area for his study of its economic history, has issued a strong caveat about their dependability (1956:104).

12. Ohadike 1988 has the most interesting collection of oral testimonies on

the founding of various west-Niger Igbo peoples. For a coherent treatment of the history of Anioma or Western Igbo society, see also Ohadike 1994:1–31.

13. On Sidahome's possible connections with the Benin monarchy, see Eghar-evba 1968:84. In the Introduction to his collection, Sidahome tells us that the tales "are Benin stories as told in Ishanland." It is also significant that unlike tales I have collected from the west-Niger Igbo—as we shall see in chapters 2 and 5—none of the Ishan tales in Sidahome's collection shows a hero destroying the Oba and ascending the Benin throne. Indeed, with regard to the horrors portrayed in Sidahome's collection, it matters a great deal whether we see those tales as "Benin stories told in Ishanland," as Sidahome would have them, or as Ishan tales that look at Benin from an antihegemonic distance. In a letter he wrote to me (dated 28 August 1995) kindly commenting on an initial draft of one of the chapters of this book, Dan Ben-Amos states: "In Edo tradition, while the Oba may be a tyrant, he is 'our' tyrant, and this duality generates a set of narrative and attitudinal problems that are missing from your stories." I would suspect that the average Ishan person—though closely linked with the Bini in the "Edo" ethnic classification—would be no more likely to see the Oba as "our" tyrant than the average west-Niger Igbo, and that Sidahome has possibly treated the Benin monarchy with a little more sympathy than it would get in a more *popular* tradition.

14. Egharevba may, of course, have been influenced to some extent by the numerous European authorities he had consulted in the course of compiling his *Short History*: in his Preface, he acknowledges his indebtedness "to European friends and visitors for their help and notes from which I have been able to gather quotations and precise dates" (xii). However, as a member of one of the palace organizations (the House of Iwebo) he must have had independent access to considerable information.

15. For the arrogance of an Ezomo and his responsibility for starting the war betwen Benin and the Ubulu, see Simayi's story of Ezemu in Okpewho 1992:195–196.

16. Characteristically, most of these figures were imperial warlords. The Ezo-mo and Ologbosere were members of the supreme military command. Igwara is for Benin "Aruanran," the governor of Udo who fought Oba Esigie fiercely for a long time until he was finally subdued. He survives in heroic lore as a frightful giant, to be discussed later in this chapter.

17. This is the only other point of contingence between the Ubulu version of the story and the Benin-Ishan versions. Ugonoba (or Ugo), in the Iyekorhiom-won region—present-day Oriomwon local government area of Edo State—was the town ruled by the Agboghidi of the latter versions. The only other reference to the Agboghidi figure I have encountered in the oral traditions of the western Igbo is in an account from Igbuzo which is partly a reference to the Benin-Ubulu war (Ohadike 1988:118–124). In it, the Ubulu king, said to be "of Benin extraction," had killed his wife Adose (= Bini Adesua), given to him by the Oba of Benin as wife "because of the friendship that existed between them"; the cause of the murder was that the princess would not genuflect in greeting to her husband, as was the custom. The Oba, enraged at the news of his daughter's death, summoned "his chiefs including the king of Isa [= Ishan], the king of Uromi and the king of Ugo" to a war with the Ubulu, and "commissioned the

king of Ugo to lead the expedition." I also understand that the name Agboghidi is one of the appellations of the Obi of Onitsha, Ofala Okagbue I.

18. The Ubulu seem to command a certain reputation in the folk traditions of this region: an Ukwuani narrative also tells how Benin was forced to a compromise with her in another conflict. See Anene-Boyle 1979:85–89.

19. Although there have been efforts in recent linguistic scholarship to identify possible Edo elements within the Ijo family of languages (Thomas and Williamson 1967, Elugbe 1979), these hardly support a hypothesis of direct Benin influence.

20. Compare Sidahome 1964:178. In his play *Ozidi* (1966), Clark-Bekederemo maximizes the image of the giant by attributing the huge moat around the old city of Benin to Ogueren's simply walking round the city walls (82). There is possible support in Benin and other oral traditions for that detail, although it does not appear to have been used by Okabou in *The Ozidi Saga.*

21. These references to red-uniformed soldiers in oral traditions about Benin are rather well attested by documentary evidence. Ling Roth (1972:126) and Blackmun (1983:84) both cite Olfert Dapper's seventeenth-century observation that, in preparing for war, Benin noblemen dressed themselves entirely in scarlet, and Kaplan tells us that in Benin symbology "[red] is associated with Ogun, god of iron and of war" (1981:79).

22. For an insight into the elaborate system of revenues—taxes, tributes, etc.—by which the Benin monarchy supported its stupendous pomp and power, see Igbafe 1980.

23. In an excellent essay on Clark-Bekederemo's uses of the Ijo literary tradition (1994), Dan Izevbaye has been admirably cautious in skirting the hegemonist risks involved in a treatment of images and motifs that Benin shares with other communities. Although he evokes Egharevba in the historical sources on which some of his argument is built, he is more inclined to speak of "cultural relationships" than to propose diffusionist directions. With regard to linguistic similarities, he suggests that "later researchers may be able to say whether these words belong to a common stock and the same family root, or whether some of them are loan words" (6). For a view of Egharevba's scholarship as one characterized by Edo nationalism and loyalty to the Benin monarchy, see Usuanlele and Falola 1994: 305, 316.

24. I must point out, however, that while I applaud the recognition by writers like Todorov, Rabkin, and others of the role of the "fantastic" in all creative literature and especially the narrative, I am a little suspicious of the sort of abstract taxonomy they indulge. Their analyses seem to rest entirely on a consideration of the reader of printed narratives (including the so-called folktales) as well as the characters of the narrative drama. They cite Propp in their discussion of these folktales, and inevitably suffer from the same failure as Proppian taxonomy, which is a lack of interest in the sociological context of the tales. For instance, for the Ubulu to represent themselves as having trounced Benin and brought her to her knees may be seen as a legitimate manipulation of historic truth for the psychological comfort of the community; now, would anyone either in Benin or in Ubulu-Uku see the details of the story as "a direct reversal of ground rules" (Rabkin 1976:14) operating in oral culture, where notions of magic and the supernatural permeate daily life and thought as deeply as the tales?

2. The Hunter Who Became a King

1. See Okpewho 1992:328 for the fundamental difference between literary scholars and historians in their approaches to the oral tradition. For the tension between historians and anthropologists in their study of oral testimonies, see Okpewho 1983:114–124.

2. Compare James Baldwin: "History, I contend, is the present—*we*, with every breath we take, every move we make, *are* History—and what goes around, comes around" (1995:xvi).

3. A classicist to the core, Collingwood obviously owes his universalist view of the historical subject to authorities like Thucydides and Tacitus. But Nagy, himself a classical philologist, cites a revealing *locus*, in his analysis of the word *historia*, from "the father of history" for whom the line between *historia* and *fabula* is extremely thin (1990:259).

4. The nationalist poet and prominent Nigerian political leader, Dennis C. Osadebay, himself an Asaba man, has a somewhat stylized translation of the song: see Finnegan 1970:149n. The song, incidentally, comes back to me with interesting personal memories. My mother used to make us take a purgative drink—often some vicious-tasting nostrum or other "made in England"—on the first Saturday of every month. My sisters and I hated the Ojea song with a passion, because we usually lay groaning with nausea while our mother (who obviously enjoyed the song) sang it with some feeling. In 1984, when I carried out the "second burial" (that is, the comprehensive funeral rites done much later) of my mother, the song was among those performed by one of the female song groups at the final celebrations. This time I danced to it in grateful memory.

5. *Osiyoje* is poetic diction for *o si ayaa je*, "how did it go?" Although the west-Niger Igbo trace from homelands east of the Niger, the vicissitudes of social and political history have often brought many of them to see the river as not simply a geographical but an ethical boundary between them and their eastern kinfolk, preferring to be identified as "Ibo" (a convenient form used by the British colonialists who could not manage the harsh plosive *gb*) while derogatorily reserving the original name for the easterners. The differences were especially exacerbated by experiences during the Nigerian Civil War, 1967–70. Early in the war, the Biafran army crossed the Niger and occupied the Midwest State. The Federal army regained the state six weeks later, and many especially in the riverine towns of Asaba and Igbuzo (Ibusa) have never forgiven the easteners for the untold horrors which federal soldiers visited on these communities for allegedly giving the Biafrans willing access to the Midwest State. For a more recent discussion of the origins of the name "Igbo" and the concept of an Igbo identity, see Oriji 1994:2–6.

6. In a slightly similar vein, compare the brothers Nilsen's sacrifice of their common lover in Jorge Luis Borges' short story "The Intruder" (1972), composed with a dash of folk flavor.

7. Although Simayi presented this as a story of an actual historical event, the names for Meeme ("I am the Doer") and Onukwu ("Buffoon") seem indicative of the more or less symbolic import of such stories.

8. He is the narrator of the focal tale in chapter 3. More on him later. In the transcription of tales in this book, CAPITALS are used for words spoken loud-

ly, ordinary roman font for words spoken in normal conversational voice, and *italics* for words spoken softly. See Okpewho 1992:350–351.

9. Ojiudu concluded a tale he told me on this night about the origin of his box-harp, *opanda*, by proudly recalling a nickname he had earned for his extraordinary virtuosity with the instrument. He had been called *Mmadu God*, "Man of God," more in the sense of a superhuman genius than of a pious man. Adopting a sensuous alto he sang, to the background music of the *opanda* and the choral support of his friend Okoojii, the following tune which he claimed made him the heartthrob of the youth of his day:

> *Mmadu God elee m-o*
> *Mmadu God-e, Mmadu God elee m-o*
> *Mmadu God-e, mak' i gbusie m i lie m-o!*
>
> *Mmadu God alaputa m-o*
> *Mmadu God-e, Mmadu God alaputa m-o*
> *Mmadu God-e, mak' i gbusie m i lie m-o!*
>
> *Eb' i no kii lote m-o*
> *Kii lote m-o, eb' i no kii lote m-o*
> *Kii lote m-o, n' ebe n no na mm' elote i-oo!*
>
> *Ofu ony' a dimm' ije n'enu-o*
> *Ofu ony' a dimm' ije, ofu ony' a dimm' ije n'enu-o*
> *Enu b' uwa, ike agwu onye na-acho ogalanya!*
>
> *Awaa, awa wawa wa waa wawa waa, awaaaaah!*
>
> *Mmadu God* has sold me
> *Mmadu God*, oh, *Mmadu God* has sold me
> *Mmadu God*, if you kill me, you must eat me!
>
> *Mmadu God* has betrayed me
> *Mmadu God*, oh, *Mmadu God* has betrayed me
> *Mmadu God*, if you kill me, you must eat me!
>
> Wherever you are, remember me
> Remember me, oh, wherever you are, remember me
> Remember me, for wherever I am, I'll remember you!
>
> One should not go through life alone
> One should not go, not go through life alone
> Oh, what a life: wearing yourself down in the pursuit of wealth!
>
> Alas, alas, alas, alas, alas!

10. Evidently the narrator substitutes rousing for shaking because he realizes the hunter has not yet opened the door for his caller.

11. The Igbo text is "Omemma," meaning one who does good, or (in this context) one who makes you feel good.

12. The narrator accompanied the detail about making the bed with a forceful nod of his head, designed to suggest a calculated resolve on the woman's part. This was what drew laughter from the audience, who obviously had a sense of what the woman had in mind.

13. Ojiudu actually used the English word "shake" rather than the Igbo (*mehube*) used by his friend and accompanist Okoojii. At this point in the narration, the children had dropped off to sleep and my sister (Mrs. Arinze), observing the rather pornographic drift of the story, had herself retired indoors.

14. This is the standard formula used by narrators in this region for abbreviating the plot of a tale. Notice that the narrator also underscores the passage of time with his extended musical interludes.

15. The Igbo is *kwii*. See note 27 below.

16. The "sons" of the Oba (112) are evidently his personal guards, or perhaps soldiers of the imperial army. The frequency with which these emissaries invade the household of the hunter—who, we are apparently meant to understand, is now advancing in years—would suggest that they are not far from his community. Because of the constancy of its campaigns against communities in this region, the Benin army—nay, the Benin kingdom itself—is often portrayed in their tales to be within earshot.

17. The New Yam Festival among the west-Niger Igbo has traditionally taken place around September—after the harvest season, when the community is now set to usher in the "new year"—and this is about the same period when the Bini observe their own new yam festival (*ague*), conducted by the Oba. It has been said that, until more recent times, the Oba's rituals involved much human sacrifice. The teeth demanded in this story could thus be read either as a synecdoche for human life or as a token of Benin's assertion of the community's vassalage under the empire. For some discussion of the aims and processes of the *ague* festival, see Ryder 1969:172n5, 219–220 (especially for the human sacrifices) and Igbafe 1979:61. The narrator's hesitation in line 125, which Mr. Okoojii unfortunately (I think) forces him to correct in line 128, arises from the fact that the hunter does not quite wish to let his curious son know what the real problem is: he thinks the boy is still too young ("Keep on growing," he tells him, 120), and does not want him driven into precipitate acts of violence.

18. The original Igbo, *uzu na-akpu n'oyi-yii*, literally means "A smith that forges in mysterious circumstances." The smith figure in the world of African myth and religion has traditionally been credited with supernatural skill and powers and charged with making the weapons needed by the hero for the performance of extraordinary martial feats. For a comparative discussion of this phenomenon in African and Indo-European traditions, see Okpewho 1979:116–119.

19. *O na-ata a n'obi*: literally, "there was a tugging in his heart," the heart being traditionally understood as the seat of sensations like anger, fear, anxiety, etc.

20. *Aha, o bu nke n' gwa i?* Literally: "[You think] what I'm telling you [is all there is to it]?"

21. The narrator uses the Igbo word, *Obi*, rather than *Oba*, which is the proper Benin title. It should be noted that Igbuzo (Ibusa), the narrator's hometown, was a thoroughly republican community without a paramount head (see Okpewho 1983:62–63 for a tale explaining how this came about) until 1995, when Professor Louis Nwoboshi of Ibadan University was installed the first king under the auspices of the Delta State government.

22. *Njinji ejie,* was how I put it in the Igbo: literally, "total darkness would have ensued," with the root verb *ji-* meaning "to be dark or black."

23. The soft locution aptly dramatizes the emissary's combined embarrassment at the ease with which all twelve of them were subdued by one youngster and fear of possible penalty for failure.

24. It is generally believed in these parts that the second child to emerge in a twin birth is the "senior," since he or she has, as it were, sent the first one on to see what the world is like! The Yoruba name for the first twin born is "Taiwo" (implying the "look-out" child), and the second, who is considered the elder, "Kehinde" (i.e. the one who brings the rear). Hence the "senior" son in this story seems to be the one deciding who goes forward first to the fight. I have preferred "champion" to "hero" as a translation for *dike* in line 169 so as not to underplay the heroic merits of the "junior" son.

25. The pitch-blackness of the army might well be from the soldiers' going to war bare-bodied. Ling Roth tells us of the Bini infantry: "Common soldiers keep the upper part of their bodies naked, but from the hips downwards they wear a garment as fine as silk" (1972:126). However, Benin iconography frequently portrays soldiers as fully clad with protective tunics, charms, etc.: see, for instance, Pitt-Rivers 1968:45, 55, 67; Dark 1973: plate pp. 15, 16, 48. The emphasis on pitch-blackness here apparently suggests the soldiers have painted their faces with charcoal or other darkening stuff, to strike fear into the enemy: cf. line 190 of Simayi's story of the Benin-Ubulu war (Okpewho 1992:197).

26. There might seem to be a confusion in the locations of the twin and the invaders. But it appears the young man had first mysteriously appeared behind the army, thus cutting them off from possible retreat to Benin. As he proceeded to cut down those nearest to him, he sowed confusion among the rest, who now (we must assume) found their way somehow around the quandary and fled toward Benin (here, the Oba's palace).

27. The Igbo original is *kwi-kwi,* "no," a semi-ideophonic negative for *kwii* (see note 15 above), "yes." The "no" is, of course, the twins' refusal to heed their father's frantic plea that they cease their pursuit and slaughter of the Bini warriors.

28. That a hero like Beowulf is driven more by pity and concern for the distressed (especially in championing the cause of the Scylding Danes) probably says something about the interpolation of Christian doctrine on the old Germanic tradition.

29. Odogwu Okwuashi of Onicha-Ugbo has a ditty with which he sometimes prefaces his tales: *Adaigbo ewek' iwe mmadu,* "Ogwashi people [Adaigbo is their founding ancestor] are too full of anger." The statement may be read partly as a reflection of the fierce contests waged for some decades now between two ruling families in the town over its paramount chieftaincy, but partly also as a celebration of the heroic daring for which citizens of that town are fabled in their traditions.

30. The real warlord fights only when the going gets tough: compare the account given of *Ezomo* Ehenua of Benin in Bradbury 1973:256. Compare also the Fulani hero Silamaka who, on learning that the Bambara leader Da Monzon has sent a cavalry of 500 against him, laughs out jubilantly and says, "Da Monzon has at last begun to move!" (Ba and Kesteloot 1968:27). From the European

tradition, compare Roland's exuberant joy on hearing how vast the Saracen army is: "I thirst the more for the fray!" (Sayers 1937:Verse 1088).

31. The hunting profession enjoys fairly generous notice in the oral traditions of various West African societies. It plays a central role, for instance, in the epics of Sunjata (e.g. Niane 1965, Innes 1974, Johnson 1986) and Kambili (Bird 1974), as well as the folk poetry (e.g. Babalola 1966, Diabate 1970, Thoyer-Rozat 1978, Ajuwon 1982) and other narrative traditions (e.g. Herskovits 1958, Innes and Sidibe 1990). Okere tells us the "Igbo are not great hunters, but hunting is a traditional activity" (1983:83). Shaw considers hunting-gathering as prior to the more sedentary occupations like agriculture and stock-keeping, which "set up the conditions necessary for what is usually called 'civilization'" (1977a:93). Hopkins thinks rather that it is "more realistic to treat hunters as semi-specialists who were integrated with the farming community, rather than as antiquated survivors from a pre-historic, pre-agricultural age" (1973:43). If Shaw's evolutionist thesis is right, it may explain why hunting occupies a secondary place to yam cultivation in Igbo oral traditions. However, in addition to Ojiudu's story discussed here, I have another hunters' tale by him (about a hunter Ogadi's encounter with the forest ogre Nwankebeli) as well as one by Charles Simayi of Ubulu-Uno, which indicates that such tales are a feature of the narrative traditions of the west-Niger Igbo.

32. An interesting exception, of hunters unequipped with charms, has been recorded by Colin Turnbull among the Pygmies and the Ik of east-central Africa, communities "characterized by an almost complete lack of magic, witchcraft, or sorcery" (1968:91). These resources are, of course, usually prepared from materials like herbs, roots, and the barks of trees, the paucity of which in the arid environments of Turnbull's subjects may well explain why they have to rely on other tricks, e.g. simulating the prey so as to infiltrate its company and kill it, as it were, from within.

33. Higbie (1995) gives a rather interesting discussion of the symbolism of names in Homeric literature, with useful citations of cognate scholarship.

34. For further insights into the place of hunter folklore in Mande history and society, see Bulman 1990.

35. For an interesting study of the hunter as culture hero in another Nigerian group (the Igala), see Boston 1964.

36. Although they speak primarily of Yoruba mythic traditions, Barnes and Ben-Amos capture the essence of Ojiudu's story: "The iron sword of Ogun was perhaps his most meaningful symbol, for it condensed the twin meanings of aggression and civilization. It cleared the forest and built the house. More significantly, it vanquished the enemy and crowned the king" (1989:57). Herskovits (1958) also has interesting insights, from Dahomean mythology, on the hunter's place in medical history (217–218), the development of religious systems (237–238, 249–250), and the evolution of ethical values (250–251).

37. In another of Ohadike's testimonies, about the origins of the neighboring town of Asaba, we are told of its founder: "Nnebisi and his descendants were named 'Ochubanta ewelu ani' meaning that 'the hunter has taken possession of the land'" (1988:194).

38. Imiidi and Umuwai (mentioned later in this discussion) are two of the nine wards that make up Igbuzo town.

39. A reference to one of the historic monuments in Igbuzo relating to the people's fight against British colonial forces.

40. One of the heroes of Igbuzo's resistance to British colonial occupation of their town, evidently as part of the Ekumeku movement brilliantly treated by Ohadike (1991).

41. This is the best I can do in rendering Ojiudu's brilliant assonance, *k'eze k'ozo. Eze* is a red-capped chief, the topmost level attainable in the titled organization of the west-Niger Igbo; the *ozo* (also called *alo*) is the title taken, by any man with the necessary means, to mark the attainment of social distinction. Nzimiro (1972:22–28), Onwuejeogwu (1972a:19–24, 1972b:37, 1981:85–94) and Ohadike (1994:85–92) are among the most dependable sources of information on the structure of titled organizations among the Nri-Igbo groups, east and west of the Niger.

42. My major sources are Onwuejeogwu's *The Traditional Political System of Ibusa* (1972a) and Ohadike's (edited with R.N. Shain) *Jos Oral History and Literature Texts: Volume 6. Western Igbo* (1988). Onwuejeogwu is from the Ogboli segment of Igbuzo foundation, while Ohadike is from the Umejei segment. The latter, which includes testimonies from representative members of both the Ogboli (pp. 79–95) and Igbuzo (pp. 105–135) segments of the town, is particularly useful in revealing the partisan interests guiding contemporary social and political relations there. By far the most brilliant of these testimonies, in terms of rationalization as well as dramatic interest, are those given by Chiefs Ikpo, Ashinze, and Ashikodi, all (Umejei- or Isu-) Igbuzo men.

43. For detailed discussions of Nri ritual culture and its relation to political culture, see Afigbo 1981:31–67, Jeffreys 1935:346–354, Leonard 1968:30–40, Onwuejeogwu 1981:31–55, and Shaw 1977b:94–102. That the "divine" king of Nri superintended the functions of productivity credited to the principal divinity of this culture—*Ala*, the Earth goddess—and had little of the control over citizens' lives that we find in the Oba of Benin, is clear enough from these studies.

44. There have been two different accounts of the origin of the name "Igbuzo." One, encouraged if not originated by the Nri (Ogboli) segment of the town, has it that the name was originally given to the area settled by the Isu colonists which marked the staging-post on the journey from the settlements of the two Nri groups (at Ogboli and Ogwashi-Uku): "Igbuzo," by this account, thus stood for the *Igbo* (who lived) along the way *uzo* (see Onwuejeogwu 1972a: 10). An alternative account, clearly favored by Isu elements and sympathizers, claims that the name was an acknowledgment (even by the Nri elements) of the fact that the Isu colonists arrived in the area before the Nri: according to this account, "Igbuzo" is a corruption of the statement *I bu uzo*, you are the first (Ohadike 1988:106, 128). This may be counter to the account by Onwuejeogwu, himself an Ogboli-Igbuzo man, of Igbo movements, which places "the Nri-movement A.D. 900 to 1911; the Isu-movement between the 15th and 16th centuries" (1972a:6).

45. In his testimony, Ashinze claims the Benin forces had been led by the Oba himself, encamped somewhere within the environs of Igbuzo. The Oba and his men were routed across River Oboshi (which claimed many Bini troops), and in the course of his flight "the Oba dropped his *ada* (a cutlass and special symbol

of royalty)," which Ezechi picked up, consequently proclaiming himself king of Igbuzo. See Ohadike 1988:120–123.

46. *Founders* here suggests a bias in favor of the Isu element, i.e. the descendants of Umejei, who would seem to have dominated the social and political organization of Igbuzo since its foundations for as long as anyone may recall. The Nri, from whom Ogboli-Igbuzo descended, have been traditionally ruled by a priest-king. But if Nosike Ikpo is right in tracing the ancestral Isu to the Orlu rather than the Awka-Nri area (Ohadike 1988:110)—in a story he told me in December 1977, Ojiudu in fact identifies the town of origin as Isukwuato, much nearer Orlu—then we must set Umejei's hometown within the Igbo republican heartland.

Incidentally, as I write this, the paramount chieftaincy of Louis Nwoboshi, the Obuzo of Igbuzo, is being contested in the law courts. The reason, as I gathered during a visit to Igbuzo (July 1996), is that, although he had been appointed to play something of the role of the community's "spokesman," the Obuzo has proceeded to appropriate to himself articles of paramountcy or kingship. For a parallel account of change, in neighboring Asaba, from a paramount *Obi* to a system of multiple *eze* (red-capped chiefs), see Isichei 1961:515.

47. Mudimbe, discussing the relationship between myth and history in the context of social formations, makes the point that "they inhabit the present as discursive practices and as such operate as political ideologies, that is, as bodies of functional ideas and truths responding to the needs of a specific community and interacting with these needs" (1991:98).

48. See, for instance, the exchanges between Simayi and his accompanist Okondu Enyi on details of the former's narration of the Ezemu story (Okpewho 1992:371n22).

49. Renato Rosaldo's observation—that "questions of culture seem to touch a nerve because they quite quickly become anguished questions of identity" (1989:ix)—may help to explain the caution observed by Ojiudu Okeze in his mythical account of his people's social history.

50. "But the hunter legends are nevertheless unsatisfactory as historical records. There is something in their make-up which resists a literal interpretation and tends to bring historical inquiry to a full stop" (Boston 1964:117). I would hope that the sort of analysis I have done of Ojiudu's story should demonstrate the futility of "literal interpretation" that some old-fashioned, empiricist historians habitually look for in the oral traditions. The position generally taken on the function of history by French thinkers—such as Paul Ricoeur's, that history should hope not to "resuscitate" but to "reconstruct" (1961:222), or Foucault's, that history "is not to be understood as a compilation of factual successions or sequences as they may have occurred" (1973:219)—should perhaps serve as a needed object lesson. Hayden White (1973) has also stressed that whatever methods we adopt in accounting for the past are no more than "processes of selection and arrangement of data from unprocessed historical record in the interest of rendering that record more comprehensible to an audience of a particular kind" (5).

3. Male Manqué

1. For a detailed account and analysis of a case of exorcism—a renunciation, or "sweeping away"—of an evil destiny, see Fortes 1987:145–174.

2. The "bronze" heads from Benin that grace numerous museums across the world were originally commissioned for the altars erected to the Oba's ancestors in the palace, and were the focus of *ugie erha Oba* (festivals in honor of the Oba's ancestors). Some of the heads, however, are later copies of the concept. Some heads are also said to be memorials to Benin's victory over hostile communities, the heads of whose kings were subsequently cut off and brought to the Oba: see Egharevba's *Descriptive Catalogue of Benin Museum* (1969?), pp. 21, 25, and 26 and Ben-Amos 1995:45.

3. The (Asaba) Igbo word for the left hand is *aka ekpei*, which is probably related to the Bini word for leopard, *ekpen*. In Asaba a left-handed person is often jocularly branded *aka ekpei awolo*, "leopard-southpaw." Little children who show this tendency are often coerced to switch from left to right hand. We are even told that in Benin it "was forbidden to give an [ambidextrous man] a chieftaincy title" (Ebohon 1979:38).

4. Cf. also Dean 1983:33: "In general, the cult of the hand celebrates masculine aggressiveness, with particular reference to warfare and hunting."

5. "Use," Bradbury tells us, means poverty. The *u* is pronounced *oo* as in *moo* and the *e* as in *egg*. For further discussion of the Edo concept of the personality, with a version of the "Use" story—more recent than, but substantially similar to, Bradbury's—see Babatunde 1992: 125–159.

6. Bradbury's footnote: "The title means 'You cannot reach the world and then *hi*'—that is 'Your destiny is settled before you are born and you cannot change it.'"

7. A king in the first dynasty of the Benin kingdom, later superseded by the second dynasty, whose rulers have since borne the title Oba: see note 8 to chapter 1. Dan Ben-Amos has kindly reminded me that the word *ogiso* breaks down etymologically into *ogie* (ruler) and *so* (sky); hence, the idea of divine kingship in Benin predates her second dynasty inaugurated by the Ife theocracy.

8. On the problematic chronology of the reigns of Igodo and Ere—the latter of whom Igbafe (1979:5–6) considers the greatest king of the Ogiso period—see Adedeji 1989:75–77.

9. As may perhaps be expected, the Bini have often frowned at the derivation of their cherished traditions from Yorubaland. They have instead seen Ife itself as an ancient Bini colony dating from the exiled son (Ekaladerhan) of Ogiso Owodo, and Oranmiyan as the grandson of Ekaladerhan, sent by his father at the request of the Bini—in other words, a son come home to the land of his fathers. For this alternative account, see Ebohon 1972:6–7. For revisionist discussions of Benin-Ife relations, see also Ryder 1965, Akinola 1976, and Igbafe 1974: 6–7.

10. In a privately printed pamphlet (1954) with the title *The Origin of Benin*, J.U. Egharevba tells us (chapter 3, "Names of the City"): "The city has been known by four names respectively. It was first called 'Igodomigodo' and then 'Ile' in the days of Ogisos or kings of the first period of the Benin Empire. Oranmiyan changed it to 'Ile-Ibinu' the land of vexation, on account of its

abundant sacrifices, Oba Ewedo [called] it 'Ubini'" (page 8). The pamphlet has been reprinted in Egharevba 1973.

11. Bradbury (1973:42n) seems to question the correctness of this dating. An account which credits the introduction of brass works to a certain "Aham-mangiwa" who came to Benin with some white men in the reign of Oba Esigie, late fifteenth or early sixteenth century (Ben-Amos 1983:13), may thus bear out his doubts.

12. See Dean 1983:36. Fagg (1978:46) mentions the discovery of bronze castings at Udo, a village west of Benin which gave it a great deal of trouble, especially in the reign of Oba Esigie (see page 176 above), and "may have defied the Oba's ban on bronze casting for anyone but himself" and, as an older metropolis than Benin city, acted as the scene of much rivalry between the new monarchy and the traditional bureaucracy, *Uzama Nihiron.* The confrontation between the Oba and this bureaucracy is especially keen in his relations with their leader, the Iyase. "The sole right to argue with or censure the Oba in public was held to lie with the Town Chiefs and, more especially, with the *Iyase.* When one of them died, the Oba sent his men to claim his lower jaw, 'the jaw he had used to dispute with the Oba'. This act symbolized the ultimate supremacy of the king over the Edo [Bini]" (Bradbury 1973:69).

13. See also Kaplan 1981:79: "Because the Oba is the embodiment of the Bini people, his health is a reflection of the state of temporal and spiritual affairs."

14. Schaefer (1983:77) cites a report by an imperial officer, Captain John Adams, in which he records his impressions of the Benin monarch: "The King of Benin is fetische, and the principal object of adoration in his dominions. He occupies a higher post here than the Pope does in Catholic Europe; for he is not only God's vice-regent upon earth, but a god himself, whose subjects both obey and adore him as such."

15. We could read a dual-sex symbol here: the plantain is straight as a penis (masculine), and hollow as a womb (feminine).

16. These early Ijo connections with eastern Yoruba communities—which we remarked on in chapter 1—may to some extent have occasioned a mytho-linguistic conflation of the names "Ondo" and "Odudua" (the Yoruba supreme deity) into "Ododoa." The reptiles, especially crocodiles, are arguably also symbols of the water divinity Olokun, recognized by the Bini as next to the supreme God, Osanobua. For crocodiles as icons of the power of the Oba, see Chambers 1983:94.

17. For the full story, see Beier 1966:23–41.

18. That is, his tale, which was told by Okoojii, Ojiudu's musical accompanist, later on the same night as the story presented in chapter 2.

19. The original Igbo, *agidigwom,* is an ideophone denoting a resounding event.

20. The Igbo word for God, "Olisebuluwa," which bears obvious but inexpli-cable resemblance to the Bini "Osanobua," implies that He carries or holds (*bulu*) the world (*uwa*), presumably in His hands.

21. The low voice is either intended to strike a note of sadness, or else to indicate a hidden element that the young woman is too infatuated to observe.

22. The igbo word, *fucham,* is an ideophone suggesting something light or empty.

23. The narrator often tries hard to avoid the use of pornographic diction. My sister (Mrs. Arinze) and her children had retired indoors, but some other children from the neighborhood were still among the rapt audience of the performance.

24. Ideophone for the precipitate haste with which the tapper struggles to descend so as to break the news of what he saw. The palm tree is usually climbed by means of a tough, twisted rope—slung around the tree—on which the tapper balances himself. With a knife, he makes a notch under the palm branches and positions a gourd or bottle to catch the potent juice that flows throughout the night from the notch. This is the palmwine.

25. The tapper does not die, of course. But the picture of him "dragging up his head" is a graphic way of demonstrating the gross over-exertion of this busy-body, even in near-death.

26. The Igbo for "a proclamation was issued" is *ekwe* (a gong) *adaa* (came down, i.e. sounded), and this is the translation I have stuck to whenever such a phrase occurs.

27. The narrator raises his voice here, both to indicate the woman's intense feeling about the boy's grave predicament and to underscore the momentous nature of the steps she is about to take to get him out of it.

28. The Igbo for "piece" (*nga*) is perhaps more commonly used in Okoojii's Igbuzo dialect of Igbo than in Asaba, Arinze's hometown only seven miles away from Igbuzo. *Nga* means piece as a measurement of length or distance covered—in other words, a "stretch"—and is etymologically derived from the root-verb *gaa* (to go). Thus, to say you have done something *ofu nga* (once) means you have done it in one "move."

29. *Tafufufu* is an ideophone for the charging force of the flames issuing from the cutlass.

30. *Mma-ekwu*: "Broad-knife" is the best I can do for a translation. This is a short and triangular knife used traditionally for peeling yams and other tubers, before the advent of the more common long-bladed knife. The spell, contained in the proverb that the broad-knife "only lies on one side," is to ensure that the sleeper—and his wife, no doubt—does not stir or turn around during the period of the metaphysical journey.

31. This talisman (*nzuzu*) is an all-purpose charm, frequently contained in a little calabash vial (*onunu*)—the kind we saw the diviner give to the farmer in Bradbury's Bini story above—and designed to protect the wielder from mishaps or provide whatever (s)he may need at any moment. For instance, it could be used to decide the right path to follow at a crossroads or, as further on in this story, to produce objects (like kolanuts) demanded of him/her.

32. The old woman has just charmed both the young man and his wife with the broad-knife. The broad-knife will assume the material form of the man, leaving the princess, who will be fast asleep, in the comforting assurance that her man is beside her. The young man will, meanwhile, be off on a metaphysical journey to spiritland, where he will come face to face with those responsible for his not having a penis.

33. That is, in the world before this one.

34. The formal Igbo blessing—*I jee, i naa*—literally means, "As you go forth, so may you return." See line 258 below.

35. Okoojii has now been using a variety of terms for the hero's weapon. *Mma* (128) is the common word for a cutlass; *agbanashi* (177)—"the inescapable"—is a figurative name for the more combat-oriented variant; and *akili* (213) means something like "the router." These poetic substitutes are evidently meant to evoke the appropriate heroic aura around the young man who has been prepared by the old woman for "war."

36. There is a slight but interesting lexical difference in the two expressions of surprise by Arinze and the narrator. Arinze's original Igbo statement is, *Egwu a ni-di atu a?*: Shouldn't he—or, oughtn't he to (*ni*)—be afraid? while Okoojii's is *Egwu a-di atuzi i?*: Are you no longer (*zi*) afraid? God should of course command awe or respect from a lesser figure, however well-endowed; but this young man seems to have lost his fear either from an overconfident reliance on the mystical resources he is wielding or because he is driven by a rather aggressive feeling of being wronged.

37. Compare Bradbury's third Bini story above ("Ehi-will-enrich-me") for the phallic symbolism of the plantain. In Yoruba pornographic folklore, a roasted plantain is credited with the power of causing penile erection (*gb'oko le*).

38. White chalk, used mostly for ritual purposes, is made from (clayey) kaolin, which being pliable can be moulded in any kind of shape. Here, the narrator indicates a cylindrical shape which approximates the physiognomy of the penis.

39. The raised tone both indicates a flashback and a change of scene. We should recall that the young man, who has been operating in the spiritual world, is the metaphysical form of the figure lying beside the princess on a bed, in the shape of a broad-knife. The princess herself is under a spell, and so does not know what has been happening.

40. This ideophone was earlier used (90) to indicate the forceful haste with which the palmwine tapper landed his leg on the climbing rope in his anxiety to report the young man's asexuality to the Oba. Here, it captures the force with which the young man eagerly puts his new-won organ to work. Also, as in the tapper's action, the *-chii* part is intended to capture a frictional sound: of leg scraping against rope, of penis grazing the pubic hair on its way into the vagina.

41. *Awutoa* (stomped in) aptly captures the bold self-assurance with which the young man steps in to expose his proud new physique, a feeling further driven home by the elaborate and suspenseful drama of his self-revelation.

42. The guards are reminding the Oba about the palmwine tapper's oath, that if he was proved wrong about the young man's manhood he should be executed, and the Oba is all too glad to have them do their usual job. They need no instructions from him, when the man called the doom upon himself! I have been unable to ascertain the etymology of the word for guards (*idoloma*) used here by Okoojii and by Okafor Odagwue in his tale (see above, page 112, line 264). However, in *The Ozidi Saga* (Clark-Bekederemo 1991:102), the word *odeleowei* is used for a warrior's deputy; Clark-Bekederemo, who thinks the word a conflation of an English word ("orderly") and an Ijo (*owei*, man), translates it as "orderly-man" (note 3, page 156). I suspect *idoloma* is, like *odeleowei*, a loanword emanating from the British colonial military vocabulary.

43. Arinze, as may be observed, frequently interjects questions and comments into the narrations of our various artists. Quite often he is tolerated, even indulged, but on one occasion he is politely cautioned by Simayi (in one of our

1981 recordings), "Please do not ruin my tale!" In the present instance, Okoojii is being rather polite in letting Arinze know he would rather not be distracted. Really, in most of these interventions, Arinze is driven partly by the desire to generate a warm, interactive atmosphere between narrator and audience and partly by his anxiety that I (a university professor, thought to have considerably lost touch with rural culture) should understand what is going on as much as possible.

44. Apparently, the narrator is grateful to his friend, Ojiudu Okeze, both for providing musical support (the thumb piano) for the narrative performance and for introducing him to me and thus bringing him some recognition.

45. In his *Descriptive Catalogue of Benin Museum* (1969:45–46), Egharevba lists the *akpata* and the *asologun* as musical instruments played by Bini and other Edo peoples in narrative and other ludic contexts (he credits the Ora and Ishan peoples as more proficient in the latter instrument). He also mentions the institutionalized place of, as well as taboo against, the instrument in the court. Although players of the instrument are excluded from the court and traditional titles, several Benin commemorative bronze plaques, recorded in Luschan (1919) and other sources, show an *akpata* player as part of a group of figures surrounding the Oba and other high chiefs. His presence may, as I believe Ben-Amos tries to suggest (1975:42ff), be seen as a lingering fossil of the old rural culture—as in Udo, where many of the surviving artworks were discovered by archaeologists—on which an alien (Yoruba-derived) monarchical structure had been superimposed.

46. Since he became a titled chief in his village, my friend Charles Simayi of Ubulu-Uno no longer does the sort of public performances—e.g., with his music group on festive occasions—he used to do in the past. But he occasionally honors requests for command performances of his tales to musical accompaniment, as he did for us in 1993 with his tale of the faithless mystic, Idabo. Okafor Odagwue of Idumuje-Uno, himself the Ozoma of his town, has not ceased performing on command and other occasions since he took his own title.

47. Naturally, these tales involving sexuality and levels of consciousness are easy grist for Freudian-style interpretation. See, for instance, Herskovits 1958 and Horton 1961.

48. See Bremond 1977 for a rather interesting structural-transformational discussion of a type of folktales in which courteous or discreet characters come into good fortune while reckless or misguided characters fail, by a process of "impossible imitation," to win the same fortune.

49. For an account of the formal components of *ikenga* among the Igbo, see Vogel 1974:3–7.

50. On *eke*, see also Meek 1937:55 and Cole 1982:53.

51. For instance, both Arinze (1970:15) and Onwuejeogwu (1981:33) seem to take seriously the idea that the personal *chi* is a portion of the essence of *Chukwu*. Our narrator Okoojii himself, like many of his contemporaries in a society circumscribed by Western culture, obviously sees God (*Olisebuluwa* = *Chukwu*) as Creator, although his story is based on the concept of a "choice" negotiated with such a figure. For an interesting discussion of the influence of Western concepts on African religious thought, see Horton 1993:161–193.

52. Other interesting insights on the concept of *chi* may be found in Nwoga

1984 (from religious and literary perspectives) and Ogunyemi 1996:35–45 (a very challenging feminist analysis).

53. In demanding the kolanut of the young man, both the gateman and the *chi* use rather polite diction. The original Igbo word for "let's have" (172 and 200) is *wete-kee*, the *kee* being a mollifying suffix that takes the edge out of the imperative *wete* (bring), so that the demand may be translated, "Do, bring . . ." Besides apologizing (like the gateman and the *chi*) for the plight of the young man on earth, God also uses the same polite form of request—"Do, bring" (*wete-kee*), 235—when he calls for the stick of plantain with which he wishes to mould the young man's penis. These manipulations of narrative diction—as well as adjustment of voice and facial expression accompanying the words—no doubt bear witness to the artistic skill of the late Mr. James Okoojii. He was a narrator with a clear tenor voice, a sense of timing and control of the constituent moments of his tales, and, like his friend Mr. Ojiudu Okeze, a thorough gentleman.

54. On God and the protective divinities (like *chi*) being located in the upper realms, while the shades of the departed are located in the lower earth (Igbo *ani mmo*), see Achebe 1975:160–162; cf. Arinze 1970:12–13 and Fortes 1987: 172.

55. The image of the old woman who saves the young man from his predicament is very central to this story; but I am reserving discussion of it for the next chapter, where I explore its full political as well as mythical implications.

56. Adediran (1991) sees Benin imperialism in eastern Yorubaland as a "pleasant" one. Even if a case can be made for Benin as an imperial power over the west-Niger Igbo, I should hope that my analysis of the image of the Oba in this chapter points in a somewhat different direction from Adediran's position. I particularly question the view that Benin's record "demonstrates that imperial rule could be tolerable to subject peoples irrespective of their cultural identity" (92)!

4. The Old Woman on the Outskirts

1. There is a cluster of motifs around the figure of the old woman who helps various figures in difficult circumstances, the most relevant to our tales being Motifs N825.3, Old Woman Helper, and H1233.1.1, Old Woman Helps on Quest.

2. Simayi uses the phrase *ite-aka-elu-oshu*, which literally translates "a pot with a vagina that cannot be plumbed": in other words, a pot whose bottom can hardly be reached. The reference is to the huge, heavy cast-iron pots used in this part of the country for mass cooking. Distortions in sound at certain points in the recording of this tale have discouraged me from attempting the typographic differentiations I have done with the other tales in this book.

3. Meaning, "There, I knew it!" The poor, mistreated wife had reason enough to suspect her mates never meant her any good, and that the strange object in her portion of the food was their evil doing.

4. *Chogai* is an ideophone for the sound of an object piercing into a soft mass. *Vuuu* is the sound of an object in rapid flight.

5. *Mbosi wa tu im' ita k' wa ji amu a.* This is a formula used by raconteurs in this

region either for abbreviating a tale or for suggesting the rapid development of events. Cf. line 109 of Ojiudu Okeze's tale, p. 42.

6. These ideophones denote excessive but worthless effort.

7. Ideophone for the heaviness or richness of the dishes set out by the women.

8. Ideophone indicates something raw and shoddily cooked.

9. "Ozoma," a traditional title, is a variant of the Benin "ezomo," equivalent to the Chief of Staff in Western military culture (cf. Ryder 1969:4, 20, 177; Igbafe 1979:5, 26, 90). In an interview held with him after his narrative performances on this day, Okafor traced the origins of his village, Idumuje-Uno, and the etymology of its name, to Benin ("Idu"). Although the military role of the *ozoma* may never have paralleled that of the *ezomo* in the militaristic organization of the old Benin kingdom, what Okafor said in the interview does echo what is known of the privileged position of the *ezomo* in Benin: "No candidate for a chieftaincy here gets to our *Obi* without going through me." Okafor has appeared in narrative performances at local and larger cultural festivals, which also featured the likes of Odogwu Okwuashi Nwaniani of Onicha-Ugbo (see Okpewho 1992: 47, 342–44 and chapter 5 below). "Odagwue" is a nickname denoting the "resounding" impact of Okafor's performances.

10. One of the west-Igbo local government areas of the present Delta State. The other three are Oshimili (with Asaba as its headquarters as well as state capital), Ndokwa, and Ika. Ubulu-Uno, Charles Simayi's village, is also in Aniocha local government area. Separated by some fifteen miles from each other, Idumuje-Uno and Ubulu-Uno trace distinct origins. While Idumuje-Uno, one of the Eze Chima group of communities, claims Benin sources, Ubulu-Uno and its sister community Ubulu-Uku claim to have been founded by two hunter brothers (Aniobodo and Ezemu) who migrated from somewhere in today's Ndokwa local government area.

11. The Ogiso was a king of the first dynasty of the Benin kingdom, from about the tenth to the twelfth century A.D., while the Oba (the present title) represents the second dynasty, starting from about 1170 A.D. (Egharevba 1968: 1–6). But the communities which suffered unrelentingly from the militarism of Old Benin seldom drew a line between one reign of terror and another, so that in their folk memory the two kinds of rulers are frequently interchangeable.

12. As Simayi frequently does in his stories, Okafor uses the ideophones *tiiii* (connoting the long distance covered), and *pelele* (which conveys the idea of landing "pat" at a point): see line 77 below.

13. On the outskirts of the city, to the east.

14. The New Yam Festival among the Western Igbo has traditionally taken place around September, and this is about the same period when the Oba of Benin celebrates the *ague* festival. It has often been said that this is the most dangerous period for non-indegenes to be within Benin and environs, for the human sacrifices carried out during *ague* are done with them (hence the capture of Oye) and not with Benin citizens (this is taboo). The old woman is thus surprised to see the young man in Benin at this time. For some discussion of the aims and processes of the *ague* festival, see Ryder 1969:172n5, 219–220 (especially for the human sacrifices) and Igbafe 1979:61.

15. *Onwu egbu onye mbosi ndu aso a*, in the Igbo. It is one of the standard salutes of the Obas of Benin (Ebohon 1979:43), although we also find it used as a salute

for various spiritual figures in Igboland (see Achebe 1958:66, 75). Obas of Benin—Akenzua II and the present Erediauwa I included—are also greeted *Uku-akpolokpolo*, which may have derived, thanks to the fabled descent of the present dynasty from Ife, from the Yoruba words for *iku* (death) and *opolopo* (many, multitudes) and been intended to impress upon the people the stupendous terror of royalty. The connection with "death" is clearly implied in the salute. In his poem "Hands Over Head," from the collection *A Decade of Tongues* (1965), Clark obviously suggests translating "Okuakpolokpolo" as "He who asks for a hundred human heads today and gets them," and I believe it is the same word that Paula Ben-Amos has translated as "Death, Great One" (1983:51). However, Ebohon's translation for the word is "The mighty that rules" (1979:42).

16. *Ushio*, one of the tools wielded by diviners. It is essentially a wooden (sometimes metal) staff with a stringed bunch of cowrie shells tied just under the top and producing a rattling sound when shaken by the diviner in a divination séance.

17. The sound of their stampede.

18. *Omel'ije* literally means the cause or maker (*omelu*) of all journeys (*ije*), in other words, the origin of all endeavors or undertakings. The epithet indicates not only the literal function of the smith in making the instruments used in a wide variety of occupations (farming, hunting, warfare, cooking, etc.) but indeed to the spiritual powers traditionally attributed to such seminal artistry. See further Okpewho 1979:116–119. For the close kinship between smith and diviner in traditional religious thought, see line 394.

19. The Igbo word used here for the diviner is *ogbu-ebunu*, literally "killer (i.e. slaughterer) of the ram," one of the highly prized animals sacrificed to major traditional divinities like Amadioha (Thunder) and Anyanwu (Sun): see Arinze 1970:81–83. See also Jeffreys 1954:36, Onwuejeogwu 1981:31–34 for Anyanwu as central to Nri religion. I am not sure, however, to what extent the connection between the ram and the sun supports Jeffreys's Egyptianist theory (1954:39–40) about Igbo religious culture.

20. For further discussion on the relationship between music and narration, see Okpewho 1979:57–66 and 1983:93–96.

21. The following is a relevant extract from our interview with Okafor: *What clubs do you belong to and why?* I belong to the club of elders known as Ikpala. I belong to the club of diviner-physicians known as Dibie. I belong to the club of smiths known as Uzu. I am a member of these clubs because I am a titled man of the town. *What are the qualifications for membership of these cults and your roles in them?* Being a titled man of the land, being a tested and renowned diviner-physician of the land, and being a famed dancer, drummer, flutist, and story-teller in the community are the special qualifications. My role in the meeting of elders, Ikpala, is blowing the trumpet to summon meetings. For the club of diviner-physicians, I preside over the meetings as their leader. I am only a member of the club of smiths.

22. Evidently, this consideration qualifies the two tales to be classified as "mythic legends" according the system that I outlined in Okpewho 1983:59–67. For although no Benin Oba is specified in either tale, the narrator's mind is operating against a historical backcloth admittedly frayed by time and interest, among other factors.

23. This is a widespread motif in African narrative traditions, a good example

of which may be found in some versions of the Mwindo tale recorded by Biebuyck and his assistants among the Banyanga of Zaire (see especially Biebuyck 1978). See also Egharevba 1968:2–3 on the plot by Ogiso Owodo's wives against Ekaladerhan, the king's only son.

24. This is the official recognition of the young man as heir apparent, *edaiken*. In customs relating to succession to the Benin monarchy, the heir apparent would be apportioned his own quarters in a section of Benin beyond the Oba's palace. Here he would live until the Oba had died and the prince had begun the processes that would formally confirm him as the new king. For these customs, see Egharevba 1968:74.

25. Although the nurturing role of mother is foregrounded in Simayi's representation of the despised wife, I believe there is subtle suggestion, especially in the images of the old women in the stories by both narrators, of an intrinsic mystical power in womanhood which is transferred to heroes destined to play leading roles in their societies. This idea is given some emphasis in one of the tales by Odogwu Okwuashi that I discuss in chapter 5 below.

26. We will recall that the Ubulu king, Ezemu, goes to Benin in response to the call for healers to save the incumbent Oba from dying, like his predecessors, shortly after coronation (see chapter 1, pp. 17–18). For similarities between the Ezemu story and Okafor Odagwue's story of the rescue of Oye, with respect to the testing of these ritualists (i.e., stabbing the earth beneath the Oba's feet), see Okpewho 1992:193–194 (lines 41–56). Among the Ubulu, in fact, Ezemu is something of a culture hero to whom various aspects of their ritual traditions are attributed. For a story of Ezemu's rescue of a (ritual) mother, similar in many respects to Okafor's story of Oye, see Dibia 1990:219–226. For the west-Niger Igbo as ritualists in the service of the Benin monarchy and generally as itinerant professionals, see Ohadike 1994:21–23, 53–54. See also Ebohon 1972:84–90.

27. In the Ezemu story told by Simayi, there is an especially impressive portrait of the conciliatory wisdom and sheer civilized fair-dealing whereby the Oba of Benin—counselled by a diviner—and Ezemu settle their differences after a long, drawn-out war (Okpewho 1992:198–200).

28. *Onye ndidi na-eli azu ukpoo*, literally, "The patient person eats the fish from the hook."

29. Charles Simayi, himself a diviner-physician, has a story in my collection about such a professional, by name Idabor, betraying the trust of fellow practitioners who innocently give him shelter while he conducts his trade in a manner that puts the reputation of his hosts in jeopardy. For an interesting study of a shaman's empathic portrait of a fellow practitioner in his stories, see Oxford 1992.

30. On the subject of liminality in cultural as well as ritual life, see especially Turner 1967 and 1977.

31. The old woman is portrayed throughout by Simayi as someone from the spirit world, but that is simply what Benin represents in the mythical imagination of these narrators: in Clark-Bekederemo's words, "the embodiment of all that is distant and mysterious, the empire of improbable happenings that together with the world of spirits help to explain the events of their own lives" (1991:xxxvii).

32. Paula Ben-Amos (1983c:79–80) cites evidence from both her fieldwork

and Olfert Dapper's seventeenth-century account (quoted by Ling Roth) that vividly illustrates this isolation of the *iyoba* (Queen Mother). Ebohon (1972:30–33) provides an elaborate account of the exiling of this figure and of the misogynist backgrounds to the exclusion of women from Benin rule (18–19).

33. See Drake 1969 for differences between the Freudian and Jungian schools on this matter.

34. The Igbo of Asaba have a rather graphic way of illustrating the stubborn personal pride and independence—even in the face of material dependency—for which they are known. If anyone brings it home to you that they are superior to you, you should ask them, "Do you feed me?" If the answer is still yes, you should further ask, "Is that all?"!

35. For further insights into the role of females and female organizations in western Igbo societies, see Amadiume 1981; Dibia 1990:143–148, 212–237; Isichei 1991; and Ohadike 1994:90–94, 204–207.

36. A sentiment by no means peculiar to the Igbo. Compare one of the lyric codas in *The Ozidi Saga* of the Ijo: "Who has no husband is a rafter tree in the bush. . . ." (Clark-Bekederemo 1991:267–268). Amadiume's and Okonjo's arguments about women's roles and privileges in traditional Igbo society should perhaps be put in the wider context of theories about the antecedence of matriarchy in human society. The concept, classically treated by J.-J. Bachofen in his study of "motherright," is very much in the foreground of Cheikh Anta Diop's reconstruction of Black Africa's cultural history in *The Cultural Unity of Negro Africa* (1962). Amadiume utilizes this work in her own book *Afrikan Matriarchal Foundations* (1981), "Dedicated to Cheikh Anta Diop—*Ebunu ji isi eje ogu*—Brave ram who fights with his head." Nsugbe (1974) is an interesting study of Ohafia society, a matrilineal exception to the general pattern of patriliny today among the Igbo: which probably explains why among them "there are no carved *ikenga*" (Boston 1977:50), the male icon of entrepreneurial success (see chapter 3 above).

37. Compare Sudarkasa 1981:51 and Ohadike 1994:178–179, 226 for marginalization of women in the combined spheres of politics and economy under colonialism. See also Ottenberg 1959. Special tribute should, however, be paid to notable female entrepreneurs, especially among the riverine Igbo, in the new dispensation. For a portrait of Omu Okwei of Ossomari, see Ekejiuba 1967.

38. See Green 1964:201–202. I have tried to give more accurate translations to the Igbo text than those by Green guided, we may be sure, by Victorian prudery. Forde and Jones have observed this sort of collective action as characteristic of women's associations in Igboland generally, whereby they "secure their demands by collective public demonstrations, including ridicule, satirical singing and dancing, and group strikes" (1950:21). Judith van Allen describes this form of activity as "sitting on a man," using it to characterize the phenomenon of the Aba Women's War. As a young boy in Asaba, I once witnessed a group of women in our quarter (Umuaji) chanting songs and baring their behinds at the front door of a nonnative herbalist who had done something they strongly disapproved of: the message of their action was that the man should leave the community forthwith. I cannot quite recall what the man had done. What I do vividly remember is my mother giving me a good hiding on the backside, because one of my aunts who had taken part in the baring action reported seeing me at the scene.

39. Compare Green 1964:212 and 214 for similar cases of insubordination in Agbaja.

40. For detailed accounts of this historic action, see especially Perham 1937: 202–212 (= Leith-Ross 1939:23–39), Onwuteaka 1965, Afigbo 1972:207–248, van Allen 1976, Nwabara 1977:181–200, and Mba 1982:73–97. For an earlier protest action—the Nwaobiala movement of 1925—by a women's dance society, see Mba 1982:68–72.

5. The Singer in the Tale

1. Lani Guinier has recently made the same case in urging a reorientation in the training of female lawyers as against their male counterparts. In conversational situations, she says, many women "participate only after listening to what others are saying. They see conversation as a way of collaborating to synthesize information rather than competing to perform or to win" (1997:15).

2. Of the large number of feminist studies of African oral and written literature that have appeared in recent years, I am impressed by the work of two authors in particular, because of the convincing authority with which they treat their subjects. Karin Barber's study (1991) of the tradition of female praise poetry in the Yoruba town of Okuku is the work of a foreigner who lived so long among her hosts that she became practically one of them. I myself watched her on Oyo State (Nigeria) television playing roles in the Oyin Adejobi folk theater—some of whose works she has recently published (Barber and Ogundijo 1994)—and doing so in such brilliant Yoruba that after a while one learnt to forget she was not even an African. Although some of her deconstructionist strategy gives me a few problems, I deeply trust and respect the empathy and understanding she brings to her study of her female Yoruba subjects. Chikwenye Okonjo Ogunyemi (1993, 1996) has also brought to the analysis of African and Afro-diasporic women's writing such a well-grounded understanding of Nigerian cultures (especially her native Igbo and her marital Yoruba) that she has pretty much constructed for her field a vernacular theory every bit as stimulating as what "Skip" Gates has done (1988) for Afro-American literature. Her scholarship recommends itself equally to male and female readers, especially because she is inclined to explore the complementary roles of men and women in culture and society.

3. In a "Rebuttal" which appears in his latest, posthumous book (1995:187–202), Lord took care to dissociate himself from the "narrow elitism . . . nothing short of perversity" which has led scholars like Eric Havelock to place the "Homeric governing class" culturally above the unlettered "peasantry" to which many an unlettered oral artist, like the Serbo-Croatian epic singers, belong.

4. Lord's "Rebuttal" begins by identifying three classes of scholars on oral culture or the "oral theory," placing Jack Goody with Eric Havelock, Walter Ong, and others in the first class of "philosophers" (psychologists, sociologists, and the like) of whom he says: "Their primary concerns are the illiterate and the preliterate, or nonliterate, and literate societies, and the 'oral mind.' Although they often give some attention to 'literature,' they are not primarily concerned with the more limited problems of composition and transmission—or, as I think I prefer, learning and performing—which are the focus of what I think of as

the first stage, as it were, of the 'oral theory'" (1995:188). I would include, in this group, Robin Horton in his comparison of African and Western cognitive systems (1967).

5. See Isichei 1973:682 for women as storytellers in Asaba.

6. Harold Scheub has been particularly privileged in coming in contact with, and giving full attention to (e.g., 1975, 1992), a narrative tradition dominated as much by female artists as Ropo Sekoni has claimed for the (Ondo) Yoruba (1994a, 1994b). Opland follows Scheub in identifying the Xhosa narrative (*ntsomi*) as an exclusively female province, while the tradition of court poetry is a male preserve (1995:162).

7. Some of her loud words (transcribed in CAPS) may be attributed to her anxiety to be heard aright, which in itself indicates the details thereof must be important to her.

8. "So" was said in English, as also on lines 12 and 176. Educated up to teacher training college, Christy used English for the following other words in this story: "choose" (line 21), "like" (23, 29, 37), "intelligent" (35), "that girl" (48, 56; "against that girl," 82), "the girl" (50, after Arinze in 49), "jolly" (166, as pidgin for "enjoy oneself"), "more" (183, after Arinze in 182), "confess" (227). Arinze, a retired teacher, frequently uses English in his own interventions (e.g, the whole of lines 51 and 236), in part because he realizes he is dealing with a narrator who has had some education. He also uses the word "okay" as is.

9. That is, the Oba had only girls—in this case, one from each wife.

10. This is Madam Mokogwu, who had earlier narrated a version of the "Omalingwo" story.

11. The loud tone was meant to introduce the Oba's response, either in his characteristic imperiousness or from excitement at the prospect of having a rich son-in-law. But evidently Christy realized she had not quite completed the suitor's requests, so she reverted to normal tone.

12. In many traditional African societies, a young man first expresses his interest in a young woman with an initial visit. Her family then undertakes to research the suitor's background, and if there are no serious obstacles to the proposed union, the young man may then proceed with his next move. In this, the young man is accompanied by chosen members of his family, bringing along kegs of wine and other traditional items of entertainment. Achebe's *Things Fall Apart* and Flora Nwapa's *Efuru* (1966) are good references for procedures of this kind. But, as we shall see later in this chapter, matters may not be quite so straightforward in the palace of the Oba of Benin.

13. This is the first time we are learning that the young woman's mother had died from being fed scraps of left-over food. She hadn't been poisoned, Christy told me (in our discussion on July 9, 1996): she just died from under-nourishment.

14. Notice the changes in tone from loud to soft. The girl's return marks a critical moment, fraught with anxiety; the sick man, however, is calling the girl quietly aside, so as not to be caught informing against the king and queen.

15. The narrator's manual histrionics are meant to signify the girl's determined act of summarily disposing of a temptation that she had almost fallen for.

16. I have translated Christy's *ofuludi*—literally, the one most fitting to her husband—as "favored mate" to signify that the queen was a perfect match, socially and otherwise, for the king.

17. Arinze is here observing the similarities between the mistreated girl in this story and the young man in "Omalingwo" (the castaway son of a despised wife of an Oba, who later returns to the palace to recover his position as heir apparent), a version of which Christy had narrated earlier.

18. Arinze, a retired teacher, is being his old pedagogic self in orchestrating the audience's applause for a story well told.

19. Benin stories of legendary females like Emotan and Igbaghon are, of course, often told by male narrators. But this may be largely because these figures have a central role in the history of struggles for monarchical power centered essentially around princes. Azuonye has also found in the repertoire of the Ohafia narrator, Kaalu Igirigiri, a tale about a heroine who goes to war to rescue her husband from enemy territory (1990:68–69).

Incidentally, Osoba does not record the name of the narrator of the story of "The Beautiful Princess" (1993:66–73), a feminist variant of Simayi's story of the castaway who returns to identify its mother in the royal household. In his introduction to the "folktales" in this collection (1), he pays general tribute to the "men and women who had acquired a life time of wisdom" in African oral traditions; but it is equally arguable that that story is the product of a female narrator's adjustment of the tradition.

Conversely, female narrators do also have male protagonists in their tales. An example is the story of Omalingwo, a version of Simayi's story in chapter 4. But it is interesting that, whereas in his story the castaway child is cast in very masculine imagery, in the version told by Christy (and another woman, Madam Mokogwu) there is a tendency to highlight the somewhat effeminate handsomeness of the boy. The name Omalingwo, which Simayi never calls the boy, may etymologically be broken down to two component ideas: *oma*, for beauty, and *ngwo*, for suppleness or flexibility.

20. In my novel *The Victims* (1970), I present a situation in which a lack of stable control by the husband spells doom for his family of two wives and their children. Falade also urges a link between the dispositions of co-wives and the role of the husband they share (1963:225).

21. In his analysis of the Tshimshian "Story of Asdiwal," Lévi-Strauss (1977: 146–197) abjures the vogue of functionalist interpretation by seeing the story in terms not so much of the hunting and fishing life, which it projects on the surface, as of a confrontation in this culture between ideas of lineage and of residence. "The myth is certainly related to the given facts," he says in defense of his analysis, "but not as a *representation* of them. The relationship is of a dialectical kind, and the institutions described in the myths can be the very opposite of the real situation."

22. I have called Arinze Christy's "brother-in-law," which is what he is by a strictly European definition. However, in traditional Asaba affinal etiquette, she would consider herself his wife by virtue of being married to his brother. Given the subtle stresses we have pointed to in her marriage, could Christy have been a bit impatient that, in his frequent interventions, Arinze was being unduly "magisterial" toward her? If this is at all true, then there is a stronger element of confrontation than of camaraderie in the exchanges between them.

23. This is the term used for the detailed funeral obsequies following the interment of the deceased—a particularly expensive affair. My mother died in

1956, when I was in high school, and was laid to rest by my uncles. When I came of age and had the means, I was obliged to do the detailed rites, which I finally accomplished in April 1984.

24. Like Ojiudu Okeze, Odogwu headed a performance group in Jos (Northern Nigeria) in the fifties. He claimed not to have known Ojiudu, but mentioned Eke Momah of Ubulu-Uku—popularly known as "M & B" (an early brand of analgesic manufactured by May and Baker)—as one of his contemporaries in Jos in the practice.

25. A prominent figure in this village is Chief Demas Nwoko, a distinguished Nigerian artist and architect. An early member (with Nigerian writers like Chinua Achebe, the late Christopher Okigbo, Wole Soyinka, and J.P. Clark [-Bekederemo]) of the Mbari Cultural Centre under the directorship of the German Ulli Beier, Nwoko was then (the 1960s and '70s) lecturer in design at Ibadan University's Department of Theatre Arts. He is also well known as the builder of notable landmarks like the Dominican Seminary at Ibadan and the (Edo) State Cultural Complex in Benin. Since retiring early to his village, he has remained a committed patron of traditional arts and organized periodic competitions in the various forms. For generous tributes and references to Nwoko's work and contributions to the development of theater and culture in Nigeria and Africa, see especially Graham-White 1974:113, 152; Banham 1976:5, 14; Banham et al 1994:88; Beier 1981:328; Kerr 1995:95; Ogunbiyi 1981:338; Wren 1991:110; Gibbs 1993:237. For the artist's own thoughts on his craft, see Nwoko 1970:49–75.

26. Okafor Odagwue of Idumuje-Uno (one of the narrators in chapter 4 above) has told my brother-in-law Patrick Arinze of an experience he once had with Odogwu in one of the cultural events staged in Idumuje-Ugboko. Okafor had brought his group along and thought to share with Odogwu the booth the latter had set up for his own group. Odogwu told him to go set up his own. Although a man of the people, Odogwu apparently drew a polite line between himself and local yokels like Okafor who saw themselves as his professional rivals.

27. For a discussion of these, see Innes 1974:17–24 and Okpewho 1992:130–135.

28. The two stories treated below were recorded by me at about 7 P.M. on September 9, 1981. Accompanying me were my brother-in-law, Patrick Arinze, and his friend Ignatius Osadebe of Ubulu-Uno, who introduced Odogwu to us. The recording took place in the living room of Odogwu's family house in Idumudiagbo quarters of Onicha-Ugbo. Besides Odogwu and the three players accompanying him, there were roughly twenty other people in the audience, mainly the artist's extended family and neighbors.

29. This is the phrase used for the desperate snapping motions of the mouth that precede the final slump of the head at death.

30. One of the principal court officials, a kind of "prime minister" to the Oba. In his booklet *Benin Titles* (reprinted in Egharevba 1973), Egharevba cites the office as created by Oba Ewedo but elevated to the headship of the Executive Council (*eghaevbonore*) by Oba Ewuare. A *Concise Lives of the Famous Iyases of Benin*, also reprinted in Egharevba 1973, makes rather interesting reading.

31. Here Odogwu evokes the image of a townsman who is said to be in the

habit of intoning (in English) "And then, and then, how you are, and then, and then . . . " to introduce a momentous issue.

32. This proverb refers to the habit of mice eating away at food items (e.g., smoked meat or fish) in such places as the rafter. The child implies that even the smallest citizen such as himself has his own rights.

33. Throughout the entire narration, Odogwu and his accompanists inter-ject choral interludes at periodic intervals. The songs deal with a variety of subjects of social relevance, but most end with an idiomatic line, "The cocoyam (*akasi*) has become a porridge (*awai*)." The idiom gains its force from a com-parison of the cocoyam, which in Igbo culture is regarded as an inferior crop, to the yam, the king of crops, which is frequently cooked in oil as a porridge. No doubt it is a token of the populism of Odogwu (and his group) to make the point that the cocoyam is just as fit a material for porridge as the yam!

I should also observe that, at this particular point in the performance, Odogwu happened to observe me monitoring the spool of tape, which was getting close to the end. He digressed to address me in a recitative tone, "Be sure to check on it." Soon afterwards, taking a cue from me, he led his men in a choral interlude that enabled a smooth transition as I turned the spool over to resume my recording. In this, he showed himself much more at ease with the technology of recording than we see in Clark-Bekederemo's narrator, Okabou.

34. A vegetable base for the stew, which has to be washed for a considerable length of time to remove its bitterness. Odogwu led his men in an ideophonic tune—*fo, foki foki foki fo, foki foki fo fo . . .* —sung to a jerking of the hips, a movement that drew laughter from those in the audience who were able to connect it with the suggestive sound of the words.

35. To his parents, who were exceedingly worried about his visit to the Oba, the Child again said, "The mouse eats, but so does the maggot."

36. Here Odogwu used a proverb—"The eye does not see the ear without the aid of a mirror"—to signify that the charmed gourdlet had rendered the boy invisible to the palace guards.

37. This is apparently the salutation for the *ohene*, the chief ritual functionary in various west-Niger Igbo communities. See especially Dibia 1990:212–237.

38. See Soyinka and Fagunwa 1968:8.

39. Emmanuel Obiechina has drawn attention (1972:24–26, 1973:95–102) to the influence of the foreign cinema on Nigerian popular culture. Part of the nickname of one of Odogwu's accompanists, "Ababa *Chico*," apparently derives from the American cowboy film. Of the influence of Indian films, Obiechina notes: "As well as European and American films, there has been, since the [second world] war, a large influx of Indian films with their 'romantic' stories and an element of magic and the supernatural, which appeal very much to the popular imagination" (1973:95). Traditional African storytelling, especially as practiced by the likes of Odogwu, certainly shares with the Indian film the fluid interaction between plot, music, and dance. On the centrality of song and dance to Indian cinema, and their appeal to foreign popular audiences in Africa and elsewhere, see especially Barnouw and Krishnaswamy 1980:155–168; cf. Dickey 1993:120, 184n1. "Albela" was a black-and-white musical comedy produced in 1951 by Bhagwan Art Productions of Bombay. Master Bhagwan, the producer-director, also played the title role. Music was by C. Ramchandra.

40. In pointing to the precocious development of the Child-wiser-than-the-Oba, Odogwu uses the conventional formula for abbreviating time, "A tale is born on the day it is conceived," which we have seen some of our earlier narrators use in their tales: Ojiudu (line 109, in chapter 2), and Simayi (line 170, first tale in chapter 4).

Odogwu's use of pornographic diction in connection with the Oba's wife in each story is also in accord with the western Igbo narrative tradition. We will recall that the revolt against Ezechi, Igbuzo's first paramount ruler, began with one of the chiefs in council defiling Ezechi's queen with a sexual insult (Okpewho 1983:63, and page 56 above). Odogwu's recourse to this convention is therefore very much in accord with the antihegemonic character of the Benin myth among the west-Niger Igbo.

41. Asked in September 1995 why Odogwu continued to return to the North despite his experience of it, his elder brother Ulichukwude said it was because he still had brothers and sisters living up there, as well as Northern friends, some of whom had saved his life in those painful days in 1966. It is equally possible that Odogwu sought to reconnect with the wider universe he had known for so long.

42. For problems over succession in Benin monarchical traditions, see Ekeh 1978.

6. Myth, Empire, and Self-Determination

1. Cited in *African Affairs*, 48 (1949), 246.

2. Consider the following judgment by a British writer who had done a detailed study of documents relating to the Benin-British encounter, before finally visiting the city several decades after its fall: "The Benin expedition was less a war of righteous revenge, muscular Christianity triumphing over barbarous paganism, than part of a sombre and complex game of political chess, and in that game the eventual winners and losers were not who they might at first appear" (Home 1982:12).

3. For a picture of Oba Akenzua II lapping his daughter Adesuwa, as he prepares to give her away in marriage, and the Oba's general tendency to break with tradition in a humane spirit consonant with the times, see Flora Kaplan's excellent discussion of the political context of domestic life in Benin (Kaplan 1997:245–313). My personal experience of the Benin monarchy dates from around November 1964 when, as one of a group of foreign service officers in training, we paid a visit to Oba Akenzua II and were received in the council room of his palace. Young as most of us were, we looked and listened in awe as the Oba (though Western-educated) addressed us through his spokesman. Many years later, as chairman of a task force planning the fortieth anniversary celebrations of the University of Ibadan, I revisited the palace in 1988 with a film crew for an interview with the present Oba, Erediauwa I (son of the late Akenzua II), who was then Chancellor of our university. The Oba, a Cambridge-educated man who had held top administrative positions in government and industry, received us most graciously and, though attended in the same council room by an imposing ring of Benin elders, spoke to us directly and in English.

I had written to Dr. Greg Akenzua, his younger brother, who was my senior contemporary both at secondary and upper levels of schooling, to help arrange an audience for me and my men with the Oba, and perhaps my friendship with Greg helped secure me the special graces of His Highness. But I must confess the Oba put me at tremendous ease, taking particular interest in my surname (which has a perfectly intelligible "Edoid" ring and meaning to it) and a few details of my personal career that might have been brought to his attention. I have never ceased to remember that occasion with fond regard for the king.

4. In discussing the practice of "cultural imperialism" by way of foreign articles of culture, Tomlinson notes that "often people don't seem to object to the importation of these products and practices: they don't perceive them as an 'imposition'; hence it is difficult to see where domination at a specifically cultural (rather than an associated economic) level is occurring" (1991:94).

5. Quoted in Afigbo 1987:16. On Ugo (or Ugonoba) as the boundary between Benin and the west-Niger Igbo, see Simayi's account of the Benin-Ubulu war in Okpewho 1992:200. Regarding the Benin moat, Afigbo asks: "Since Benin was a mighty military empire surrounded on all sides by weak and politically fragmented peoples, what made the building of a defensive wall and ditch around the imperial metropolis necessary?"

6. I hardly see why Ekeh (1990:676–677) finds it necessary to join Ryder in absolving the Benin monarchy of large-scale slaving. If Benin did not sell slaves directly to Europeans, it was evidently because Itsekiri middlemen like Nana Olomu had secured franchise for the entire supply zone between Warri-Sapele and Benin, thus disabling direct contact between the Europeans and the Benin nobility. Incidentally, Ryder goes to some length to discuss the slaving and other enterprises of the French Captain Landolphe, who built himself factories on the Benin River and entered into privileged trading relations with local potentates (1969:198–228). In any case, for what purpose would Benin have kept such an advanced and effective army as it was reputed to have had at the time, if not for slaving and kindred operations? Ekeh indeed goes on (680) to cite Wrigley's claim (1971:123) that Benin art began to suffer "aesthetic decadence" at about the end of the seventeenth century, "when the slave trade was becoming the dominant mode of economic and social life."

7. We need to look more closely at the histories of other communities we have sometimes glibly traced from Benin, like the Ijo. For a detailed investigation of the foundations of Ijo society and culture, which renders claims of origination from Benin basically irrelevant and consequently attenuates evidence of Benin influences on Ijo culture, see Alagoa et al. 1988. The thrust of this collection of specialist essays is that Ijo groups had been migrating to various geographical locations, especially along the Atlantic seaboard, for centuries before the rise of Benin as a nation, let alone military power. For a myth of cult origins which locates an Ijo group (Apoi) within the cosmology of the Ilaje Yoruba of Okitipupa, Ondo State of Nigeria, see Okpewho 1992:262–264.

8. For his responses to this and other attacks, see Shaw 1975.

9. In her studies of copper use in West Africa (1973, 1984), Eugenia Herbert has suggested that although copper was imported in large quantities into West Africa from the fifteenth century, large deposits of it existed and were exploited long before the advent of Europeans, even in the centuries before the Christian

era. It was found to be aesthetically pleasing and more pliable than iron, and its scarcity made it restricted to ritual and other ceremonial purposes as well as use as a medium of exchange. It also featured in various cosmogonic myths. In his account of his finds, Thurstan Shaw himself suggests that, probably after some disaster, the craftsmen who made the famed Igbo-Ukwu bronzes disappeared; later on it became necessary for the people to send to Benin, now full-fledged makers of their own bronzes, for the brass pectoral mask that was part of the ritual regalia of the Nri king (1970:285).

10. Quoted in Afigbo 1981:60. For the Nri factor in the history of the west-Niger Igbo, see chapter 2 above.

11. No doubt a corruption of the Igbo word *Ogboma*, meaning "wizard," which was probably how the man was viewed or described in relation to his professional excellence.

12. For further details on the Aro and their slaving and other historical traditions see, for example, Dike 1956:37–41, Afigbo 1981:187–281, and Dike and Ekejiuba 1990. For an early (eighteenth-century) account of Aro slaving raids, see Equiano's *Interesting Narrative* (1995:46–48).

13. Dike pursued his study of Aro history at Harvard and published the first stage of it (1978) in collaboration with his former Ibadan student, Felicia Ekejiuba. For a detailed assessment of Dike as scholar, researcher, and administrator, see Ajayi 1990:40–69.

14. Compare Fanon: "By its very nature, colonialism is separatist and regionalist. Colonialism does not simply state the existence of tribes; it also reinforces it and separates them" (1968:94).

15. "The colonial states," as Appiah has rightly observed, "were made for raising—not spending—government revenues" (1992:164).

16. One unfortunate phenomenon has been observed in the periodic agitation for creation of more states in Nigeria. The leaders of such a movement are frequently middle-class types who hope that their lot will be immensely improved with the creation of the desired state. True enough, the establishment of the new state comes with the creation of a new administrative structure, which means new "permanent secretaries" or "director-generals," as they are now called; the setting up of new parastatals, which means new "chairpersons"; the building of a state university, which means new professors, registrars, bursars; and so on.

17. While it is agreed that ethnic identity is generally too fluid to facilitate firm delimitation (Rothchild and Olorunsola 1983:11, 12; Nnoli 1994:21; cf. Tomlinson 1991:97)), it is at any rate safe to predicate any efforts at delimitation on some basis of what Nnoli calls "group factors," roughly similar to what I have here called "communitarian" considerations. It should be noted I am not recommending delimitation along *ethnic* or *tribal* lines. The tales which I have discussed in this study obviously make fundamental claims about culture and history, but only in response to the superior claims on these represented by the Oba or the monarchical machine that made life difficult for Benin's neighbors. Otherwise, it is evident that the west-Niger Igbo and other communities in the region have interacted and lived so long with the Bini (Edo) that no *ethnic* or even linguistic lines are immediately drawn in the tales: for how would the young ritualist in Okafor Odagwue's tale about Oye (chapter 4) have communi-

cated with the old woman in whose house he landed on the outskirts of Benin? All of which lends support to Ekeh's effort to trace the growth of the hegemonist prejudices of tribalism and ethnicity to Nigeria's colonial history (1990).

18. Consider the following statement from Claude Ake's presidential address to a conference of the Nigerian Political Science Association: "State power is highly developed and used rather freely and the role of the state in the economy and society of Nigeria is very substantial. The remarkable growth of state power in Nigeria began under colonialism. The colonial state needed the apparatus to be effectively repressive and to ensure monopoly control of the economy. Since independence the power and interventionism of the Nigerian state have increased even more because the state had to spearhead economic development in the absence of a strong indigenous capitalist class. As things stand now, the Nigerian state appears to intervene everywhere and to own virtually everything" (1981:1162).

I must add that, while I respect Eghosa Osaghae's detailed analysis (1991) of the fate of "ethnic minorities" in the federal structure, I am not so enamored of the concept of a strong center that he seems to be suggesting as the pivot of our restructuring goals. I am also saddened that, in recommending a devolutionary formula, he has had recourse to the well-worn consumerist idiom of "share of the national cake" (249).

19. Each zone will provide the president (if that's what the national leader will be called) for a specified number of years, after which another zone will have its turn. A final, small list of candidates from the zonal elections will be presented to the country at large for voting, and the cost of their closely guided campaigns will be covered by the federal treasury. The zonal centers will have neither the structure nor the power of state capitals. They may either be fixed by mutual agreement, or else movable. Essentially, they should serve as centers for the coordination of electoral and related matters.

20. Ohadike's account (1991:147–150) of the collusion between British colonial administrators and agents (especially Crewe-Read) and the reconstituted Benin monarchy against the anticolonial redoubt of the west-Niger Igbo has been corroborated by at least two of my narrators. Usuanlele and Falola also suggest this collusion in their characterization of the era of "reconstruction" after the fall of Benin (1897), in the reign of Oba Eweka II: "Before 1938 the political climate in the Benin Division had been relatively calm and many changes were initiated by colonial officers using the Oba as an instrument" (1994:315).

21. I refer here to the distinctions subsumed by Lyotard in *The Postmodern Condition* (1984) and *The Differend* (1988), in the latter of which he shows a surer sympathy for "local narratives," as legends of self-assertion, against the superior claims of meta- or "master-narratives" (*maitre-récits*) as accounts endorsed or legitimized by the state. For a dependable analysis of the development of Lyotard's thought in this regard across his works, see Klein 1995. Although Lyotard is dealing with the relations between European totalizing histories and the localized accounts of peoples thought to be without history, the similarity between these relations and the ones we have explored between Benin and the communities within her zone of influence should demonstrate that we have here in Africa the same hegemonic attitudes that we have all too easily condemned in European colonial accounts about African societies.

It remains for me to add a few words about statements that Africa's most distinguished writers, Chinua Achebe and Wole Soyinka, have made in recent times about the political predicament of their country Nigeria. Both have rightly identified tribalism and the manipulation of ethnic and other differences as the major culprit in the country's failures in nation-building (Achebe 1984:5, Soyinka 1996:130). But it would seem their criticism of these failures leads them somewhat easily to a certain nihilist despair, so that Soyinka has recommended "the reconsideration of the nation status as it now exists" (131). I agree the country has been persistently traumatized by one brand of leadership after another. But the summary dissolution of the union, which I suspect Soyinka to be recommending in statements like the above scattered across his justly angry book, is hardly a solution, for it might leave the emergent entities at the mercy of the sort of future we feared looming ahead had Biafra's secession succeeded.

22. Compare Walter Rodney on nationalist portraits of old African empires: "The Western Sudanic empires of Ghana, Mali, and Songhai have become bywords in the struggle to illustrate the achievements of the African past. That is the area to which African nationalists and progressive whites point when they want to prove that Africans too were capable of political, administrative, and military greatness in the epoch before the white men. However, a people's demands at any given time change the kinds of questions to which historians are expected to provide answers" (1974:56).

23. Lupenga Mphande's study (1993) of the poetic traditions of the "Nguni diaspora"—communities in southern Africa formed by those dispersed by Shaka the Zulu's wars of territorial expansion (the *mfecane*)—is one of the rare moves made by African scholars to correct the shortcomings in our reconstructions of the past, caused by the tendency to privilege the voice of one group over others'.

Bibliography

Abraham, W.E. 1962. *The Mind of Africa.* Chicago: University of Chicago Press.

Achebe, Chinua. 1958. *Things Fall Apart.* London: Heinemann.

Achebe, Chinua. 1975. Chi in Igbo Cosmology. In *Morning Yet on Creation Day.* Garden City: Doubleday Anchor.

Achebe, Chinua. 1984. *The Trouble With Nigeria.* London: Heinemann.

Adedeji, Olohigbe O. 1989. The Mythical Imagination in the Legends of Old Benin. Ph. D. Thesis. Department of English, University of Ibadan, Ibadan, Nigeria.

Adediran, Biodun. 1991. Pleasant Imperialism: Conjectures on Benin Hegemony in Eastern Yorubaland. *African Notes,* 15:83–95.

Afigbo, Adiele E. 1972. *The Warrant Chiefs: Indirect Rule in South-eastern Nigeria, 1891–1929.* London: Longman.

Afigbo, Adiele E. 1981. *Ropes of Sand: Studies in Igbo History and Culture.* Ibadan: University Press Ltd.

Afigbo, Adiele E. 1987. *The Igbo and Their Neighbours.* Ibadan: University Press Ltd.

Ajayi, J.F. Ade. 1990. *History and the Nation and Other Addresses.* Ibadan: Spectrum Books.

Ajuwon, Bade. 1982. *Funeral Dirges of Yoruba Hunters.* New York: Nok Publishers.

Ajuwon, Bade. 1989. Ogun's Iremoje: A Philosophy of Living and Dying. In Barnes 1989.

Ake, Claude. 1981. Off to a Good Start, But Dangers Await . . . *West Africa,* May 25:1162.

Akegwure, Paul O. 1978. The Hero in Isoko Heroic Narratives. Honors Essay. Department of English, University of Ibadan, Nigeria.

Akinola, G.A. 1976. The Origins of the Eweka Dynasty: A Study in the Use and Misuse of Oral Tradition. *Journal of the Historical Society of Nigeria.* 3. 3:21–36.

Akintoye, S.A. 1971. *Revolution and Power Politics in Yorubaland 1840–1893.* New York: Humanities Press.

Alagoa, Ebiegberi J. 1964. *The Small Brave City State.* Madison: University of Wisconsin Press.

Alagoa, Ebiegberi J. 1966. Ijo Origins and Migrations: I. *Nigeria Magazine,* 91: 282.

Alagoa, Ebiegberi J. 1972. *A History of the Niger Delta.* Ibadan: Ibadan University Press.

Amadiume, Ifi. 1981. *Afrikan Matriarchal Foundations: The Igbo Case.* London: Karnak House.

Amadiume, Ifi. 1987. *Male Daughters, Female Husbands: Gender and Sex in an African Society.* London: Zed Books.

Anderson, Benedict. 1983. *Imagined Communities: Reflections on the Origin and Spread of Nationalism.* London: Verso.

Anene-Boyle, F.A. 1979. The Hero in Ukwuani Heroic Narrative. Honors Essay. Department of English, University of Ibadan, Nigeria.

Appiah, Kwame Anthony. 1992. *In My Father's House: Africa in the Philosophy of Culture.* New York: Oxford University Press.

Appiah, Kwame Anthony. 1993. Thick Translation. *Callaloo,* 16:808–819.

Arinze, Francis A. 1970. *Sacrifice in Igbo Religion.* Ibadan: Ibadan University Press.

Ayewoh, M.E. 1979. Tradition and Originality in Ishan Poetry and Weaving. Honors Essay. Department of English, University of Ibadan, Nigeria.

Azuonye, Chukwuma. 1990. Kaalu Igirigiri: An Ohafia Igbo Singer of Tales. In Okpewho 1990b. Pp. 42–79.

Azuonye, Chukwuma. 1995. *Igbo enwe eze*: Monarchical Power versus Democratic Values in Igbo Oral Narratives. In *Power, Marginality and African Oral Literature,* ed. Graham Furniss and Liz Gunner. Cambridge: Cambridge University Press.

Ba, A.H. and Lilyan Kesteloot. 1968. Une Epopee Peule: 'Silamaka.' *L'Homme,* 8:5–36.

Babalola, S. Adeboye. 1966. *The Content and Form of Yoruba Ijala.* Oxford: Clarendon Press.

Babalola, S. Adeboye. 1989. A Portrait of Ogun as Reflected in Ijala Chants. In Barnes 1989.

Babatunde, Emmanuel D. 1992. *A Critical Study of Bini and Yoruba Value Systems of Nigeria in Change: Culture, Religion, and the Self.* Lewiston: Edwin Mellen.

Baldwin, James. 1995 [1986]. *The Evidence of Things Not Seen.* New York: Henry Holt.

Banham, Martin, with Clive Wake. 1976. *African Theatre Today.* London: Pitman Publishing.

Banham, Martin, Errol Hill, and George Woodyard, with Olu Obafemi, eds. 1994. *The Cambridge Guide to African and Caribbean Theatre.* Cambridge: Cambridge University Press.

Barber, Karin. 1991. *I Could Speak Until Tomorrow: Oriki, Women, and the Past in a Yoruba Town.* Washington, DC: Smithsonian Institution Press.

Barber, Karin and Bayo Ogundijo, eds. 1994. *Yoruba Popular Theatre: Three Plays by the Oyin Adejobi Company.* [Atlanta?]: African Studies Association Press.

Barnes, Sandra T., ed. 1989. *Africa's Ogun: Old World and New.* Bloomington: Indiana University Press.

Barnes, Sandra T. and Paula G. Ben-Amos. 1989. Ogun, the Empire Builder. In Barnes 1989.

Barnouw, Erik and S. Krishnaswamy. 1980. *Indian Film.* New York: Oxford University Press.

Basden, G.T. 1921. *Among the Ibos of Nigeria.* London: Seeley Service.

Basden, G.T. 1938. *Niger Ibos.* London: Seely Associates.

Bauman, Richard. 1977. *Verbal Art as Performance*. Rowley: Newbury House.

Bauman, Richard. 1983. The Field Study of Folklore in Context. In *Handbook of American Folklore*, ed. Richard Dorson. Bloomington: Indiana University Press.

Bauman, Richard. 1986. *Story, Performance, and Event: Contextual Studies of Oral Narrative*. Cambridge: Cambridge University Press.

Bauman, Richard and Charles L. Briggs. 1990. Poetics and Performance as Critical Perspectives on Language and Social Life. *Annual Review of Anthropology*, 19:59–88.

Beidelman, T.O. 1970. Myth, Legend, and Oral History. *Anthropos*, 65:74–79.

Beier, Ulli. 1966. *The Origin of Life and Death: African Creation Myths*. London: Heinemann.

Beier, Ulli. 1981. E.K. Ogunmola: A Personal Memoir. In *Drama and Theatre in Nigeria: A Critical Source Book*, ed. Yemi Ogunbiyi. Lagos: Nigeria Magazine.

Ben-Amos, Daniel. 1971. Toward a Definition of Folklore in Context. *Journal of American Folklore*, 84:3–15. Reprinted in *Toward New Perspectives in Folklore*, ed. America Paredes and Richard Bauman. Austin: University of Texas Press.

Ben-Amos, Daniel. 1972. Two Benin Storytellers. In *African Folklore*, ed. Richard Dorson. Bloomington: Indiana University Press.

Ben-Amos, Daniel. 1975. *Sweet Words: Storytelling Events in Benin*. Philadelphia: Institute for the Study of Human Issues.

Ben-Amos, Daniel. 1977. The Context of Folklore: Implications and Prospects. In *Frontiers of Folklore*, ed. William R. Bascom. Boulder: Westview Press.

Ben-Amos, Daniel. 1993. "Context" in Context. *Western Folklore*, 52:209–225.

Ben-Amos, Paula. 1976. Men and Animals in Benin Art. *Man*, 11:243–252.

Ben-Amos, Paula. 1983a. Introduction: History and Art in Benin. In Ben-Amos and Rubin 1983.

Ben-Amos, Paula. 1983b. The Powers of Kings: Symbolism of a Benin Ceremonial Stool. In Ben-Amos and Rubin 1983.

Ben-Amos, Paula. 1983c. In Honor of Queen Mothers. In Ben-Amos and Rubin 1983.

Ben-Amos, Paula. 1995. *The Art of Benin*. London: British Museum.

Ben-Amos, Paula and Arnold Rubin, eds. 1983. *The Art of Power, the Power of Art: Studies in Benin Iconography*. Los Angeles: Museum of Cultural History, UCLA.

Biebuyck, Daniel P. ed. 1978. *Hero and Chief: Epic Literature from the Banyanga, Zaire Republic*. Berkeley: University of California Press.

Biebuyck, Daniel P. and K.C. Mateene, eds. 1969. *The Mwindo Epic from the Banyanga, Congo Republic*. Berkeley: University of California Press.

Bietenholz, Peter G. 1994. *Historia and Fabula: Myths and Legends in Historical Thought from Antiquity to the Modern Age*. Leiden: E. J. Brill.

Bird, Charles S. 1972. Heroic Songs of the Mande Hunters. In *African Folklore*, ed. Richard M. Dorson. Bloomington: Indiana University Press.

Bird, Charles S. and M.B. Kendall. 1980. The Mande Hero. In *Explorations in African Systems of Thought*, ed. Ivan Karp and Charles S. Bird. Bloomington: Indiana University Press.

Bird, Charles S. et al., eds. 1974. *The Songs of Seydou Camara: 1. Kambili*. Bloomington: African Studies Center, Indiana University.

Blackmun, Barbara Winston. 1983. Wall Plaque of a Junior Titleholder Carrying an *Ekpokin*. In Ben-Amos and Rubin.

Borges, Jorge Luis. 1981. The Intruder. In *Borges: A Reader*, ed. E.R. Monegal and A. Reid. New York: E.P. Dutton.

Boston, John S. 1964. The Hunter in Igala Legends of Origin. *Africa*, 34:116–126.

Boston, John S. 1977. *Ikenga Figures Among the North-west Igbo and the Igala*. London: Ethnographica (in association with Federal Department of Antiquities, Nigeria).

Bowra, C.M. 1952. *Heroic Poetry*. London: Macmillan.

Bowra, C.M. 1972. *Homer*. London: Duckworth.

Bradbury, R.E. 1957. *The Benin Kingdom and the Edo-speaking Peoples of Southwestern Nigeria*. London: International African Institute.

Bradbury, R.E. 1973. *Benin Studies*. Ed. Peter Morton-Williams. London: Oxford University Press (for the International African Institute).

Bremond, Claude. 1977. *The Clandestine Ox*: The Transformation of an African Tale. *New Literary History*, 8:393–410.

Briggs, Charles L. 1988. *Competence in Performance: The Creativity of Tradition in Mexicano Verbal Art*. Philadelphia: University of Pennsylvania Press.

Briggs, Charles L. 1992. "Since I Am a Woman, I Will Chastize My Relatives": Gender, Reported Speech, and the (Re)production of Social Relations in Warao Ritual Wailing. *American Ethnologist*, 19:337–361.

Bulman, Stephen. 1990. The Buffalo-Woman Tale: Political Imperatives and Narrative Constraints in the Sunjata Epic. In *Discourse and Its Disguises: The Interpretation of African Oral Text*, ed. Karin Barber and P.F. de Moraes Farias. Birmingham: Centre of West African Studies, University of Birmingham, U.K.

Burkert, Walter. 1983. *Homo Necans: The Anthropology of Ancient Greek Sacrificial Ritual and Myth*. Trans. Peter King. Berkeley: University of California Press.

Campbell, Joseph. 1972. *The Hero With a Thousand Faces*. Bollingen Series. Princeton: Princeton University Press.

Chambers, Lee. 1983. Crocodiles. In Ben-Amos and Rubin 1983:94.

Chikwendu, V.E., P.T. Craddock, R.M. Farquhar, Thurstan Shaw, and A.C. Umeji. 1989. Nigerian Sources of Copper, Lead and Tin for the Igbo-Ukwu Bronzes. *Archaeometry*, 31:27–36.

Chodorow, Nancy. 1974. Family Structure and Feminine Personality. In Rosaldo and Lamphere 1974. Pp. 43–66.

Chukwukere, I. 1983. Chi in Igbo Religion and Thought. *Anthropos*, 78:519–534.

Cisse, Youssouf. 1964. Notes sur les Societes de Chasseurs Malinke. *Journal de la Societe des Africanistes*, 34:175–226.

Clark, J.P. 1966. *Ozidi: A Play*. London: Oxford University Press.

Clark, J.P. 1981. *A Decade of Tongues*. London: Longman.

Clark-Bekederemo, J.P., ed. 1991 [1977]. *The Ozidi Saga: Collected and Translated from the Oral Ijo Version of Okabou Ojobolo*. Washington, DC: Howard University Press.

Clifford, James. 1988. *The Predicament of Culture: Twentieth-Century Ethnography, Literature, and Art*. Cambridge, MA: Harvard University Press.

Clignet, Remi. 1970. *Many Wives, Many Powers*. Evanston: Northwestern University Press.

Cole, Herbert M. 1982. *Mbari: Art and Life Among the Owerri Igbo*. Bloomington: Indiana University Press.

Collingwood, R.G. 1965. *Essays in the Philosophy of History*, ed. William Debbins. Austin: University of Texas Press.

Collingwood, R.G. 1993 [1946]. *The Idea of History*, ed. J. van der Dussen. Oxford: Clarendon Press.

Connah, Graham. 1966. Archaeological Research in Benin City, 1961–64. *Journal of the Historical Society of Nigeria*, 2:465–477.

Connah, Graham. 1967. New Light on the Benin City Walls. *Journal of the Historical Society of Nigeria*, 3:593–609.

Connah, Graham. 1975. *The Archaeology of Benin: Excavations and Other Researches in and around Benin City, Nigeria.* Oxford: Clarendon Press.

Cosentino, Donald. 1982. *Defiant Maids and Stubborn Farmers: Tradition and Invention in Mende Story Performance.* Cambridge: Cambridge University Press.

Dark, Philip C. 1960. *Benin Art.* London: Paul Hamlyn.

Dark, Philip C. 1973. *An Introduction to Benin Art and Technology.* Oxford: Clarendon Press.

de Vries, Jan. 1963. *Heroic Song and Heroic Legend.* London: Oxford University Press.

Dean, Carolyn. 1983. The Individual and the Ancestral: *Ikegobo* and *Ukhure.* In Ben-Amos and Rubin 1983:33–40.

Diabate, Massa M. 1970. *Janjon et Autres Chants Populaires du Mali.* Paris: Presence Africaine.

Dibia, Bernard O. 1990. Title Taking in Ubululand. PhD Dissertation, Indiana University. Ann Arbor: University Microfilms.

Dickey, Sara. 1993. *Cinema and the Urban Poor in South India.* Cambridge: Cambridge University Press.

Dike, Kenneth Onwuka. 1956. *Trade and Politics in the Niger Delta 1830–1885: An Introduction to the Economic and Political History of Nigeria.* Oxford: Clarendon Press.

Dike, K. Onwuka and F. Ekejiuba. 1978. The Aro State: A Case Study of State Formation in Southeastern Nigeria. *Journal of African Studies*, 5:268–300.

Dike, K. Onwuka and Felicia Ekejiuba. 1990. *The Aro of South-eastern Nigeria, 1650–1980: A Study of Socio-economic Formation and Transformation in Nigeria.* Ibadan: University Press Ltd.

Diop, Cheikh Anta. 1962. *The Cultural Unity of Negro Africa.* Paris: Presence Africaine.

Drake, Carlos. 1969. Jungian Psychology and Its Uses in Folklore. *Journal of American Folklore*, 82: 118–130.

DuBois, W.E.B. 1995 [1903]. *The Souls of Black Folk.* New York: Signet Classics.

Duran, Lucy. 1995. *Jelimusow:* The Superwomen of Malian Music. In Furniss and Gunner 1995. Pp. 197–210.

Ebohon, Osemwegie. 1972. *Cultural Heritage of Benin.* Benin City: Midwest Newspapers Corporation.

Ebohon, Osemwegie. 1979. *Eguae Oba n'Edo: The Palace of the Oba of Benin.* Benin City: Eribo Printers.

Echeruo, Michael J.C. 1979. *A Matter of Identity.* Ahiajoku Lecture. Owerri: Ministry of Information, Culture, Youth, and Sports.

Edemode, John. 1977. The Agboghidi Epic. Project Essay. Department of English, University of Ibadan, Nigeria.

Edoh, A.O. 1979. The Epic Narrative Tradition in the Torubiri Epic, Kiagbodo Town, Bendel State. Honors Essay. Department of English, University of Ibadan, Nigeria.

Egharevba, Jacob U. 1946. *Concise Lives of the Famous Iyases of Benin.* Reprinted in Egharevba 1973.

Egharevba, Jacob U. 1949 [1946]. *Benin Law and Customs.* Port Harcourt: CMS Press.

Egharevba, Jacob U. 1954. *The Origin of Benin.* Reprinted in Egharevba 1973.

Egharevba, Jacob U. 1956. *Benin Titles.* Reprinted in Egharevba 1973.

Egharevba, Jacob U. 1962. *Marriage of the Princesses of Benin City.* Reprinted in Egharevba 1973.

Egharevba, Jacob U. 1966. *Fusion of Tribes.* Reprinted in Egharevba 1973.

Egharevba, Jacob U. 1968 [1934]. *A Short History of Benin.* Ibadan: Ibadan University Press.

Egharevba, Jacob U. 1969. *Descriptive Catalogue of Benin Museum.* Reprinted in Egharevba 1973.

Egharevba, Jacob U. 1973. *Twelve Works.* Nendeln: Kraus Reprint.

Ekeh, Peter P. 1975. Colonialism and the Two Publics in Africa: A Theoretical Statement. *Comparative Studies in Society and History,* 17:91–112.

Ekeh, Peter P. 1978. Benin and Thebes: Elementary Forms of Civilization. In *The Psychoanalytic Study of Society, Vol. 7,* ed. W. Muensterberger, A.H. Esman, and L.B. Boyer. New Haven: Yale University Press.

Ekeh, Peter P. 1990. Social Anthropology and Two Contrasting Uses of Tribalism in Africa. *Comparative Studies in Society and History,* 32:660–700.

Ekejiuba, Felicia. 1967. Omu Okwei, the Merchant Queen of Ossomari: A Biographical Sketch. *Journal of the Historical Society of Nigeria,* 3:633–646.

Elaigwu, J. Isawa and Victor A. Olorunsola. 1983. Federalism and Politics of Compromise. In Rothchild and Olorunsola 1983.

Elugbe, B.O. 1973. A Comparative Edo Phonology. PhD Thesis. University of Ibadan, Nigeria.

Elugbe, B.O. 1979. Some Tentative Historical Inferences from Comparative Edoid Studies. *Kiabara: Journal of the Humanities,* 2. 1:82–101.

Emecheta, Buchi. 1979. *The Joys of Motherhood.* New York: George Braziller.

Equiano, Olaudah. 1995 [1789]. *The Interesting Narrative and Other Writings,* ed. Vincent Carretta. Harmondsworth: Penguin Books.

Erikson, Thomas Hylland. 1991. The Cultural Context of Ethnic Differences. *Man,* 26:127–144.

Eyo, Ekpo. 1977. *2000 Years of Nigerian Art.* Lagos: Department of Antiquities.

Fadipe, N.A. 1970. *The Sociology of the Yoruba,* ed. F.O. Okediji and O.O. Okediji. Ibadan: Ibadan University Press.

Fagg, William. 1978. *Divine Kingship in Africa.* Second Edition. London: British Museum Publications.

Falade, Solange. 1963. Women of Dakar and the Surrounding Urban Area. In Paulme 1963.

Fanon, Franz. 1968. *The Wretched of the Earth.* Trans. Constance Farrington. New York: Grove Weidenfeld.

Farrer, Claire R., ed. 1975. *Women and Folklore.* Austin: University of Texas Press.

Finnegan, Ruth. 1970. *Oral Literature in Africa.* Oxford: Clarendon Press.

Finnegan, Ruth. 1988. *Literacy and Orality: Studies in the Technology of Communication.* Oxford: Blackwell.

Forde, D. and G.I. Jones. 1950. *The Ibo and Ibibio-Speaking Peoples of South Eastern Nigeria.* London: Oxford University Press.

Fortes, Meyer. 1983. *Oedipus and Job in West African Religion*. With an essay by Robin Horton. Cambridge: Cambridge University Press.

Fortes, Meyer. 1987. *Religion, Morality and the Person: Essays on Tallensi Religion*. Cambridge: Cambridge University Press.

Foucault, Michel. 1973. *The Order of Things: An Archaeology of the Human Sciences*. New York: Vintage Books.

Fraser, Douglas and Herbert M. Cole, eds. 1972. *African Art and Leadership*. Madison: University of Wisconsin Press.

Furniss, Graham and Liz Gunner, eds. 1995. *Power, Marginality, and African Oral Literature*. Cambridge: Cambridge University Press.

Gage-Brandon, Anastasia J. 1992. The Polygyny-Divorce Relationship: A Case Study of Nigeria. *Journal of Marriage and the Family*, 54:285–292.

Gallagher, Jacki. 1983. Between Realms: The Iconography of Kingship in Benin. In Ben-Amos and Rubin 1983:21–26.

Gates, Henry Louis, Jr. 1988. *The Signifying Monkey: A Theory of Afro-American Literary Criticism*. New York: Oxford University Press.

Gibbs, James. 1993. Tear the Painted Masks. Join the Poison Stains: A Preliminary Study of Wole Soyinka's Writings for the Nigerian Press. In *Research on Wole Soyinka*, ed. James Gibbs and Bernth Lindfors. Trenton: Africa World Press, 1993. Pp. 225–261.

Gilroy, Paul. 1991. *There Ain't No Black in the Union Jack: The Cultural Politics of Race and Nation*. Chicago: University of Chicago Press.

Gilroy, Paul. 1993. *The Black Atlantic: Modernity and Double Consciousness*. Cambridge, MA: Harvard University Press.

Gleason, Judith. 1987. *Oya: In Praise of the Goddess*. Boston: Shambhala Publications.

Goody, Jack. 1977. *The Domestication of the Savage Mind*. Cambridge: Cambridge University Press.

Goody, Jack. 1987. *The Interface Between the Written and the Oral*. Cambridge: Cambridge University Press.

Goody, Jack and Ian Watt. 1968. The Consequences of Literacy. In *Literacy in Traditional Societies*, ed. Jack Goody. Cambridge: Cambridge University Press.

Graham-White, Anthony. 1974. *The Drama of Black Africa*. New York: Samuel French.

Green, Margaret M. 1964 [1947]. *Igbo Village Affairs: Chiefly with Reference to the Village of Umueke Agbaja*. London: Frank Cass.

Guinier, Lani et al. 1997. *Becoming Gentlemen: Women, Law School, and Institutional Change*. Boston: Beacon Press.

Hafkin, Nancy J. and Edna G. Bay, eds. 1976. *Women in Africa: Studies in Social and Economic Change*. Stanford: Stanford University Press.

Hahn, Johann G. von. 1876. *Sagwissenschaftliche Studien*. Jena: F. Mauke (E. Schenk).

Havelock, Eric. 1963. *Preface to Plato*. Cambridge, MA: Belknap Press of Harvard University Press.

Havelock, Eric. 1976. *Origins of Western Literacy*. Toronto: Ontario Institute for Studies in Education.

Havelock, Eric. 1982. *The Literate Revolution in Ancient Greece and Its Cultural Consequences*. Princeton: Princeton University Press.

Henderson, Richard M. 1972. *The King in Every Man: Evolutionary Trends in Onitsha Igbo Society and Culture*. New Haven: Yale University Press.

Herbert, Eugenia W. 1973. Aspects of the Use of Copper in Pre-colonial West Africa. *Journal of African History*, 14:179–194.

Herbert, Eugenia. 1984. *Red Gold of Africa*. Madison: University of Wisconsin Press.

Herskovits, Melville J. and Frances S. Herskovits. 1958. *Dahomean Narrative: A Cross-Cultural Analysis*. Evanston: Northwestern University Press.

Higbie, Carolyn. 1995. *Heroes' Names, Homeric Identities*. New York: Garland.

Hobsbawm, Eric and Terence Ranger, eds. 1983. *The Invention of Tradition*. Cambridge: Cambridge University Press.

Hollos, Marija and Philip E. Leis. 1989. *Becoming Nigerian in Ijo Society*. New Brunswick: Rutgers University Press.

Home, Robert. 1982. *City of Blood Revisited: A New Look at the Benin Expedition of 1897*. London: Rex Collings.

Hook, Sidney. 1943. *The Hero in History: A Study in Limitation and Possibility*. New York: Humanities Press.

Hopkins, A.G. 1973. *An Economic History of West Africa*. New York: Columbia University Press.

Horton, Robin. 1961. Destiny and the Unconscious in West Africa. *Africa*, 31: 110–116.

Horton, Robin. 1962. Kalabari World-view: An Outline and Interpretation. *Africa*, 32:197–220.

Horton, Robin. 1967. African Traditional Thought and Western Science. *Africa*, 37:50–71, 155–187.

Horton, Robin. 1993. *Patterns of Thought in Africa and the West: Essays on Magic, Religion and Science*. Cambridge: Cambridge University Press.

Hull, Richard W. 1981. Benin Art as Power. In Kaplan 1981:8–19.

Hymes, Dell. 1981. *"In Vain I Tried To Tell You": Essays in Native American Ethnopoetics*. Philadelphia: University of Pennsylvania Press.

Igbafe, Philip A. 1974. Benin in the Precolonial Era. *Tarikh*, 5.1:1–16.

Igbafe, Philip A. 1979. *Benin Under British Administration: The Impact of Colonial Rule on an African Kingdom, 1897–1938*. New York: Humanities Press.

Igbafe, Philip A. 1980. The Precolonial Economic Foundations of Benin. In *Topics in Nigerian Economic and Social History*, ed. I.A. Akinjogbin and S.O. Osoba. Ile-Ife: University of Ife Press.

Ikime, Obaro. 1969. *Niger Delta Rivalry*. London: Longman.

Ikime, Obaro. 1972. *The Isoko People: A Historical Survey*. Ibadan: Ibadan University Press.

Innes, Gordon, ed. 1974. *Sunjata: Three Mandinka Versions*. London: School of Oriental and African Studies, London University.

Innes, Gordon. 1990. Formulae in Mandinka Epic: The Problem of Translation. In Okpewho 1990b.

Innes, Gordon and Bakari Sidibe, eds. 1990. *Hunters and Crocodiles: Narratives of a Hunters' Bard*. Sandgate, UK; Paul Norbury/UNESCO.

Irigaray, Luce. 1991. *The Irigaray Reader*, ed. Margaret Whitford. Oxford: Blackwell.

Irigaray, Luce. 1993. *An Ethics of Sexual Difference*. Trans. Carolyn Burke and Gillian C. Gill. Ithaca: Cornell University Press.

Isichei, Elizabeth. 1976. *A History of the Igbo People*. London: Macmillan.

Isichei, Elizabeth. 1991. Myth, Gender, and Society in Pre-colonial Asaba. *Africa*, 16:513–529.

Isichei, Patrick A.C. 1973. Sex in Traditional Asaba. *Cahiers d'Études Africaines*, 13:682–699.

Izevbaye, Dan S. 1994. J.P. Clark-Bekederemo and the Ijo Literary Tradition. *Research in African Literatures*, 25:1–21.

Jackson, Michael. 1982. *Allegories of the Wilderness: Ethics and Ambiguity in Kuranko Narratives*. Bloomington: Indiana University Press.

Jeffreys, M.D.W. 1935. The Divine Umundri Kings. *Africa*, 8:346–354.

Jeffreys, M.D.W. 1954. Ikenga: The Ibo Ram-headed God. *African Studies*, 13: 25–40.

Johnson, John W., ed. 1986. *The Epic of Son-Jara: A West African Tradition*. Bloomington: Indiana University Press.

Jordan, Rosan A. and Susan J. Kalcik, eds. 1985. *Women's Folklore, Women's Culture*. Philadelphia: University of Pennsylvania Press.

Kalcik, Susan. 1975. " . . . like Ann's gynecologist or the time I was almost raped." In Farrer 1975.

Kaplan, Flora S. 1981. Of Symbols and Civilizations. In *Images of Power: Art of the Royal Court of Benin*, ed. Flora S. Kaplan. New York: New York University.

Kaplan, Flora S. 1997. "Runaway Wives," Native Law and Custom in Benin, and Early Colonial Courts, Nigeria. In *Queens, Queen Mothers, Priestesses, and Power*, ed. Flora S. Kaplan. Pp. 245–313. New York: New York Academy of Sciences.

Kerr, David. 1995. *African Popular Theatre from Pre-Colonial Times to the Present Day*. London: James Currey.

King, Katherine C. 1987. *Achilles: Paradigms of the War Hero from Homer to the Middle Ages*. Berkeley: University of California Press.

Klein, Kerwin Lee. 1995. In Search of Narrative Mastery: Postmodernism and the People without History. *History and Theory*, 34:275–298.

Kuper, Adam. 1994. Culture, Identity and the Project of a Cosmopolitan Anthropology. *Man*, 29:537–554.

Langellier, Kristin M. and Eric E. Peterson. 1992. Spinstorying: An Analysis of Women Storytelling. In *Performance, Culture, and Identity*, ed. Elizabeth C. Fine and Jean Haskell Speer. Westport: Praeger.

Lawal, Babatunde. 1973. Dating Problems at Igbo-Ukwu. *Journal of African History*, 14:1–8.

Leith-Ross, Sylvia. 1939. *African Women: A Study of the Ibo of Nigeria*. London: Routledge and Kegan Paul.

Leonard, A.G. 1968 [1906]. *The Lower Niger and Its Tribes*. London: Frank Cass.

Lévi-Strauss, Claude. 1977. The Story of Asdiwal. In *Structural Anthropology*, vol. 2. London: Allen Lane.

Lévi-Strauss, Claude. 1979. *Myth and Meaning*. New York: Schocken Books.

Levtzion, Nehemia. 1973. *Ancient Ghana and Mali*. London: Methuen.

Lewis, I.M., ed. 1968. *History and Social Anthropology*. London: Tavistock.

Lord, Albert B. 1960. *The Singer of Tales*. Cambridge, MA: Harvard University Press.

Lord, Albert Bates. 1991. *Epic Singers and Oral Tradition*. Ithaca: Cornell University Press.

Lord, Albert B. 1995. *The Singer Resumes His Tale*. Ithaca: Cornell University Press.

Lyotard, Jean-François. 1984. *The Postmodern Condition: A Report on Knowledge*. Trans. Geoff Bennington and Brian Massumi. Minneapolis: University of Minnesota Press.

Lyotard, Jean-François. 1988. *The Differend: Phrases in Dispute*. Trans. George van den Abeele. Minneapolis: University of Minnesota Press.

Mba, Nina E. 1982. *Nigerian Women Mobilized: Women's Political Activity in Southern Nigeria, 1900–1965*. Berkeley: Institute of International Studies.

Mbiti, John S. 1969. *African Religions and Philosophy*. London: William Heinemann.

McKeganey, Neil and Michael Bloor. 1991. Spotting the Invisible Man: The Influence of Male Gender on Fieldwork Relations. *British Journal of Sociology*, 42:195–210.

Meek, C.K. 1937. *Law and Authority in a Nigerian Tribe*. London: Oxford University Press.

Mitchell, Carol. 1985. Some Differences in Male and Female Joke-Telling. In Jordan and Kalcik 1985:163:186.

Mphande, Lupenga. 1993. Ngoni Praise Poetry and the Nguni Diaspora. *Research in African Literatures*, 24. 4:99–122.

Mudimbe, V.Y. 1988. *The Invention of Africa: Gnosis, Philosophy, and the Order of Knowledge*. Bloomington: Indiana University Press.

Mudimbe, V.Y. 1991. *Parables and Fables: Exegesis, Textuality, and Politics in Central Africa*. Madison: University of Wisconsin Press.

Mudimbe, V.Y. 1994. *The Idea of Africa*. Bloomington: Indiana University Press.

Nagy, Gregory. 1979. *The Best of the Achaeans: Concepts of the Hero in Archaic Greek Poetry*. Baltimore: Johns Hopkins University Press.

Nagy, Gregory. 1990. *Pindar's Homer: The Lyric Possession of an Epic Past*. Baltimore: Johns Hopkins University Press.

Niane, Djibril T. 1965. *Sundiata: An Epic of Old Mali*, tr. G.D. Pickett. London: Longmans.

Nketia, J.H.K. 1963. *Drumming in Akan Communities of Ghana*. Edinburgh: Thomas Nelson.

Nnoli, Okwudiba. 1994. *Ethnicity and Democracy in Africa: Intervening Variables*. Lagos: Malthouse Press.

Nsugbe, Philip O. 1974. *Ohaffia: A Matrilineal Ibo People*. London: Oxford University Press.

Nwabara, S.N. 1977. *Iboland: A Century of Contact with Britain*. London: Hodder and Stoughton.

Nwapa, Flora. 1966. *Efuru*. London: Heinemann.

Nwoga, Donatus I. 1984. *The Supreme God As Stranger in Igbo Religion and Thought*. Ahiazu Mbaise: Hawk Press.

Nwoko, Demas. 1970. Search for a New Nigerian Theatre. *Presence Africaine*, 75:49–75.

Nzimiro, Ikenna. 1972. *Studies in Ibo Political Systems: Chieftaincy and Politics in Four Niger States*. London: Frank Cass.

Obiechina, Emmanuel N., ed. 1972. *Onitsha Market Literature*. London: Heinemann Educational Books.

Obiechina, Emmanual N. 1973. *An African Popular Literature: A Study of Onitsha Market Pamphlets.* Cambridge: Cambridge University Press.

Ogieiriaixi, Evinma. 1974. Inconsistencies in the Old *edo* Orthographies. In *Edo Language and Its Orthography.* Benin City: Ministry of Education, Midwest State.

Ogot, Bethwell A. 1967. *A History of the Southern Luo, Vol 1: Migrations and Settlement 1500–1900.* Nairobi: East Africa Publishing House.

Ogunbiyi, Yemi. 1981. The Popular Theatre: A Tribute to Duro Ladipo. In Ogunbiyi 1981.

Ogunbiyi, Yemi, ed. 1981. *Drama and Theatre in Nigeria: A Critical Source Book.* Lagos: Nigeria Magazine.

Ogundipe-Leslie, Omolara and Carole Boyce Davies, eds. 1994. *Women As Oral Artists.* Special issue of *Research in African Literatures,* vol. 25.

Ogunyemi, Chikwenye Okonjo. 1993 [1985]. Womanism: The Dynamics of Black Female Writing in English. In *Revising the Word and the World: Essays in Feminist Literary Criticism,* ed. Vévé Clark, Ruth-Ellen B. Joeres, and Madelon Sprengnether. Chicago: University of Chicago Press.

Ogunyemi, Chikwenye Okonjo. 1996. *Africa Wo/Man Palava: The Nigerian Novel by Women.* Chicago: University of Chicago Press.

Ohadike, Don C. 1991. *The Ekumeku Movement: Western Igbo Resistance to the British Conquest of Nigeria, 1883–1914.* Athens: Ohio University Press.

Ohadike, Don C. 1994. *Anioma: A Social History of the Western Igbo People.* Athens: Ohio University Press.

Ohadike, Don C. et al., eds. 1988. *Jos Oral History and Literature Texts: Vol. 6. Western Igbo.* Jos: Department of History, University of Jos, Nigeria.

Ojo, G. J. Afolabi. 1966. *Yoruba Culture: A Geographical Analysis.* Ife: University of Ife Press/London: University of London Press.

Okere, L. C. 1983. *The Anthropology of Food in Rural Igboland, Nigeria: Socioeconomic and Cultural Aspects of Food and Food Habit in Rural Igboland.* Lanham: University Press of America.

Okojie, C. G. 1960. *Ishan Native Laws and Customs.* Lagos: CMS Press.

Okonjo, Kamene. 1976. The Dual-Sex Political System in Operation: Igbo Women and Community Politics in Midwestern Nigeria. In Hafkin and Bay 1976.

Okonjo, Kamene. 1981. Women's Political Participation in Nigeria. In Steady 1981.

Okonjo, Kamene. 1992. Aspects of Continuity and Change in Mate-Selection Among the Igbo West of the River Niger. *Journal of Comparative Family Studies,* 23:339–360.

Okpewho, Isidore. 1970. *The Victims.* London: Longman.

Okpewho, Isidore. 1979. *The Epic in Africa: Toward a Poetics of the Oral Performance.* New York: Columbia University Press.

Okpewho, Isidore. 1983. *Myth in Africa: A Study of Its Aesthetic and Cultural Relevance.* Cambridge: Cambridge University Press.

Okpewho, Isidore. 1990a. Towards a Faithful Record: On Transcribing and Translating the Oral Narrative Performance. In Okpewho 1990b.

Okpewho, Isidore. 1992. *African Oral Literature: Backgrounds, Character, and Continuity.* Bloomington: Indiana University Press.

Okpewho, Isidore. 1995. The Cousins of Uncle Remus. In *The Black Columbiad: Defining Moments in African American Literature and Culture*, ed. Werner Sollors and Maria Diedrich. Cambridge, MA: Harvard University Press. Pp. 15–27.

Okpewho, Isidore, ed. 1990b. *The Oral Performance in Africa*. Ibadan: Spectrum Books.

Ong, Walter J. 1982. *Orality and Literacy: The Technologizing of the Word*. London: Methuen.

Onwuejeogwu, M. Angulu. 1972a. *The Traditional Political System of Ibusa*. Occasional Publications of Odinani Museum, Nri: No. 1. Ibadan: Institute of African Studies, University of Ibadan.

Onwuejeogwu, M. Angulu. 1972b. An Outline Account of the Dawn of Igbo Civilization in the Igbo Culture Area. *Odinani: The Journal of Odinani Museum, Nri*, 1:14–57.

Onwuejeogwu, M. Angulu. 1981. *An Igbo Civilization: Nri Kingdom and Hegemony*. London: Ethnographica.

Onwuteaka, V. C. 1965. The Aba Riot of 1929 and Its Relation to the System of Indirect Rule. *Nigerian Journal of Economic and Social Studies*, 7:24–36.

Opland, Jeff. 1995. Nontsizi Mgqwetho: Stranger in Town. In Furniss and Gunner 1995. Pp. 162–184.

Oriji, John N. 1994. *Traditions of Igbo Origin: A Study of Pre-Colonial Population Movements in Africa*. New York: Peter Lang.

Osaghae, Eghosa. 1991. Ethnic Minorities and Federalism in Nigeria. *African Affairs*, 90:237–258.

Osoba, Funmi, ed. 1993. *Benin Folklore: A Collection of Classic Folktales and Legends*. London: Hadada Books.

Otite, Onigu. 1974. Who Are the Edo? In *Edo Language and Its Orthography*. Benin City: Ministry of Education, Midwest State.

Otite, Onigu. 1977. Historical Aspects of the Sociology of the Bendel State of Nigeria. *Journal of the Historical Society of Nigeria*, 9:40–54.

Ottenberg, P. V. 1959. The Changing Economic Position of Women Among the Afikpo Ibo. In *Continuity and Change in African Cultures*, ed. William R. Bascom and Melville J. Herskovits. Chicago: University of Chicago Press.

Oxford, Cheryl. 1992. Ray Hicks: The Storyteller as Shaman. In *Performance, Culture, and Identity*, ed. Elizabeth C. Fine and Jean Haskell Spear. Westport: Praeger.

Paulme, Denise, ed. 1963. *Women of Tropical Africa*. Berkeley: University of California Press.

Pender-Cudlip, Patrick. 1972. Oral Traditions and Anthropological Analysis: Some Contemporary Myths. *Azania*, 7:3–24.

Perham, Margery. 1937. *Native Administration in Nigeria*. London: Oxford University Press.

Preston, George Nelson. 1981. Reading the Art of Benin. In Kaplan 1981:62–76.

Rabkin, E. 1976. *The Fantastic in Literature*. Princeton: Princeton University Press.

Raglan, Lord. 1936. *The Hero: A Study in Tradition, Myth, and Drama*. London: Methuen.

Rank, Otto. 1959 [1909]. *The Myth of the Birth of the Hero*. New York: Vintage.

Ricoeur, Paul. 1961. Histoire de la philosophie et historicité: In *L'histoire et ses interprétations*, ed. Raymond Aron. Paris: Mouton.

Rivers, Pitt. 1968 [1900]. *Antique Works of Art from Benin.* New York: Hacker Art Books (rpt).

Rodney, Walter. 1974 [1972]. *How Europe Underdeveloped Africa.* Washington, DC: Howard University Press.

Rosaldo, Michelle Zimbalist and Louise Lamphere, eds. 1974. *Woman, Culture, and Society.* Stanford: Stanford University Press.

Rosaldo, Renato. 1989. *Culture and Truth: The Making of Social Analysis.* Boston: Beacon Press.

Roth, H. Ling. 1972 [1903]. *Great Benin: Its Customs, Art, and Horrors.* Northbrook: Metro Books (rpt).

Rothchild, Donald and Victor A. Olorunsola. 1983. Managing Competing State and Ethnic Claims. In Rothchild and Olorunsola 1983.

Rothchild, Donald and Victor A. Olorunsola, eds. 1983. *State versus Ethnic Claims: African Policy Dilemmas.* Boulder: Westview Press.

Ryder, Alan F.C. 1965. A Reconsideration of the Ife-Benin Relationship. *Journal of African History,* 6:25–37.

Ryder, Alan F.C. 1969. *Benin and the Europeans, 1485–1897.* New York: Humanities Press.

Sayers, D.L. 1937. *The Song of Roland.* Harmondsworth: Penguin.

Schaefer, Stacy. 1983. Benin Commemorative Heads. In Ben-Amos and Rubin 1983:71–78.

Scheub, Harold. 1975. *The Xhosa Ntsomi.* Oxford: Clarendon Press.

Scheub, Harold. 1985. A Review of African Oral Traditions and Literature. *African Studies Review,* 28:1–72.

Sekoni, Ropo. 1994a. Yoruba Market Dynamics and the Aesthetics of Negotiation in Female Precolonial Narrative Tradition. In Ogundipe-Leslie and Davies 1994. Pp. 33–46.

Sekoni, Ropo. 1994b. *Folk Poetics: A Sociosemiotic Study of Yoruba Trickster Tales.* Westport: Greenwood.

Shaw, Thurstan. 1970. *Igbo-Ukwu: An Account of Archaeological Discoveries in Eastern Nigeria.* London: Faber and Faber.

Shaw, Thurstan. 1975. Those Igbo-Ukwu Radiocarbon Dates: Facts, Fictions, and Probabilities. *Journal of African History,* 16:503–517.

Shaw, Thurstan. 1977a. Hunters, Gatherers and First Farmers in West Africa. In *Hunters, Gatherers and First Farmers Beyond Europe: An Archaeological Survey,* ed. J. V. S. Megaw. Leicester: Leicester University Press.

Shaw, Thurstan. 1977b. *Unearthing Igbo-Ukwu.* Ibadan: Oxford University Press.

Sidahome, Joseph E. 1964. *Stories of the Benin Empire.* London: Oxford University Press.

Sidibe, M. 1959. Soundiata Keita, heros historique et legendaire, empereur du Manding. *Notes Africaines,* 81:41–51.

Soyinka, Wole and D. O. Fagunwa. 1968. *The Forest of a Thousand Daemons.* London: Thomas Nelson.

Soyinka, Wole. 1976. *Myth, Literature and the African World.* Cambridge: Cambridge University Press.

Soyinka, Wole. 1996. *The Open Sore of a Continent: A Personal Narrative of the Nigerian Crisis.* New York: Oxford University Press.

Spivak, Gayatri Chakravorty. 1988. Can the Subaltern Speak? In *Marxism and the Interpretation of Culture*, ed. Gary Nelson and Lawrence Grossberg. Urbana: University of Illinois Press.

Steady, Filomina C., ed. 1981. *The Black Woman Cross-Culturally*. Cambridge, MA: Schenkman.

Sudarkasa, Niara. 1981. Female Employment and Family Organization in West Africa. In Steady 1981.

Talbot, P. Amaury. 1926. *Peoples of Southern Nigeria*. 4 vols. London: Oxford University Press.

Tatham, Peter. 1992. *The Makings of Maleness: Men, Women, and the Flight of Daedalus*. New York: New York University Press.

Tedlock, Dennis. 1983. *The Spoken Word and the Work of Interpretation*. Philadelphia: University of Pennsylvania Press.

Tegnaeus, Harry. 1950. *Le Heros Civilisateur: Contribution à l'Étude Ethnologique de la Religion et de la Sociologie Africaines*. Studia Ethnographica Upsaliensa II. Stockholm: Victor Pettersons.

Thomas, Northcote. 1969 [1914]. *Anthropological Report on Ibo-speaking Peoples of Nigeria: IV. Law and Custom of the Ibo of the Asaba District. S. Nigeria*. New York: Negro Universities Press.

Thomas, E. and Kay Williamson. 1967. *Wordlists of the Delta Edo*. Occasional Publications, No. 8. Ibadan: Institute of African Studies, University of Ibadan, Nigeria.

Thompson, Linda. 1992. Feminist Methodology for Family Studies. *Journal of Marriage and the Family*, 54:3–18.

Thoyer-Rozat, Annik, ed. 1978. *Chants des Chasseurs du Mali par Mamadu Jara*. Paris: [privately published].

Todorov, Tzvetan. 1975. *The Fantastic: A Structural Approach to a Literary Genre*. Tr. R. Howard. Ithaca: Cornell University Press.

Tomlinson, John. 1991. *Cultural Imperialism: A Critical Introduction*. Baltimore: Johns Hopkins University Press.

Tonkin, Elizabeth. 1992. *Narrating Our Pasts: The Social Construction of Oral History*. Cambridge: Cambridge University Press.

Turnbull, Colin. 1968. Discussion. In *Man the Hunter*, ed. Richard B. Lee and Irven DeVore. Chicago: Aldine.

Turner, Victor. 1967. *The Forest of Symbols: Aspects of Ndembu Ritual*. Ithaca: Cornell University Press.

Turner, Victor. 1977. Variations on a Theme of Liminality. In *Secular Rituals*, ed. Sally F. Moore and Barbara G. Myerhoff. Assen: Van Gorcum.

Uchendu, Victor C. 1965. *The Igbo of Southeastern Nigeria*. New York: Holt, Rinehart, and Winston.

Usuanlele, Uyilawa and Toyin Falola. 1994. The Scholarship of Jacob Egharevba of Benin. *History in Africa*, 21:303–318.

Vail, Leroy and Landeg White. 1991. *Power and the Praise Poem: Southern African Voices in History*. Charlottesville: University Press of Virginia.

van Allen, Judith. 1976. "Aba Riots" or Igbo "Women's War"? Ideology, Stratification, and the Invisibility of Women. In Hafkin and Bay 1976.

Vansina, Jan. 1961. *Oral Tradition: A Study in Historical Methodology*. Trans. H.M. Wright. Harmondsworth: Penguin Books.

Vogel, Susan. 1974. *Gods of Fortune: The Cult of the Hand in Nigeria*. New York: Museum of Primitive Art.

von Luschan, Felix. 1919. *Die Altertumer von Benin*. Berlin: Museum für Volker-
kunde.

Warren, C. 1988. Gender Issues in Field Research. In *Qualitative Research Methods
Series*, no. 9. London: Sage.

Weigle, Marta. 1978. Women as Verbal Artists: Reclaiming the Daughters of
Enheduanna. *Frontiers: A Journal of Women Studies*, vol. 3, no. 3:1–9.

Weigle, Marta. 1989. *Creation and Procreation: Feminist Reflections on Mythologies of
Cosmogony and Parturition*. Philadelphia: University of Pennsylvania Press.

Welch, J.W. 1935. The Isoko Clans of the Niger Delta. PhD Thesis. University
of Cambridge, Cambridge, UK.

White, Hayden. 1973. *Metahistory: The History of Imagination in Nineteenth-Century
Europe*. Baltimore: Johns Hopkins University Press.

Wren, Robert M. 1991. *Those Magical Years: The Making of Nigerian Literature at
Ibadan 1948–1966*. Washington, DC: Three Continents Press.

Wrigley, C.C. 1971. Historicism in Africa: Slavery and State Formation. *African
Affairs*, 70:113–124.

Yesufu-Giwa, Moru. 1949. Once Fair City. *African Affairs*, 48:246.

Yocom, Margaret R. 1985. Woman to Woman: Fieldwork and the Private Sphere.
In Jordan and Kalcik 1985. Pp. 45–53.

Zenani, Nonengile Masithathu. 1992. *The World and the Word: Tales and Observations from the Xhosa Oral Tradition*, ed. Harold Scheub. Madison: University of
Wisconsin Press.

Index

Aba Women's War. *See* women
Aboh, 9
Abraham, W.E., 28
Abraka (Avbeka), 11
Achebe, Chinua, 75, 88, 90, 91, 96, 136, 194, 209, 215, 217, 223
Achilles, 30
ada (sword of office), 178, 202
Adaigbo (or Odaigbo), 10, 55, 56, 200
Adams, Captain John, 205
Adedeji, Olohigbe, 69, 204
Adesua, 15, 56, 195
Ado (=Edo), 19
Adose. *See* Adesua
aesthetics, 2
Afigbo, Adiele E., 92, 129, 178, 182, 183, 214, 220, 221
Afoluwa (narrator of Ozidi story), 19
Africa: contemporary, xi, 185, 191, 215, 222; "heroic" past of, xi, 191; scholarship on, 139
Agboghidi, 11, 15–20, 23, 195
Agbor, 117; Patriotic Union, 117, 191
age grades. *See* social structure, age grades
agogo. See musical instruments
ague. See festivals
Ahamangiwa, 205
Ajayi, J.F.A., 2, 190, 221
Ajuwon, Bade, 49, 52, 201
Akan, 51
Akaraogun, 167
Ake, Claude, 222

Akengbuda. *See* Oba—some Obas
Akenzua I, Akenzua II. *See* Oba—some Obas
Akenzua, Dr. Greg, 220
Akinola, G.A., 204
Akintoye, S.A., 177
akpata. See musical instruments
Akugbene, 9, 24
Alagoa, E.J., 4, 9, 25, 73
Albela (Indian film), 168
alo (chieftaincy title), 6, 202
Amadioha (Igbo god of thunder), 211
Amadiume, Ifi, 130–33, 213
Anazonwu (Obi of Onitsha), 133
ancestors, 62, 88, 127; Oba's, 70
Ancient Near East, 140
Anderson, Benedict, 185
Anene-Boyle, F.A., 11, 14, 23, 24, 196
Ani Udo, 55
Ani, Ana, Ala (Igbo earth deity), 182
Anioma. *See* Igbo, Western or West-Niger
anthropology, ix, 62
Anumenechi, John ("the Reverend"), 156, 157
Anyanwu, 211
Apocalypse Now, 30
Appiah, Kwame Anthony, xi, 183, 185, 221
archaeology, 1, 178–79
archetypes, 13
Arinze, Christy, xi, xii, 142–54, 156, 215, 216; biodata, 149
Arinze, Francis, 91, 208, 209, 211

Arinze, Patrick, xi–xiii, 38, 40–45, 53–54, 76–83, 92, 106, 142–49, 151, 153, 206, 207, 215, 217
Aro, 32, 33, 90, 180–83; oracle (Ibini Ukpabi or "Long Juju"), 180
art, art history, 1
Arualan. See Aruanran
Aruanran, 19–24, 36, 85, 195
Asaba, xiii, 10, 32, 33, 141, 149, 151, 155, 165, 169, 194, 197, 201, 203, 204, 206, 213, 216; local government areas, 210; etymologies of name, 10
Ashikodi, L.N., 53, 202
Ashinze, Chief, 202
Askia Mohammed. See Traore, Toure, Taraware
asologun. See musical instruments
Attoh, Chief S.N. Ofili, xii
audience input, 50, 92, 126, 138, 165, 166, 199, 206, 208
Avbeka. See Abraka
Awka, 9, 10
Ayewoh, M.E., 8
Azinge, Chief J.B., xiii
Azuonye, Chukwuma, 95–96, 216

Babalola, S. Adeboye, 52, 201
Babatunde, Emmanuel D., 204
Bachofen, J.-J., 213
badenya, 50
Bhagwan Art Productions (Bombay), 218; Master Bhagwan, 218
Baldwin, James, 197
Balewa, Abubakar Tafawa, 193
Banham, Martin, 217
Barber, Karin, 27, 214
Barnes, Sandra, 177, 201
Barnouw, Erik, 218
Basden, G.T., 88, 92
Bauman, Richard, 136
Beidelman, T.O., 55, 193
Beier, Ulli, 205, 217
Ben-Amos, Daniel, xiii, 13–15, 21, 22, 26, 84–86, 136, 195, 205, 208
Ben-Amos, Paula Girshik, xiii, 70, 71, 201, 204, 205, 211, 212
Benin: arts and crafts, ix, 1, 13, 69–70, 83–84, 176, 179, 208, 221; as a monar-chical culture, 91, 92; ethnomusicology, 13–14; fall of, ix, 222; images of, 11–14, 19, 63; influence of others on, 178–83, 191; influence on others, 95, 118, 173–78, 182, 191; myth of Yoruba origins, 6, 69, 175–76, 204, 210; ontology and religion, 13, 63–68, 70–72, 89, 91–93; oral traditions or folklore, 13, 15, 21, 68
—earlier names: Igodomigodo, 175, 204; Ile, 204; Ile Ibinu, 69, 204; Ubini, 205
Benin City, 20, 23, 157, 173, 205; as "City of Skulls," 11
the "Benin cycle" (of myths), 63
the Benin empire, 3, 54, 177, 183; extent of, 3, 193
the Benin Kingdom, ix, 1, 10, 59, 75, 95, 97, 173–83, 209, 219; achievements of, 174–76; and the Portuguese, 177, 194; conflicts with the aristocracy, 12, 69–70, 123, 178, 205; dynastic conflicts, 12, 68–70, 117, 123, 219; iconography, 70, 200; military campaigns, ix, 9, 10, 54, 199; relations with neighbors, x, 3, 4–25, 123, 173; trade with Europeans, ix, 12, 220
—rulers. See Oba; Ogiso
—wars with: Asaba, 10, 33; Igbuzo, x, 27, 39–46; Okhumwu, 21–22; Ubulu-Uku, 15–19, 25, 30, 49, 98, 105, 166, 195, 200, 220
Benin River, 73, 220
The Benin Scheme. See The Scheme for the Study of Benin History and Culture
Benue rift valley, 179
Beowulf, 200
Biafra, 184, 197, 223
Biebuyck, Daniel P., 212
Bietenholz, Peter G., 29
Bini (citizens of Benin), xii, 4, 5, 13, 17, 18, 63, 68, 72, 74, 75, 87, 89, 173, 177, 194, 204, 221
biographical issues, 136–72
Bird, Charles, 49, 50, 201
the "Black Atlantic," 185
Blackmun, Barbara Winston, 176
Bloor, Michael, 137, 138, 154

Borges, Jorge Luis, 197
Bosnia-Hercegovina, 186
Boston, John S., 87–89, 96, 201, 203, 213
Bowra, C.M., 24
Bradbury, R.E., 1–3, 8, 13, 63–65, 67, 71, 72, 87–89, 181, 184, 193, 200, 204, 205, 207; and The Benin Scheme, 2, 184; functionalist anti-aestheticism, 2, 193; on Benin religion, 13, 63–68, 72
brass, 69–70, 179, 204
Bremond, Claude, 208
brigandage, 32
Briggs, Charles, 136
the British: and Benin, 11, 12, 73, 175, 180, 182, 219, 222; colonization by, 33, 128, 130, 133, 134, 174, 222; commercial interests, 149; social research, 2
bronze, 70, 204, 205, 208
Bulman, Stephen, 201
Burkert, Walter, 49–50

Calabar, 12
Camara, Seydou, 49
"center" vs. "periphery," ix, 188, 222
chalk, white, 81
Chambers, Lee, 205
charms (mystical resource). See magic
chi, 75, 80, 87–92, 208; as spiritual double, 91
Chikwendu, V.E., 179
Chima. See Eze Chima
Chodorow, Nancy, 137
Christianity, 90
Chukwu. See God—names for
Chukwukere, I., 90–92
cinema, influence on storytelling, 162, 218
cire perdu (lost-wax) casting, 69, 179
Cisse, Youssouf, 52
Clark[-Bekederemo], J.P., 3, 20, 196, 207, 212, 217, 218; A Decade of Tongues, 211; Ozidi: A Play, 196; The Ozidi Saga, 3, 9, 19, 23, 196, 213
Clifford, James, 171, 185
Clignet, Remi, 151–52
cocoyam (as "female" crop), 132

Cole, Herbert, 70, 208
collective, collectivity, 47, 48, 50, 89
Collingwood, R.G., 27–31, 53, 60, 197; Eurocentrism of, 28; on "historical contemplation," 30, 53, 60; on "presentism," 31; on "purposive action," 28
colonialism, colonial rule, 186–88, 221. See also the British; Ekeh, P.P.
communalism, 62, 68
Connah, Graham, 2
context, x, 60, 136
copper, 179, 220
Cosentino, Donald, 127
creation, 62, 73, 75, 76, 93
Crewe-Read, S.O. (colonial officer), 222
Cross River, 180
cults, 63–64; Igbile, 73; Ododoa, 73, 205; hand (obo), 64, 65, 204; head (uhumwu), 64, 65; of Oba's ancestors, 70
culture, x, 1, 29, 61, 135, 203, 220, 221; cultural imperialism, 220; cultural values, 123–24; culture area, 129; oral culture, 140–41

Da Monzon, 200
Dahomey (Republic of Benin), 63, 201
Dapper, Olfert, 196, 213
Dark, Philip, 2, 70, 83, 200
Davies, Carole Boyce, 139
Dean, Carolyn, 70, 205
destiny, fate, 63, 67, 71, 72, 74, 86, 87, 90, 91; prenatal or prechosen, 62, 64, 65, 86, 90, 93; psychological factors in, 86–87
Diabate, Massa M., 201
Dibia, Bernard O., 213, 218
Dickey, Sara, 218
différance, différence, xii
diffusion (of tales), xii, 25, 128
Dike, K.O., 1, 27, 183, 184, 194, 221
Diop, Cheikh Anta, 213
divine kingship, 73. See also Oba, as divine king
diviner, divination, 63, 65, 72, 75, 84, 87, 104, 106–17, 123–25, 160, 211
Drake, Carlos, 213
dual organization, 5

DuBois, W.E.B., 184

Ebohon, Osemwegie, 68, 71, 95, 150, 180, 204, 210, 213
Echeruo, Michael J.C., xiii, 92
Edaiken (heir apparent), 212
Edeleyo, Princess, 117, 128
Edemode, John, 8, 11, 18
Edini, 10, 55, 57
Edo: eponymous ancestor of Benin, 4; ethno-linguistic group, 4, 5, 8, 19, 22, 84, 95, 173, 181, 194, 196, 205, 221; state in Nigeria, 193
Edoh, A.O., 194
"Edoid," 182, 220
Edozien, Obi Chike (Asagba of Asaba), xiii, 194
egalitarianism, 95
Egbamarhuan, 22
Eghaevbo (ruling councils), 85, 176, 217
Egharevba, Jacob U., 4, 7, 10, 12, 13, 15–18, 20, 21, 29, 68, 73, 128, 177, 182, 183, 193–96, 210, 212; as a historian, 22, 25, 181, 196; member of the House of Iwebo, 195; *Benin Titles*, 217; *Concise Lives of the Famous Iyases of Benin*, 217; *Descriptive Catalogue of Benin Museum*, 204, 208; *Fusion of Tribes*, 193; *Marriage of the Princesses of Benin*, 85; *Origin of Benin*, 204; *A Short History of Benin*, 20, 177, 195
Ehengbuda. *See* Oba—some Obas
ehi, 63–68, 72, 75, 87, 90, 92
Ejime, 57, 58
Ejohwomu, Ovie Luke (Adakaji of Abraka), 194
Eka (Agbor), 177
Ekaladerhan, 204, 211
Ekatakpi (Aruanran), 21
eke (lot, portion in life), 208
Ekeh, P.P., xiii, 117, 186–87, 219, 220; on colonialism and the "two publics," 186–87, 222
Ekejiuba, Felicia, 213, 221
Ekiti, 176
Eko (Lagos), 25, 193
Ekumeku Movement, 202
Elaigwu, J. Isawa, 188

Elugbe, Ben, 182, 196
Emecheta, Buchi, 151
Emokpaogbe (Agboghidi), 15–16
Emokpolo, 16, 17
Emotan, 215
empire, xii, 52, 135, 183, 222. *See also* the Benin empire
English, narrators' use of: Christy, 153–54, 172, 214; Odogwu, 167, 172, 218; Ojiudu, 199
Enyi, Okondu, 203
epics, 18, 19, 24, 34, 191, 201
Equiano, Olaudah, 221
Ere. *See* Ogiso
Erikson, Thomas Hyland, 186
Erivini (narrator of Ozidi story), 19
Esan. *See* Ishan
Esigie. *See* Oba—some Obas
ethnicity, 184, 189, 221; "ethnic minorities," 221
ethnography, 138
ethnopoetics, xi
Etsako, 3, 4, 8, 18, 19, 174
Eweka I, Eweka II. *See* Oba—some Obas
execution (order), 11, 61, 66, 93, 99, 102, 117, 162, 164, 207
Eyo, Ekpo, 179
eze (king, red-capped chief), 95, 96, 203
Eze Chima, 10, 178, 181, 210
Ezechi, 56–59, 203, 219
Ezemu, 17, 18, 37, 49, 116, 195, 203, 210, 212
Ezomo (war minister), 3, 8, 12–15, 17, 18, 61, 68, 70, 193, 195, 210; Ehenua, 3, 65, 200; Omoruyi, 65

fabula, 29, 197
fadenya, 50
Fadipe, N.A., 52
Fagg, William, 70, 71, 175, 205
Fagunwa, D.O., 167, 218
Falade, Solange, 150, 216
Falola, Toyin, 196, 222
the family, 62, 87, 88, 137
Fanon, Franz, 221
the fantastic, 25, 26, 196
Farrer, Claire, 138
federalism, 187–89

feminism, 130–33, 137–40, 143, 214; African, 150; American, 138
festivals: *ague*, 128, 199, 210; *igue*, 64, 70, 174, 175; New Yam, 123, 160, 199, 210; *ugie erha Oba*, 204
fieldwork, 3, 207
Fine Arts Museum of San Francisco, 84
Finnegan, Ruth, 139, 141, 197
folklore, 138
Forde, D., 213
form, narrative, x
formulas, 116, 199, 209, 218
Fortes, Meyer, 62–63, 86, 87, 204, 209
Foucault, Michel, 203
Fraser, Douglas, 70
Freudianism, 208, 213
functionalism, 2

the Ga (of Ghana), 193
Gage-Brandon, Anastasia, 151
Gallwey, Vice-Consul, 11, 12
Gates, Henry Louis ("Skip"), 214
Gboma-Gbesin (Agboghidi's sword), 17
gender issues, x, 126–34, 137–40
gerontocracy, 6, 70, 124. *See also* social structure, age grades
Gibbs, James, 217
Gilroy, Paul, 185–86
Gleason, Judith, 52
God, supreme, 62–65, 78, 80–81
—names for: Chineke, 90; Chukwu, 90, 180, 208; Olisebuluwa, 205, 208; Osanobua, 72, 205; Woyengi (Our Mother), 74, 86
Goody, Jack, 140–41, 214
Gowon, General Yakubu, 193
Graham-White, Anthony, 217
the "Great Divide," 141
Green, Margaret M., 90, 130, 131, 133, 213
griot, 140
Guinier, Lani, 214

Havelock, Eric, 140, 141, 214
head-hunting, 6, 22, 33, 88
—head-hunting groups: Abam, 32, 182, 183; Abiriba, 32; Edda, 32, 183; Ohafia, 32, 183

Hegel, G.W.F., 28
hegemony, ix, 5, 20, 26, 132, 136, 190, 195, 218, 221, 222
heirs apparent, 84, 118
Henderson, Richard N., 92
hereditary rulership, 6, 7, 51
hero, 27, 30–33, 46, 211; precocity of, 161, 218; testing of, 162–64; weapons of, 17, 43, 199, 206
heroism, 27, 30–48, 59; private and public, 34–36, 47–48
Herskovits, M., and F. Herskovits, 63, 201, 208
Higbie, Carolyn, 201
history, x, 1, 25, 27, 60, 197; "evidence" in, 30; myth and, 60; oral vs. literate, 60; past and present in, 28, 29; philosophy of, 27–31; *historia*, 29, 197; historians, 27, 30, 51, 104
histrionics, 198, 209, 218
Hobsbawm, Eric, 176, 185
Hollos, Marija, 7
Home, Robert, 219
Homer, 30; Homeric literature, 140, 201
Hook, Sidney, 30
Hopkins, Anthony, 201
Horton, Robin, 63, 74, 208, 215
Hull, R.W., 70
human sacrifice, 11, 105, 123, 160, 199
hunter, 37–46, 100, 199, 201; as culture hero, 51–53, 201; as defender, 17, 37–46, 50, 52, 59; hunter tales, 48–50, 167, 201, 203; hunters' guilds, 52
hunting, 64, 87, 200, 204, 211; hunting and war, 49–50; hunting culture, 52; qualities of the hunting life, 48–51
Hymes, Dell, xi

Ibadan University, ix, 1, 3, 155, 169, 173, 179, 194, 199, 217, 219
Ibakpolo, 24
icha aka, 157
ichi (facial scarification), 179
ichi mmo, 157
Idemili (goddess), 131
identity, x, 3, 37, 136, 171, 190, 203, 221
ideophone, 205, 207, 209, 210
Idu, Iduu (=Edo or Benin), 14, 23, 95

Idubo (=Aruanran), 21
Idumuje-Ugboko, 156, 217
Idumuje-Uno, 210, 217
Ife, 69, 204; as a theocracy, 176, 204; arts, 179; Oni of, 69, 70, 175, 194
Igala, 8, 182, 201; Ata of, 71
Igbafe, Philip, 196, 199, 204, 210
Igbaghon (Jamieson River), 16, 17, 216
Igbesamwan (guild of artists), 69
Igbo, 4, 32–60, 75, 89, 129–34; and Benin ceremonialism, 95, 118, 129, 176, 179; as acephalous, 96; cosmology, 10, 87–96; influences on Benin, 178–83; language, 180–82
Igbo, Western or West-Niger (=Anioma), 3, 26, 31–60, 73, 92, 96, 151, 174, 189; and Britain, 33, 202, 222; relations with Benin (general), 9–10
Igbo-Ukwu, 179, 221
Igbuzo (Ibusa), xiii, 10, 25, 34, 38, 47, 75, 151, 177, 195, 197, 199, 206; etymologies of name, 202; social history, 10, 53–60, 96, 203
—sections of: Imiidi, 53, 57, 201; Ogboli, 55–56, 202; Umuwai, 54, 57, 201
Igirigiri, Kaalu, 216
igue. See festivals
Igueghae, 70, 177
Igwara (=Aruanran), 14, 195
ijala poetry, 48
Ijo (Ijaw), 3, 4, 7, 8, 19, 73–75, 193–94, 196, 205; among the Yoruba, 220; relations with Benin (general), 9
—clans: Apoi, 220; Kalabari, 74; Mein, 9, 73; Tarakiri Orua, 9, 19, 73
ikegobo, 2, 3, 64, 70, 87, 89, 181
ikenga, 87–90, 181–82, 208, 213
Ikime, Obaro, 5, 10, 13
Ikpo, Chief Nosike, xiii, 202, 203
Ikpoba Hill (Benin), 109, 112, 213
Ima of Ogbelaka (=Imaran Adiagbon), 17
images and symbols, 20, 23–24, 34, 58–61, 67, 68, 83, 84, 96, 127, 135, 152, 196, 201, 205, 207, 211
imagination: female, 153–54; historical, 8, 31; narrative (mythic), 13, 134, 153, 171

Imaran Adiagbon, 16
individual, individualism, 62, 75, 87–89, 91, 92, 178, 190, 213
Innes, Gordon, xi, 50, 201, 217
"invention" theory, 185
Irele, F. Abiola, xiii
Irigaray, Luce, 137, 138
iron, use of, 64, 176
Ironsi, General Johnson Aguiyi, 156
Isele-Uku, 9, 92
Isembi (Ijo god), 74
Ishan (Esan), 13, 14, 21, 23, 170, 194, 195
—relations with Benin: historical, 6–8; mythic, 13, 21, 23
Isichei, Elizabeth, 92, 213
Isichei, Patrick, 215
Isoko, 3, 4, 8–10, 24, 25, 194
ivory (in Benin arts), 69, 176
Iyase (prime minister), 12, 68, 69, 160, 162, 164, 205, 217
Iyenuroho (=Iyenugholo), 21
Iyololu, 11, 18, 19
Izevbaye, D.S., 196
Izomo (=Ezomo), 14

Jackson, Michael, 127
Jeffreys, M.D.W., 87–90, 181–83, 211
Johnson, John W., 50, 201
joking styles, 138
Jones, G.I., 213
Jordan, Rosan, 138
Jungianism, 213

Kalabari. *See* Ijo—clans
Kalcik, Susan, 138, 143
Kamara clan, 52
Kambili, 50, 201
Kaplan, Flora, 196, 205, 219
Keita clan, 52; Sunjata Keita, 47, 191, 201
Kendall, M.B., 49, 50
Kerr, David, 217
King, Katherine, 30
Klein, Kerwin Lee, 222
kolanut, 79–80, 86, 88, 93, 117
Konate clan, 52
Kone clan, 52

Krishnaswamy, S., 218
Kuper, Adam, xi, 184, 186
Kwa language group, 4, 182

Ladipo, Duro, 179–80
Lamphere, Louise, 137
Landolphe, Captain, 220
Langelier, Kristin M., 138
Lawal, Babatunde, 179
Leith-Ross, Sylvia, 214
letter-writers, 154
Lévi-Strauss, Claude, 216
Lewis, I.M., 193
liminality, 85, 127, 128, 150. *See also* marginality
lineage, 62, 89
literacy. *See* orality; Western culture
literary scholars (vs. historians), 27
local narratives, 29; vs. master-narratives, 191, 222
Lord, Albert B., 136, 140, 214
Lyotard, Jean-François 191, 222

magic (charms, mystical aid), 15, 18, 21, 49, 145, 160, 162, 185, 201, 207; *dalilu*, 49
maleness, 31, 137, 138, 154; male authority, 135; men as oral performers, 137–40, 153
Mali, 52, 140
Mande, Manding, Mandinka, 49, 50, 52
marginality, 85, 98, 126–28, 135, 150
the margins (vs. the center), ix
matriarchy, 213
matriliny, 213
Mauritius, 186
Mba, Nina E., 128, 132, 214
Mbari Cultural Center (Ibadan), 217
Mbiti, J.S., 28
McKeganey, Neil, 137, 138, 154
Meek, C.K., 208
Meeme Odogwu, 36, 37
melting-pot, 186
Melzian, H.J., 181
memory, 61; collective, 29, 31, 53, 59, 134
metaphysics, x; Benin, 63–75; Igbo, 75–92

mfecane. *See* Shaka the Zulu
Mgbile (Ijo ancestor), 9, 73, 104
migration, 8, 12, 55–57, 69, 92, 123, 141, 178
military dictatorship, 59, 60
Mitchell, Carol, 138
modern technology, 7. *See also* Western culture
modernity, 142, 151–54
Mohammed, Askia. *See* Traore, Toure, Taraware
Momah, Eke ("M & B"), 217
Morton-Williams, Peter, 2
motherhood, 118, 125, 127, 136
"motherright," 213
motifs, tale, x, xii, 209: death by drowning, 18, 19, 21, 22; hero samples women's dishes to identify mother, 103; hero's precocious growth, 161, 218; hero's weapons not strong enough, 43, 47, 78; infernal gateman, 79–80; male child cast away, 99, 127; medicine-pot borne by emigrant, 55–56; mistreated wife, 98–104, 143, 144, 164; old woman helper, 84, 85, 97–134, 209; penile problems, 76–83; red-uniformed (child) soldiers, 16–20, 24, 196, 211; (river) boundary between human and spiritual worlds, 72, 79; tooth-plucking, 23–24, 37, 42–43, 61, 199; wife-snatching, 35–37
Mphande, Lupenga, 223
Mudimbe, V.Y., 185, 203
music, x, 38–39, 85–86, 116, 198, 199, 208
musical instruments, 27, 58, 85, 115; *agogo*, 38; *akpata*, 84–85, 208; *asologun*, 84–85, 208; *opanda*, 38, 58, 198; thumb-piano, 76; *ubo*, 85
Mwindo, 211
myth, mythology, x, 27, 50, 57, 73, 131, 135, 141, 185, 211; and history, 60, 203; and reality, 152, 193, 216; *mythologique*, 96

Nagy, Gregory, 46, 197
nation, nationalism, 183–91
Ndichie (college of elders), 129

Ndokwa, 3, 9
New Yam Festival. *See* festivals
Nguni diaspora, 223
Niane, Djibril Tamsir, 201
Niger River, 5, 8, 10, 32, 55, 123, 178, 181, 183; Niger Delta, 8, 9, 73, 180
Niger-Congo language family 4
Nigeria: Civil War, 149, 153, 156, 184, 187, 197; contemporary, 1, 125, 153, 183–90, 221, 222; intergroup relations, 4, 166, 180, 183, 186–90, 221; language and ethnicity, 4, 186–90; political divisions, x, 4, 5, 193, 194, 197
Nnebisi (Asaba ancestor), 9, 201
Nnobi, 130–33; origin myth, 131
Nnoli, Okwudiba, 189
Nri (Nshi), 10, 31, 55–58, 90, 179–83, 202, 203, 211, 221; bronzecasting, 179–80; decline of, 182; ritual expertise, 123, 180–81; relations with Benin, 179–83
Nsugbe, Philip O., 213
Nupe, 8
Nwabara, S.N., 214
Nwabueze, Joseph Chimgo, xiii
Nwajei, Adaeze, 141
Nwambuonwo, Okafor (Odagwue), xii, 105–16, 123–27, 135, 143, 208, 211, 212, 217, 221; as ritualist, 211; as *ozoma*, 115, 208; biodata, 115; meaning of "Odagwue," 210; performance style, 115–16
Nwaobiala Movement, 214
Nwapa, Flora, 215
Nwoboshi, Obi Louis (Obuzo of Igbuzo), xiii, 57, 199, 203
Nwoga, Donatus Ibe, 208
Nwoko, Demas, 217
nyama (spiritual agencies), 49
nyenne (spirits of the bush), 127
Nzimiro, Ikenna, 92, 129, 202

Oba (ruler in second Benin dynasty), 2, 6, 8–10, 14, 23, 37, 42–46, 54, 57, 61, 66–72, 76–78, 92–97, 110–12, 178, 215, 218, 219, 222; as pivot of Benin life, 13, 70, 205; as divine king, 71–72, 93, 205; images of, 11, 18, 19, 77, 95–96, 116–18, 126–29, 143–49, 161–64, 175, 195; praise salutes of, 71, 95, 110, 118, 158, 162, 210
—some Obas: Akengbuda, 15–16; Akenzua I, 3, 65, 180; Akenzua II, 175, 211, 219; Ehengbuda, 12, 15, 25, 84; Erediauwa I, 194, 210, 219; Esigie (Osawe), 20–22, 71, 85, 128, 195, 205; Ewedo, 69, 70, 205, 217; Eweka I, 6, 69, 84, 194; Eweka II, 175, 222; Ewuakpe, 7, 22, 85; Ewuare, 4, 7, 8, 71, 128, 217; Obanosa, 12; Oguola, 69, 70, 173; Ohuan (Odogbo), 84; Ovonramwen, 12; Ozolua, 12, 20–22
"Oba Nkpeze," 24
Obanosa. *See* Oba—some Obas
Obi, 13, 15, 56, 95, 105, 166, 199, 203, 209
Obiechina, Emmanuel N., 218
Obolo, Oboro-Uku. *See* Ubulu-Uku
Odighi n'Udo, 21
odion, odionwere (pl. *edion*), 6
Odogbo, Prince. *See* Oba—some Obas, Ohuan
Odogwu of Abba, 36
Odudua, 205
Oedipalism, 62
ofo, 88
Ogbechie, Okonji ("Ababa Chico"), 156, 157, 218
Ogboinba, 74–75, 86, 87
Ogboli. *See* Igbuzo
ogene, 164
Ogie, 9, 15
Ogieiriaixi, Evinma, 193
Ogiobolo (king of Ubulu-Uku), 16
Ogiso (ruler in first Benin dynasty), 8, 10, 14, 66–69, 129, 175, 194, 204, 210; cruelty of, 68–69; etymology of title, 204
—some Ogisos: Ere, 68, 69, 204; Igodo, 68, 204; Owodo, 68, 204, 211
Ogot, Bethwell, 27
Ogueren (or Oguaran), 19, 23, 196
Ogun, 52, 64, 196
Ogunbiyi, Yemi, 217
Ogundijo, Bayo, 214

Ogundipe-Leslie, Omolara, 135

Ogunyemi, Chikwenye O., xiii, 208, 214

Oguta, 129

Ogwashi-Uku, xiii, 10, 36, 55–56, 156, 180, 200, 202

Ohadike, Don, xiii, 31, 53, 55, 57, 92, 194–96, 201, 202, 212, 213, 222

Ohene Abubu-ugo, 54

oil palm produce, 132

Ojea, 32–34, 197

Ojo, G.J. Afolabi, 52, 177

Ojobolo, Okabou, 19, 196, 218

Okagbue I, Ofala (Obi of Onitsha), 196

Okere, L.C., 201

Okeze, Christopher Ojiudu, x, xii, 24, 27, 31, 34, 36–60, 75–78, 83, 197–99, 201–203, 205, 208, 216, 218

Okhumwu, 20

Okigbo, Christopher, 217

Okocha, Sunday ("Timekeeper"), 156, 157

Okojie, C.G., 8

Okomma Ogbodogbo, 54

Okonjo, Kamene, 130, 132, 151, 213

Okoojii, James, xii, 38, 40–46, 58, 61, 63, 75–86, 91, 92, 96–98, 198, 199, 205–208; narrative style, 209

okpako (pl. *ekpako*), 6

Okuo-Ukpoba (River of Blood), 21

Okwuashi, Odogwu (Nwaniani), xii, 35, 154–72, 191, 200, 210, 212, 216, 217, 219; nicknamed *akawo mai-gash*, 156, 167; nicknamed "Albela," 154, 160, 165, 168, 218; and recording technology, 217–18; as letter-writer, 168–69; biodata, 155–57; narrative repertory, 169–70; performance style, 157, 217–18; two tales, 158–65

Olisebuluwa. *See* God—names for

Ologbose (Ologbosere), 12, 14, 16, 180, 195

Olokun, 71, 205

Olomu, Nana, 220

Olorunsola, Victor, 188, 221

"Omalingwo," 216

"Omemma," 51

Omezi, 35–36

Omofobhon, 24

Omoha, 56, 57

Omu (grand matron), 129–30, 132, 164

—some Omus: Ejime Obi-Elue (of Asaba), 149; Nwagboka (of Onitsha), 129, 133; Okwei (of Ossomari), 213

Ondo (Ijo ancestor), 9, 73, 205

Ong, Walter J., 140, 214

Onicha-Olona, 10

Onicha-Ugbo, 10, 35, 54, 155–57, 160, 165, 166, 168, 169, 217

Onicha-Ukwuu, 10, 54

Onitsha, 10, 92, 129–30, 133, 181, 196

Onogie (pl. Enigie), 6, 13, 14

Onwina (guild of artists), 69

Onwuejeogwu, M. Angulu, 55, 90, 92, 129, 182, 202, 211

Onwueme, Tess, xiii

Onwuteaka, V.C., 214

Opia Nwammemee, 35, 36

Opland, Jeff, 215

oppositions, 127, 174

Ora, 194

oral composition, 140; parataxis, 140, 167; repetition, 116, 124; parallelism, 116

oral testimonies, 55

oral tradition, xiii, 2, 11, 25, 31, 47, 60, 73, 97, 140, 178, 191; African, 216; as history, 27–30, 53–60; approaches to the study of, 1, 27, 197

orality, 140–41; and literacy, 140–41, 214; "oral mind," 214; "oral theory," 214

Oranmiyan (architect of second Benin dynasty), 6, 69, 175–77, 194, 204

Orea, 19

Orua, Oruabou, 9, 19

Osadebay, Dennis C., 197

Osadebe, Ignatius, xii, 38, 217

Osaghae, Eghosa, 222

Osanobua. *See* God—names for

Osawe. *See* Oba—some Obas, Esigie

Osoba, Funmi, 216

Ossomari, 92

Otiono, Nduka, xii

otu inyemedi, 130

otu umuada, 130

Oturkpo, 156

Ovie (king), 9, 13
Ovio (Benin chief), 10
Owodo. *See* Ogiso—some Ogisos
Oxford, Cheryl, 212
Oye, 106–109 112–15, 123
Oyo, 176
Ozidi, 19, 20, 23, 47
The Ozidi Saga. See Clark[-Bekederemo], J.P.
ozo, 202
Ozolua. *See* Oba—some Obas
ozoma 115

Pan-Africanism, 174, 187
Parry, Milman, 140
patriarchy, 51, 129, 131, 134, 137
Patton, 30
Paulme, Denise, 139
"peace week," 31
Pender-Cudlip, Patrick, 193
Pere (Ijo ruler), 9, 73, 194
performance, x, xii, 13, 16, 27, 38, 58, 124, 136, 138, 160, 218. *See also* context
Perham, Margery, 214
personality, 61, 63, 71, 187; of narrators, 149
personhood, 61, 62, 90; prenatal, 61, 62
Peterson, Eric E., 138
pluralism, x, 188, 190
polygyny, 97, 116, 117, 136, 143, 149–51, 153
postmodernism, 185
postnarrative discussion, 53–55, 58, 60, 160, 165, 210
power, 7, 118, 126, 136, 137, 140, 151; abuse of, 7; monarchical, 97
Preston, George Nelson, 73
primogeniture contests, 12, 20–22, 84
Propp, Vladimir, 196
protolife, 63
protoself, 62–64, 86, 90
proverbs, 29, 42, 91, 93, 95, 100–102, 124, 218
psychoanalysis, 137
punitive expeditions: Benin, 13, 57, 177; British, 73, 219

queen: omu as, 129, 132; Queen Victoria, 129; queen-mother (*iyoba*), 70, 128, 129; Queen-Mother Idia, 21

Rabkin, Eric, 196
Ramchandra, C.V., 218
Ranger, T.O., 176, 185
recording (by tape), xii, 167
religion, x, 182; Benin, 63–75; Igbo, 75–92
repetition. *See* oral composition
republicanism, 190; Igbo, 51, 87, 91, 92, 118, 129, 133, 166, 178, 199, 203; Ijo, 73–75
Research in African Literatures, 203
resistance, revolt, x, 132–34, 164
ritual, ritualism, 64, 127, 131, 180, 207, 212, 218. *See also* Nri
Rivers, Pitt, 195, 201
Rodney, Walter, 222
Roland, 201
Rosaldo, Michelle Zimbalist, 130
Rosaldo, Renato, 203
Roth, H. Ling, 196, 200, 213
Rothchild, Donald, 188
Ryder, Alan F.C., 2, 8, 11, 128, 184, 199, 204, 210, 220

Sagbama-Igbedi Creek, 9
"same differences," xii
Santayana, George, 28
Sayers, Dorothy, 201
Schaefer, Stacy, 205
The Scheme for the Study of Benin History and Culture (=The Benin Scheme), ix, 1–2, 25, 183, 184, 190, 191
Scheub, Harold, 60, 215
"second burial," 155, 197, 216
Sekoni, Ropo, 139–40
self, projections of the, x, 3, 26, 31, 75, 88, 89, 135, 137, 138, 141, 152, 153, 160, 171, 190
Serbo-Croatia, 140
Shaka the Zulu, 191, 193, 223; *mfecane* (dispersal, caused by his conquests), 193, 223

Shaw, Thurstan, 178–79, 201, 221
Sidahome, Joseph, 3, 4, 11, 14, 16–18, 21–23, 170–71, 196; and Benin monarchy, 195
Sidibe, Bakari, 50, 201
Silamaka, 200
Simayi, Charles, xii, 17, 29, 31, 36, 58, 98–104, 115, 116, 118, 126, 129, 135, 143, 155, 166, 167, 195, 197, 200, 201, 207, 208, 212, 216, 219, 220; as a ritualist, 212; narrative style, 104–105
slaves: raiding for, 10, 17, 32, 33, 180; trading in, 12, 32, 33, 177, 180, 220
the smith, 47, 52, 64, 124, 199, 211
social structure, 62, 89; elements of: age grades (age-sets), 5–7, 124; clan, 5; dual-sex political system, 130; kinship, 7, 130, 131; titled organizations, 6, 7, 85, 124, 202; town or village, 5, 194
songs, 32–33, 133. See also storytelling
Soyinka, Wole, 217, 218, 223
Spencer, Herbert, 28
Spengler, Oswald, 28
Spivak, Gayatri Chakravorty, 191
storytelling, 15, 53, 85, 116, 141–42; songs within stories, 115, 116, 124, 157, 165, 166, 168, 217–18; traditional African, 218
subalternity, 85–86, 118, 175, 190–91
Sudarkasa, Niara, 213
Sunjata. See Keita clan

Tacitus, 197
Talbot, P. Amaury, 8
the Tallensi, 62, 63
Tatham, Peter, 31, 49
Tegnaeus, Harry, 51
terra-cotta (in Benin art), 70
"Third World," 31, 186
Thomas, E., 196
Thompson, Linda, 137, 139
Thoyer-Rozat, Annik, 201
Thucydides, 197
titled organizations. See social structure
Todorov, Tzvetan, 196
Tomlinson, John, 220

Tonkin, Elizabeth, 27
tradition, 135, 136, 143, 171, 220. See also oral tradition
transcription and translation, xi
Traore, Toure, Taraware, 52; Askia Mohammed (Toure), 191; Samori (Toure), 191
Trevor-Roper, Hugh, 28
tribalism, 221
tributes (exacted), 6, 10, 13, 24, 25, 27, 129, 177
trickster tales, 139–40
Trinidad, 186
Turnbull, Colin, 201
"twin birth," 200
type, tale, xii, 48, 208. See also hunter, hunter tales

Ubini. See Benin—earlier names
the Ubulu, 17, 18, 37, 56, 118, 196, 212
Ubulu-Uku, 15–17, 35, 178, 210
Ubulu-Uno, 17, 98, 166, 210
Uchendu, V.C., 92
Udo, 7, 8, 22, 173, 195, 205, 208
Ughoton (Gwatto), 73
Ugo (Ugonoba), 15–18, 178, 195, 196, 220
ukhure, 88
Ukwuani (Kwale), 11, 14, 23–25, 36, 196
Umejei, 53, 56, 57, 202, 203
Umueke Agbaja, 130, 131, 133
the Urhobo, 4, 5, 8, 9, 155, 165, 194; relations with Benin, 5–6
Use, 67–68, 74, 87
ushio, 210
Usuanlele, Uyilawa, 196, 222
Uthman dan Fodio, 191
Uwangue (Benin title), 8
Uzama Nihiron, 69, 70, 85, 176, 205
Uzi, 68–69

Vail, Leroy, 27
van Allen, Judith, 131–32, 213
Vansina, Jan, 27
variants, tale, 19
vassalage, 8, 13, 24, 199
Victoria, Queen, 129

Vogel, Susan, 70, 208
vow, prenatal, 62

war, warfare, 6, 10, 12, 13, 26, 28, 49, 64, 78, 79, 87, 176, 204, 207, 211. *See also* the Benin kingdom
warrant chief system, 134
Warren, C., 137
Weigle, Marta, 138
Western culture, 7, 167–68, 208, 214; literacy, 136, 140–41, 171, 214; technology, 137, 167–68
White, Hayden, 203
White, Landeg, 27
Williamson, Kay, 196
wish-fulfillment, 58, 96, 118, 193
witches, 85, 127
women: as entrepreneurs, 132, 142, 152; as oral performers, 98, 136, 138–40, 141–142, 150, 153–154, 216; as rulers, 98, 117, 125, 128; womanhood, 135, 137; women's liberation movement, 137; women's psychology, 139; Women's War, Aba, 130, 133–34, 213
wood (in Benin art), 69, 176
World War II, 30
Woyengi. *See* God—names for
Wren, Robert, 217
Wrigley, C.C., 220

Xhosa oral literature, 214

Yabuku of Inekorogha, Madam, 19
yam (as "male" crop), 132
yang and *yin*, 31
Yesufu-Giwa, Moru, 173, 174
Yocom, Margaret C., 138
Yoruba, 4, 49, 52, 139, 179, 201, 204, 205, 207, 211, 214; Ilaje, 220

Isidore Okpewho has been Professor and Chair of English at Ibadan University, Visiting Professor of English at Harvard University, and Chair of Africana Studies at Binghamton University (SUNY). Among his numerous books are scholarly studies such as *The Epic in Africa* (1979), *Myth in Africa* (1983), *The Oral Performance in Africa* (1990), and *African Oral Literature* (1992). Two of his three published novels, *The Last Duty* (1976) and *Tides* (1993), have won international prizes.